Wills
OF THE
RICH
AND
FAMOUS

Herbert E. Nass, Esq.

For David Stone,
With my best wishes,

Wills
OF THE
RICH
AND
FAMOUS

Herbert E. Nass, Esq.

GRAMERCY BOOKS
New York

This 2000 edition is published by Gramercy Books™, an imprint of Random House Value Publishing, Inc., 201 East 50th Street, New York, NY 10022, by arrangement with the author.

Gramercy Books™ and design are trademarks of Random House Value Publishing, Inc.

Printed in the United States of America

Random House
New York • Toronto • London • Sydney • Auckland
http://www.randomhouse.com

Library of Congress Cataloging–in–Publication Data

Nass, Herbert E.
  Wills of the rich and famous / Herbert E. Nass.
p. cm.
  ISBN 0-517-20827-X
  1. Celebrities--United States--Biography. 2. Rich people--United States--Biography. 3. Wills--United States. I. Title.

CT215 .N37 2000
920.073--dc21
[B]   00-025143

9 8 7 6 5 4 3 2

Acknowledgments

So many people have been supportive of me and this endeavor, and I would like to thank all of you. In particular, the following people deserve special thanks for their inspiration and/or assistance:

Ann and Richard Sarnoff

Liz and Seth Neubardt

Roseann Worthington

Barbara and Tom Kornreich

Matthew Cantor, Esq

Eillen and Andy Kamins

Jennifer and Mike Kaminsky, Esqs.

Carol and Franklin Speyer

Henry Zimet

Renata and Martin Zimet

Shelley and Donald Meltzer

Abbe and Greg Large

Aracely and David Janis

Jeffrey Sarnoff

Greta Guggenheim

Douglas Martin

Sandy and Bud Neubardt

Betty and Fred Hayman

Marilyn and Joe Nass

Stephen Vlock, Esq.

Jerry Ordover, Esq.

William Sarnoff

Linda and Brian Tell

James H. Miller/Isabel Iglesias

Jennifer and Steve Warner

Linda and Mitchell Berger

Vicki and Michael Grossman

Daryn and David Grossman

Tom Danziger, Esq.

Joan Rivers

Sandy and Michael Besen

Matthew Rich

Melissa and Brandon Sall, Esq.

Linda and David Simon

Louis Ellenport

William D. Zabel, Esq.

Dayna Langfan and Larry Heller

Billie and Laurence A. Tisch

Amy and David Nachman, Esqs.

Peggy and Andrew Wallach

Steve Eckhaus, Esq.

Oprah Winfrey

Milton Levitan, Esq.

Jack O'Neil, Esq.

Peter C. Valente, Esq.

Alan Halperin, Esq.

Sidney Mandel, Esq.

Hannah C. Pakula

Susie and Harlan M. Stone

Denise and Robert Hayman

Robert Gries

Mark Kriendler-Nelson, Esq.

Andrew Neubardt, Esq.

Steven Lowy

Nancy Friedman-Margolin

Julie Harris

Wendy and Lewis Rubin, Esq.

Ivan Jenson

Victor Matthews

Dr. Ruth Nass

Vera List

Cynthia Manson

Susanne Jaffe

Amanda and Seth Miller

Glen Meehan

Mark Stadtmauer, Esq.

Ronald Herbst, Esq.

J. Edward Meyer, Esq.

Adina Zion, Esq.

Jeff Taub, Esq.

Ellen and Henry Korn, Esq.

Debra and Howard Ressler, Esq.

Jill and Andrew Herz, Esq.

Ellen and Richard Chassin, Esq.

Marie Falango

Fran and Jim McGonigle

Kenneth J. Stumpf

Rhoda Kadin

Robin Leach

Lia and Larry Shire, Esq.

Lucy and Richard Halperin, Esq.

Ginny and Brian Ruder

Barbara and Herb Louis

Marcy and Paul Kadin

David Jacoby, Esq.

Claire and Larry Benenson

Alice and Tom Tisch

Burt and Leni Welte

Robert Steinberg, Esq.

Roger D. Olson, Esq.

Larry King

Buck Finkelstein, Esq.

David Washburn, Esq.

Alan Brockman, Esq.

Richard Bowler, Esq.

Keith Nebel, Esq.

Meg and Bob Ebin, Esqs.

Paul Dewey

Hermine Kamins

Kathie and Mark Teich

Ted James

Marc Kazmac

Sandy and Marc Freidus

Biff Liff

Diane and Gary Diamond

Silda and Eliot Spitzer, Esqs.

Andrew Solt

Jerry Wolfe, Esq.

Claudia and Mario Covo

Gail and Walter Harris

Mallory Factor

John Olson, Esq.

Gilbert Parker

Chris and Douglas Diamond

Finally, I must give special credit to my associate, Jesse B. Schwartz, Esq., for his contribution to the section about Babe Ruth, and to my former associate, Seth D. Slotkin, Esq. for his contribution to the section about Sammy Davis, Jr.

Contents

Introduction

"Where There's a Will, There's a . . ."

A. Relative
B. Lawyer
C. Way
D. All of the above

With the personal lives of the rich and famous increasingly subject to public scrutiny, so, too, have their deaths and their Wills become a further subject of interest for the stargazing public. Knowing what a person directed or requested in his or her Will can shed light on that person's most private thoughts, feelings, and relationships. Each one of the one hundred Wills excerpted in this volume reflects interesting quirks, facts, or eccentric characteristics about the illustrious person who signed that Will.

> *"Thy will be done"*
> -John Greenleaf Whittier

For those who have prepared and signed their Wills, a Will can be used as a vehicle to express love or gratitude by giving property of value to specified surviving relatives, friends, or institutions. For example, actress **Mari-**

lyn Monroe showed her devotion to her acting teacher, **Lee B. Strasberg**, by giving him all of her tangible personal property and 75 percent of her residuary estate to dispose of as *he* wished. Six years after Monroe's death, Strasberg showed his devotion to his third wife, Anna, by giving her his entire estate, including his substantial continuing interest from the Monroe estate.

Gifts made under Wills need not be made only in cold cash, but may be of an object of special sentimental value. Ironically, comedian **Groucho Marx**, who once said that he would not want to be a member of any club that would have him, specifically bequeathed his membership in the Hillcrest Country Club in Beverly Hills to his son. Fittingly, comedian **W. C. Fields**, whose death was partly attributable to his excessive drinking, expressly gifted one-third of "my liquor" to each of three of his drinking buddies.

A Will may also be a person's last opportunity to vent pent-up emotions, settle a score, or set the record straight. The Will of actress **Joan Crawford** expressly disinherits two of her four children. Of course, one of those Crawford children who was "cut out" proceeded to write a best-selling book about life with her dear mommie.

Sometimes, a Will can be used to attempt to control the activities of surviving relatives "from the grave" by including bequests conditioned on the performance of specified conduct in the future. For example, pianist **Vladimir Horowitz** made a $300,000 gift to The Juilliard School of Music on the condition that Juilliard agrees "never to hold any piano or other musical competition in [Horowitz's] name or honor." That "strings attached" bequest was obviously made by one of music's most high-strung performers.

"With malice towards none, and charity for All . . .
-Abraham Lincoln

Many of the Wills contained within include provisions for charities. Bequests made under Wills have often been the catalyst behind the establishment of great educational and medical institutions, museums, and private foundations. Billionaire **J. Paul Getty** gave most of his enormous estate toward the fulfillment of his dream to create a great museum bearing his name. In their Wills, artists **Mark Rothko**, **Andy Warhol**, **Norman Rockwell**, and **Robert Mapplethorpe** all created or funded private foundations to support the arts.

"To be of No Church Is Dangerous"
-Samuel Johnson

A Will might also be seen as a person's last opportunity to prove his or her religious faith. In the first article of his Will, **J. P. Morgan** expressed the following deeply religious sentiments: "I commit my soul into the bands of my Saviour, in full confidence that having redeemed it and washed it in His most precious blood He will present it faultless before the throne of my Heavenly Father." Despite his tremendous success and wealth, perhaps Morgan was just hedging his bets and understood that "you can't take it with you."

"Let no one pay me honor with tears,
nor celebrate my funeral with mourning"
-Cicero

Although lawyers usually advise against it because it may be too late when the Will is finally located, a Will can be used to give funeral, burial, cremation, or embalming instructions. Not surprisingly, many of our most public entertainers and movie stars specifically direct that their funerals be kept private and restricted to family members. In her Will, **Gloria Swanson** emphatically states: "I wish no public funeral or display of any sort. It is my wish that my body be cremated. I direct that my cremation be private and confined to members of my family only."

At the other extreme, some of our rich and famous dead took a very active role in planning their own funerals. **Cole Porter** requested that a certain biblical quotation he found especially comforting be read at his funeral. Great escape artist and magician **Harry Houdini** provided in his Will that his body should be embalmed and buried in a vault constructed in the same manner as his beloved mother's, and that a bronze bust of him be placed on his tomb so as to facilitate his projected return from the dead.

The Wills discussed in this book have been divided into the following chapters: The Beautiful People; The Leading Ladies; The Leading Men; The Musicians; The Comedians; The Showmen; The Presidents; The Writers; The Sporting Life; The Producers and Directors; The Artists; One of a Kind; and last but certainly not least, The Super Rich.

They don't get much more beautiful than **Jackie O**, her son **JFK Jr.**, and the People's Princess, **Lady Di**. Each of the Wills of the Beautiful People show them to be thoughtful and caring, from JFK Jr.'s bequest to his nephew, John B. Kennedy Schlossberg, of "my scrimshaw set previously owned by my father", to his mother's gift of a Greek portrait bust of a woman to her boyfriend, Maurice Templesman. It appears from their Wills that The Beautiful People also liked and appreciated beautiful things.

The Leading Ladies have multiple husbands, romantic links to Clark Gable and two generations of Kennedys, star-struck mothers, and tragic deaths in common among them. **Marilyn Monroe, Jean Harlow, Carole Lombard,** and **Natalie Wood** all died tragic and untimely deaths, One might speculate as to whether such untimely deaths added to the legendary luster surrounding this subgroup of these ladies. Despite their deaths, these leading ladies will live forever on television screens and in movie theaters around the globe. Whether she be Harlow or Monroe, she is sometimes with us first thing in the morning, or on "The Late Show."

Our group of Leading Men appears to have been a hardworking bunch. Three of them had just completed filming movies shortly before they died. **Clark Gable** died two weeks after wrangling with horses and **Marilyn Monroe** on the set of *The Misfits,* Spencer Tracy had recently welcomed his daughter's fiance, Sidney Poitier, to his home in *Guess Who's Coming to Dinner,* and **Henry Fonda** had acted with his daughter, Jane, in *On Golden Pond.* Shortly after Fonda received an Academy Award (in absentia) as Best Actor for his performance in that film, he went beyond Golden Pond.

The Musicians lived lives ranging from twenty-seven years in the case of rock singer **Jim Morrison** to the eighty-six years of concert pianist **Vladimir Horowitz.** As for their Wills, this select group of Music Men either paid little or no attention to their Wills or alternatively, focused their thoughts on their Wills. Rebel **Jim Morrison's** Will was a one-pager, **Ricky Nelson's** was three, and multimillionaire **John Lennon's** was four. At the other extreme was songmaster **Cole Porter**, whose twenty-nine-page Will was prepared by one of New York's finest law firms, Paul, Weiss, Rifkind Wharton & Garrison, and meticulously disposes of all his varied properties. **Elvis Presley** had a thirteen-page Will in which he gives broad discretion to his named executor, his father, Vernon Presley, to dispose of Elvis's "trophies" and other personal property.

Even the Comedians seem to take their own Wills seriously. There are no parting one-liners or any "magic words" in the Will of **Groucho Marx**. The Will of the tragically overdosed, burned-out "Saturday Night Live" comedian **John Belushi** is surprisingly and unusually structured, calculated, and family-oriented.

Phil Silvers's handwritten Will and Codicil read more like a rambling, intensely personal letter to family and friends than a legal document. Nonetheless, Silvers's stream of consciousness Will and Codicil were admitted to probate by the California probate court.

The Wills of a few of the Showmen indicate their desire that the show involving them should go on after their deaths. **Harry Houdini** left specific instructions in his Will regarding his embalming and entombment, indicating his expectation that he would someday perform the ultimate trick and return from the dead. **Bob Fosse** wanted to be celebrated by sixty-six friends at numerous last suppers underwritten by Fosse's estate. **George M. Cohan's** Will gives a detailed discussion of the importance of his estate's retaining the copyrights to his lyrics and music, which would continue to produce income for his heirs long after he was gone.

Ranging from the one-sentence Will of taciturn **Calvin Coolidge** to the thirty-page, handwritten Will of the father of our country, **George Washington**, the Wills of the Presidents are representative of Wills of testators with comparable wealth and similar family situations. After all, even presidents put their pants on one leg at a time just like the rest of us. However, there is one important type of tangible personal property that only our presidents can claim as their own—presidential papers and other records associated with only the highest office in the land.

George Washington was of course the first to be concerned with the question of the proper disposition of his presidential records. **Thomas Jefferson** bequeathed his extensive library to the University of Virginia, and his "papers of business" passed to his executor for disposition. Coolidge's one-sentence Will makes no mention of any presidential papers. Perhaps the succinct Coolidge did not have too many papers of which to dispose. Despite its length and detailed attention to the disposition of his personal items, **Franklin Roosevelt's** Will is silent on the subject of the disposition of his presidential papers. Roosevelt died before any legislation related to the disposition of presidential papers was enacted. **John Kennedy's** Will, which was signed seven years *before* he became president and was never updated, obviously does not address the disposition of presidential papers. Kennedy's failure to update his Will after becoming president is somewhat odd in light of his brother Joseph's death at an early age, the substantial Kennedy family wealth, and the subsequent birth of Kennedy's two children, Caroline and "John-John." But what is even more perplexing is that Robert Kennedy, who was tragically assassinated in 1968 five years *after* his brother John, had an even older Will, dating back to 1953. Perhaps the Kennedy brothers shared some superstitions about signing their Wills. Unfortunately, old Wills did not shield them from misguided assassins' new bullets.

A few of the Writers seemed to see their Wills as an opportunity to make some final comments on certain facts of life. For example, **F. Scott Fitzgerald's** handwritten Will begins with a cynical allusion to "the uncertainty of life *and the certainty of death"* (emphasis added). Playwright **Lillian Hellman** used her Will as a stage to describe the background, sentimental and historical, of the various objects of tangible property that she was giving to selected friends. Most of these writers' Wills express their gratitude, and their egos, by bequests to various educational institutions or by the establishment of literary awards under their Wills, such as "The Truman Capote award for Literary Criticism in memory of "Newton Arvin" or "The Dashiell Hammett Fund" established by Lillian Hellman.

In strange ways, the Wills of the Producers and Directors well reflect their creative styles. The one-page, handwritten will of stark and truthful film director **John Cassavetes** minces no words and gets the job done in a direct, blunt manner. The Master of Suspense, **Alfred Hitchcock,** had a Will and then six subsequent changes to that Will by codicils spanning over seventeen years. Always controversial director **Orson Welles** makes a substantial gift to a woman who was not his wife. Romantic film director **Vincente Minnelli** increased the bequest to his third wife by a codicil, but gives the bulk of his estate to his beloved daughter from his marriage to Judy Garland, Liza (with a Z) Minnelli. And **Walt Disney** seems to have had the all-American Will. From the starkness of Cassavetes's to the professional polish of Walt Disney's, the Wills of the Producers and the Directors display the temperaments of men who had already given many directions in the productions of their lives.

Inherently, estates of the Artists contain something

that the rest of ours do not to the same extent—art. Very often, artists look at their artistic creations as their "children," so the final placement of their artworks takes on a profoundly personal meaning. For example, **Mark Rothko's** two-page Will mentions certain paintings for special disposition. Alternatively, in his relatively innocuous Will, pop artist **Andy Warhol** does not mention a single work of his art or anyone else's. Warhol's nine-page Will is certainly more polished than Rothko's two-pager, but both lacked the focused foresight required of persons disposing of exceptional estates. One other ironic fact that unites all of these artists is that as much as their work may have been admired during their lives, the value of their artworks increased dramatically after their deaths. Upon their deaths their artworks became a finite, fixed supply with the demand for that fixed supply significantly increased. Pop prophet **Andy Warhol** could not have been more correct when he said, "Death means a lot of money, honey."

In a universe all his own, brilliant scientist **Albert Einstein** left a Will in which his prized violin receives special treatment.

The Athletes included in The Sporting Life reached the pinnacle of success in their sports partly as a result of their great control and discipline. Although **Babe Ruth** was reportedly sometimes out of control, his Will and the Wills of **Joe DiMaggio** and **Arthur Ashe** reflect the personalities of persons in control of their game, and of their families.

Last, but certainly not least under any criteria, are the Wills of the Super Rich. Almost every person written about in this book has been rich by most people's standards. But a few of our group of the Super Rich had fortunes counted in the billions of dollars. **J. Paul Getty and Howard Hughes** were billionaires before there were more than a handful of billionaires around. Hilton Hotels' commander and founder, **Conrad Hilton**, may not have been a billionaire, but he always knew that he could find a place to spend the night and get some room service.

As one might expect, the Wills of the Super Rich are often super long. It must be remembered that these Wills (with the notable exception of **Howard Hughes's**) were prepared by the attorneys for the Super Rich. No self-respecting attorney who expects to get paid a super fee would dare give a short Will to a Super Rich client. Every single contingency must be covered and accounted for, even it includes the notion in **Conrad Hilton's** Will that if every single one of his descendants and heirs conspired to contest his Will and lost, then the property would pass to the State of California.

J. Paul Getty's Will and the codicils to that Will win the prize for length. Getty's 1958 Will was a mere seventeen pages, but the aggregate of the twenty-one following codicils greatly exceeds that number, **Nelson Rockefeller's** Will was a princely sixty-four pages. As for mysterious **Howard Hughes**, if you added all the separate napkins, scraps of paper, and even legal paper that allegedly contained his Will, they might add up to something. In the end, they added up to nothing, and Hughes's billion-dollar estate passed by intestacy to Hughes's "laughing heirs," and to Uncle Sam.

It was first said by Benjamin Franklin that there are only two certainties in life—death and taxes. But for the Super Rich it may be said that there is only one certainty in life—death, but not necessarily taxes. By establishing private foundations or giving their fortunes exclusively to charity, these tremendous estates could avoid paying estate taxes. With the vast majority of J. Paul Getty's estate passing to the not-for-profit Getty Museum, there were relatively small estate taxes as a result of the unlimited charitable deduction available.

The Will excerpts reproduced in this book are the testators', or testatrices (and lawyers') own words. In almost every case, except in the one-page Wills included here, the excerpted portions do not include the entire dispositive scheme, but only the sections of greatest interest. Entire sections of these Wills have been omitted or are not discussed due to an excess of "legalese" and a minimum of interesting material. Following are the excerpted highlights from the Wills of some of the most popular and celebrated people from the historical past and of our times.

The Beautiful People

Out of this World

JOHN F. KENNEDY, JR.
The (Future?) President's Plane is Missing
JULY 16, 1999

LADY DIANA
Darkness After Midnight in the City of Lights
AUGUST 31, 1997

JACQUELINE KENNEDY ONASSIS
Ensnare a Greek Bearing Gifts
MAY 19, 1994

PERRY ELLIS
Last Year's Fashion
MAY 30, 1986

John F. Kennedy, Jr.

DATE AND PLACE OF BIRTH
November 25, 1960
Washington, D.C.

DATE AND PLACE OF DEATH
July 16, 1999
Ocean off the coast of
Martha's Vineyard, Massachusetts

The (Future?) President's Plane is Missing

When dashing John F. Kennedy Jr.'s single engine Piper Saratoga II HP private airplane plummeted him to his instantaneous death in the cold waters off the coast of Martha's Vineyard, Massachusetts, the whole world lost one of its favorite sons. There are few, if any, American names as famous as "Kennedy", and there were only two "John F. Kennedys" that were part of one of the greatest political dynasties of the 20th Century. The first JFK died tragically at age 46 from an assassin's bullet in 1963, and the second JFK died equally tragically and even more prematurely at age 38, thirty-six years later in 1999.

Some cynics might say that JFK Jr.'s demise was merely a 20th century version of the Greek myth of Icarus, in which young Icarus flew too close to the sun, his wings melted, and he drowned. Did JFK Jr., who was not an experienced pilot, also tempt fate and the gods by flying his own small plane on a hazy, low visibility night with a recently broken ankle? Despite the tragedy and celebrity of his name and famous family, and his substantial personal wealth, most who knew him said that JFK Jr. was a very regular kind of guy.

JFK Jr.'s Will, dated December 19, 1997, indicates who and what were important to him after the death of his mother Jacqueline Kennedy Onassis on May 19, 1994 and slightly over one year after his marriage to Carolyn Bessette in 1996.

The Will of "JOHN F. KENNEDY, JR. of New York, New York" was prepared by a Boston law firm and signed in Kennedy family offices at 500 Fifth Avenue in New York City.

Article FIRST of the Will gives all of JFK's

"tangible personal property (as distinguished from money, securities and the like), wherever located, **other than my scrimshaw set previously owned by my father,** to my wife, Carolyn Bessette-Kennedy, if she is living on the thirtieth day after my death . . ." (emphasis added).

The Will provides further that if John were survived by issue, then that important scrimshaw set was bequeathed to Carolyn, or if she did not survive, to their children. If John were not survived by children, which he was not, the scrimshaw set was bequeathed to "my nephew, John B. K. Schlossberg." Few people in America can honestly say that they know what "scrimshaw" is, but JFK Jr. certainly did, and in his relatively short Will he left very specific instructions related to this single family heirloom. It is indeed ironic that JFK Jr. died in a spot on the sea, above which some of that scrimshaw prominently mentioned in his Will may have been crafted by those Massachusetts sailors, whalers and seaman of bygone times. All the rest of JFK Jr.'s tangible personal property, other than that scrimshaw set, was bequeathed to Carolyn, if she had survived. Since she did not, all the tangible personal property, excluding that scrimshaw set, is to be divided into three equal shares among JFK Jr.'s 6 year old nephew John, and nieces, 11 year old Rose and 9 year old Tatiana.

At the time of his death, JFK Jr. was living with his wife in a cooperative apartment that he owned on "N. Moore Street" in the trendy neighborhood known as "Tribeca" in New York City. The name of that street is often erroneously referred to as "North" Moore Street, as it was on JFK Jr.'s death certificate, but in fact, the "N" stands for "Nathaniel", and not "North." The Boston law firm which prepared the Will avoided the initial issue altogether and simply referred to the residence "at 20-26 Moore Street, Apartment 9E, in said New York." That cooperative apartment was given to John's wife Carolyn, "if she is living on the thirtieth day after my death." Sad to say, but from the autopsy and other forensic reports, neither John nor Carolyn survived even thirty seconds after that fateful impact at approximately 9:41 p.m. on a foggy Friday night.

Article THIRD pertains to the valuable real estate and residences on Martha's Vineyard, and elsewhere, which John and his sister Caroline Kennedy Schlossberg had inherited from their mother, Jacqueline. JFK Jr.'s Will provides that those properties should go to his children, if any, or if none, in equal shares to his sister Caroline's three children. Apparently John wanted to be sure that those particular properties stayed in the family.

Article FOURTH provides for the disposition of "the residue of all the property, of whatever kind and wherever located, that I own at my death to the then trustees of The John F. Kennedy, Jr. 1983 Trust. . . ." The exact terms of that trust are not required to be filed with the Surrogate's Court, but we do know that the beneficiaries of that trust included the following: Carolyn Bessette Kennedy, Caroline Kennedy Schlossberg, JFK Jr.'s cousins, Anthony Stanislaus Radziwill, Timothy P. Shriver, and Robert F. Kennedy, Jr.; two "god children" of JFK Jr.'s; and friends or former employees, Rosemarie Terenzio, Robert Littell, Ephigenio Pinheiro, Marta Sgubin, and the charity known as "Reaching Up, Inc." which JFK Jr. had helped to create. It is noteworthy that the John Fitzgerald Kennedy Library Foundation, Inc., is only a contingent beneficiary of that trust. What the operative contingency is, we do not know.

It is very revealing that although he had numerous Kennedy and Bouvier cousins, he selected only three to share in his substantial estate. In fact, he named his closest cousin, Anthony Stanislaus Radziwill, "as my executor." Anthony had been the best man at John's wedding, but Anthony died after a long fight with cancer only three weeks after John's death, and never began acting as Executor of John's Will. The Will named John's cousin Timothy P. Shriver, as the back-up executor. Tim Shriver is the son of Eunice Kennedy Shriver and is the President of the "Special Olympics." It is certainly telling that John named two male cousins for the important role ahead of his wife and sister. Perhaps he felt that his wife and sister would be too grief-stricken to be able to do an effective job with his undoubtedly complicated estate. The three cousins included in the Will were all well known for their *pro bono* and other humanitarian activities, and John may have felt inclined to reward them rather than any "poster boys of bad behavior", as he once referred to two other Kennedy cousins.

The shortest article in JFK Jr.'s short Will provides in full as follows:

"I appoint my wife, Carolyn Bessette-Kennedy, as guardian of each child of our marriage during minority. No guardian appointed in this will or a codicil need furnish any surety on any official bond."

It is entirely unnecessary to appoint the natural mother as the guardian of her own children, so it is not clear why this clause was included. Despite his obvious hope to eventually have children, John died without any children of his own to continue the name and legacy as John F. Kennedy III.

John F. Kennedy, Jr. signed his famous name on every page of his relatively short Will. Perhaps sensing their future footnote in history, the witnesses to that Will took the unusual step of adding their own initials to each page of his Will. Normally, witnesses sign their names only at the end of the Will, and do not initial each page, but for the "Sexiest Man Alive", wouldn't you want to initial each page also?

John F. Kennedy Jr. left a Will which showed him to be a thoughtful and generous, but ultimately a simple man. At age 38, he definitely died too young, and were it not for that fateful flight on a hazy July night, the world will never know just how high Jr. might have flown.

/s/ *John F. Kennedy, Jr.*

Will dated December 19, 1997
Will signed at 500 Fifth Avenue, New York, New York

I, JOHN F. KENNEDY, JR., of New York, New York, make this my last will, hereby revoking all earlier wills and codicils. I do not by this will exercise any power of appointment.

FIRST: I give all my tangible personal property (as distinguished from money, securities and the like), wherever located, other than my scrimshaw set previously owned by my father, to my wife, Carolyn Bessette-Kennedy, if she is living on the thirtieth day after my death, or if not, by right of representation to my then living issue, or if none, by right of representation to the then living issue of my sister, Caroline Kennedy Schlossberg, or if none, to my said sister, Caroline, if she is then living. If I am survived by issue, I leave said scrimshaw set to my said wife, Carolyn, if she is then living, or if not, by right of representation to my then living issue. If I am not survived by issue, I give said scrimshaw set to my nephew John B. K. Schlossberg, if he is then living, or if not, by right of representation to the then living issue of my said sister, Caroline, or if none, to my said sister, Caroline, if she is then living. I hope that whoever receives my tangible personal property will dispose of certain items of it in accordance with my wishes, however made known, but I impose no trust, condition or enforceable obligation of any kind in this regard.

SECOND: I give and devise all my interest in my cooperative apartment located at 20-26 Moore Street, Apartment 9E, in said New York, including all my shares therein and any proprietary leases with respect thereto, to my said wife, Carolyn, if she is living on the thirtieth day after my death.

<u>THIRD</u>: If no issue of mine survive me, I give and devise all my interests in real estate, wherever located, that I own as tenants in common with my said sister, Caroline, or as tenants in common with any of her issue, by right of representation to Caroline's issue who are living on the thirtieth day after my death, or if none, to my said sister, Caroline, if she is then living. References in this Article THIRD to "real estate" include shares in cooperative apartments and proprietary leases with respect thereto.

<u>FOURTH</u>: I give and devise the residue of all the property, of whatever kind and wherever located, that I own at my death to the then trustees of The John F. Kennedy, Jr. 1983 Trust established October 13, 1983 by me, as Donor, of which John T. Fallon, of Weston, Massachusetts, and I are currently the trustees (the "1983 Trust"), to be added to the principal of the 1983 Trust and administered in accordance with the provisions thereof, as amended by a First Amendment dated April 9, 1987 and by a Second Amendment and Complete Restatement dated earlier this day, and as from time to time hereafter further amended whether before or after my death. I have provided in the 1983 Trust for my children and more remote issue and for the method of paying all federal and state taxes in the nature of estate, inheritance, succession and like taxes occasioned by my death.

<u>FIFTH</u>: I appoint my wife, Carolyn Bessette-Kennedy, as guardian of each child of our marriage during minority. No guardian appointed in this will or a codicil need furnish any surety on any official bond.

<u>SIXTH</u>: I name my cousin Anthony Stanislaus Radzi-

will as my executor; and if for any reason he fails to qualify or ceases to serve in that capacity, I name my cousin Timothy P. Shriver as my executor in his place. References in this will or a codicil to my "executor" mean the one or more executors (or administrators with this will annexed) for the time being in office. No executor named in this will or a codicil need furnish any surety on any official bond. In any proceeding for the allowance of an account of my executor, I request the Court to dispense with the appointment of a guardian ad litem to represent any person or interest. I direct that in any proceeding relating to my estate, service of process upon any person under a disability shall not be made when another person not under a disability is a party to the proceeding and has the same interest as the person under the disability.

SEVENTH: In addition to other powers, my executor shall have power from time to time at discretion and without license of court: To retain, and to invest and reinvest in, any kind or amount of property; to vote and exercise other rights of security holders; to make such elections for federal and state estate, gift, income and generation-skipping transfer tax purposes as my executor may deem advisable; to compromise or submit to arbitration any matters in dispute; to borrow money, and to sell, mortgage, pledge, exchange, lease and contract with respect to any real or personal property, all without notice to any beneficiary and in such manner, for such consideration and on such terms as to credit or otherwise as my executor may deem advisable, whether or not the effect thereof extends beyond the period of settling my estate; and in

distributing my estate, to allot property, whether real or personal, at then current values, in lieu of cash.
WITNESS my hand this 19 day of Dec 1997.

/s/ *John F. Kennedy, Jr.*

Diana, Princess of Wales

DATE AND PLACE OF BIRTH	DATE AND PLACE OF DEATH
Sandringham, Norfolk	Paris, France
England	Salpetriere Hospital
July 1, 1961	August 31, 1997

Darkness after Midnight in the City of Lights

In view of the horrific car crash which caused Lady Diana's death, there is a certain macabre irony in the fact that on the first page of her Will there is a reference to her "chattels" as including "any car or cars that I may own at the time of my death." It was indeed an expensive, luxury Mercedes-Benz, not owned by Diana, that crashed in an underground tunnel near the Seine River in Paris around midnight that caused her untimely death at the age of 36. She and her boyfriend, Emad Mohammed al-Fayed, called "Dodi" by his friends, were together in the back seat reportedly without their seatbelts buckled. Ultimately, it was found by a French court after a lengthy investigation that it was the recklessness of their very drunk driver trying to outrace swarming "paparazzi" that ended Diana's fairy tale life. If only Lady Diana had devoted some of her world renowned charitable attentions to Mothers Against Drunk Driving. . . .

"DIANA PRINCESS OF WALES of Kensington Palace London" signed her Will dated June 1, 1993 shortly after she had formally and publicly separated from her husband, Prince Charles, the future King of England. Excluding her "chattels", Lady Diana's entire estate was bequeathed, in equal shares, to her two sons, Prince William and Prince Harry, to be held in trust for each until he attained the age of twenty-five.

Reproduced here are the complete Wills and Codicils of Lady Diana, including her signature on her Will as "HER ROYAL HIGHNESS". Fortunately or unfortunately for Diana, that royalness wore off when her divorce from Prince Charles was final on August 28, 1996.

It is noteworthy that on February 1st, 1996, Lady Diana signed a Codicil amending her Will to provide that "my sister Elizabeth Sarah Lavinia McCorquondale (known as The Lady Sarah McCorquondale) of Stoke Rochford Grantham Lincolnshire" should replace Commander Patrick Desmond Christian Jermy Jephson as co-Executor and co-Trustee to serve with Lady Di's mother, Frances Shand Kydd. Despite all the unusual names, can one really blame Lady Di for replacing someone with a name like "Jermy"?

Commander Jephson had been Diana's trusted "Private Secretary" until he resigned after a falling-out with her in January of 1996. As we can see from the date of her Codicil, Lady Di did not waste any time in replacing "P.D.C.J. Jephson" with her sister Sarah.

At the time of her death, Lady Diana was a wealthy divorcee, thanks primarily to the royal largesse in the form of her divorce settlement. She left an estate worth approximately $35,000,000 U.S. Dollars. However, because Lady Diana was no longer part of the royal family, her estate was taxed by the British government at the standard forty percent (40%) estate tax rate. After the British government got its $14,000,000 share, her sons were left with approximately $11,000,000 each. Ultimately, that may be a drop in the royal bucket for 15 year old Prince William, who is second in line to the throne, or to his understudy, Prince Harry.

After Lady Di's unexpected death it was reported that there were some post-mortem gifts from her estate, not mentioned in her Will, that included a gift of $82,000 for Lady Diana's butler, Paul Burrell, and also allowed her 17 godchildren to select from among her personal "chattels". There's that word again. Finally, it was determined by the powers-that-be after her death that it would be appropriate for her wardrobe, picture and name to be used for charitable purposes, as she had done during her lifetime.

The sudden death of the People's Princess at the end of summer holidays sent shock waves across the globe. For a person who had braved landmine fields in Angola, and traveled to the far reaches of Zimbabwe, Pakistan and Bosnia, it is indeed ironic that she met her end after leaving the ritziest of hotels in one of the world's most cosmopolitan cities. The senseless, sudden death of the Queen of Our Hearts caught the whole world unprepared for the end of the tales of the fairy princess named Diana.

/s/ *Diana*

Will dated June 1, 1993
First Codicil dated February 1, 1996

I DIANA PRINCESS OF WALES of Kensington Palace London W8 HEREBY REVOKE all former Wills and testamentary dispositions made by me AND DE-CLARE this to be my last Will which I make this first day of June One thousand nine hundred and ninety three

1   I APPOINT my mother THE HONOURABLE MRS FRANCES RUTH SHAND KYDD of Callinesh Isle of Seil Oban Scotland and COMMANDER PATRICK DESMOND CHRISTIAN JERMY JEPHSON of St James's Palace London SW1 to be the Executors and Trustees of this my Will

2   I WISH to be buried

3   SHOULD any child of mine be under age at the date of the death of the survivor of myself and my husband I APPOINT my mother and my brother EARL SPENCER to be the guardians of that child and I express the wish that should I predecease my husband he will consult with my mother with regard to the upbringing education and welfare of our children

4(a) I GIVE free of inheritance tax all my chattels to my Executors jointly (or if only one of them shall prove my Will to her or him)

(b) I DESIRE them (or if only one shall prove her or him)

(i)   To give effect as soon as possible but not later than two years following my death to any written memorandum or notes of wishes of mine with regard to any of my chattels

    (ii) Subject to any such wishes to hold my chattels (or the balance thereof) in accordance with Clause 5 of this my Will

(c) FOR the purposes of this Clause "chattels" shall have the same meaning as is assigned to the expression "personal chattels" in the Administration of Estates Act 1925 (including any car or cars that I may own at the time of my death)

(d) I DECLARE that all expenses for the safe custody of and insurance incurred prior to giving effect to my wishes and for packing transporting and insurance for the purposes of the delivery to the respective recipients of their particular chattels shall be borne by my residuary estate

5   SUBJECT to the payment or discharge of my funeral testamentary and administration expenses and debts and other liabilities I GIVE all my property and assets of every kind and wherever situate to my Executors and Trustees Upon trust either to retain (if they think fit without being liable for loss) all or any part in the same state as they are at the time of my death or to sell whatever and wherever they decide with power when they consider it proper to invest trust monies and to vary investments in accordance with the powers contained in the Schedule to this my Will and to hold the same UPON TRUST for such of them my children PRINCE WILLIAM and PRINCE HENRY as are living three months after my death and attain the age of twenty five years if more than one in equal

shares PROVIDED THAT if either child of mine dies before me or within three months after my death and issue of that child are living three months after my death and attain the age of twenty one years such issue shall take by substitution if more than one in equal shares per stirpes the share that the deceased child of mine would have taken had he been living three months after my death but so that no issue shall take whose parent is then living and so capable of taking

6   MY EXECUTORS AND TRUSTEES shall have the following powers in addition to all other powers over any share of the Trust Fund

(a) POWER under the Trustee Act 1925 Section 31 to apply income for maintenance and to accumulate surplus income during a minority but as if the words "my Trustees think fit" were substituted in sub-section (1)(i) thereof for the words "may in all the circumstances be reasonable" and as if the proviso at the end of sub-section (1) thereof was omitted

(b) POWER under the Trustee Act 1925 Section 32 to pay or apply capital for advancement or benefit but as if proviso (a) to sub-section (1) thereof stated that "no payment or application shall be made to or for any person which exceeds altogether in amount the whole of the presumptive or vested share or interest of that person in the trust property or other than for the personal benefit of that person or in such manner as to prevent limit or postpone his or her interest in possession in that share or interest"

7   THE statutory and equitable rules of apportionment shall not apply to my Will and all dividends and other payments in the nature of income received by the Trustees shall be treated as income at the date of receipt irrespective of the period for which the dividend or other income is payable

8   IT is my wish (but without placing them under any binding obligation) that my executors employ the firm of Mishcon de Reya of 21 Southampton Row London WC1B 5HS in obtaining a Grant of Probate to and administering my estate

9   ANY person who does not survive me by at least three months shall be deemed to have predeceased me for the purpose of ascertaining the devolution of my estate and the income thereof

10   IF at any time an Executor or Trustee is a professional or business person charges can be made in the ordinary way for all work done by that person or his firm or company or any partner or employee

THE SCHEDULE

MY Executors and Trustees (hereinafter referred to as "my Trustees") in addition to all other powers conferred on them by law or as the result of the terms of this my Will shall have the following powers

1(a) FOR the purposes of any distribution under Clause 5 to appropriate all or any part of my said property and assets in or toward satisfaction of any share in my residuary estate without needing the consent of anyone

(b) FOR the purposes of placing a value on any of my personal chattels (as defined by the Administration of Estates Act 1925) so appropriated to use if they so decide such value as may have been placed on the same by any Valuers they instruct for inheritance tax purposes on my death or such other value as they may in their absolute discretion consider fair and my Trustees in respect of any of my personal chattels which being articles of national scientific historic or artistic interest are treated on such death as the subject of a conditionally exempt transfer for the purposes of the Inheritance Tax Act 1984 Section 30 (or any statutory modification or re-enactment thereof) shall in respect of any such appropriation place such lesser value as they in their absolute discretion consider fair after taking into account such facts and surrounding circumstances as they consider appropriate including the fact that inheritance tax for which conditional exemption was obtained might be payable by the beneficiary on there being a subsequent chargeable event

(c) TO insure under comprehensive or any other cover against any risks and for any amounts (including allowing as they deem appropriate for any possible future effects of inflation and increasing building costs and expenses) any asset held at any time by my Executors and Trustees And the premiums in respect of any such insurance may be discharged by my Executors and Trustees either out of income or out of capital (or partly out of one and partly out of the other) as my Executors and Trustees shall in their absolute discretion determine and any monies received by my Executors and Trustees as the result of any insurance insofar as not used in rebuilding reinstating replacing or repairing the asset lost or damaged shall be treated as if they were the proceeds of sale of the asset insured PROVIDED ALWAYS that my Executors and Trustees shall not be under any responsibility to insure or be liable for any loss that may result from any failure so to do

2(a) POWER to invest trust monies in both income producing and non-income producing assets of every kind and wherever situated and to vary investments in the same full and unrestricted manner in all respects as if they were absolutely entitled thereto beneficially

(b) POWER to retain or purchase as an authorised investment any freehold or leasehold property or any interest or share therein of whatever nature proportion or amount (which shall be held upon trust to retain or sell the same) as a residence for one or more beneficiaries under this my Will and in the event of any such retention or purchase my Trustees shall have power to apply trust monies in the erection alteration improvement or repair of any building on such freehold or leasehold property including one where there is any such interest or share And my Trustees shall have power to decide (according to the circumstances generally) the terms and conditions in every respect upon which any such person or persons may occupy and reside at any such property (or have the benefit of the said interest or share therein)

(c) POWER to delegate the exercise of their power to invest trust monies (including for the purpose of holding or placing them on deposit pending investment) and to vary investments to any company or other person or person whether or not being or including one or more of my Trustees and to allow any investment or other asset to be held in the names or name of such person or persons as nominees or nominee of my Trustees and to decide the terms and conditions in every respect including the period thereof and the commission fees or other remuneration payable therefor which commission fees or other remuneration shall be paid out of the capital and income of that part of the Trust Fund in respect of which they are incurred or of any property held on the same trusts AND I DECLARE that my Trustees shall not be liable for any loss arising from any act or omission by any person in whose favour they shall have exercised either or both their powers under this Clause

(d) POWER to retain and purchase chattels of every description under whatever terms they hold the same by virtue of the provisions of this my Will And in respect thereof they shall have the following powers

   (i) To retain the chattels in question under their joint control and custody or the control and custody of any of them or to store the same (whether in a depository or warehouse or elsewhere)

(ii) To lend all or any of the chattels to any person or persons or body or bodies (including a museum or gallery) upon such terms and conditions as my Trustees shall determine

(iii) To cause inventories to be made

(iv) Generally to make such arrangements for their safe custody repair and use as having regard to the circumstances my Trustees may from time to time think expedient

(v) To sell the chattels or any of them and

(vi) To treat any money received as the result of any insurance in so far as not used in reinstating replacing or repairing any chattel lost or damaged as if it were the proceeds of sale of the chattel insured

(e) POWER in the case of any of the chattels of which a person of full age and capacity is entitled to the use but when such person's interest is less than an absolute one

(i) To cause an inventory of such chattels to be made in duplicate with a view to one part being signed by the beneficiary for retention by my Trustees and the other part to be kept by the beneficiary and to cause any such inventory to be revised as occasion shall require and the parts thereof altered accordingly

(ii) To require the beneficiary to arrange at his or her expense for the safe custody repair and insurance of such chattels in such manner as my Trustees think expedient and (where it is not practicable so to require the beneficiary) to make such arrangements as are referred to under paragraph (iv) of sub-clause (d) of this Clause

PROVIDED THAT my Trustees shall also have power to meet any expenses which they may incur in the exercise of any of their powers in respect of chattels out of the capital and income of my estate or such one or more of any different parts and the income thereof as they shall in their absolute discretion determine AND I FURTHER DECLARE that my Trustees shall not be obliged to make or cause to be made any inventories of any such chattels that may be held and shall not be liable for any loss injury or damage that may happen to any such chattels from any cause whatsoever or any failure on the part of anyone to effect or maintain any insurance

IN WITNESS whereof I have hereunto set my hand the day and year first above written

SIGNED by HER ROYAL HIGHNESS)
in our joint presence and)
then by us in her presence)

/s/ Diana

I DIANA PRINCESS OF WALES of Kensington Palace London W8 DECLARE this to be a First Codicil to My Will which is dated the first day of June One thousand nine hundred and ninety three

1. My Will shall be construed and take effect as if in clause 1 the name and address of Commander Patrick Desmond Christian Jermy Jephson were omitted and replaced by the following:

   my sister Elizabeth Sarah Lavinia McCorquodale (known as The Lady Sarah McCorquodale) of Stoke Rochford Grantham Lincolnshire NG33 5EB

2. In all other respects I confirm my said Will.

IN WITNESS whereof I have hereunto set my hand this
First day of February One thousand nine hundred and
ninety six

                    SIGNED by HER ROYAL HIGHNESS)
                         in our joint presence and then)
                             by us in her presence)

                    /s/ Diana
                    _____

Jacqueline K. Onassis

DATE AND PLACE OF BIRTH
July 28,1929
Southampton
Southampton, New York

DATE AND PLACE OF DEATH
May 19, 1994
1040 Fifth Avenue
New York, New York

Ensnare a Greek Bearing Gifts

The lengthy and sophisticated Will of Jacqueline Kennedy Onassis reveals what a sensitive, generous and thoughtful person she was. Jackie's Will, which was signed less than two months before she died, includes numerous detailed bequests, such as the following gifts of tangible personal property to certain people who were obviously important to her:

A. ". . . to my friend, MAURICE TEMPELSMAN . . . my Greek alabaster head of a woman . . ."

B. ". . . to my friend, RACHEL (BUNNY) L. MELLON, in appreciation of her designing the Rose Garden in the White House . . . my Indian miniature 'Lovers watching rain clouds,' Kangra, about 1780 . . . and my large Indian miniature with giltwood frame 'Gardens of the Palace of the Rajh,' a panoramic view of a pink walled garden blooming with orange flowers, with the Rajh being entertained in a pavilion by musicians and dancers. . . .

C. ". . . to my friend [attorney and co-Executor] ALEXANDER D. FORGER . . . my copy of John F. Kennedy's Inaugural Address signed by Robert Frost. . . .

After those very specific bequests, Jackie provided that the balance of her tangible personal property, including "my collection of letters, papers and documents, my personal effects, my furniture, furnishings, rugs, pictures, books, silver, plate, linen, china, glassware, objects of art, wearing apparel, jewelry, automobiles and their accessories, and all other household goods owned by me . . . [including the kitchen sink] were to pass in equal shares to her two children, Caroline and John.

It is noteworthy that Jackie's Will also contained a legal mechanism whereby the children could renounce and disclaim their respective interests in the tangible property within nine months of their mother's death. Any property so disclaimed by the children would have then passed as follows:

1. . . . such items. . . . which relate to the life and work of my late husband, John F. Kennedy, to JOHN FITZGERALD KENNEDY LIBRARY INCORPORATED, Boston, Massachusetts. . . .

2. . . . the balance of said tangible personal property shall be sold and the net proceeds of sale shall be added to my residuary estate. . . .

In fact, Caroline and John chose not to renounce the vast bulk of the tangible personal property bequeathed to them and it was that property which sold at a memorable auction at Sotheby's that grossed close to thirty-five million dollars ($35,000,000) for Caroline and John. Unfortunately, John and Caroline's well-known Uncle Sam wanted his piece of the Kennedy/Onassis pie, and there were substantial United States and New York State estate taxes paid by Jackie's estate. It was those taxes and substantial administration expenses which ultimately depleted the residuary estate so that the charitable lead trust contemplated under the Will (and praised as a brilliant estate planning technique in the press after Jackie's death) was never funded.

Regarding her copyright interests in her "personal papers, letters or other writings by me", Jackie bequeathed those equally to her two children. However, the Will also expressly provided that

> "I request, but do not direct, my children to respect my wish for privacy with respect to such papers, letters and writings and, consistent with that wish, to take whatever action is warranted to prevent the display, publication or distribution, in whole or in part, of these papers, letters and writings."

Jackie's well-know predilection for privacy even extended after her death, and it is no surprise that her surviving children endeavored to respect her wishes.

As a result of her marriage to, and the subsequent death of, Greek shipping magnate, Aristotle Onassis, "Jacqueline K. Onassis" as she refers to herself in her Will, died a very wealthy woman. Her Will indicates her wealth by the number of generous cash bequests which she makes to various friends, relatives, and employees.

There is a $500,000 ten year ten percent (10%) annuity trust established for each child of her sister, Lee B. Radziwell. Ever the politician's wife, Jackie states in her Will:

> "I have made no provision in this my Will for my sister, LEE B. RADZIWILL, for whom I have great affection be-

cause I have already done so during my lifetime. I do wish, however, to remember her children . . ."

The Will also includes the following cash bequests to the following persons on the condition that they survive her:

1. $250,000 to NANCY L. TUCKERMAN.
2. $125,000 to MARTA SQUBIN.
3. $100,000 to niece, ALEXANDRA RUTHERFURD.
4. $50,000 to PROVIDENCIA PAREDES.
5. $25,000 to LEE NASSO.
6. $25,000 to MARIE AMARAL.
7. $25,000 to EFIGENIO PINHEIRO.

There was also a bequest of $250,000 "to each child of mine who survives me.", which brings the grand total of the cash bequests to over one million dollars ($1,000,000).

Jackie's other investments included valuable real estate and a magnificent cooperative apartment located at 1040 Fifth Avenue, New York, New York. That cooperative apartment, which subsequently sold for close to ten million dollars ($10,000,000), and all of her real property in the Towns of Gay Head and Chilmark, Martha's Vineyard, Massachusetts, Jackie devised and bequeathed to her two children in equal shares. Tragically, it was only several nautical miles away from her property in Martha's Vineyard that Jackie's son John died in a tragic plane crash in 1999, five years after she did.

There was also a devise of her real property in Newport, Rhode Island, known as "Hammersmith Farm," which Jackie had inherited from her mother, Janet Lee

Auchincloss, to her half-brother, Hugh D. Auchincloss, Jr., or if he had not survived, then to his children in equal shares.

Although Jackie does not refer to the name "Kennedy" in her own name, instead opting for the initial "K", there are numerous references to her late husband, who died over thirty (30) years before she did. For example, Jackie's Will states:

> "Under the Will of my late husband, JOHN FITZGER-ALD KENNEDY, a marital deduction trust was created for my benefit over which I was accorded a general power of appointment. I hereby exercise such power of appointment and direct that, upon my death, all property subject to such power be transferred, conveyed and paid over to my descendants who survive me, <u>per stirpes</u>."

After all of the foregoing bequests, Jackie's Will contemplated a charitable lead trust comprised of her residuary estate. The charity which was intended to receive the income from that lead trust for 24 years was to be The C & J Foundation (named after her two children), with the remainder passing to Jackie's descendants living at that time. If no descendants of John or Caroline were then living, the remainder was directed to pass one-half ($\frac{1}{2}$) to the living descendants of Jackie's cousin, Michel Bouvier, and one-half ($\frac{1}{2}$) to the living descendants of her sister Lee B. Radziwill, or the entire amount to either if no descendants of the other survived.

The Trustees of the C & J Foundation—Caroline, John, attorney Forger, and friend Tempelsman—were directed to pay the income to qualified charitable organizations, but with Jackie stating her "wish" that "in selecting the particular qualified charitable beneficiaries which shall be the recipients of benefits from the Foundation the independent Trustees give preferential consideration to such eligible organization or organizations the purposes and endeavors of which the independent *Trustees feel are committed to making a significant difference in the cultural or social betterment of mankind or the relief of human suffering.*"(emphasis added)

The Will also expressly provided that "To assist the independent Trustees I authorize, but do not direct, that they retain my close friend and confidante Nancy L. Tuckerman to assist them in the administration of the Foundation."

Unfortunately, the best laid charitable plans went astray in this case as there was no residuary estate remaining after taxes and expenses to fund that charitable trust.

Jackie's choice of Executors is noteworthy. Despite the fact that each of her children, John and Caroline, were attorneys and quite close to their mother, she did not name either one as an Executor of her Will. Instead she named her attorney, Alexander D. Forger, and boyfriend, Maurice Tempelsman, as Executors. Perhaps she felt that her children would have been too grief-stricken to properly fulfill the numerous obligations of an Executor of a Will.

The First Widow who fascinated the world left a Will which also continues to fascinate. She signed that Will in her apartment on Fifth Avenue less than two months before she died from cancer at the age of 64. Although she survived her two husbands, one has to wonder whether she could have survived the untimely death of her 38 year old son. John died with his wife and sister-in-law while piloting his own plane in a tragic nosedive into the ocean short of his mother's former property on the island of Martha's Vineyard off the coast of Massachusetts where the Kennedy family had already made so many big splashes.

/s/ *Jacqueline K. Onassis*

Will dated March 22, 1994

Will signed at 1040 Fifth Avenue, New York, New York

Perry Ellis

DATE AND PLACE OF BIRTH
March 3, 1940
Churchland, Virginia

DATE AND PLACE OF DEATH
May 30, 1986
New York Hospital
New York, New York

Last Year's Fashion

Named Edwin Ellis at birth, fashion designer Perry Ellis was the only child of Edwin L. and Winifred Ellis of Virginia. His father owned a fuel company and his mother was a homemaker. From that humble beginning, Perry Ellis rose steadily through designer showrooms until he became chairman and chief designer for Perry Ellis International, a major fashion player. Ellis's fashion look was a soft, casual style which he referred to as "the slouch look." But financially Ellis was no slouch; he died with a substantial estate.

According to the Will, Ellis's estate is paid over to a pre-existing trust he had established. As was the intent, the exact provisions of that trust are private information. However, we do know from papers filed with the Surrogate's court that Ellis' daughter, Tyler Alexandra Gallagher Ellis, who was born out-of-wedlock, is a beneficiary of that trust. At the time of her father's death, Tyler was not yet two years old and resided with her mother in Los Angeles, California.

The court papers also reveal that Mr. Robert L. McDonald, who resided with Mr. Ellis, was also a beneficiary of that *inter vivos* trust and was named as the Executor of Ellis' Will. Mr. Ellis's Will is not a model of artful or thoughtful draftsmanship. It was particularly unusual to read the Will's final clause which states, "As used in this will, the term 'discretion' shall mean the widest discretion which it shall be legally permissible for a fiduciary to exercise." That might have gone without saying, but perhaps the fiduciary just wanted to be sure. Mr. Ellis signed this Will about six months before he died while suffering from his final illness, which was reported to be AIDS-related.

What may be most interesting about Ellis's Will is the following provision at the start of the Will:

> I direct that my body be cremated immediately upon my death and that my remains be sent to my mother, Mrs. Winifred Ellis, and buried in the family burial plot in Norfolk, Virginia.

It seems that the boy wonder of fashion wanted his final remains to return to his mother and the Virginia soil from whence he came.

/s/ *Perry Ellis*

Will dated January 27, 1986
Residing at 37 West 70th Street, New York, New York

The Leading Ladies

Diamonds To Dust

MARILYN MONROE
"Something's Got to Give"
AUGUST 5, 1962

JOAN CRAWFORD
Whatever Happened to Baby Joan ?
MAY 10, 1977

MAE WEST
Go West, Young Man
NOVEMBER 22, 1980

CAROLE LOMBARD
Till Death Do Us Part
JANUARY 17, 1942

JEAN HARLOW
Platinum Turns to Dust
JUNE 7, 1937

NATALIE WOOD
West Coast Story
NOVEMBER 30, 1981

GLORIA SWANSON
Sunset on Sunset Boulevard
APRIL 4, 1983

Marilyn Monroe

DATE AND PLACE OF BIRTH
June 1, 1926
Los Angeles General Hospital
Los Angeles, California

DATE AND PLACE OF DEATH
August 5, 1962
12305 Fifth Helena Drive
Los Angeles, California

"Something's Got to Give"

Dead from an overdose of sleeping pills at age thirty-six, Marilyn Monroe became an international symbol of glamour and sex who commanded the attention of presidents, Pulitzer Prize-winning playwrights, and all-star ballplayers.

When Marilyn Monroe signed her Will on January 14, 1961, she was already divorced from three husbands, including baseball legend Joe DiMaggio and playwright Arthur Miller. She had first been married at age sixteen to an aircraft worker named James Dougherty. Monroe had also been romantically linked with the Kennedy family. None of her three marriages or other liaisons produced any children, but there were reportedly some close calls. Speaking of calls, there is provocative evidence of a flurry of telephone calls from Monroe's home to Robert Kennedy's Justice Department office in the days just before her death.

Not surprisingly, Monroe's career was at its lowest ebb at the time of her suicide in 1962. Her last two films, *Let's Make Love* and *The Misfits* (written by her soon to be ex-husband Arthur Miller and co-starring Clark Gable shortly before his own death), had been commercial failures.

Monroe had been dismissed from the set of *Something's Got to Give* two months before her death.

It has been reported that both Monroe's mother and grandmother were committed to mental institutions during their lives. Article five of Monroe's Will establishes a $100,000 trust for "the maintenance and support of my mother, GLADYS BAKER," and another relative.

The remaining portion of that trust and 25 percent of the residuary estate is left to Monroe's psychotherapist, Dr. Marianne Kris, "to be used by her for the furtherance of the work of such psychiatric institutions or groups as she shall elect." When Dr. Kris died in 1980, she left her share of the Monroe estate to an institution that subsequently became the London-based Anna Freud Centre for the Psychoanalytic Study and Treatment of Children.

The largest portion of Marilyn Monroe's estate was left to the man she seemed to revere the most shortly before her death, legendary "method" acting teacher Lee Strasberg. Monroe displays her trust and faith in Strasberg by the following bequest of her personal property:

> I give and bequeath all of my personal effects and clothing to LEE STRASBERG, or if he should predecease me, then to my Executor hereinafter named, it being my desire that he distribute these, in his sole discretion, among my friends, colleagues and those to whom I am devoted.

Monroe's own devotion to Strasberg is evident from her substantial gift of "the entire remaining balance," or 75 percent, of her estate that Strasberg received under the following residuary clause of her Will:

All the rest, residue and remainder of my estate . . . I give, devise and bequeath as follows:

(a) to MAY REIS the sum of $40,000.00 or 25% of the total remainder of my estate, whichever shall be the lesser.

(b) to DR. MARIANNE KRIS 25% of the balance thereof, to be used by her as set forth in ARTICLE FIFTH (d) of this my Last Will and Testament.

(c) to LEE STRASBERG the entire remaining balance.

It has been reported that the Monroe estate is continuing to earn income in excess of $1 million over twenty-five years after her death, through the licensing of her image on selected products and through film royalties. When Strasberg himself died in 1982, his share of the Monroe estate passed under his Will (see page 185 for excerpts from Strasberg's Will) to his surviving widow, Anna Strasberg. Strasberg had married Anna in 1968, six years *after* the death of Monroe.

As the primary beneficiary of the Monroe estate, Anna was recently named the sole administrator of it after the death of Monroe's named executor and the draftsman of her Will, attorney Aaron R. Frosch. One has to wonder whether Marilyn would truly have wanted her estate to pass to Strasberg's widow or the Anna Freud Centre in London. But in the end, Monroe may not have had anyone else whom she wanted to have it.

Monroe's body was finally laid to rest in the "Corridor of Memories" in the Westwood Village, California, Memorial Park cemetery. According to employees of that cemetery, Monroe's ex-husband Joe DiMaggio placed red roses on Monroe's crypt for many years after her death. However, despite persistent rumors, the unoccupied crypt right next to the one in which Monroe was laid is not owned in the name of Joe DiMaggio and may be available for purchase from the owner at a cost of over $50,000. For that price, one can lie next to the immortal remains of the most illustrious sex goddess of our times for an eternity. That is much longer than any of Monroe's ex-husbands made it.

/s/ Marilyn Monroe

Will dated January 14, 1961

Joan Crawford

DATE AND PLACE OF BIRTH
March 23, 1908
San Antonio, Texas

DATE AND PLACE OF DEATH
May 10, 1977
150 East 69th Street
New York, New York

Whatever Happened to Baby Joan?

Actress Joan Crawford appeared in over eighty movies, including her first screen success, *Our Dancing Daughters,* in 1928 and her shocking thriller *Whatever Happened to Baby Jane*? in 1962. Crawford was one of Hollywood's most glamorous movie queens, but behind the glamour, Crawford apparently had stormy relationships with three of her four husbands and at least two of her four adopted children.

Crawford's three marriages to actors Douglas Fairbanks, Jr., Franchot Tone, and Phillip Terry all ended in divorce. In 1955 she married Alfred N. Steele, who was the chairman and chief executive officer of the Pepsi-Cola Company. In 1959, Steel died of a heart attack. Steel's widow, Crawford, served on the Pepsi Board of Directors until she herself died of a heart attack eighteen years later in 1977.

During her four marriages, Crawford never bore any children. Instead, she adopted four children—Cathy, Cynthia, Christina, and Christopher. From her Will it appears that Crawford had good relationships with only two of her four children. The second-to-last article of her will states bluntly:

> It is my intention to make no provision herein for my son Christopher or my daughter Christina for reasons which are well known to them.

In her book entitled *Mommie Dearest,* Crawford's daughter Christina Crawford Koontz describes her reaction when she first saw those words in the Will that her mother had signed only seven months before her death: "My first impression was that these words she'd ordered put into her Last Will and Testament were from over twenty years ago. . . . She had tried to reach out of her grave and slap me one last time, just to prove who had really been in control all these years. . . . I was speechless and stunned. Not because of the money. It would have been a nice gesture, but it wasn't the money. It was the insult." *Mommie Dearest* also states that until she was legally adopted by the unmarried Crawford in Las Vegas, Nevada, at the age of eleven months, Christina's name had been Joan Crawford, Jr.

However, Crawford's two favored daughters, Cathy and Cynthia, did not receive too much to write home about either. It appears that daughter Cathy was number one in Crawford's heart as she is given all of Crawford's tangible personal property, if she survived. If she did not survive her mother, the tangible personal property was to go to daughter Cynthia. Furthermore, for daughters Cathy and Cynthia the Will establishes trust funds in the amount of $77,500 for each of them, with principal payments to be gradually doled out as follows until they each reached the age of fifty.

If such daughter shall have attained the following age at the time of my death:	I give and bequeath outright to her the following amount:
30 years	$5,000
35 years	15,000
40 years	30,000
45 years	45,000

I give and bequeath the remaining portion of the amount set apart for such daughter, or the entire amount set apart for her if she shall not have attained the age of 30 years at the time of my death, to my trustees hereinafter named in trust.

For each of the children of only these two daughters, Crawford made $5,000 bequests. There are also seven bequests ranging from $5,000 to $35,000, totally $70,000, to employees and friends but to no other relatives.

Crawford divided her residuary estate into eight shares to be used for the general purposes of six named charities: the Muscular Dystrophy Association of America, the American Cancer Society, the American Heart Association, the Wiltwyck School for Boys, the USO of New York City, and the Motion Picture Country Home & Hospital. The Motion Picture Country Home received three of the eight shares and the other charities each received one share.

As one might have expected, cut-out daughter Christina and son Christopher chose to contest their mother's Will. According to an Agreement of Compromise filed with the New York Surrogate's Court, Christina and Christopher agreed to settle their claim against the estate for a total of $55,000 (less their attorney's fees). In addition, it was agreed that one plaster bust of the deceased Crawford inscribed "To Christina" would be delivered to her.

We need not be too concerned about the plight of Christina because the cover of the lastest edition of her book *Mommie Dearest* proclaims that it has sold over 3 million copies. Ironically, Christina may have profited more from her exposé than her two sisters favored under their mother's Will.

The last article of Crawford's Will simply states: "I direct that my remains be cremated." Crawford's funeral took place on Friday the thirteenth, in May of 1977, but the bad luck may have begun long before then.

/s/ *Joan Crawford Steele*

Will dated October 28, 1976

Mae West

DATE AND PLACE OF BIRTH
August 17, 1893
Brooklyn, New York

DATE AND PLACE OF DEATH
November 22, 1980
570 North Rossmore
Los Angeles, California

Go West, Young Man

The legendary Hollywood goddess of sex, Mae West once purred, "It isn't what I do, but how I do it. It isn't what I say, but how I say it, and how I look when I say and do it."

It was during her Vaudeville days that West met and secretly married her one and only husband, Frank Wallace, whom she later divorced. As West states in her Will:

SECOND: I declare that I am unmarried, having been previously married and divorced from FRANK WALLACE, and that I have no children, living or dead. I further declare that I have a sister, MILDRED KATHERINE WEST, also known as BEVERLY WEST, of 16022 Rayen Street, Sepulveda, California; that I had a brother, John Edwin West, now deceased; and that I have a nephew, JOHN FRANK WEST, of 16022 Rayen Street, Sepulveda, California, the son of my brother, JOHN EDWIN WEST. I further declare that I have no other brothers or sisters, living or dead.

THIRD: I declare that all property which I own, of

whatever nature and wheresoever situated, to be my
sole and separate property.

According to papers filed with the Los Angeles court,
the value of West's personal and real property at the time
of her death was in excess of $1,000,000. With the West
image continuing to pop up the world over, the annual
income accruing to her estate could have been much
greater than that amount.

In her Will, West makes cash bequests ranging from
$1,000 to $25,000 to her nephew, sister, private secretary
and friends. To the "MAE WEST FAN CLUB of Ontario,
Canada" she made a bequest of $3,500. One has to won-
der why there were no Mae West fan clubs in the United
States worthy of a bequest from her.

To her then 85 year old sister, Mildred Katherine
West, West gave the sum of $25,000, "my automobile,
all of my personal jewelry and personal belongings."
Furthermore, sister Katherine is the beneficiary of a
trust containing sister Mae's entire residuary estate. The
trust provided for a minimum monthly payment to sister Katherine of "not less than THREE THOUSAND
($3,000) DOLLARS per month, and such additional
sums, if any, as the Trustee . . . deems proper or necessary for the health, support and maintenance of my sister, it being my desire that my sister be maintained in
the same manner as I have done for her during my lifetime. . . ."

After sister Katherine's death, the remaining property
in the trust was to be divided with one-half divided
among six named relatives. It is interesting to note that of
the five West cousins named in her 1964 Will, four of

them are listed on the court papers as "Address un-known."

The other half of the remaining property in West's estate was to be divided into sevenths and distributed in equal shares to the following seven charitable organizations: the Motion Picture Relief Fund, City of Hope, United Crusade, the Salvation Army, American Brotherhood of Blind, the Hollywood Comedy Club, Cedars-Sinai Hospital of Los Angeles, California. On the probate papers filed with the court, the American Brotherhood of Blind and the Hollywood Comedy Club are both listed with "Address unknown."

As her Executor and Trustee, West designated the United California Bank.

The Will includes a $1.00 *In Terrorem* clause and states that "I have intentionally omitted making provision for all my heirs who are not specifically mentioned herein, and I generally and specifically disinherit each. . . ." West was one of the three children of John and Matilda West who lived in Brooklyn. Mae's predeceased brother is mentioned in the Will and sister Katherine is the primary beneficiary.

There is no mention of any special burial provisions in West's Will. Reportedly, her no longer hot body was shipped back to the borough of her birth, Brooklyn, New York, to be buried in a crypt in the same cemetery as her mother, father and predeceased brother were buried.

When Mae West first moved to Hollywood, California in 1932, she moved into the Ravenswood Apartments. When she died 48 years later, at the age of 87, she died in that very same apartment. Although she was a Presbyterian, West reportedly had her last rites given by a Roman

Catholic priest whose church was nearby. Apparently, he was the only priest able to "come up and see [her] in time."

/s/ *Mae West*

Will dated November 9, 1964

Carole Lombard

DATE AND PLACE OF BIRTH
October 6, 1909
Fort Wayne, Indiana

DATE AND PLACE OF DEATH
January 17, 1942
Table Rock Mountain, Nevada

Till Death Do Us Part

Born Carol Jane Peters in Fort Wayne, Indiana, Carole (who added an *e* to her name when she adopted her stage name) Lombard became one of the brightest stars in Hollywood.

In 1931, Lombard was married to her costar in *My Man Godfrey,* William Powell, but that marriage lasted only two years before ending in divorce. In 1939, Miss Lombard married film star Clark Gable, and the couple were reported to be among Hollywood's happiest at the time of Miss Lombard's tragic death three years later.

As indicated in her Will dated August 8, 1939, Carole Lombard left her entire estate to her husband, Clark Gable, and named him as the sole executor. For the provisions of the Will of Clark Gable, who died eighteen years later in 1960, see page 37 of this volume.

Carole Lombard's death came suddenly and tragically when the airplane in which she, her mother, and twenty others were flying crashed and burned near Las Vegas, Nevada. In light of her fiery end, it is indeed ironic that the first article of Lombard's Will provides the following:

I request that no person other than my immediate family and the persons who shall prepare my remains for interment be permitted to view my remains after death has been pronounced. I further request a private funeral and that I be clothed in white and placed in a modestly priced crypt in Forest Lawn Memorial Park, Glendale, California.

The search party that located all of the crash victims included cowboys, Indians, and soldiers. Miss Lombard's body was not initially recognizable because it was so badly burned and was only identified with the aid of dental records and from a wisp of her blond hair. It is not known whether she was "clothed in white" before being placed in a "modestly priced" crypt at Forest Lawn Memorial Park cemetery as she had requested in her Will.

When the remarried Clark Gable died in 1960, his body was placed in the crypt next to the one holding his former wife's remains. (Where Gable's fifth wife, to whom he was married when he died, is buried is another story.) It was death that brought the King and Queen of Hollywood back together again.

/s/ *Carole Lombard*
_____

Will dated August 8, 1939

Jean Harlow

DATE AND PLACE OF BIRTH
March 3, 1911
Kansas City, Missouri

DATE AND PLACE OF DEATH
June 7, 1937
Good Samaritan Hospital
Hollywood, California

Platinum Turns to Dust

Born Harlean Carpenter in Kansas City, in 1927 at the age of sixteen, Harlean eloped with a Chicago bond broker named Charles McGrew 2d, and the couple moved to Beverly Hills, California. With her stunning platinum-blond hair and alluring sexuality, she began appearing on the silver screen under the name of Jean Harlow. However, it was not until after the date she signed her Will that she legally changed her name to Jean Harlow, according to papers filed by her mother with the Los Angeles court.

Seven months after moving to Hollywood, the McGrews separated and were subsequently divorced. Harlow's second husband, Paul Bern, committed suicide in 1932 two months after their marriage by shooting himself at home in Harlow's bedroom. In September of 1933, the actress married a cameraman named Harold G. Rosson, but in March 1955, the actress commenced a divorce action against him, complaining in part that his reading in bed did not allow her to receive the proper amount of rest.

It is noteworthy that the Will includes a "One Dollar

($1.00)" *in terrorem* clause enjoining anyone from contesting the will. Based on her marital history, Harlow appears to have been terrifying indeed.

At the time of her death in 1937 at the age of twenty-six, it was reported in *The New York Times* that Jean Harlow had an estate that was worth in excess of $1 million. After an illness of only a few days, she died of complications arising from uremic poisoning. At her bedside when she died was her fiancé, actor William Powell, and as one would expect, her mother and sole heir, Jean Harlow Bello.

Harlow was laid to rest in a crypt in a private sanctuary room in Glendale's Forest Lawn Cemetery. The room contained marble from France, Italy, and Spain and was reportedly purchased by Powell for $25,000 as a tribute to the woman he then loved. The second crypt in the room is occupied by the body of Harlow's number one fan—her mother.

　　　　　　　　　　　　　　　　/s/ Harlean Rosson
　　　　　　　　　　　　　　　　————————————————————

Will dated September 5, 1935

Natalie Wood

DATE AND PLACE OF BIRTH
July 20, 1938
San Francisco, California

DATE AND PLACE OF DEATH
November 30, 1981
Water off Santa Catalina Island
California

West Coast Story

Born Natasha Gurdin to Russian immigrant parents in San Francisco, Natalie Wood got her new name at age six. Wood was one of the few child stars of Hollywood who successfully made the transition to adult film roles, including roles in *Rebel Without a Cause, Marjorie Morningstar,* and *West Side Story.*

Wood married actor Robert Wagner in 1957, was divorced from him in 1962, and then remarried him in 1972. Between her marriages to Mr. Wagner, she was also married to, and subsequently divorced from, English film producer Richard Gregson. Her marriage to Mr. Gregson produced a daughter named Natasha Gregson. Her second marriage to Mr. Wagner produced another daughter, Courtney Brooke Wagner. At the outset of her Will Wood expressly describes her family relationships as follows:

> I declare that I am married, and that my husband's name is ROBERT J. WAGNER. I have one child by a previous marriage, namely my daughter, NATASHA GREGSON, who was born September 29, 1970, and one child by my present marriage, namely my daughter, COURTNEY BROOKE WAGNER, who was born March 9, 1974.

My said husband has one child by a previous marriage, namely his daughter KATHARINE WAGNER, who was born May 11, 1964.

Later in the Will, Natalie Wood provides that husband Robert should be the guardian of her daughter Natasha from her prior marriage and expressly states her reasons for doing so as follows:

Under circumstances now existing, I feel that in the event that I am survived by my husband, ROBERT J. WAGNER, the best interest of my daughter NATASHA would be served if he were appointed guardian of her person and estate. My husband has assured me that in such event he would cooperate with NATASHA's father in the same manner that I would cooperate with him in maintaining his relationship with NATASHA. Accordingly it is my desire and request that ROBERT J. WAGNER be appointed to serve in those capacities. . . . Accordingly, in the event that both my husband and I are deceased during the minority of my daughter COURTNEY, it is my desire and request that she and NATASHA be raised together in the same household, in California, and that they be cared for by my housekeeper WILLIE MAE WORTHEN.

The role of mother was evidently important to her, as Wood singles out one painting she owned entitled *The Three Ages of Motherhood* for special disposition under her Will.

To her sister Olga Viripaeff, Wood made a bequest of $15,000, and she gave to her sister "LANA GURDIN, also known as LANA WOOD, all of my furs and clothing." To her husband, Robert Wagner, Wood left "all of my interest in automobiles, household furnishings, paintings and other works of art (except as hereinafter provided), jewelry and remaining personal effects" and a portion of her residuary estate. The balance of her residuary estate was to be held in trust for the benefit of her parents and children. Wagner was appointed the executor and trustee of his wife's Will.

Natalie Wood signed her Will about a year and a half prior to her tragic drowning near Santa Catalina Island off the coast of Los Angeles. At the time of her death, she had been cruising on a fifty-five-foot cabin cruiser with her husband, Robert Wagner, and actor Christopher Walken, who was costarring with Wood in a film entitled *Brainstorm*. After a seven-hour search by the Coast Guard, Wood's body was found in a rocky cove near Santa Catalina. Her death was called an accidental drowning by investigators.

Wood is buried in the Westwood Village Memorial Park, a short distance from the crypt of another West Coast girl, named Marilyn Monroe.

/s/ *Natalie Wagner*

Will dated April 17, 1980

Gloria Swanson

DATE AND PLACE OF BIRTH
March 27, 1899
Chicago, Illinois

DATE AND PLACE OF DEATH
April 4, 1983
New York Hospital
New York, New York

Sunset on Sunset Boulevard

The only child of Joseph and Adelaide Svensson, Gloria May Josephine Svensson was born in Chicago in 1899. Gloria Svensson adopted the name "Swanson," and she became the glittering goddess of Hollywood's roaring twenties. Ms. Swanson summed up her larger-than-life presence in films with her famous line in the 1950 film *Sunset Boulevard:* "I *am* big. It's the movies that got small."

By the time of her death, Gloria Swanson had been married six times and divorced five times. Her last marriage was in 1976 to writer William Dufty, but he receives nothing under her Will. Early in her career, she was also romantically linked with a Boston financier and patriarch of an American political dynasty, Joseph P. Kennedy.

Her six marriages produced two daughters, Gloria Daly and Michelle Amon, and she adopted a son, Joseph, who predeceased her in 1977. She named her two daughters and her attorney as executors of her Will. Her Will divides her estate to give 40 percent to each of her daughters and 10 percent to each of the surviving daughters of her predeceased son as follows:

. . . I give, devise and bequeath all the rest residue and remainder of my Estate, real, personal or mixed and wherever situated as follows:

(a) Forty percent (40%) to my daughter, GLORIA S. DALY of . . . New York City . . .

(b) Forty percent (40%) to my daughter, MICHELLE AMON of Neuilly, 92200 France. . . .

(c) Ten percent (10%) to my granddaughter CHRISTINA SWANSON and ten percent (10%) to my granddaughter PATRICIA SWANSON.

However, a subsequent codicil to the Will executed in 1981 inexplicably drastically changes the disposition of the residuary estate, providing that daughter Gloria would receive the odd percentage of 13⅓ of her mother's estate outright, and the other 26⅔ of her 40-percent share was to be held in trust for the benefit of Swanson's *other* daughter, Michelle. Daughter Michelle continued to receive 40 percent of her mother's estate outright.

Swanson was known for her extravagance and lavish lifestyle. It is reported that she earned $8 million between 1918 and 1929 and that she spent nearly all of that. When she died at the age of eighty-four, her gross estate was in excess of $1,440,000 according to papers filed with the New York court.

The first article of the Will directs that Swanson's cremation be private and confined to members of her family only and that there be "no public funeral or display of any sort." Dead in her eighties, the shining star of the twenties guarded her image until the very end.

_____/s/ *Gloria Swanson*_____

Will dated March 4, 1981
Codicil dated September 11, 1981
Residing at 920 Fifth Avenue, New York, New York

The Leading Men

Last Curtain Calls

CLARK GABLE
Gone with the Wind
NOVEMBER 16, 1960

DOUGLAS FAIRBANKS
The Public Life of Don Juan
DECEMBER 12, 1939

YUL BRYNNER
The King Must Die
OCTOBER 10, 1985

SPENCER TRACY
Guess Who's Not Coming to Dinner
JUNE 10, 1967

EDWARD G. ROBINSON
The End of Rico
JANUARY 26, 1973

JOHN WAYNE
Put Down Your Dukes
JUNE 11, 1979

HUMPHREY BOGART
Cigarette Smoking Was Hazardous to His Health
JANUARY 14, 1957

WILLIAM HOLDEN
Sunset on Ocean Avenue
NOVEMBER 16, 1981

HENRY FONDA
Beyond Golden Pond
AUGUST 12, 1982

ROCK HUDSON
Bad Day at Castle Rock
OCTOBER 2, 1985

CARY GRANT
He Was No Angel
NOVEMBER 29, 1986

Clark Gable

DATE AND PLACE OF BIRTH
February 1, 1901
Cadiz, Ohio

DATE AND PLACE OF DEATH
November 16, 1960
Hollywood Presbyterian Hospital
Hollywood, California

Gone With the Wind

Called "the King of Hollywood," Clark Gable starred as southern gentleman Rhett Butler in the 1939 screen classic *Gone With the Wind* and in the ill-fated *The Misfits* with Marilyn Monroe shortly before they both died. Known as the consummate lady-killer, Gable did not appear to be too lucky in love. He was married five times. His first marriage, to Josephine Dillon, ended in divorce in 1930. His second marriage, to Rhea Langham, ended in divorce in 1939. His third marriage ended tragically when his wife, actress Carole Lombard, was killed in a plane crash on January 17, 1942. Gable and Lombard were reported to have had one of Hollywood's happiest marriages. It is noteworthy that after his death eighteen years later, Gable's body was placed in a crypt next to that of his former wife. One has to wonder how Gable's fifth and final wife, Kay, felt about where husband Clark was finally laid to rest.

After the plane crash killing Carole Lombard, Gable joined the United States Air Force and became a private at the age of forty-one. Gable flew in dangerous combat bombing missions over Europe, and with those war stories behind him, Clark Gable made a triumphant return to Hollywood.

After his return Gable married Lady Sylvia Ashley in 1949, but that marriage ended in divorce in 1952. In 1955, Gable married Kathleen ("Kay") Williams Spreckles, a model and actress, and he was married to her when he died of a heart attack at the age of 59 in 1960. It has been claimed that the tension on the set of *The Misfits* between the tardy Marilyn Monroe and her playwright (and soon to be ex-) husband, Arthur Miller, partially contributed to the emotional and physical strain on Gable.

Gable's last Will, which he signed in 1955, is just over two pages long and initially states, "I hereby declare that I am married to Kathleen G. Gable and that I have no children." Next, there is evidence of the gentleman Gable was known to be, as shown by a very unusual gift. To "JOSEPHINE DILLON, my former wife," Gable devised a piece of real property and a house located in North Hollywood, California. One doesn't usually see gifts to former wives in Wills, but Gable did it in his. Other than that one piece of property, Gable gave all the rest of his estate "to my beloved wife, KATHLEEN G. GABLE" and appointed her as the sole executrix of his Will. Perhaps as a precaution against the former wives who were not mentioned, Gable's Will also includes a $1.00 *in terrorem* clause.

Despite five marriages, Gable never had any children while he was alive. However, papers filed with the Los Angeles court revealed that Gable's wife, Kathleen, was pregnant with a child at the time of his death, referred to in the court papers as "Unborn Baby Gable." John Clark

Gable was born on March 20, 1961, in the same hospital in which his father had died 124 days earlier.

/s/ *Clark Gable*

Will dated September 19, 1955

Douglas Fairbanks

DATE AND PLACE OF BIRTH
May 23, 1883
Denver, Colorado

DATE AND PLACE OF DEATH
December 12, 1939
705 Ocean Front
Santa Monica, California

The Public Life of Don Juan

One of the greatest stars of the silent-film era, Douglas Fairbanks was known worldwide for his roles as Robin Hood, the Thief of Baghdad, Don Q., and Don Juan. Fairbanks, who had a smile that charmed the world, was married three times, first to Beth Sully in New York in 1907. That marriage ended in divorce in 1919. In 1920, Fairbanks married screen star Mary Pickford in Los Angeles in a wedding that was one of the most sensational Hollywood had ever seen, and their home in Beverly Hills, dubbed "Pickfair," was reportedly out of this world. It seems that the Fairbanks-Pickford relationship lost its magic in the mid-1930s; they were finally divorced on January 14, 1936. After their divorce, Pickford remained at Pickfair and lived there with her next husband until her death in 1979.

On March 7, 1936, in Paris, Fairbanks married Lady Ashley, former wife of London's Lord Ashley and formerly a musical comedy actress named Sylvia Hawkes.

In his Will dated November 2, 1936, Fairbanks leaves 20/40ths of his estate to his "beloved wife, SYLVIA FAIR-BANKS," with the provision that such amount shall not exceed $1 million. He leaves 12/40ths to his "beloved son DOUGLAS FAIRBANKS, JR.," but not to exceed $600,000. Two-fortieths are left to his "beloved brother" Robert Fairbanks, but not to exceed $100,000, and one-fortieth to his "beloved brother" Norris Wilcox. One-fortieth of the estate equal to $50,000 was placed in trust for each of Fairbanks's four nieces, and the final fortieth ("not to exceed the sum of Fifty Thousand Dollars ($50,000.00)"), was left to Douglas Fairbanks, Jr., "absolutely but with the request that he distribute said sum to the people and in the proportions as I advise him by letter addressed to him to be found with this Will." The contents of that letter were never revealed. Any property remaining after the foregoing fractional amounts were paid was to be divided equally between Fairbanks's wife, Sylvia, and son, Douglas, Jr.

The Will also provides for a $10,000 bequest to the Motion Picture Actors' Relief Fund of Los Angeles, California, to be known as the "Douglas Fairbanks Fund." Fairbanks named the Bank of America National Trust & Savings Association as executor of his Will for property located in California, and the Guaranty Trust Company of New York "as Executor to administer upon all of my estate located outside the State of California." It is unusual to appoint two different executors to administer different property, but Fairbanks liked to do things his way.

Fairbanks died of a sudden heart attack at the age of fifty-six while sleeping in his home overlooking the Pacific Ocean in Santa Monica, California. After Fairbanks's death, it was reported the Fairbanks's 150-pound mastiff named Marco Polo whined for hours near Fairbanks's bed, refusing to move after his master's death. Apparently, the famed Fairbanks smile affected fans not only of the human species.

/s/ *Douglas Fairbanks*

Will dated November 2, 1936

Yul Brynner

DATE AND PLACE OF BIRTH
July 11, 1915
Siberia, Russia

DATE AND PLACE OF DEATH
October 10, 1985
New York Hospital
New York, New York

The King Must Die

Born on the island of Sakhalin off the coast of Siberia in the Soviet Union to a Rumanian mother and father who was a Mongolian mining engineer, Yul Brynner's exotic background added to the regal aura about him. As the perennial King in the theater and film versions of "The King and I", Brynner commanded that particular role the way no other actor ever had and has come to be identified with that particular part. It was well stated in a review by the *New York Times*, "Yul Brynner's performance in 'The King and I' . . . can no longer be regarded as a feat of acting or of endurance. After 30-odd years of on-and-off barnstorming, Mr. Brynner is quite simply, The King. Man and role long since merged into a fixed image that is as much a part of our collective consciousness as the Statue of Liberty."

At least the Statue of Liberty has hair. Brynner's bald head was as much a part of his image as his oriental features. Brynner also had leading roles in big pictures including, "The Ten Commandments", "The Brothers Karamazov" and "The Magnificent Seven."

When he died, Brynner was survived by his wife,

Kathy, and five children—Rock, Lark, Victoria, Mia and Melody. To his son Rock, he gave a $50,000 bequest and any stock he owned in "Hard Rock Café PLC, an English corporation, or Hard Rock Holdings (USA), Inc., a Delaware corporation, (or other entity owing or operating the Hard Rock Café in New York, New York)." It might have been easier said if Brynner gave his son any stock with the name "Rock" in it.

To his daughter Lark Lippert, Brynner made a $25,000 bequest. Daughter Victoria Brynner received a $50,000 bequest and a $100,000 trust fund for her benefit. Daughters Mia and Melody got to share any tangible property that was left if Brynner's wife had not survived. They were also beneficiaries of a separate *inter vivos* trust Brynner had established in 1983. Talk about playing favorites with your children. Just so there would be no mistake on that subject, Brynner's Will includes the following:

> I have intentionally made no provision in this my Will, for any of my children not named in this Will.

Brynner left the bulk of his estate to his wife Kathy Lee, including the following gifts of his two residences in New York and in France:

> I give and bequeath to my wife, KATHY LEE BRYNNER, if she shall survive me, all of my right, title and interest in the capital stock of 860 West Tower, Inc. and propri-etary lease relating to cooperative apartment No. 27-A at 860 United Nations Plaza, New York, New York. . . .
>
> (b) If my said wife, KATHY LEE BRYNNER, shall survive me, I give, devise and bequeath to her a life estate in and to my house and land known as Le Ma-

noir de Criquebeuf, Bonnebosq, 14340 Cambremer, France. . . .

Kathy Lee Brynner also received all of Yul's "automobiles, jewelry, books, artwork, silverware, paintings, household and personal effects and similar tangible personal property. . . ."

Brynner was known to be an accomplished photographer and a lover of the arts. His Will includes the following bequests of art works to two special friends:

> (a) I give and bequeath to my friend Robert Lantz, if he shall survive me, the ink and watercolor view of boats at Trouville by Boudin, if I own same at my death.
>
> (b) I give and bequeath to my friend, Michael Lynne, if he shall survive me, the abstract painting by Vasarely, if I own the same at my death.

From Siberia to Siam, Yul Brynner will always be remembered as the King, especially around his own castle.

/s/ *Yul Brynner*

Will dated July 14, 1985

Spencer Tracy

DATE AND PLACE OF BIRTH
April 5, 1900
Milwaukee, Wisconsin

DATE AND PLACE OF DEATH
June 10, 1967
9191 St. Ives Drive
Beverly Hills, California

Guess Who's Not Coming to Dinner

Appearing in over sixty films during his long career, Spencer Tracy won the Academy Award for Best Actor two years in a row but may be best known for his appearances in nine films with Katharine Hepburn, with whom he was romantically linked. Hepburn and Tracy's final appearance together was in Tracy's last movie, *Guess Who's Coming to Dinner*, which was completed shortly before he died.

Mr. Tracy, who was a devout Catholic, had married an actress named Louise Treadwell in 1923. Despite his romance with Ms. Hepburn, Spencer remained married to Louise until death did them part. As he Will states, the Tracys had two children.

I am married. My wife is LOUISE TREADWELL TRACY. I have two children, the issue of our marriage, a son, JOHN TEN-BROECK TRACY, and a daughter, LOUISE TREADWELL TRACY, also known as SUSIE TRACY.

John was born totally deaf in 1924. As a result of his

son's deafness, Tracy and his wife founded the John Tracy Clinic for the Deaf in Los Angeles in 1942.

In his 1961 Will, Tracy makes the following bequests of his tangible personal property:

FOURTH: I bequeath all of my jewelry to my daughter, Susie, and to my son, John, to be divided as they may agree.

FIFTH: I bequeath to my brother, CARROLL E. TRACY, that automobile owned by me and used by me as my personal automobile, whichever automobile that shall be at the time of my death. I further bequeath to my said brother my wardrobe, or such part thereof as he selects. . . .

SIXTH: I devise and bequeath to my wife, Louise Tracy, my interest in our residence or residences and such item or items as she may select from my remaining articles of personal, domestic or household use or ornament, including my remaining automobiles.

In the codicil to his Will, which he executed about two years later, Tracy revoked article five of his Will and substituted the following:

FIFTH: I bequeath to my brother, CARROLL E. TRACY, all of the furniture, fixtures, paintings and other articles of ornament and household use at 9191 St. Ives Drive, Los Angeles, California, and the two automobiles owned by me and used by me for my personal use which are kept at said address. I further bequeath to my said brother my wardrobe, or such part thereof as he selects. . . .

This change increased the property passing to Tracy's brother and at the same time reduced the tangible personal property passing to Tracy's wife. However, the same codicil changed the distribution of Tracy's residuary estate so that one-half was to be distributed outright to his wife and the balance held in trust for her benefit, rather than the entire amount's being held in trust as the Will had provided. Seems as if Tracy did not want his wife to get her hands on his "wardrobe," automobiles, or "other articles of ornament and household use."

When he died, Tracy had not been living with his estranged wife. After learning that Tracy had been stricken by a heart attack at his home at six A.M., Tracy's brother, Carroll, arrived with a doctor, but it was too late. Arriving at Tracy's house soon thereafter were Tracy's wife, daughter, and son. Next came Tracy's longtime "companion" Katharine Hepburn, director George Cukor (who had been a witness to Tracy's Will), and Tracy's business manager, Ross Evans. Tracy's funeral was attended by many of Hollywood's notables, including Gregory Peck, Edward G. Robinson, and Frank Sinatra. However, conspicuously absent from Tracy's funeral was his favorite co-star, Katharine Hepburn.

/s/ Spencer Tracy

Will dated May 6, 1961
Codicil dated October 23, 1963

Edward G. Robinson

DATE AND PLACE OF BIRTH
December 12, 1893
Bucharest, Rumania

DATE AND PLACE OF DEATH
January 26, 1973
Mount Sinai Hospital
Hollywood, California

The End of Rico

When he was born in Rumania, he was named Emanuel Goldenberg, but after his family emigrated to the United States, young Emanuel quickly mastered the English language and changed his name to the American-sounding Edward G. Robinson. Robinson's most famous role was that of Little Caesar in the 1931 film by that name in which he uttered his classic line after being shot by the police: "Mother of God, is this the end of Rico?"

In 1927, Robinson had married actress Gladys Lloyd. That marriage lasted for twenty-eight years before ending in divorce in 1955. In 1958, while appearing on Broadway and playing an older man who marries a much younger woman, Robinson married a thirty-eight-year-old woman named Jane Arden.

During his life, Robinson was known to be a serious collector of artworks. During the aftermath of his divorce, in 1957, Robinson reportedly sold the bulk of his art collection for $3,250,000. However, it appears there were still at least a few valuable paintings remaining, as the Will provides:

DISPOSITION OF PAINTINGS

A. If I am survived by my wife, JANE, I give and bequeath my painting by Pisarro [sic] entitled "The Dead
Tree", my painting by Vuillard of an interior scene with
child in red dress entitled "Madame Vuillard au Deje-
uner", my painting by Berthe Morisot entitled "Avant le
Theatre" and all paintings painted by me (other than
the portrait of my friend, Sam Jaffe) to my Trustees
hereinafter named, in trust. . . .

Finally, Robinson alludes to the prominence and future provenance of his art collection by stating:

I also recommend that my Executors or Trustees consider the possibility of conducting a sale of such paintings and other art objects at public auction under the
most advantageous terms available; further, I suggest
that such public auction might be held at Sotheby in
London, unless in the light of all circumstances and
conditions existing at that time it appears advantageous to conduct the sale at the Parke-Bernet Galleries,
Inc. of New York City or Christies in London. It is my
further belief that it would be proper and advantageous
to sell my paintings and other art objects as "THE ED-
WARD G. ROBINSON COLLECTION."

Besides paintings, Robinson also appears to have been
a collector of books, and for his beloved books he made
the following provisions in his Will:

If I am survived by my wife, JANE, I give and bequeath
all of my books to my said wife. If my said wife shall
predecease me, then I direct that said books be distrib-

uted to my Trustees hereinafter named and that my Trustees retain said books for a period of two years from the time of my death. <u>If, at the end of said two year period, my son, EDWARD, is then living and if during said two year period he has, in the opinion of my Trustees, exhibited sufficient responsibility and stability to warrant distribution of a portion of my books to him, said books shall be divided by my Executor or Trustees between my son, EDWARD, and my granddaughter, FRANCESCA, in shares to be determined by my Trustees to be of approximate equal value</u> [emphasis added]. . . . I recommend that my Trustees consider the possibility of selling such books as a collection at Parke-Bernet Galleries, Inc. in New York City.

Next there is this provision for a one-of-a-kind piano that Robinson owned:

I now own a certain piano which is unique in that it has been autographed by many of the great contemporary musicians. If I own said piano at the time of my death . . . I give and bequeath said piano to the UNIVERSITY OF CALIFORNIA for the use of the School of Music at the Los Angeles campus of said University.

Finally, Robinson disposed of all his remaining tangible personal property as follows:

If I am survived by my wife, JANE, I give and bequeath all of my clothing, linens, pipes, souvenirs, mementos, and jewelry not otherwise disposed of hereunder, and similar personal effects to my said wife. . . . I request, but do not direct, that my wife give mementos from my personal effects to my brother, my nieces and nephews, and to such of our friends as she shall select, which mementos may have a particular sentimental meaning to the particular person selected as the recipient by my said wife.

I give and bequeath to my wife, JANE, for life, all my photographs, scripts, my self-portraits, records and similar personal effects, pertaining to my career. Upon the death of my said wife . . . I give and bequeath the aforesaid property to the UNIVERSITY OF SOUTHERN CALIFORNIA, a California corporation.

One has to wonder what wife Jane did with her husband's pipe collection. Besides, people always thought of Robinson as a cigar chomper.

During his life, Robinson was known to be generous with friends and charity. The following provisions in his Will are in line with that reputation.

BEQUESTS TO FRIENDS AND RELATIVES

The following gifts are small token gifts and do not in any way measure my affection for the beneficiary. I give and bequeath the following property to the following persons:

A. To my friend, SAM JAFFE, the portrait of Sam Jaffe painted by me.

G. To my niece, BEULAH GOLDBERG (also known as BEAULA ROBINSON) the following amounts:

    1. If my said niece survives me, the sum of Five Thousand Dollars ($5,000).

    2. If my said niece survives me and she is unmarried at the time of my death, I give and bequeath to her an additional Two Thousand Five Hundred Dollars

($2,500.00) [Was a husband worth only $2,500 back then?]

BEQUESTS TO CHARITY

I give and bequeath five percent (5%) of my net estate
. . . in equal shares to the following charitable organizations:

A. CITY COLLEGE OF NEW YORK, City of New York;

B. ACTORS FUND OF AMERICA (for the benefit of indigent actors);

C. MOTION PICTURE RELIEF FUND (for the care of residents of Motion Picture Country Home);

D. AMERICAN ACADEMY OF DRAMATIC ARTS, City of New York;

E. JEWISH COMMUNITY FOUNDATION OF THE JEWISH FEDERATION—COUNCIL OF LOS ANGELES;

F. N.A.A.C.P. LEGAL DEFENSE & EDUCATIONAL FUND.

Robinson's residuary estate was placed in trust for the benefit of his wife, son, and granddaughter. If none of them had survived him, which they all did, one-half of the estate was to be paid to the Motion Picture Relief Fund and the balance to Robinson relatives.

As befitting a product of the gangster era, Robinson's Will includes the following unusual "Contest Clause," which provides in part:

Except as otherwise provided in this Will, I have intentionally and with full knowledge omitted to provide for my heirs. If any person other than my son, EDWARD, shall claim to be a child of mine or the descendant of a child of mine (other than my granddaughter, FRANCESCA, or her descendants), I direct my Executors to resist such claim; but if any court shall nevertheless determine that such person is a descendant of mine, I give to such person the sum of Ten Dollars ($10.00) and no more. . . .

Any offspring of Little Caesar out there thinking about asserting a claim had only ten dollars to look forward to receiving.

Despite his long film career, Robinson never received an Academy Award for any of his performances. Robinson was to have received a special Oscar for his "outstanding contribution to motion pictures" at the Academy Awards ceremony scheduled for March of 1973. Unfortunately, the end for Rico came two months too soon.

/s/ *Edward G. Robinson*

Will dated February 15, 1972

John Wayne

DATE AND PLACE OF BIRTH
May 26, 1907
Winterset, Iowa

DATE AND PLACE OF DEATH
June 11, 1979
U.C.L.A. Medical Center
Los Angeles, California

Put Down Your Dukes

The paradigm of bygone American masculinity and virility, John Wayne swashbuckled his way though over two hundred films during his fifty-year film career. Finally, the man known as The Duke put down his guns and succumbed to multiple cancer of the lungs, abdomen, stomach, and intestines at the age of seventy-two.

Despite the All-American image, Wayne had been divorced twice, and as his Will indicates, his third marriage was on shaky ground. Wayne's Will begins:

> I am married to PILAR WAYNE, but she and I are separated, and for this reason I intentionally make no provision in this Will for her. I have seven (7) children whose names and respective birth dates are as follows: MICHAEL ANTHONY WAYNE, November 23, 1934; MARY ANTONIA LA CAVA, February 25, 1936; PATRICK JOHN WAYNE, July 15, 1939; MELINDA ANN MUNOZ, December 3, 1940, AISSA WAYNE, March 31, 1956; JOHN ETHAN WAYNE, February 22, 1962; and MARISA CARMELA WAYNE, February 22, 1966. The first four of the above-named children are the issue of my former marriage with Josephine A.

Wayne; the last three of the above-named children are the issue of my marriage with said Pilar. I and all of my said children except Mary Antonia La Cava and Melinda Ann Munoz are sometimes also known by the surname "Morrison."

Wayne's wife, Pilar Palette Wayne, was born in Peru. Wayne's first two wives, Josephine Saenz and Esperanzo Bauer, were also Latin Americans. It appears that one other part that Wayne played offscreen was that of Latin lover.

Based on the provisions of the Will, it appears that the Duke favored his eldest son, Michael. Michael is named as co-executor of his father's Will, was appointed custodian of any minor child's funds, and received a bequest of all Wayne's preferred stock in his film company, Batjac Productions, Inc. Wayne divides his tangible property, including any "motion picture memorabilia or items whose value arises primarily from their connection with my motion picture career," but not including any "paintings, sculpture, American Indian artifacts, and other items having intrinsic merit and value," equally among his seven children. Those excluded "art objects" were to be donated to a charitable organization, selected by the executors.

In the Will, Wayne makes a $10,000 bequest to a former secretary and a $30,000 bequest to his current secretary. Wayne establishes a trust fund for the benefit of his former wife Josephine Morrison, which was to pay her the sum of $3,000 per month, with the remainder to pass to her four children after her death.

Living up to his reputation as a gunslinger, Wayne's Will includes a final *in terrorem* clause stating:

If any beneficiary under this Will in any manner, directly or indirectly, contests or attacks this Will or any of its provisions, any share or interest in my estate given to that contesting beneficiary under this Will is revoked and shall be disposed of in the same manner provided herein as if that contesting beneficiary had predeceased me without issue.

Now, that's true grit.

　　　　　　　　　　　　　　　/s/ John Wayne
　　　　　　　　　　　　　　　_____

Will dated October 5, 1978

Humphrey Bogart

DATE AND PLACE OF BIRTH
December 25, 1899
West 103rd Street
New York, New York

DATE AND PLACE OF DEATH
January 14, 1957
Holmby Hills, California

Cigarette Smoking Was Hazardous to His Health

Dead from throat cancer at the age of fifty-seven, actor Humphrey Bogart appeared in many screen classics and made Casablanca famous. Despite his often brusque style and tough-guy image, Humphrey Bogart was apparently also very lovable, being married to four different actresses. He divorced his first wife, Helen Menken, in 1927 after one year of marriage. His subsequent marriage to Mary Phillips lasted until 1937. In 1938, Bogart married Mayo Methot. Mayo finally allowed Bogart to obtain a Nevada-style divorce from her in 1945. Shortly after that, Bogart married his *To Have and Have Not* costar, actress Lauren Bacall. Bacall was still happily married to Bogart when he died twelve years later.

The first article of Bogart's Will, which he signed in 1956 about six months before he died, states:

I am married to Betty Bogart (also known as LAUREN BACALL BOGART) and have two children, namely, my son STEPHEN HUMPHREY BOGART, who was born

January 6, 1949, and my daughter LESLIE BOGART, who was born August 23, 1952.

To his wife "Betty," as Bogart affectionately referred to her, he left all of his "clothing and personal effects . . . jewelry, automobiles and accessories thereto, and such interest as I may have in household furniture, furnishings, equipment and effects of every sort and nature." If his wife did not survive him, then Bogart provided that his friend and business manager, A. Morgan Maree, Jr., should dispose of the property "in such manner as he may believe would comply with my desires." Mr. Maree, who was a trusted adviser to both Humphrey and Betty Bogart, was also named as co-executor of the Will, together with Betty Bogart and the Security-First National Bank of Los Angeles. For her own reasons, Betty declined to serve as an executor of her husband's estate according to papers filed with the court, but she did serve as a trustee of her children's trusts.

In his Will, Bogart places one-half of his residuary estate in trust for his wife, "Betty." That trust provides:

> The purpose of this trust shall be to provide for the security and welfare of my beloved wife BETTY during the remainder of her life. In establishing this trust I am particularly aware of her high earning potential, the impact of income taxes thereon, the standard of living to which she has been accustomed during our marriage, and the uncertainties of the many years during which I hope her life will continue in the event of my decease.

The balance of Bogart's estate was to be held in trust for his two children until they reached the age of forty-five. The trustees had the discretion to invade principal or income for his children's benefit, and in this regard the Will states:

> In exercising such discretion my trustees shall take into account the provisions that my wife BETTY shall be able to make for such child from time to time out of funds available to her and shall be guided as near as may be by the standard of living to which said children have been accustomed during my lifetime. It is my desire that their care, comfort and welfare be adequately provided for during their tender years, that they be afforded every opportunity for such higher education as may be appropriate in view of their interest and ability, and that consideration for their support and maintenance after completion of their education shall be secondary.

If neither Betty nor any children survived, there were provisions for "BETTY's mother, NATALIE GOLDBERG, so long as she shall live, and thereafter in equal shares to BETTY's cousins, JUDITH DAVIS ORSHAN and JOAN DAVIS." Just for the record, Bacall's mother, Natalie Goldberg, lived on Cranberry Street in Brooklyn, New York.

In addition to providing for his wife's family, Bogart also makes modest bequests to two of his employees. Finally, the Will also includes an unusual clause in which any persons claiming to be heirs of Bogart would receive only a $1.00 bequest.

One screen habit that Bogart has come to be identified with is smoking cigarettes. The cigarette dangling from the mouth is probably more closely identified with Bogart than with any other actor in history. It is not then surprising that Bogart died of cancer of the esophagus at the relatively young age of fifty-seven. Nor is it then surprising that the one charitable bequest that Bogart makes in his Will is as follows:

> If the circumstances shall ever be such that THE HUMPHREY BOGART FOUNDATION shall become entitled to receive any property . . . I direct my trustees to cause to be formed a nonprofit corporation bearing that name to receive such property. Said corporation shall have as its primary purpose the making of grants <u>for the aid of medical research, with special reference to the field of cancer</u>. [emphasis added]

One wonders whether if Bogart had known that the cigarette habit would be hazardous to his health (and that of millions of others), he would have been so willing to use the cancer stick as a prop throughout his career.

/s/ *Humphrey Bogart*

Will dated June 6, 1956
Residing at 232 S. Mapleton Drive, Los Angeles, California

William Holden

DATE AND PLACE OF BIRTH
April 17, 1918
O'Fallon, Illinois

DATE AND PLACE OF DEATH
November 16, 1981
535 Ocean Avenue (#5B)
Santa Monica, California

Sunset on Ocean Avenue

Known in Hollywood circles as a dependable and normal family man for most of his career, actor William Holden made a Will and subsequent codicil that lived up to that reputation.

Holden's Will is devoted to family, friends, and the charitable causes that he believed in. The Will begins by stating:

> I am not now married. I was previously married to ARDIS HOLDEN, but our marriage was subsequently dissolved. We have two (2) children now living whose names are: PETER WESTFIELD HOLDEN, and SCOTT PORTER HOLDEN. I have no deceased children. My former wife, ARDIS HOLDEN, has a child by a former marriage, VIRGINIA BAYLOR. For purposes of this Will . . . VIRGINIA BAYLOR shall be considered as my child and descendant, and her descendants shall be considered as my descendants.

Despite the divorce from his wife in the 1960s, Holden nonetheless provided for her and for her child from a previous marriage in his Will. Holden provided for his former wife by making her a beneficiary of the trust holding his residuary estate, which provided that income was to be paid to Holden's descendants, former wife, and mother. In a codicil to the Will, Holden added his niece, the child of Holden's deceased brother, as a beneficiary of his estate. Now, that is a family man.

But the plot gets thicker. Holden also made a $250,000 bequest to actress Stephanie Powers, who was his frequent companion in his later years. There were also $50,000 bequests to a woman residing in Switzerland, where Holden spent several years, and to a woman who lived in Newport Beach, California. Furthermore, the Will forgives any debts owed to Holden or his estate by anyone from a group of eleven people named in the Will, including Miss Powers.

During the middle of his career, Holden took seven years off from filmmaking and moved abroad to Switzerland, Hong Kong, and Kenya, Africa. During that period, Holden became a wildlife conservationist and was the founder of the Mount Kenya Safari Club. In his Will, Holden provides that if he owned any property or business interests in the Republic of Kenya in Africa, that property should be given to a charity "which is interested in the preservation of wild life and the environment and, if at all possible, has ties to or interests in Africa and, more specifically, the Republic of Kenya." At the same time, Holden bequeathed his extensive gun collection in equal shares to his two sons, Peter and Scott. His two sons also received $75,000 bequests and were beneficiaries of the residuary trust.

Holden named the Title Insurance and Trust Company of Los Angeles, California, as the executor of his Will and as trustee of the trust.

At the age of sixty-three, William Holden was found dead in his seaside apartment in Santa Monica, California. According to the police report, Holden had died of natural causes two or three days prior to being found by the manager of the apartment building. Though his permanent home was in Palm Springs, California, and he spent time on his land in Kenya, the sun set on the golden boy while alone in an apartment on Ocean Avenue overlooking the Pacific Ocean.

/s/ William F. Holden

Will dated April 6, 1979
Codicil dated August 24, 1979
Signed in Los Angeles, California

Henry Fonda

DATE AND PLACE OF BIRTH
May 16, 1905
Grand Island, Nebraska

DATE AND PLACE OF DEATH
August 12, 1982
Cedars-Sinai Medical Center
Los Angeles, California

Beyond Golden Pond

One of America's most beloved actors, Henry Fonda starred in more than one hundred films and theatrical productions, but an Academy Award for Best Actor eluded Fonda until his last film, *On Golden Pond,* which Mr. Fonda made shortly before his death with his daughter, Jane, and costar Katharine Hepburn. Henry Fonda was married to five women during his life. His first marriage, to actress Margaret Sullavan, ended in divorce in 1933. His second wife, Frances Seymour Brokaw, was the mother of Jane and Peter. Reportedly, she killed herself in a sanitarium in 1950. During his third marriage, to Susan Blanchard, Fonda adopted a daughter, Amy. That marriage ended in divorce. So did Fonda's fourth marriage, to Contessa Afdera Franchetti. At the time of his death, Fonda was involved in his fifth marriage, to Shirlee Mae Adams. The first article of Fonda's Will states:

> I declare that I am married to Shirlee Adams Fonda, and that we have no issue. I further declare that I have three children by previous marriages: My daughters Jane Fonda Hayden and Amy Fonda Fishman, and my son Peter Henry Fonda.

The Will that is excerpted herein was signed about a year and a half before Fonda died. The codicil, which was signed six months later, shows a significant change of mind by Fonda regarding who should handle his affairs after his death.

In his Will, Fonda appoints wife Shirlee, son Peter, and his attorney as executors of his Will. In the codicil to his Will Fonda removes son Peter as an executor and substitutes a new attorney, and wife Shirlee stays in place.

The three-page Will includes a $200,000 bequest to Fonda's daughter Amy, if she survived him by ninety days, which she did. There are no bequests for daughter Jane or son Peter in the Will, and about that Fonda states:

> I am providing primarily for my wife Shirlee and my daughter Amy because they are dependent upon me for their support. I have made no provision in this Will for Jane or Peter, or for their families, solely because in my opinion they are financially independent, and my decision is not in any sense a measure of my deep affection for them.

With that said, Fonda's Will also includes an *in terrorem* clause to inhibit any possible attacks or objections to the Will. However, it was no secret that Fonda's relations with his politically activist daughter Jane and *Easy Rider* son Peter were known to be occasionally stormy.

Under the Will, Fonda leaves all his "personal effects, clothing and automobiles . . . furniture, furnishings and objects of art" and his entire residuary estate to his wife, Shirlee. If Shirlee did not survive him, then his entire residuary estate was left to the Omaha Community Playhouse, at Omaha, Nebraska, to be used for such capital improvements, and for the maintenance and operation thereof, as the governing body of said Playhouse deems proper, this gift to be known as "The Henry and Shirlee Fonda Bequest."

Fonda, who was born near Omaha, was a generous supporter of its local playhouse during his lifetime.

Known as an honest and self-effacing man with a great ability to act, Henry Fonda did not want a grandiose or large funeral. On that question, the Will simply states:

It is my wish that there be no funeral or memorial service at the time of my death, and that my remains be promptly cremated and disposed of without ceremony of any kind.

A few months after winning his first Oscar for his heart-warming performance in *On Golden Pond*, Henry Fonda went beyond Golden Pond and died from a weak heart at the age of seventy-seven. At Fonda's bedside when he died were wife Shirlee, daughters Jane and Amy, and son Peter, but all of America mourned the loss of one of the most beloved actors of our time.

/s/ *Henry Fonda*

Will dated January 22, 1981
Codicil dated July 9, 1981

Rock Hudson

DATE AND PLACE OF BIRTH
November 17, 1925
Winnetka, Illinois

DATE AND PLACE OF DEATH
October 2, 1985
9402 Beverly Crescent Drive
Beverly Hills, California

Bad Day at Castle Rock

That one of the silver screen's most rugged, handsome "lady-killers" died of acquired immune deficiency syndrome (AIDS) allegedly stemming from his homosexual activities was one of the great ironies of the 1980s. Hudson's AIDS-related death resulted in a widely reported lawsuit against his estate brought by Rock's former lover Marc Christian. Mr. Christian claimed he had suffered serious injury by not being informed of Hudson's contagious medical condition. And a Los Angeles jury agreed, awarding Mr. Christian millions of dollars in damages against Hudson's estate.

Hudson, who was named Roy Scherer, Jr., at birth and subsequently took the surname of his stepfather, Wallace Fitzgerald, changed his name to the more masculine-sounding "Rock Hudson" at the suggestion of his agent around 1947.

Hudson was married for three years during the 1950s to his agent's secretary, Phyllis Gates. Whether this marriage was for the sake of appearances or true love or a combination of both, we will never know for sure, but in any case, the gate closed on their marriage in 1958. After that, Hudson's homosexual tendencies were a well-kept

Hollywood secret until word leaked to the public shortly before Hudson's death. Toward the end of his life, Hudson was less secretive about his homosexuality and often had homosexual romps around his Beverly Hills home known as The Castle. It was in his bedroom in The Castle that Hudson finally stopped rocking, dying in his sleep.

Since the early 1970s Hudson was intimately involved with Tom Clark, who for many years was Hudson's live-in lover and handled Hudson's personal affairs. For Tom Clark, the fourth article of Hudson's 1981 Will provides the following:

> I give to TOM H. CLARK all of my automobiles, household furniture and furnishings, clothing, art objects, jewelry, motion picture equipment, my collection of motion picture films, cassettes and all other tangible personal property and personal effects of mine. TOM H. CLARK may retain for himself those items that he would like to as a memento and may distribute the other items among such other friends of mine whom he may select and the persons and organizations named in the revocable trust created by me, dated April 3, 1974 and all amendments thereto made prior to my death which TOM H. CLARK deems would be appropriate for them to have. The balance of such items may be given to such charitable organizations which TOM H. CLARK deems it would be appropriate for them to have. . . .

This provision affords Clark great discretion in the disposition of Hudson's tangible property, which was quite substantial. Unfortunately for Clark, in a codicil that Hudson signed at his New York lawyers' offices on August

23, 1984, Hudson bluntly revokes that gift with the following:

> I hereby delete in its entirety Article FOURTH of my said Last Will and Testament. I purposely make no provision for the benefit of TOM H. CLARK.

It appears that Clark had fallen from Rock's grace, but no one was named to take his place.

According to his Will, Hudson's entire residuary estate was to be "poured over" into the revocable trust created in 1974. The terms of that trust are private and did not have to be filed with the court. Hudson's business manager and accountant, Wallace Sheft, was named as the executor of the Will and was trustee of the 1974 trust.

Hudson's Will included a "One Dollar ($1.00)" *in terrorem* clause and the statement that "except as otherwise provided in this Will, I have intentionally and with full knowledge, and not by accident or mistake, omitted to provide herein for my heirs living at the time of my death."

Despite the *in terrorem* clause young Christian was not deterred from making a claim against the estate. Because Christian was not mentioned in the Will and had no family relationship with Hudson, he did not contest the Will, but instead made a claim for damage against Hudson's estate for the decendent's failure to disclose his fatal illness to his former lover. Christian had nothing to lose, other than his life.

Finally, Hudson's Will, which he had signed before being diagnosed with AIDS, provided for the following disposition of his remains: "I request that I be cremated and that my cremated remains be scattered in the channel between Wilmington and Catalina Island." It has been reported that the cut-out Clark insisted on being the only one to hold the urn with Rock's remains and to scatter Rock's ashes in his last channel.

/s/ *Roy H. Fitzgerald*

Will dated August 18, 1981
Codicil dated August 23, 1984
Signed at 410 Park Avenue, New York, New York

Cary Grant

DATE AND PLACE OF BIRTH
January 18, 1904
Bristol, England

DATE AND PLACE OF DEATH
November 29, 1986
Davenport, Iowa

He Was No Angel

Born to a working-class family in the English port city of Bristol and named Archibald Alexander Leach, film star Cary Grant had a suave and elegant manner that drove women mad. Based on his own marital history, it appears that at least four women drove Grant mad; he was divorced four times.

Mr. Grant's first wife was actress Virginia Cherrill. His second wife was the heiress Barbara Hutton. His third wife was another actress, Betsy Drake. His fourth wife was the actress Dyan Cannon, with whom Grant had his beloved daughter, Jennifer. At the time of his death, Grant was married to his fifth wife, Barbara Harris.

To avoid any possible confusion, Grant's 1984 Will describes the two women most important to him as follows:

I am married to BARBARA HARRIS GRANT; and all references in this Will to "my wife" are to her.

I declare that I have had and now have only one child, a daughter, JENNIFER GRANT, born February 27, 1966. Said JENNIFER GRANT was born of my marriage to DYAN GRANT [presently known as DYAN CANNON], which marriage was dissolved by a final judgement of divorce dated March 21, 1969. All references in this Will to "my daughter" are to said JENNIFER GRANT.

In his Will, Grant divides his residuary estate equally between his said wife and in trust for his daughter until she reached age thirty-five. At the time of Grant's death, Jennifer was twenty years old. In addition, he gave to his wife his residence at 9966 Beverly Grove Drive in Los Angeles, California, and all his "household furniture, furnishings, appliances, works of art of all kinds, silver and silverware, automobiles and other tangible items," excluding his personal effects. To dispose of his personal effects, Grant provided the following:

> I give and bequeath all of my wearing apparel, ornaments and jewelry . . . to STANLEY E. FOX, with the understanding that although this bequest to him is absolute, and not impressed with any trust, it is nevertheless my wish and desire that he shall distribute certain of my tangible effects as I may at any time hereafter designate . . . to any of the following persons: (1) my wife, BARBARA HARRIS GRANT; (2) my daughter, JENNIFER; (3) my friends, MRS. LESLEY HARRIS, BETSY DRAKE GRANT, IRENE SELZNICK, MARGE EVERETT, NORMAN ZEILER, CHARLES RICH, KIRK KERKORIAN, FRANK SINATRA, RODERICK MANN, STANLEY DONEN, WILLIE LEE WATSON, and STANLEY E. FOX; and (4) such other of my friends and relatives whom I may mention to STANLEY E. FOX from time to time . . . it is my hope that he shall endeavor to make distribution of said items in a manner satisfactory and fair to all concerned.

It appears that Grant was not chicken about letting Fox, who was Grant's friend and business adviser, make some important decisions after he had departed.

Besides taking care of his wife and daughter, Grant was also generous with several employees and friends. To one employee he bequeathed $100,000 and to another $25,000. For the Motion Picture Relief Fund, Inc., Grant left the sum of $50,000. He bequeathed the Variety Club International and the John Tracy Clinic in Los Angeles the sum of $25,000 each.

The final article of Grant's Will states, "I desire that my remains be cremated, and that there be no formal services to note my passing." Grant died suddenly from a stroke at the age of eighty-two before appearing at a fund-raising event in Davenport, Iowa. It would be hard to imagine that the death of acting great Cary Grant could pass without notice, as he had requested in his Will.

/s/ *Cary Grant*

Will dated November 26, 1984
Signed at Beverly Hills, California

The Musicians

Not A Bunch of Dead Beats

FRANK SINATRA
"From Here to Eternity", or "That's Life"
MAY 14, 1998

JERRY GARCIA
Skeletons from the Closet
AUGUST 9, 1995

IRVING BERLIN
God Bless Irving Berlin
SEPTEMBER 22, 1989

COLE PORTER
Everything Goes
OCTOBER 15, 1964

JIM MORRISON
"This is the End, Beautiful Friend"
JULY 3, 1971

ELVIS PRESLEY
The King is Dead
AUGUST 16, 1977

KATE SMITH
God Bless Kate Smith
JUNE 17, 1986

JASCHA HEIFITZ
High Strung
DECEMBER 10, 1987

BING CROSBY
The Nineteenth Hole
OCTOBER 14, 1977

JOHN LENNON
Strawberry Fields Forever
DECEMBER 8, 1980

SAMUEL BARBER
A Different Drummer
JANUARY 23, 1981

COUNT BASIE
Out for the Count
APRIL 26, 1984

RICKY NELSON
"The Miss Adventures of Ricky Nelson"
DECEMBER 31, 1985

VLADIMIR HOROWITZ
Strings Attached
NOVEMBER 5, 1989

Frank Sinatra

DATE AND PLACE OF BIRTH
December 12, 1915
Hoboken, New Jersey

DATE AND PLACE OF DEATH
May 14, 1998
Cedars-Sinai Medical Center
Los Angeles, California

"From Here to Eternity," or "That's Life"

It is not surprising that the world famous entertainer often referred to as the "Chairman of the Board" left a lengthy and complex Will which generously provided for numerous people. The primary beneficiaries of his Will are his fourth wife Barbara, and his three children from his first marriage: Nancy Sinatra Lambert, Christina Sinatra and Francis Wayne Sinatra. The Last Will and Testament of "Francis Albert Sinatra, also known as, Frank Sinatra" is lengthy enough that the lawyer who prepared it thought it should include a "Table of Contents", and the Will is organized into thirteen lucky Sinatra "Clauses."

CLAUSE FIRST of the Will addresses Frank's "Marital Status and Family" as follows:

I am married to BARBARA SINATRA, who in this Will is referred to as "my Wife." I was formerly married to NANCY BARBATO SINATRA, to AVA GARDNER SINATRA, and to MIA FARROW SINATRA, and each of said marriages were subsequently dissolved. I have three children, all of whom are the issue of my marriage to NANCY BARBATO SINATRA: NANCY SINATRA LAMBERT, FRANCIS WAYNE SINATRA, and CHRISTINA SINATRA. All of the above-named children are adults. I have never had any other children.

That is certainly a respectable line-up of former wives, but there was only one Frank Sinatra. Although his marriages to Ava Gardner and Mia Farrow were rather brief, those women helped confirm and create Frank's reputation as one of the great playboys of the western world, attractive to women of all shapes and ages. As for Frank's disclaimer that, "I have never had any other children", we won't go there.

It is noteworthy that all the bequests and devises under the Will to fourth wife, Barbara, are conditioned on Frank and Barbara being "married and living together" at the time of Frank's death. Barbara went the distance and she and Frank were married for over twenty-two (22) years, but in view of Frank's marital track record, it seems reasonable for him to include that condition on the substantial gifts to wife number four. Frank probably knew that there was always the possibility that one of the young nurses taking care of him in his old age might catch his eye.

In his Will dated September 3, 1991, Frank shows the exceptionally generous impulses for which he was well-known, and well-loved. He makes cash bequests in the following amounts to each of the following persons who survived him:

1. "To my former wife, NANCY BARBATO SINATRA . . ."—$250,000

2. "To DOROTHY UHLEMANN"—$50,000

3. "To ELVINA JOUBERT"—$50,000

4. "To JILLY RIZZO"—$100,000

5. "To my Wife's son, ROBERT OLIVER MARX"—$100,000

6. "To my daughter, CHRISTINA SINATRA"—$200,000

7. "To my son, FRANCIS WAYNE SINATRA"—$200,000

8. "To my daughter, NANCY SINATRA LAMBERT"—$200,000

Frank also took advantage of the $1,000,000 generation-skipping tax exemption available to his estate by giving "To the Trustees of that certain Trust established by me and my former Wife, NANCY BARBATO SINATRA, by Trust Agreement dated December 13, 1983, for the benefit of the children of NANCY SINATRA LAMBERT, the sum of ONE MILLION DOLLARS ($1,000,000), to be added to the assets of said trust and allocated equally between the separate trusts being administered thereunder for the benefit of my two grandchildren, ANGELA JENNIFER LAMBERT and AMANDA KATHERINE LAMBERT".

Those cash bequests add up to a cool $2.1 million dollars. However, by a Codicil to his Will dated May 1, 1993, Frank increased the bequest to Elvina Joubert from $50,000 to $150,000 and deleted bequest number 4 above "by reason of the death of JILLY RIZZO." Jilly Rizzo had been Sinatra's favorite restaurant owner, and always kept his kitchen open late for Sinatra and his pack.

In addition to the cash bequests mentioned above, Frank's three children were also bequeathed all of his interest in a partnership known as "Wilshire-Camden Associates", (the old New Jersey/California connection) in equal shares. He also gives "in equal shares to CHRISTINA SINATRA, FRANK WAYNE SINATRA, and NANCY SINATRA LAMBERT, or to the issue of any of them who do not survive me . . ." the remainder interest in an entity called the "Somerset Trust", which Frank had established in 1989. Finally, under his Will Frank forgives all loans or indebtedness owed to him by any of his children.

The disposition of the tangible personal property of Frank Sinatra reveals what a rich and materially wealthy life he led. In CLAUSE SEVENTH of his Will, Frank gives to wife Barbara, on the express condition that "we are married and living together at the time of my death, all of the silverware, books, displayed paintings, and household furniture" in their many homes. One has to wonder what Frank's collection of "undisplayed" paintings included.

Regarding the disposition of other tangible personal property, including "my jewelry, art objects, clothing, household furniture and furnishings, personal automobiles (except the 1988 Rolls Royce and 1990 Mercedes which are the separate property of my Wife), train collections, music and recording collections, memorabilia, and other articles of a personal nature", the Will provides the following thoughtful procedures for dividing up those numerous items of tangible personal property, and for Frank Sinatra, that could get pretty personal:

1. My Executor shall first return to any child of mine any of such items which said child may have given to me;

2. My Executor shall then honor such written contractual commitments, if any, which I may have entered into during my lifetime for delivery of such items of personal property at my death;

3. I give all of my sheet music to my son, FRANCIS WAYNE SINATRA;

4. Thereafter, each of my Wife, if she survives me and we are married and living together at the time of my death, and each of my children who survive me may designate to my Executor any of the aforementioned items of property which that beneficiary is desirous of receiving. My Executor shall have all such objects appraised in the manner he deems appropriate, and the appraised value shall be allocated to the requesting beneficiary. My Wife shall be entitled to receive up to a maximum of twenty-five percent (25%) of the total aggregate value of such property, and my children shall be entitled to receive the remaining maximum aggregate value of seventy-five percent (75%) of such property, with each of my three children being entitled to receive a maximum of one-third of said remainder, or twenty-five percent (25%) of the total aggregate value of the whole of said property, upon the principle of

representation. If my Wife should fail to survive me or we are not married and living together at the time of my death all of said property shall be divided amongst my children. If none of my children or their issue survive me, such property shall be considered as part of the residue of my estate. Notwithstanding the foregoing, my Executor shall have the authority, in my Executor's sole and absolute discretion, to distribute any of my personal items and memorabilia to such of my friends and my employees as he may deem appropriate.

It is not surprising that the Chairman of the Board gave discretion to his Executor to distribute "any of my personal items and memorabilia to such of my friends and my employees as he may deem appropriate." Pure Frankness. Fourth wife Barbara appears to be well provided for under Frank's Will. Besides an outright cash bequest of $3,500,000, Barbara is also given all of Frank's interest in "Sheffield Enterprises, Inc.", and "that certain Master Recording entitled Trilogy, and all rights to royalties and future distribution related thereto." Wife Barbara is devised all of Frank's interest in the magnificent houses and real properties located in Rancho Mirage, California on both Starlight Lane and, where else, Frank Sinatra Drive. Not many people can devise real estate located on a road named after them in their own Will. Wife Barbara also received the houses and real properties owned by Frank located in Beverly Hills, Cathedral City and Malibu, California. For a boy born in Hoboken, New Jersey he sure enjoyed California real estate, and there was a reason that Frank Sinatra was often called the "Inn Keeper".

Frank gives the "Residue" of his estate to his three children in equal shares. However, after the satisfaction of all of the foregoing gifts of cash, partnership interests houses, real property, and tangible personal property, one has to wonder what would be left as part of the Residue.

No doubt mindful of the Type A Sinatra personality, and the tensions which often arise between the children from a former marriage, and a later wife, Frank's Will includes an unusually comprehensive "No Contest" clause, which is worth reproducing in full here:

CLAUSE TENTH: <u>No Contest Clause</u>

A. If any devisee, legatee or beneficiary under this Will, or any legal heir of mine or person claiming under any of them directly or indirectly engages in any of the following conduct, then in that event I specifically disinherit each such person, and all such legacies, bequests, devises and interests given under this Will or any trust created by me at any time to that person shall be for forfeited as though he or she had predeceased me without issue, and shall augment proportionately the shares of my estate going under this Will, to or in trust for, such of my devisees, legatees and beneficiaries who have not participated in such acts or proceedings:

1. contests this Will or, in any manner, attacks or

seeks to impair or invalidate any of its provisions,

2.   claims entitlement to any asset of my estate by way of any written or oral contract (whether or not such claim is successful),

3.   unsuccessfully challenges the appointment of any person named as an executor or a trustee,

4.   objects in any manner to any action taken or proposed to be taken in good faith by my Executor, whether my Executor is acting under court order, notice of proposed action or otherwise, whether such objection is successful or not,

5.   objects to any construction or interpretation of my Will, or any provision of it, that is adopted or proposed in good faith by my Executor,

6.   unsuccessfully seeks the removal of any person acting as an executor,

7.   files any creditor's claim in my estate that is based upon a claim arising prior to the date of this Will (without regard to its validity),

8.   Claims an interest in any property alleged by executor to belong to my estate (whether or not such claim is successful),

9.   challenges the characterization proposed by my Executor of any property as to whether it is separate or community (without regard to the ultimate resolution of the merits of such challenge),

10. challenges the position taken by my Executor as to the validity or construction of any written agreement entered into by me during my lifetime,

11. attacks or seeks to impair or invalidate any of the following:

    a.   any designation of beneficiaries for any insurance policy on my life;

    b.   any designation of beneficiaries for any pension plan or IRA account;

    c.   any trust which I created or may create during my lifetime or any provision thereof;

    d.   any gift which I have made or will make during my lifetime;

    e.   any transaction by which I have sold any asset to any child or children of mine (whether or not any such attack or attempt is successful)

12. conspires with or voluntarily assists anyone attempting to do any of these things; or

13. refuses a request of my Executor to assist in the defense against any of the foregoing acts or proceedings.

B. Further, if any of my Wife's issue or my grandchildren do any of the things referred to in this CLAUSE TENTH, then any legacy, bequest, device [sic] or other interest which would otherwise pass to my Wife or the parents of my grandchildren who so act, as the case may be

shall likewise be forfeited, and such forfeiting
legatees shall be deemed to have predeceased
me without issue.

C. Expenses to resist any contest or other attack of
any nature upon any provision of this Will shall be
paid from my estate as expenses of administration.

The reference in Subdivision (B) above to a "device"
. . . which would otherwise pass to my Wife" has to make
one wonder what kind of devices Barbara and Frank were
playing with. Of course, the sloppy typist meant "devise",
which is the passing of real, as opposed to tangible, property, under a Will.

The reference to a possible conspiracy or refusing "a request of my Executor" under numbers 12 and 13 above
could have been Frank's own concepts of honor, but are
more likely the product of a cautious lawyer.

Speaking of lawyers, on page one of the Will, Frank
names two as the Executors of his Will: Eliot Weisman
and Harvey L. Silbert. Those two Executors are "empowered" to designate and appoint any bank or other corporate fiduciary to act as Co-Executor with them, or as
an Agent on their behalf. Later in the Will on page 17,
the touchy legal issues of "Conflicts of Interest and Ex-
culpation" are addressed in the lawyers' best interest as
follows:

A. Any fiduciary, or any firm with which a fiduciary is
affiliated, that performs services in connection with
the regular operations of any business, partnership,
firm or corporation in which my estate is financially
interested may be compensated for services inde-

pendently of compensation for services as a fiduciary hereunder.

B. The general rule of law whereby actions, decisions, or transactions are held to be void or voidable if a fiduciary is directly or indirectly interested therein in a non-fiduciary capacity shall not be applicable to transactions between my estate and any business entity in which the individual fiduciary is involved. I recognize that the dual role of my fiduciary may result in situations involving conflicts of interest or self-dealing, and it is my express intent that my fiduciary shall not be liable as aforesaid, except in the event of his own bad faith or gross negligence. Notwithstanding the foregoing, all such transactions shall be fair and reasonable. The fiduciary's power hereunder shall be exercised in good faith for the benefit of my estate and in accordance with the usual fiduciary obligations, except that the rule against self-dealing shall not be applicable as provided in this paragraph.

C. A fiduciary who is an attorney, accountant, investment advisor or other professional shall not be disqualified from rendering professional services to my estate and from being compensated on a reasonable basis therefor in addition to any compensation which he or she is otherwise entitled to receive as fiduciary; neither shall a firm with which a fiduciary is associated be disqualified from dealing with, rendering services to or discharging duties for my estate and from being compensated therefor on a reasonable basis.

D.   No fiduciary under this Will shall be liable to any
person interested in my estate for any act or default
of that fiduciary or of any other fiduciary or any
other person, unless resulting from that fiduciary's
own bad faith or gross negligence.

The Will includes a thirty (30) day survivorship clause
which requires each beneficiary under the Will to survive
Frank by at least 30 days in order to inherit under his Will.
With the exception of the legendary restauranteur, Jilly
Rizzo, they all did. Also, the definition of "child" or "issue" under the Will includes only children "born in wedlock." No doubt that was often an issue of concern for the
man with the golden voice.

From a humble beginning as the son of an immigrant
from Italy in Hoboken, New Jersey, Frank Sinatra achieved
such fame and fortune that he commanded the attention
of Princesses, Presidents, Godfathers and Goddesses. It
has been said that it was Frank's assistance to the cam-
paign of John F. Kennedy that helped Kennedy to win the
Presidency in 1960 with the slimmest of victory margins.
As an icon of America, Frank Sinatra truly made it everywhere. In view of the vast wealth which he accumulated
and many close friends that he had during his eventful 82
years, we would all have to agree that for Francis Albert
Sinatra, those were very good years.

/s/ *Francis Albert Sinatra*

Will dated September 3, 1991

Will signed in Los Angeles, California

First Codicil dated May 1, 1993

First Codicil signed in Rancho Mirage, California

LAST WILL AND TESTAMENT

OF

FRANCIS ALBERT SINATRA,

also known as

FRANK SINATRA

I, FRANCIS ALBERT SINATRA, also known as FRANK SINATRA, declare this to be my Will and revoke all former Wills and Codicils. I am a resident of Riverside County, California.

CLAUSE FIRST: Marital Status And Family.

I am married to BARBARA SINATRA, who in this Will is referred to as "my Wife." I was formerly married to NANCY BARBATO SINATRA, to AVA GARDNER SINATRA, and to MIA FARROW SINATRA, and each of said marriages were subsequently dissolved. I have three children, all of whom are the issue of my marriage to NANCY BARBATO SINATRA: NANCY SINATRA LAMBERT, FRANCIS WAYNE SINATRA, and CHRISTINA SINATRA. All of the above-named children are adults. I have never had any other children.

CLAUSE SECOND: Nomination Of Executor; Executor's Powers.

A.   I nominate ELIOT WEISMAN and HARVEY L. SILBERT to act as Co-Executors of this Will. I specifically empower my Co-Executors at any time to designate and appoint any bank or other corporate fiduciary to act as Co-Executor with them, or as Agent on their behalf, and with the further power to change the designation of the said bank or other corporate fiduciary from time to time. If either ELIOT WEISMAN or HARVEY L. SILBERT is unable, unwilling or ceases to act as Co-Executor, I nominate NATHAN S.

GOLDEN to act as Co-Executor with the other of them. If two of said three individuals become unable, unwilling or ceases to act as Executor, I nominate CITY NATIONAL BANK, Beverly Hills, California, to act as Co-Executor with the remaining individual, or as sole Executor if all three of said individuals become unable, unwilling, or cease to act hereunder. Whenever the word "Executor" or "Co-Executor" is used in this Will, it shall be deamed to refer to whichever one or more of them is acting from time to time. I direct that no bond shall be required of any Executor or Co-Executor as a condition to qualifying to serve hereunder, whether acting jointly or alone.

B.　I authorize my Executor to sell, lease, mortgage or encumber the whole or any part of my estate, with or without notice; to transfer registered securities into street name or to hold them in the name of a nominee, without any liability on the part of my Executor; and at the option and sole discretion of my Executor, to continue to hold, manage and operate any property, business or enterprise that may be an asset of my estate from time to time, whether in corporate, partnership (limited or general) or other form, and whether or not such asset is one in which my Executor is personally interested, the profits or losses therefrom to inure to or be charged against my estate and not my Executor. My Executor shall have absolute discretion as to how much cash, if any, to invest at interest.

C.　I authorize my Executor to invest and reinvest funds of my estate, including surplus moneys and the proceeds from the sale of any assets of my estate, in every kind of property, specifically including, but not by way of limitation, corporate or governmental obligations of every kind, securities of any regulated investment trust, and stocks, preferred or common and any common trust fund administered by any corporate fiduciary under this Will.

D.   It is my intention that my Executor be permitted to take advantage of any tax savings that the law of any juridiction allows, without regard to conflicting interests of those interested in my estate and without making any adjustments among such persons. To that end, I authorize my Executor, in my Executor's absolute discretion, to take any one or more of the following actions as may appear advisable:

1.   To join with my Wife in executing joint income tax returns;

2.   To value my gross estate for federal estate tax purposes as of the date of my death or as of the alternative valuation date as allowed for such purposes;

3.   To claim as estate or inheritance tax deductions, or both, expenses which would otherwise qualify as income tax deductions;

4.   To elect to have gifts by my Wife treated as made one-half by me for federal gift tax purposes; and

5.   To make any other elections allowed by the Internal Revenue Code or the tax law of applicable jurisdiction.

E.   If at my death I hold any stock purchase warrants, stock subscription or conversion rights, or any rights under any stock option plan, I authorize my Executor to exercise any or all of those warrants and rights if my Executor, in my Executor's discretion, deems such exercise to be in the best interests of my estate and the beneficiaries thereof, and to borrow money for that purpose if my Executor, in my Executor's discretion, deems it advisable.

F.   I authorize my Executor to administer my estate under The California Independent Administration of Estates Act.

G.   Upon any preliminary or final distribution of the residue of my estate, my Executor may distribute the residue in undivided interests or in kind, or in money, or partly in any of them at such valuations and according to such method or procedure as my Executor shall determine, including the power to distribute all or part of any particular asset to any beneficiary as my Executor shall determine.

H.   All decisions of my Executor made in good faith shall be binding and conclusive on all persons interested in my estate, but shall be subject to such confirmation or Court authority as is required by law.

CLAUSE THIRD: Amount Of Property Disposed Of.

I intend that my Will shall govern the disposition of all property wherever situated that I have the power to will at the time of my death, including both my separate property and my one-half interest in such community property as my Wife and I may own at the time of my death.

CLAUSE FOURTH: Payment of Debts and Taxes.

I direct my Executor to pay in full any and all lawful debts which may be owing by me at the time of my death, both secured and unsecured, and regardless of when they might otherwise be due and payable, in the following order of priority and from the following sources:

1.   My Executor shall first pay and discharge in full from our community assets, including my Wife's share thereof to the full extent her share is liable for such debts and to the full extent of such community property, any and all debts chargeable to the community estate of myself and my Wife, other than payments in satisfaction of any promissory notes secured by mortgages and/or trust deeds which are a lien on the Rancho Mirage residential real property owned by us.

2.   My Executor shall next pay and discharge in full from my share of our community property the full amount of any promissory notes secured by mortgages and/or trust deeds which are a lien on the Rancho Mirage residential real property owned by us, and regardless of whether said real property is owned by us as joint tenants with the right of survivorship, as community property, or as my sole and separate property. If my share of our community property is insufficient to pay said debt in full after payment of our unsecured debts, then any shortfall in payment of this secured debt shall be paid from my separate property. No other debts secured by residential real property in which I have an interest shall be paid in full as a result of my death.

3.   I direct that all estate, inheritance or other death taxes occasioned or payable by reason of my death, whether related to the bequests set forth in this will, and whether attributable to property subject to probate administration or not, and all of

the expenses of administration of my estate, including but not limited to executor commissions, attorneys fees, court, publication and filing fees, and funeral expenses and expenses of my last illness, if any, shall next be paid from my share of our community property, to the full extent remaining after payment of the debts described in subparagraphs 1 and 2 above. If my share of our community property is insufficient to pay said taxes and expenses, they shall be paid from the residue of my separate property.

CLAUSE FIFTH: <u>Specific Bequests.</u>

I make the following specific bequests from my share of our community property to the extent such remains after payment in full of the items described in CLAUSE FOURTH above, and if my share of our community property shall be insufficient to satisfy these bequests, from my separate property:

A.   To my former Wife, NANCY BARBATO SINATRA, if she survives me, the sum of Two Hundred Fifty Thousand Dollars ($250,000). If NANCY BARBATO SINATRA does not survive me, this gift shall lapse and shall be considered as part of the residue of my estate.

B.   To DOROTHY UHLEMANN of North Hollywood, California, if she survives me, the sum of Fifty Thousand Dollars ($50,000). If DOROTHY UHLEMANN does not survive me, this gift shall lapse and shall be considered as part of the residue of my estate.

C.   To ELVINA JOUBERT of Rancho Mirage, California, if she survives me, the sum of Fifty Thousand Dollars ($50,000). If ELVINA JOUBERT does not survive me, this gift shall lapse and shall be considered as part of the residue of my estate.

D.   To JILLY RIZZO, if he survives me, the sum of One Hundred Thousand Dollars ($100,000). If JILLY RIZZO does not survive me, this gift shall lapse and shall be considered as part of the residue of my estate.

E.   To my Wife's son, ROBERT OLIVER MARX, if he survives me, the sum of One Hundred Thousand Dollars ($100,000). If ROBERT OLIVER MARX does not survive me, this gift shall lapse and shall be considered as part of the residue of my estate.

F.   To my daughter, CHRISTINA SINATRA, if she survives me, the sum of Two Hundred Thousand Dollars ($200,000). If CHRISTINA SINATRA does not survive me, this gift shall lapse and shall be considered as part of the residue of my estate.

G.   To my son, FRANCIS WAYNE SINATRA, if he survives me, the sum of Two Hundred Thousand Dollars ($200,000). If FRANCIS WAYNE SINATRA does not survive me, this gift shall lapse and shall be considered as part of the residue of my estate.

H.   To my daughter, NANCY SINATRA LAMBERT, is she survives me, the sum of Two Hundred Thousand Dollars ($200,000). If NANCY SINATRA LAMBERT does not survive me, this gift shall lapse and shall be considered as part of the residue of my estate.

I.   To the Trustees of that certain Trust established by me and my former Wife, NANCY BARBATO SINATRA, by Trust Agreement dated December 13, 1983, for the benefit of the children of NANCY SINATRA LAMBERT, the sum of One Million Dollars

($1,000,000), to be added to the assets of said trust and allocated equally between the separate trusts being administered thereunder for the benefit of my two grandchildren, ANGELA JENIFER LAMBERT and AMANDA KATHERINE LAMBERT.

J.   To my Wife, BARBARA SINATRA, provided that we are married and living together at the time of my death, all of my rights as licensor pursuant to that certain License Agreement dated February 29, 1988 with Sheffield Enterprises, Inc., including my twenty-five percent (25%) royalty thereunder, or in the alternative such shares of Capital Stock of Sheffield Enterprises, Inc. as I may have acquired during my lifetime in exchange for said rights. If my Wife does not survive me or we are not married and living together at the time of my death, this gift shall lapse and shall be considered as part of the residue of my estate.

K.   To my Wife, BARBARA SINATRA, provided that we are married and living together at the time of my death, my interest in that certain Master Recording entitled "Trilogy", and all rights to royalties and future distribution related thereto. If my Wife does not survive me or we are not married and living together at the time of my death, this gift shall lapse and shall be considered as part of the residue of my estate.

L.   I give to my children, in undivided interests as tenants in common, upon the principle of representation, my community interest in that certain partnership known as Wilshire-Camden Associates, in which I am a limited partner.

M.   I hereby forgive any and all loans or indebtedness which may exist at the time of my death, whether in writing or otherwise, which may be owed to me by any of my children.

CLAUSE SIXTH: <u>Confirmation Of Separate and Joint Tenancy Assets.</u>

A.   I confirm to my Wife, if she survives me, my interest in the real property situated in Riverside County, California, and commonly known as 70-588 Frank Sinatra Drive, Rancho Mirage, California, including all adjacent guest houses on the grounds thereof, commonly known as 70-200, 70-548, and 70-630 Frank Sinatra Drive, Rancho Mirage, California, which property is held of record by my Wife and I as joint tenants with the right of survivorship.

B.   I confirm to my Wife, if she survives me, my interest in the real property situated in Los Angeles County, California, and commonly known as 915 Foothill Road, Beverly Hills, California 90210, which property is held of record by my Wife and I as joint tenants with the right of survivorship.

C.   I confirm to my Wife, if she survives me, my interest in the real property situated in Riverside County, California, and commonly known as 1130 Starlight Lane, Rancho Mirage, California, which property is held of record by my Wife and I as joint tenants with the right of survivorship.

D.   I confirm to my Wife as her sole and separate property the parcel of real property situated in Riverside county, California, and commonly known as 36928 Pinto Palm Drive, Cathedral City, California.

E.   I confirm to my Wife, if she survives me, my interest in the real property situated in Los Angeles County, California, and commonly known as 30966

Broad Beach Road, Malibu, California 90265, subject
to all existing encumbrances. If said parcel of real
property is not held of record by my Wife and I as
joint tenants with the right of survivorship on the
date of my death, I give my interest in the said parcel
of real property to my Wife, if she survives me and if
we are married and living together at the time of my
death, and in such event, if my Wife fails to survive
me, or we are not married and living together at the
time of my death, the above-described real property
shall be considered as part of the residue of my estate.

CLAUSE SEVENTH: <u>Gifts Of Tangible</u>
<u>Personal Property and</u>
<u>Community Property.</u>

A.   I give to my Wife, if she survives me, and we
are married and living together at the time of my
death, all of the silverware, books, displayed paintings, and household furniture and furnishings located
in the homes described in CLAUSE SIXTH above, and
my interest in any policies of insurance covering the
foregoing items of personal property. If my Wife fails
to survive me or we are not married and living together at the time of my death, the above-described
personal property and any policies of insurance covering such personal property shall be considered as part
of the residue of my estate.

B.   I give all of my jewelry, art objects, clothing,
household furniture and furnishings, personal automobiles (except the 1988 Rolls Royce and the 1990
Mercedes which are the separate property of my
Wife), train collections, music and recording collections, memorabilia and other tangible articles of a

personal nature, and my interest in any such property not otherwise specifically disposed of by this Will or in any other manner, together with any insurance of such property existing at the time of my death, in the following manner:

1.   My Executor shall first return to any child of mine any of such items which said child may have given to me;

2.   My Executor shall then honor such written contractual commitments, if any, which I may have entered into during my lifetime for delivery of such items of personal property at my death;

3.   I give all of my sheet music to my son, FRANK WAYNE SINATRA;

4.   Thereafter each of my Wife, if she survives me and we are married and living together at the time of my death, and each of my children who survive me may designate to my Executor any of the aforementioned items of property which that beneficiary is desirous of receiving. My Executor shall have all such object appraised in the manner he deems appropriate, and the appraised value shall be allocated to the requesting beneficiary. My Wife shall be entitled to receive up to a maximum of twenty-five percent (25%) of the total aggregate value of such property, and my children shall be entitled to receive the remaining maximum aggregate value of seventy five percent (75%) of such property, with each of my three children being entitled to receive a maximum of one-third of said remainder, or twenty-five percent (25%) of the total aggregate value of the whole of said property, upon the principle of representa-

tion. If my Wife should fail to survive me or we are not married and living together at the time of my death all of said property shall be divided amongst my children. If none of my children and their issue survive me, such property shall be considered as part of the residue of my estate. Notwithstanding the foregoing, my Executor shall have the authority, in my Executor's sole and absolute discretion, to distribute any of my personal items and memorabilia to such of my friends and my employees as he may deem appropriate.

C.   I give to my Wife, if she survives me and we are married and living together on the date of my death, from my share of our community property remaining after the payment and distribution of all amounts and specific bequests hereinabove in this Will set forth, such additional assets, valued at the date of my death, as equals the total sum of Three Million Five Hundred Thousand Dollars ($3,500,000); provided, however, that if my share of our community property remaining after the payment and distribution of all amounts and specific bequests hereinabove in this Will set forth, is insufficient to provide my Wife with said total sum of Three Million Five Hundred Thousand Dollars ($3,500,000), I give my Wife all of my then remaining community property; provided, further, if my Wife fails to survive me, or we are not married and living together on the date of my death, this gift shall lapse and shall be considered a part of the residue of my estate.

CLAUSE EIGHTH: <u>Power Of Appointment.</u>

I hold a limited power of appointment conferred

upon me by the Somerset Trust established by that certain declaration of trust dated January 1, 1989 in which I am the Trustor, which power is given me pursuant to numbered paragraph 5 on page 8 of said declaration of trust. I hereby exercise said power of appointment by appointing and giving all assets subject to it in equal shares to CHRISTINA SINATRA, FRANK WAYNE SINATRA, and NANCY SINATRA LAMBERT, or the issue of any of them who do not survive me, according to the principle of representation, and if any of them should predecease me leaving no issue, to the survivors of them.

CLAUSE NINTH: Gift Of Residue.

A.   I give the residue of my community property estate and all of my separate property remaining after giving effect to the foregoing provisions of this Will, in equal shares to CHRISTINA SINATRA, FRANK WAYNE SINATRA, and NANCY SINATRA LAMBERT, or the issue of any of them who survive me, according to the principle of representation, and if any of them should predecease me leaving no issue, to the survivors of them.

B.   If none of my issue survive me, I give the residue of my estate of my heirs, according to the laws of succession of the State of California in force at the date of this will.

CLAUSE TENTH: No Contest Clause.

A.   If any devisee, legatee or beneficiary under this Will, or any legal heir of mine or person claiming under any of them directly or indirectly engages in any of the following conduct, then in that event I specifically disinherit each such person, and all such legacies, bequests, devises and interests given under this Will or any trust created by me at any time to that person shall be forfeited as though he or she had predeceased me without issue, and shall augment proportionately the shares of my estate going under this Will to, or in trust for, such of my devisees, legatees and beneficiaries who have not participated in such acts or proceedings:

1.   contests this Will or, in any manner, attacks or seeks to impair or invalidate any of its provisions,

2.   claims entitlement to any asset of my estate by way of any written or oral contract (whether or not such claim is successful),

3.   unsuccessfully challenges the appointment of any person named as an executor or a trustee,

4.   objects in any manner to any action taken or proposed to be taken in good faith by my Executor, whether my Executor is acting under court order, notice of proposed action or otherwise, whether such objection is successful or not.

5.   objects to any construction or interpretation of my Will, or any provision of it, that is adopted or proposed in good faith by my Executor,

6.   unsuccessfully seeks the removal of any person acting as an executor,

7.   files any creditor's claim in my estate that is based upon a claim arising prior to the date of this Will (without regard to its validity),

8.   claims an interest in any property alleged by executor to belong to my estate (whether or not such claim is successful),

9.   challenges the characterization proposed by my Executor of any property as to whether it is sep-

arate or community (without regard to the ultimate resolution of the merits of such challenge),

    10.   challenges the position taken by my Executor as to the validity or construction of any written agreement entered into by me during my lifetime,

    11.   attacks or seeks to impair or invalidate any of the following:

        a.   any designation of beneficiaries for any insurance policy on my life;

        b.   any designation of beneficiaries for any pension plan or IRA account;

        c.   any trust which I created or may create during my lifetime or any provision thereof;

        d.   any gift which I have made or will make during my lifetime;

        e.   any transaction which I have sold any asset to any child or children of mine (whether or not any such attack or attempt is successful),

    12.   conspires with or voluntarily assists anyone attempting to do any of these things; or

    13.   refuses a request of my Executor to assist in the defense against any of the foregoing acts or proceedings.

    B.   Further, if any of my Wife's issue or my grandchildren do any of the things referred to in this CLAUSE TENTH, then any legacy, bequest, device or other interest which would otherwise pass to my Wife or the parents of my grandchildren who so act, as the case may be shall likewise be forfeited, and such forfeiting legatees shall be deemed to have predeceased me without issue.

    C.   Expenses to resist any contest or other attack

of any nature upon any provision of this Will shall be paid from my estate as expenses of administration.

D. In the event that any provision of this CLAUSE TENTH, including any of the provisions of the subparagraphs of paragraph A hereof, is held to be invalid, void or illegal, the same shall be deemed severable from the remainder of the provisions in this CLAUSE TENTH and shall in no way affect, impair or invalidate any other provision in this CLAUSE TENTH. If such provision shall be deemed invalid due to its scope and breadth, such provision shall be deemed valid to the extent of the scope or breadth premitted by law.

CLAUSE ELEVENTH: <u>Conflicts of Interest; Exculpation</u>.

The following provisions shall be applicable to any Executor or Co-Executor under this will (hereafter "fiduciary"):

A. Any fiduciary, or any firm with which a fiduciary is affiliated, that performs services in connection with the regular operations of any business, partnership, firm or corporation in which my estate is financially interested may be compensated for services independently of compensation for services as a fiduciary hereunder.

B. The general rule of law whereby actions, decisions, or transactions are held to be void or voidable if a fiduciary is directly or indirectly interested therein in a non-fiduciary capacity shall not be applicable to transactions between my estate and any business entity in which the individual fiduciary is involved. I recognize that the dual role of my fiduciary may result in situations involving conflicts of interest or self-dealing, and it is my express intent that my fiduciary shall not be liable as aforesaid, except in the event of his own bad faith or gross negligence. Notwithstanding the foregoing, all such transactions shall be fair and reasonable. The fiduciary's power hereunder shall be exercised in good faith for the benefit of my estate and in accordance with the usual fiduciary obligations, except that the rule against self-dealing shall not be applicable as provided in this paragraph.

C.   A fiduciary who is an attorney, accountant, investment advisor or other professional shall not be disqualified from rendering professional services to my estate and from being compensated on a reasonable basis therefor in addition to any compensation which he or she is otherwise entitled to receive as fiduciary; neither shall a firm with which a fiduciary is associated by disqualified from dealing with, rendering services to or discharging duties for my estate and from being compensated therefor on a reasonable basis.

D.   No fiduciary under this Will shall be liable to any person interested in my estate for any act or default of that fiduciary or of any other fiduciary or any other person, unless resulting from that fiduciary's own bad faith or gross negligence.

CLAUSE TWELFTH: <u>Custodianship.</u>

If on the date of the order of distribution of any of my property, the legatee thereof is a minor, such property may, in my Executor's discretion, be delivered to a custodian chosen by my Executor to be held by such custodian for such minor under the California Uniform Transfers To Minors Act. At the time of such delivery, my Executor may also designate one or more successor custodians to act if such custodian becomes unable, unwilling or ceases to so act, and my Executor may specify whether or not any such custodian or successor custodian shall be required to post bond.

CLAUSE THIRTEENTH: Interpretation of This Will.

A.   As used in this Will, the terms "child," "children," "grandchild", "grandchildren", and "issue" shall include only children born in wedlock and lawfully adopted children and issue of such children.

B.   As used in this Will, and to the extent appropriate, the masculine, feminine and neuter gender shall include the other two genders, the singular shall include the plural, and the plural shall include the singular.

C.   If there is no sufficient evidence that my Wife and I died otherwise than simultaneously, it shall be presumed, for the purposes of this Will, that my Wife died before me.

D.   For the purposes of this Will, any beneficiary who dies within thirty (30) days after my death shall be deemed to have died before me.

E.   No interest shall be paid on any gift, legacy or right to income under this Will or any Codicil to it.

F.   The Table of Contents and the headings used herein are solely for the purpose of setting forth the organizational outline of this Will and are not to be considered provisions hereof.

G.   If any provision of this Will shall be invalid or unenforceable, the remaining provisions hereof shall subsit and be carried into effect.

H.   Except as otherwise specifically provided, the validity and construction of this Will and all rights hereunder shall be governed by the laws of the State of California.

SIGNED at Los Angeles, California, on Sept. 3rd, 1991.

Francis Albert Sinatra

FRANCIS ALBERT SINATRA
also known as FRANK SINATRA

The foregoing instrument was on the date hereof, by FRANCIS ALBERT SINATRA, also known as FRANK SINATRA, the testator, subscribed and declared to be his Will in the presence of us, who, at his request, in his presence and in the presence of each other, do sign the same at witnesses. At the time of signing this Will the testator and each of us who is acting as a witness is over 18 years of age. The testator appears to be of sound and disposing mind and memory, and each of us has no knowledge of any fact indicating that the foregoing instrument, or any part of it, was procured by duress, menace, fraud or the undue influence of any person whomsoever.

Each of us declares under penalty of perjury under the laws of the State of California that the foregoing statement is true and correct and that this declaration is signed at Los Angeles, California on September 3, 1991.

FIRST CODICIL
TO WILL OF
FRANCIS ALBERT SINATRA
also known as
FRANK SINATRA

I, FRANK ALBERT SINATRA, also known as FRANK SINATRA, do hereby declare this to be a First Codicil to my Last Will and Testament dated September 3, 1991.

I.

I hereby delete Section C of Clause FIFTH of said Last Will and Testament and in lieu and in place thereof insert the following new Section C:

"C. To ELVINA JOUBERT of Rancho Mirage, California, if she survives me, the sum of One Hundred Fifty Thousand Dollars ($150,000). If ELVINA JOUBERT does not survive me, this gift shall lapse and shall be considered as part of the residue of my estate."

II.

I hereby delete in its entirety Section D of Clause FIFTH of said Last Will and Testament by reason of the death of JILLY RIZZO.

III.

In all other respects I hereby reaffirm and republish my Last Will and Testament dated September 3, 1991.

Signed at Rancho Mirage, California on May 1, 1993.

Frank Sinatra
_____
FRANCIS ALBERT SINATRA
also known as
FRANK SINATRA

ATTESTATION AND DECLARATION

The testator, FRANCIS ALBERT SINATRA, also known as FRANK SINATRA, on the date written above, declared to us, the undersigned, that the foregoing instrument, consisting of two (2) pages, including the page signed by us as witnesses, is his First Codicil to his Last Will dated September 3, 1991 and requested us to act as witnesses to it. Then the testator signed this First Codicil in our presence, all of us being present at the same time. We now, at his request, in his presence, and in the presence of one another, subscribe our names as witnesses.

Each of us states that the testator and each of us are over eighteen (18) years of age, that the testator appears to be of sound mind, and that we have no knowledge of any facts indicating that the foregoing instrument or any part of it was procured by duress, menace, fraud, or undue influence.

We, each for himself or herself, declare under penalty of perjury under the laws of the State of California that the foregoing is true and correct and that this attestation and this declaration are executed on the 1st day of May, 1993, at Rancho Mirage, California.

Jerry Garcia

DATE AND PLACE OF BIRTH
August 1, 1942
San Francisco, California

DATE AND PLACE OF DEATH
August 9, 1995
Serenity Knolls
Forest Knolls, California

Skeletons from the Closet

As the laid back captain of the musical and cultural phenomenon known as The Grateful Dead, Jerry Garcia has been considered a prophet and an Oracle by the Dead's ultra-loyal legions of fans. For many "Dead-heads", the band was Uncle Jerry's band, as he navigated its course from the psychedelic 60's, trucking through the Workingman's seventies, into the excesses and the dark of the 80's, and concluding with more than a Touch of Grey in the 90's. Jerry Garcia died in his sleep at the age of 53 while in a residential drug treatment center near his home in California.

Part of the reason for the broad popularity of the Grateful Dead was their egalitarian and inclusive approach towards their fans and business matters involving the band. That spirit of inclusion is evident in the Will of "Jerome J. Garcia, also known as Jerry Garcia", dated May 12, 1994. Jerry's Will also manifests his personal and legal entanglements with numerous women during his 53 year strange trip.

As one might have expected from a fellow as affable and easygoing as Jerry, his estate has been besieged by creditors ranging from his former wives, managers and even an acupuncturist.

Jerry's Will begins with the following Declarations:

> I declare that I am married; my wife's name is DEBO-RAH KOONS. We have no children by our marriage. I have four children now living from prior relationships, namely, HEATHER GARCIA KATZ, born December 8, 1963, ANNABELE WLAKER [sic] GARCIA, born February 2, 1970, THERESA ADAMS GARCIA, born September 21, 1974, and KEELIN GARCIA, born December 20, 1987. I have no deceased children leaving issue, and I have not adopted any children. The terms "child" or "children" as used in this Will shall refer only to my children and if any person shall claim and establish any right to participate in my estate other than as provided in this Will, whether as heir or in any other capacity whatsoever, I give and bequeath to each such person the sum of One Dollar ($1.00).

Jerry or his attorneys wanted it quite clear that only the four children expressly named, or misnamed in the case of Annabelle Wlaker [sic] Garcia, were the ones he was admitting to, and any others would be entitled to "One Dollar ($1.00)," and nothing more.

With one notable exception, all of Jerry's personal effects including his jewelry, clothing, household furniture and furnishings, personal automobiles, books, pictures, objects of art and other tangible articles of a personal nature were bequeathed to his third wife, Deborah Koons Garcia, if she survived him for sixty (60) days, which she did.

Under Article FIFTH of the Will, Jerry expressly bequeaths "all my guitars made by DOUGLAS ERWIN, to DOUGLAS ERWIN, or to his estate if he predeceases me." Jerry obviously believed that those instruments should return to their maker. It is interesting and somewhat unusual that Garcia provided the items to pass to Erwin's Estate if Erwin predeceased him.

The balance of Garcia's residuary estate, after the payment of debts, was divided in the following somewhat unusual manner:

DISTRIBUTION OF RESIDUE OF ESTATE

A.   If my wife survives me for sixty (60) days, I give her one-third (1/3) of my estate outright and free of trust. If my wife fails to survive me for sixty days this bequest shall lapse and the amount shall be included with the remainder of my estate under paragraph B.

B.   I give the remaining two-thirds (2/3) of my estate, or if my wife fails to survive me, my entire remaining estate, to my daughters, my friends, and my brother as follows:

1.   The following shares shall be distributed outright and free of trust, by right of representation, to the persons indicated:

HEATHER GARCIA KATZ	ONE-FIFTH ($\frac{1}{5}$)
ANNABELLE WALKER GARCIA	ONE-FIFTH ($\frac{1}{5}$)
SUNSHINE MAY WALKER KESEY	ONE-TENTH ($\frac{1}{10}$)
CLIFFORD GARCIA	ONE-TENTH ($\frac{1}{10}$)

That disposition would result in the imposition of a tax on Jerry's estate because an amount well in excess of $600,000 passes to persons other than Jerry's spouse. Jerry could have placed all of his assets in a marital trust and avoided any estate tax at the time of his death, but he apparently did not want those younger persons and his older brother Clifford to have to wait for Jerry's widow to catch up with him again.

Garcia's Will is also unusual in its allusion to specific outstanding debts. His Will expressly provides that:

> After payment of all my debts, my last illness and funeral expenses and provision for my child support obligations for KEELIN GARCIA, my marital settlement agreement with CAROLYN ADAMS GARCIA which is being drafted at the time of signing this Will, and my agreement with Manasha Matheson regarding the house to be owned one-half by her and one-half by the Trust established for Keelin Garcia which is being drafted at the time of signing this Will, my Executor shall divide and distribute the remainder of my estate for my wife/husband and children.

Jerry's Will named his wife Deborah and his attorney David Hellman as co-Executors and Trustees.

Finally, Jerry's Will also provided that:

> If MANASHA MATHESON does not survive me, I hereby nominate and appoint SUNSHINE MAY WALKER KESEY, as the guardian of KEELIN GARCIA, if she is then a minor. No bond shall be required of any person who acts as guardian hereunder.

> /s/ *Jerome J. Garcia*
> _____

Will dated May 12, 1994

We can only hope that Sunshine May Walker Kesey does not serve young Keelin Garcia any of Sunshine's natural father Ken Kesey's favorite kool-aid mix.

TABLE OF CONTENTS
WILL OF
JEROME J. GARCIA

WILL
OF
JEROME J. GARCIA

I, JEROME J. GARCIA, also known as JERRY GARCIA, a resident of Marin County, California, hereby make, publish and declare this to be my Last Will and Testament.

FIRST
REVOCATION OF PRIOR WILLS
I revoke all Wills and Codicils heretofore made by me.

SECOND
DECLARATIONS
I declare that I am married; my wife's name is DEBORAH KOONS. We have no children by our marriage. I have four children now living from prior relationships, namely, HEATHER GARCIA KATZ, born December 8, 1963, ANNABELLE WLAKER GARCIA, born February 2, 1970, THERESA ADAMS GARCIA, born September 21, 1974, and KEELIN GARCIA, born December 20, 1987. I have no deceased children leaving issue, and I have not adopted any children. The terms "child" or "children" as used in this Will shall refer only to my children and if any person shall claim and establish any right to participate in my estate other than as provided in this Will, whether as heir or in any other capacity whatsoever, I give and bequeath to each such person the sum of One Dollar ($1.00).

THIRD
COMMUNITY PROPERTY
I declare my intention hereby to dispose of all property, real and personal, of which I have the right to dispose by Will, including any and all property as to which I may have at the time of my death a power of appointment by Will. I confirm to my wife her interest in our community property. It is my intention by this Will to dispose of all my separate Property and of my one-half (1/2) interest in our community property.

FOURTH
PERSONAL PROPERTY
Except as specifically provided hereinbelow, I give

my jewelry, clothing, household furniture and furnishings, personal automobiles, books, pictures, objects of art and other tangible articles of a personal nature, of my interest in such property, which I may have at the time of my death, not otherwise specifically disposed of by this Will or in any other manner, together with any insurance on such property, to my wife, if she survives me for sixty (60) days, and if she does not, then to such of my children, by representation, who survive me for sixty (60) days in equal shares as they shall agree, or as my Executor shall, in my Executor's discretion, determine if my children do not agree within one hundred fifty (150) days of my death.

In the absence of a conflict of interest, my Executor shall represent any child under age eighteen (18) in matter relating to any distribution under this Article FOURTH, including selection of the assets that shall constitute that child's share, and my Executor may, in my Executor's discretion, sell for the child's account any part of that child's share. Any property or its proceeds distributable to a child under age eighteen (18) pursuant to this Paragraph may be delivered without bond to the guardian of such child or to any suitable person with whom he or she resides or who has the care or control of him or her.

If neither my wife nor any of my children shall survive me, then this gift shall lapse and such property, and any insurance thereon, shall become part of the residue of my estate.

FIFTH

GUITARS

I give all my guitars made by DOUGLAS ERWIN, to DOUGLAS ERWIN, or to his estate if he predeceases me.

SIXTH

DISTRIBUTION OF RESIDUE OF ESTATE

After payment of all my debts, my last illness and funeral expenses, and provision for my child support obligations for KEELIN GARCIA, my marital settlement agreement with CAROLYN ADAMS GARCIA which is being drafted at the time of signing this will, and my agreement with MANASHA MATHESON regarding the house to be owned one-half by her and one-half by the trust established for KEELIN GARCIA which is being drafted at the time of signing this will, my Executor shall divide and distribute the remainder of my estate for my wife/husband and children as follows:

A.   If my wife survives me for sixty (60) days, I give her one-third (1/3) of my estate outright and free of trust. If my wife fails to survive me for sixty days this bequest shall lapse and the amount shall be included with the remainder of my estate under paragraph B.

B.   I give the remaining two-thirds (2/3) of my estate, or if my wife fails to survive me, my entire remaining estate, to my daughters, my friends, and my brother as follows:

1.   The following shares shall be distributed outright and free of trust, by right of representation, to the persons indicated:

HEATHER GARCIA KATZ	ONE-FIFTH (⅕)
ANNABELLE WALKER GARCIA	ONE-FIFTH (⅕)
SUNSHINE MAY WALKER KESEY	ONE-TENTH (¹⁄₁₀)
CLIFFORD GARCIA	ONE-TENTH (¹⁄₁₀)

2.   I give to the Trustee hereinafter named, IN TRUST, for the benefit of my younger daughters, THERESA ADAMS GARCIA and KEELIN GARCIA, one-

fifth (1/5) of my estate for each, to be held, administered and distributed as a separate trust for each child
as follows:

     a.   So long as my child is living and is un-
der age twenty-one (21), the Trustee shall pay to or apply for her benefit, as much of the net income and
principal of the Trust as the Trustee, in the Trustee's
absolute discretion, shall deem necessary for her
proper support, health, maintenance and education, after taking into consideration, to the extent the Trustee
shall deem advisable, any other income or resources of
my child, known to the Trustee. Any net income not
distributed shall be accumulated and added to principal.

     b.   When the child attains the age of
twenty-one (21), the trust share allocated on account of
such child shall thereupon be distributed free of trust to
that child.

     c.   If my child dies prior to receipt of her
entire share of principal and income provided herein,
and that child is survived by issue, then the remaining
principal and income shall be held in trust for those issue under the terms of this subparagraph 2. If my child
is not survived by issue, then the remaining principal
and income shall be distributed free of trust to the
other residual beneficiaries receiving fractional interests in my estate under this paragraph B in proportion
to those fractional interests, by right of representation;
provided, however, if a part of that balance would otherwise be distributed to a person for whose benefit a
trust is then being administered under this Will, that
part shall instead be added to that trust and shall thereafter be administered according to its terms.

      d.   Whenever provision is made in this Article SIXTH for payment for the "education" of a beneficiary, the term "education" shall be construed to include college and postgraduate study, so long as pursued to advantage by the beneficiary at an institution of the beneficiary's choice; and in determining payments to be made for such college or postgraduate education, the Trustee shall take into consideration the beneficiary's related living expenses to the extent that they are reasonable.

      e.   Notwithstanding the directions given as to the distribution of income and principal in this Article SIXTH, any trusts established by this Article shall terminate, if they have not previously terminated, twenty-one (21) years after the death of the survivor of the class composed of my wife/husband and all my issue living at my death, and the then remaining principal and undistributed income of such trusts shall be paid to my issue or other beneficiaries then living to whom income payments could be made under such trusts immediately prior to its termination under this clause, such issue to take by right of representation.

SEVENTH
ULTIMATE DISTRIBUTION

      If at the time of my death, or at any later time before full distribution of any Trust established under Article SIXTH, all my issue are deceased, and no other disposition of the property is directed by this Will, the estate or the portion of it then remaining shall thereupon be distributed to those persons who would then be my heirs, their identities and respective shares to be determined as though my death had then occurred and according to the laws of the State of California then in effect relating to the succession of separate property not acquired from a predeceased spouse.

EIGHTH
TRUSTEE'S POWERS

I give to the Trustee of all of the Trusts established under this Will the following powers, in addition to and not in limitation of the common-law and statutory powers, and without application or permission of any court.

A.   To retain any property, real or personal, which the Trustee may receive, even though such property (by reason of its character, amount, proportion to the total Trust Estate or otherwise) would not be considered appropriate for a Trustee apart from this provision.

B. To sell, exchange, give options upon, partition, or otherwise dispose of any property which the Trustee may hold from time to time at public or private sale or otherwise, for cash or other consideration or on credit, and upon such terms and for such consideration as the Trustee shall think fit, and to transfer and convey the same free of all trust.

C.   To invest and reinvest the Trust Estate from time to time in any property, real or personal, including (without limiting the generality of the foregoing language) securities of domestic and foreign corporations and investment trusts, common trust funds, including those established by any successor corporate fiduciary which acts as Executor and Trustee hereunder, bonds, preferred stocks, common stocks, mortgages, mortgage participation, even though such investment (by reason of its character, amount, proportion to the total Trust Estate or otherwise) would not be considered appropriate for a Trustee apart from this provision, and even though such investment causes a greater proportion of the principal to be invested in investment of one type or of one company than would be considered appropriate for a Trustee apart from this provision; to lend money to any and all persons, including any or all of the beneficiaries hereof, upon such terms and conditions as the Trustee in the Trustee's sole discretion deems proper; in connection with such loans the Trustee may or may not demand security therefor or interest thereon as the Trustee in the Trustee's sole discretion deems proper.

D.   To improve any real estate held in the Trust Estate, including the power to demolish any buildings in whole or in part and to erect buildings; to lease real estate on such terms as the Trustee thinks fit, including leases for periods that may extend beyond the duration of the Trusts, and to grant renewals thereof; and to foreclose, extend, assign, partially release and discharge mortgages.

E.   To borrow money from any lender even though a successor fiduciary hereunder, execute promissory notes therefor, and to secure said obligations by mortgage or pledge of any of the Trust property.

F.   To compromise or arbitrate any claim in favor of or against the Trust Estate; to commence or defend any litigation concerning the Trust Estate which the Trustee in the Trustee's absolute discretion considers prudent, and costs and expenses of such, including reasonable attorney's fees, to be borne by the Trust Estate; to give or receive consideration in any settlement to reduce the rate of return on any investment, with or without consideration; to prepay or accept prepayment of any debt; to enforce, abstain from enforcing, release or modify, with or without consideration, any right, obligation, or claim; to extend and renew any obligation or hold the same after maturity without extension or renewal; to accept deeds in lieu of foreclosure and pay consideration for the same; to determine that any property is worthless or of insufficient value to warrant keeping or protecting, and to abandon any such property or convey the same with or without consideration; and to use any portion of the Trust Estate to protect any other portion of the Trust Estate.

G.   To vote all securities held as a part of the Trust Estate, or to join in a voting trust or other lawful form of stockholders' agreements respecting the voting of shares for such period as the Trustee deems proper; to pay all assessments on such securities, to exercise options, subscriptions and conversion rights on such securities, with respect thereto; to employ such brokers, banks, counsel, custodians, attorneys or other agents, and to delegate to them such powers (including, among others, the right to vote shares of stock held in trust) or join in a voting trust or other lawful form of stockholders' agreements respecting the voting of shares for such periods as the Trustee deems proper; and to cause securities held from time to time to be registered in the name of the Trustee, or in the name of the Trustee's nominee with or without mention of the Trust in any instrument of ownership, and to keep the same unregistered or to retain them in condition that they will pass by delivery.

H.   To incur and pay all taxes, assessments, costs, charges, fees and other expenses of every kind which the Trustee deems necessary or advisable in connection with the administration of the Trust created hereby, including reasonable Trustee's fees.

I. To join in or oppose any reorganization, recapitalization, consolidation or merger, liquidation or foreclosure, or any plan therefor; to deposit property with, and delegate discretionary power to any committee or depository; to pay assessments, expenses and compensation; and to retain any property issued therein; to exercise or sell conversion or subscription rights, and to retain the property received.

J. To hold, manage, invest and account for the several shares which may be held in trust, either as separate funds or as a single fund, as the Trustee deems proper; if as a single fund, making the division thereof only upon the Trustee's books of account and allocating to each share its proportionate part of the principal and income of the common fund and charging against each share its proportionate part of the common expenses.

K. To keep any or all of the Trust property at any place or places in California or elsewhere in the United States or abroad, or with a depository or custodian at such place or places.

L. In dividing the Trust Estate into shares or in distributing the same, to divide or distribute in cash or in kind as the Trustee thinks fit. For purposes of division or distribution, to value the Trust Estate reasonably and in good faith, and such valuation shall be conclusive on all parties. Where distribution or division is made in kind, the Trustee shall, so far as the Trustee finds practicable, allocate to the beneficiaries proportionate amounts of each kind of security; or other property of the Trust Estate.

M. The Trustee is authorized in the Trustee's discretion to retain from income distributable to any beneficiary an amount equal to the income tax (Federal and State) the Trustee estimates will be imposed upon such income; any sums so withheld shall be applied to the tax liability of such beneficiary. Nothing herein shall be construed as imposing an obligation upon the Trustee to retain any sums for the purpose mentioned, nor that said tax shall be assumed or borne by the assets held for such beneficiary. No liability shall attach to the Trustee if the Trustee acts or fails to act as authorized in Subparagraph M.

N. To partition, without sale, any real or personal property held jointly or in common with others or distributable to one or more persons hereunder; to pay or receive consideration to effect equality of partition; to unite with any other owner in the management, leasing, use or improvement of any property.

O. To determine, as to all property received, whether and to what extent the same shall be deemed to be principal or income and as to all charges or expenses paid, whether and to what extent the same shall be charged against principal or against income, including, without limiting the generality of the foregoing language, power to apportion any receipt or expense between principal and income and to determine what part, if any, of the actual income received upon any wasting investment or upon any security purchased or acquired at a premium shall be retained and added to principal to prevent diminution of principal upon exhaustion or maturity thereof. In this regard, the Trustee in the Trustee's absolute discretion, may, but shall not be required to, if the Trustee deems it proper, allocate receipts or charges and expenses to income or principal according to the Principal and Income Law of the State of California as it may from time to time exist. All allocation of receipts or charges and expenses shall be conclusive on all persons interested in any trusts created thereby.

P.   In all matters to administer and invest the Trust Estate as fully and freely as an individual owner might do, without any restrictions to which fiduciaries are ordinarily subject, except the duty to act in good faith and with reasonable care.

Q.   The Trustee shall also have the power to do all things necessary to continue any business enterprise, in whatever form, owned or controlled by me upon my death for such period as the Trustee shall deem to be in the best interests of the Trust Estate.

R.   The Trustee is authorized to employ attorneys, accountants, investment advisors, specialists and such other agents as he shall deem necessary or desirable. The Trustee shall have the authority to appoint an investment manager or managers to manage all or any part of the assets of the Trust Estate, appointment shall include the power to acquire and dispose of such assets. The Trustee may charge the compensation of such attorneys, accountants, investment advisors, specialists and other agents and any other expenses against the Trust Estate.

NINTH
PAYMENT OF TAXES AND EXPENSES

I direct that all estate, succession or other death taxes, duties, charges or assessments that may by reason of my death be attributable to my probate estate or any portion of it, or to any property or transfers of prop-

erty outside my probate estate, including but not limited to burial expenses, expenses of last illness, attorney's fees, executor's fees, appraisers's fees, accountant's fees and other expenses of administering my
estate shall be paid by the Executor from the estate in
the same manner as if said taxes were a debt of my
estate, without apportionment, deduction, or reimbursement thereof and without adjustment thereof
among my beneficiaries. Provided, however, if there is
inadequate cash in my estate to pay such taxes and
expenses, then my executor may borrow such funds as
I have given authority in Article TWELFTH below.

TENTH
NO CONTEST CLAUSE

If any beneficiary of my Will or any Codicil hereto
or of the Trusts created hereunder before or after the
admission of this Will to probate, directly or indirectly,
contests or aids in the contest of the same or any provision thereof, or contests the distribution of my estate in
accordance with my Will or any Codicil, the provisions
herein made to or for the benefit of such contestant or
contestants are hereby revoked and for the purpose of
my Will and any Codicil, said contestant or contestants
shall be deemed to have predeceased me.

ELEVENTH
SPENDTHRIFT PROVISION

Each and every beneficiary under the Trust or Trusts
created by this Will is hereby restrained from and is and
shall be without right, power, or authority to sell, transfer, pledge, hypothecate, mortgage, alienate, anticipate, or in any other manner affect or impair his, her or
their beneficial and legal rights, titles, interests, claims
and estates in and to the income and/or principal of said

trusts, and the rights, titles, interests and estate of any beneficiary thereunder shall not be subject nor liable to any process of law or court, and all of the income and/or principal under said trusts shall be paid over to the beneficiary in person, or, in the event of the minority or incompetency of any beneficiary, to the guardian of that beneficiary in such manner as in the Trustee's discretion seems most advisable at the time and in the manner provided by the terms of the trust.

TWELFTH
EXECUTOR'S APPOINTMENT AND POWERS

I hereby nominate and appoint my wife DEBORAH KOONS, and my attorney DAVID M. HELLMAN, as Executor of this Will. If either of them shall be, or become unable or unwilling to act, then the survivor shall act with JEFFREY E. EHLENBACH. No bond or other security shall be required of any person who acts as Executor hereunder.

A. I hereby expressly authorize and empower my Executor to sell and dispose of the whole or any portion of my estate, real or personal, and wherever situate, as and when and upon such terms as my Executor deems proper, at public or private sale, with or without notice, and without first securing any order of court therefor. I further grant to my Executor all the powers granted to the Trustee under Article EIGHTH hereof, insofar as such powers are appropriate for the administration of my estate and the probate of my Will;

B. If my Executor in good faith decides that there is uncertainty as to the inclusion of particular property in my gross estate for federal estate tax purposes, my Executor shall exclude such property from my gross estate in the estate tax return. My Executor shall not be liable for any loss to my estate or to any beneficiary, which loss results from the decision made in good faith that there is uncertainty as to the inclusion of particular property in my gross estate.

C.   The decision of my Executor as to the date which should be selected for the valuation of property in my gross estate for federal estate tax purposes shall be conclusive on all concerned;

D.   When a choice is available as to whether certain deductions shall be taken as income tax deductions or estate tax deductions, the decision of my Executor in this regard shall be conclusive on all concerned and no adjustment of income and principal account shall be made as a result of such decision;

E.   Beginning as of the date of my death and until the establishment of the trusts provided for herein, my Executor shall make such payments of estate income, which is allocable to trust assets, as would be required if the trusts had actually been established at the date of my death.

F.   My Executor is authorized to execute and deliver disclaimers under Internal Revenue Code §2518 and California Probate Code §§260 through 295 or any successor statute.

THIRTEENTH
TRUSTEE'S APPOINTMENT AND COMPENSATION

I hereby nominate and appoint my wife DEBORAH KOONS, and my attorney DAVID M. HELLMAN, as Trustee of this Will. If either of them shall be, or become unable or unwilling to act, then the survivor shall act with JEFFREY E. EHLENBACH. No bond or other security shall be required of any person who acts as Trustee hereunder.

The individual Trustees shall be entitled to receive reasonable commissions similar to those charged by corporate Trustees in the San Francisco Bay Area. Any successor Trustee shall be entitled to reasonable compensation for its services.

FOURTEENTH
GUARDIAN

If MANASHA MATHESON does not survive me, I hereby nominate and appoint SUNSHINE MAY WALKER KESEY, as the guardian of KEELIN GARCIA, if she is then a minor. No bond shall be required of any person who acts as guardian hereunder.

FIFTEENTH
DELAYED DISTRIBUTION

I direct that no interest shall be payable on account of any delay in distributing any devise, bequest, or legacy under my Will or any Codicil thereto.

SIXTEENTH
DEFINITIONS

The words "Executor," "Trustee," "child," "children," and "beneficiary," as used herein, shall comprehend both the singular and the plural, and the masculine or feminine shall be deemed to include the other wherever the context of this Will requires. This Will and any Codicil shall be interpreted under the California law as in effect at the date of signature of such document.

IN WITNESS WHEREOF, I have hereunto set my hand this May 12, 1994.

/s/ *Jerome J. Garcia*
_____
JEROME J. GARCIA

On the date indicated below, JEROME J. GARCIA, declared to us, the undersigned, that this instrument, consisting of sixteen (16) pages, including the page signed by us as witnesses, was the testator's Will and requested us to act as witnesses to it. The testator thereupon signed this Will in our presence, all of us being present at the same time. We now, at the testator's request, in the testator's presence and in the presence of each other, subscribe our names as witnesses.

It is our belief that the testator is of sound mind and memory and is under no constraint or undue influence whatsoever.

We declare under penalty of perjury that the foregoing is true and correct and that this declaration was executed on May 12, 1994, at San Rafael, California.

Irving Berlin

DATE AND PLACE OF BIRTH
May 11, 1888
Tyumen, Russia

DATE AND PLACE OF DEATH
September 22, 1989
17 Beekman Place
New York, New York

God Bless Irving Berlin

Born near Siberia in Russia and named Israel Baline, Irving Berlin became one of America's most beloved and prolific songwriters. He was one of eight children of Cantor Moses Baline and Leah Baline. Fleeing from the Russian pogroms against Jews, the Baline family moved to New York in 1893 and settled on the Lower East Side. Mr. Baline died shortly thereafter and young "Izzy" helped support the family by selling newspapers and singing at Bowery bars and other music halls. Despite the language barrier and his lack of formal education, Berlin began composing the words and music to songs with his first hit song being "Alexander's Ragtime Band" which was published in 1911 when Berlin was 23 years old. For the next fifty-five years, Berlin wrote over 1,500 songs with his most well known songs including "Puttin' on the Ritz", "Easter Parade", "White Christmas," which was popularized by Bing Crosby's rendition, and "God Bless America" which Berlin wrote especially for popular radio star, Kate Smith.

With the huge success of America's unofficial national anthem, "God Bless America," Berlin and Smith agreed to donate all their royalties from the song to the benefit of the Boy Scouts and Girl Scouts of America. In his lengthy Will, Berlin makes the following provision pertaining to the "God Bless America Fund" he had established:

> . . . . I specifically request that in the event of a sale of the stock or the business and assets of Irving Berlin Music Corporation, a condition be imposed upon the purchaser that the purchaser will publish for the Trustees of the GOD BLESS AMERICA FUND the composition "God Bless America" and such other compositions as have been or will be transferred by me to the Trustees of the GOD BLESS AMERICA FUND, upon the same terms and conditions as the compositions are published by Irving Berlin Music Corporation, at the time of my death. . . .

Berlin was first married in 1912 to Dorothy Goetz. Tragically, she died six months later from typhoid fever which she had contracted during their honeymoon in Havana, Cuba. In his grief, Berlin wrote the touching "When I Lost You" which was his first popular sentimental ballad. Around 1925, Berlin married his second wife, Ellin Mackay, who was the daughter of a wealthy and prominent businessman in New York. Mr. Mackay vehemently opposed the marriage. Despite her father's opposition, Ellin married Irving in a Civil Ceremony in New York's municipal building. Later, Berlin reportedly had to bail his father-in-law out financially after Mr. Mackay suffered some reversal of fortunes. The Berlins reportedly had a very happy marriage until Ellin's death in 1988 at the age of 85. The Berlin's had four children, including a son, Irving Jr., who died in his infancy. When he died at the age of 101, Berlin was survived by his three daughters, nine grandchildren and two great-grandchildren.

In his Will, Berlin makes cash bequests ranging from $10,000 to $40,000 to various, employees, friends and relatives. As for charitable gifts, Berlin's Will points out:

> I have made no provision in this my Will for gifts to charities as I have heretofore established IRVING BERLIN CHARITABLE FUND, INC. for the purpose of charitable giving, which is adequately endowed for such purpose.

Because Berlin's wife did not survive him, the bulk of his estate is placed in trust for the benefit of Berlin's daughters, grandchildren and great-grandchildren. The only Executor of the Will was the Morgan Guaranty Trust Company of New York because neither Mrs. Berlin nor another named individual survived and Berlin's 1968 Will was never updated.

Dying peacefully in his sleep at the ripe old age of 101, the melodious minstrel of music Irving Berlin left a legacy that America could never forget. His music will live forever. "Not for just an hour, not for just a day, not for just a year, but always" as the man himself said.

/s/ *Irving Berlin*

Will dated May 17, 1968

Cole Porter

DATE AND PLACE OF BIRTH
June 9, 1892
Peru, Indiana

DATE AND PLACE OF DEATH
October 15, 1964
Santa Monica Hospital
Santa Monica, California

Everything Goes

Songwriter Cole Porter composed the lyrics and music to scores of the most memorable songs the world would ever hear. Porter's songs were known for lyrics that were sophisticated and witty and include such classics as "Anything Goes," "I Get a Kick out of You," and the titillating "Let's Do It."

In the summer of 1937, when he was forty-five years old and at the height of his success, Porter was in a horseback-riding accident that broke both his legs, seriously injured his central nervous system, and changed his outlook on life—from a wheelchair. After his wife of thirty-five years, the former Linda Lee Thomas, died in 1954, and Porter's right leg was amputated in 1958, Porter became even more reclusive, spending most of his time holed up in his memorabilia-filled apartment at New York's Waldorf-Astoria.

Cole Porter's lengthy and detailed Will is as much a product of his fascinating life and collections (both of objects and friends) as the drafting techniques of the fancy Park Avenue law firm that prepared it. Despite the intricate legalese, Cole Porter's own style and priorities nonetheless shine through.

The first section of Porter's Will indicates his desire to return to the soil of his birthplace in Peru, Indiana, and Porter's last personal requests of a religious nature.

I DIRECT my Executors to arrange for my burial in Peru, Indiana. I FURTHER DIRECT my Executors to arrange for no funeral or memorial service, but only for a private burial service to be conducted by the Pastor of the First Baptist Church of Peru, in the presence of my relatives and dear friends. At such service I request said Pastor to read the following quotation from the Bible:

> "I am the resurrection and the life;
> he that believeth in me, though he were
> dead, yet shall he live; And whosoever
> liveth and believeth in me shall never die,"

and to follow such quotation with The Lord's Prayer. I request that the foregoing be substantially the entire burial service, and that neither said Pastor nor anyone else deliver any memorial address whatsoever. I particularly direct that there be no service of any kind for me in New York City.

Following the burial instructions, the Will proceeds to divide Porter's varied estate among educational and charitable institutions, friends, and employees, but primarily among Porter's relatives.

To Williams College, Porter gave the 350-acre estate, known as Buxton Hill, that he owned in Williamstown, Massachusetts. He gave all the pianos in his New York apartment to The Juilliard School of Music and all his cigarette cases and scrapbooks to the Museum of Modern Art. Porter divides his papers and books among Williams

College, Yale University, and the University of California at Los Angeles. Finally, he bequeathed all his clothing to the Salvation Army.

The following are some of the more unusual and provocative personal bequests made in Porter's Will:

> I GIVE AND BEQUEATH to each of the following persons who shall survive me the article or articles of tangible personal property, which I shall own at my death, set forth below opposite the name of such person:
>
> C. The DUKE OF VERDURA, the Justiani-Capo de Monte china service and my Ginori dessert plates . . .
>
> E. MRS. WILLIAM (EDITH) GOETZ, the Cambodian head sculpture, which is now located in my apartment in New York, New York, and the small (9" x 12") water color painting of a seashore scene framed in a gilt frame.
>
> F. EDGAR M. (MONTY) WOOLLEY, the star sapphire cuff links, waistcoat buttons and studs for shirt.
>
> G. DOUGLAS FAIRBANKS, JR., the diamond dress stud.
>
> H. BARON NICOLAS DE GUNZBURG, the Russian ikon, which is now located in my apartment in New York, New York; the sculpture of an Egyptian woman's head, which is now located in my cottage on my Buxton Hill Realty; and the book by Paul Muratoff, which was published by A La Vielle Russie and which is entitled "Thirty-Five Russian Primitives."
>
> I. MISS AVA ASTAIRE, the aquamarine and ruby necklace which formerly belonged to my beloved wife, Linda Porter.

All the rest of his tangible property, "including, without limitation, my automobiles, silver, household furniture furnishings and utensils, rugs, carpets, tapestries, bric-a-brac, sculpture, paintings, china, glassware, objects of art, jewelry and personal effects," Porter left to his cousin, Jules Omar Cole, or if he did not survive, to Jules's son, James Omar Cole. One has to wonder about the meaning of "bric-a-brac" within that comprehensive context. The distinction between "carpets" and "rugs" for this purpose might also be a bit of legal overkill. How about "floor coverings of any kind"? I know, more letters.

Porter also made cash bequests ranging from $1,000 to $10,000 to certain friends and employees. The bulk of Porter's wealthy estate and continuing royalty payments is held by a trust for the benefit of Porter family relatives. Over thirty-five years after Porter's death, his estate is generating millions of dollars in income per year. With that kind of money, anything goes.

/s/ Cole Porter
_____

Will dated November 28, 1962

Jim Morrison

DATE AND PLACE OF BIRTH

December 8, 1943

Melbourne, Florida

DATE AND PLACE OF DEATH

July 3, 1971

Paris, France

"This Is the End, Beautiful Friend"

When rock superstar Jim Morrison died at the age of twenty-seven in a bathtub in Paris, he left a lyrical legacy that is etched into the consciousness of a generation. As the incendiary lead singer for the sixties rock group The Doors, Morrison helped light the flames and fan the fires of that decade. One of The Doors' first and best-known songs was "Light My Fire," which became an anthem for the flower children of the sixties. Another song, performed particularly graphically by Morrison, was "The End," in which the protagonist in the song has an Oedipal encounter with his mother and ends up murdering both of his parents. Strange days, indeed.

Morrison signed his one-page Will in Beverly Hills, California, in the office of his lawyer, Max Fink. Fink is named a co-executor, together with Morrison's then girlfriend and future wife, Pamela S. Courson. The Will begins as follows:

I, JAMES D. MORRISON, being of sound and disposing mind, memory and understanding, and after consideration for all persons, the objects of my bounty, and with full knowledge of the nature and extent of my assets, do hereby make, publish and declare this my Last Will and Testament, as follows:

FIRST: I declare that I am a resident of Los Angeles County, California; that I am unmarried and have no children.

To his then girlfriend, Pamela S. Courson, Morrison left "each and every thing of value of which I may die possessed, including real property, personal property and mixed properties," or in other words, his entire estate. If Pamela had not survived Morrison for three months after his death, then the estate was to be left to Morrison's brother, Andrew Morrison of Monterey, California, and to his sister, Anne R. Morrison of Coronado Beach, California, "to share and share alike." Neither of Morrison's parents, George S. Morrison and Clara Morrison, were mentioned in his Will. During his lifetime, Morrison had often stated that both his parents were dead. In fact, they both survived their prodigal son.

Morrison's girlfriend, Pamela Courson, married Morrison after he had signed his Will. She survived her husband by the requisite three-month period, but died about three years later on April 25, 1974. Pamela Courson Morrison's father, Columbus B. Courson, succeeded his daughter as administrator of Jim Morrison's estate and as its sole beneficiary. One has to wonder whether Mr. Columbus Courson had approved of the lifestyle and antics of his daughter's boyfriend and then husband. As might be expected, attorney Max Fink filed all the legal documents required.

After his death in Paris, Morrison was buried in the famous Parisian cemetery Père Lachaise. He was buried near some of the symbolist and surrealist poets whose writings had inspired his own poetry (with the help of large quantities of a variety of intoxicants). Dead before he was even close to thirty, Jim Morrison left a rock-and-roll legacy of fire and passion that will not be forgotten. As Morrison himself once sang, "I'll tell you this/ No eternal reward will forgive us now for wasting the dawn." Jim Morrison did not waste his dawns, his dawns wasted him.

/s/ *James D. Morrison*

Will dated February 12, 1969

Elvis Presley

DATE AND PLACE OF BIRTH
January 8, 1935
Tupelo, Mississippi

DATE AND PLACE OF DEATH
August 16, 1977
Baptist Memorial Hospital
Memphis, Tennessee

The King Is Dead

The undisputed King of Rock and Roll, Elvis Presley, died at the age of forty-two shortly after he was found unconscious in his bedroom at his home in Memphis called Graceland. The cause of death was officially termed a "cardiac arrhythmia," which may have been a result of Presley's excess weight and the pills he took to suppress his appetite. Presley reportedly had an appetite for Cadillacs, "Girls, Girls, Girls," drugs, and liquor, as well as food.

On May 1, 1967, Presley married Priscilla Beaulieu, who was an Air Force brat he had met during his own Army stint. On February 1, 1968, a daughter they named Lisa Marie was born. In 1973, Elvis and Priscilla Presley were divorced.

When Presley died about five months after signing his Will, he was survived by his nine-year-old daughter, Lisa Marie, his father, Vernon, and his grandmother, Minnie Mae Presley. Presley's 1977 Will provides primarily for these three people. A trust of the entire residuary estate is established for their benefit, and for any other Presley relatives "who in the absolute discretion of my Trustee are in need of emergency assistance for any of the above mentioned purposes," which included "health, education, support, comfortable maintenance and welfare."

Presley appointed his father, Vernon E. Presley, as the executor of the Will and as trustee. Pop Presley is given broad discretion over the affairs of the estate. For example, there is the following "Item" in the Will concerning Elvis's "trophies":

Instructions Concerning Personal
Property: Enjoyment in Specie

I anticipate that included as a part of my property and estate at the time of my death will be tangible personal property of various kinds, characters and values, including trophies and other items accumulated by me during my professional career. I hereby specifically instruct all concerned that my Executor, herein appointed, shall have complete freedom and discretion as to disposal of any and all such property so long as he shall act in good faith and in the best interest of my estate and my beneficiaries, and his discretion so exercised shall not be subject to question by anyone whomsoever.

Presley's Will was prepared by local Tennessee attorneys. At one point in the Will, Elvis gets technical when he states, "Having in mind the rule against perpetuities, I direct that (notwithstanding anything contained to the contrary in this Last Will and Testament) . . ." It is a good thing that Presley's attorneys did not write his songs.

The Will, which was apparently prepared in 1976 but not signed until 1977, concludes with the following:

IN WITNESS WHEREOF, I, the said ELVIS A. PRESLEY, do hereunto set my hand and seal in the presence of two (2) competent witnesses, and in their presence do publish and declare this instrument to be my Last Will and Testament, this 3 day of March, 1977

/s/ *Elvis A. Presley*
_____

That witness clause would have been fine, except there were, in fact, three witnesses to Presley's Will. The Will had been prepared for the signatures of only two witnesses, but it appears that an extra Presley fan slipped in there when he was signing.

Elvis's father, Vernon Presley, died in 1979. In 1989, the estate was terminated, with all the property, including Graceland, held in trust for the benefit of Presley's then twenty-one-year-old daughter, Lisa Marie, until she reaches age twenty-five. At twenty-five, Lisa Marie Presley will inherit a fortune, if not fame, and is probably not lonesome tonight.

Will dated March 3, 1977
Will signed in Memphis, Tennessee

Bing Crosby

DATE AND PLACE OF BIRTH
May 2, 1904
Tacoma, Washington

DATE AND PLACE OF DEATH
October 14, 1977
La Moraleja Golf Club
Madrid, Spain

The Nineteenth Hole

Bing Crosby had a melodious singing voice and easygoing manner that made him one of America's most beloved entertainers for over five decades. However, it was revealed in a 1983 book by son Gary Crosby called *Going My Own Way* that the publicly easygoing Bing was a strict disciplinarian at home with his children.

Crosby was named Harry Lillis Crosby at his birth in Tacoma, Washington. The nickname Bing came early, and it stuck. In 1930 Bing married Wilma Winifred Wyatt, who was a film star known professionally as Dixie Lee. They had four sons before Dixie Lee Crosby died in 1952. In 1957, Crosby married a woman less than half his age, Kathryn Grant, a twenty-three-year old actress from Texas. They had three children—Harry Lillis Crosby 3d, Nathaniel Patrick Crosby, and Mary Frances Crosby. Bing's June 1977 Will describes his family as follows:

> I am married to KATHRYN GRANT CROSBY, who in this Will is referred to as "my Wife." I have the following children:
> GARY EVAN CROSBY;
> PHILIP LANG CROSBY;

DENNIS MICHAEL CROSBY;
LINDSAY HARRY CROSBY;
HARRY LILLIS CROSBY, III;
MARY FRANCES CROSBY; and
NATHANIEL PATRICK CROSBY.

In his Will Crosby makes the following cash bequests to his wife, certain other family relatives (but not his children), and three charities in Spokane, Washington, where Crosby had studied law at Gonzaga University before dropping out to pursue his interest in music:

I make the following cash gifts:

(a) To my Wife, KATHRYN GRANT CROSBY, $150,000.

(b) To my niece, CAROLYN MILLER, $15,000.

(c) To my niece, MARILYN McLACHLAN, $15,000.

(d) To my sister, MARY ROSE POOL, $20,000.

(e) To my niece, CATHERINE CROSBY, the daughter of my brother, TED, $10,000.

(f) To my niece, MARY SUE SHANNON, $10,000.

(l) To SAINT ALOYSIUS CHURCH, Spokane, Washington, $5,000.

(m) To GONZAGA UNIVERSITY, Spokane, Washington, $50,000.

(n) To GONZAGA HIGH SCHOOL, Spokane, Washington, $50,000.

In addition, Crosby gave all his personal property including "my automobiles, jewelry, silverware, books, paintings, works of art, household furniture and furnishings, clothing, and other personal effects" to his wife, Kathryn, if she survived. If she did not survive him, that property was to pass as part of Crosby's residuary estate.

According to his Will, Crosby's residuary estate is given to the Harry L. Crosby Trust, which he established on the same day he signed his Will. The provisions of that trust are private, but it is telling that publicly easygoing Bing included a very comprehensive *in terrorem* clause in his Will that refers to Crosby's children as follows.

Provision Against Contest.

Except as otherwise provided in this Will and the trust referred to in CLAUSE EIGHTH I have intentionally and with full knowledge omitted to provide for my heirs, and I have specifically failed to provide for any child of mine whether mentioned in this Will or in said trust or otherwise. . . .

Finally, it is noteworthy that the funeral instructions in his Will show Crosby to be a self-effacing and religious person:

I direct that my funeral services be conducted in a Catholic church; that they be completely private with attendance limited to my wife and the above mentioned children; that a low mass [emphasis added] be said and that no memorial service of any kind be held. I further direct that insofar as possible services be held without any publicity, other than that which my family permits after my burial, which shall be in a Catholic cemetery.

Crosby collapsed of a heart attack on a golf course in Spain after having completed a very respectable eighteen holes of golf. Shortly after learning of her husband's death, Kathryn Crosby was quoted at a news conference as saying, "I can't think of any better way for a golfer who sings for a living to finish the round."

/s/ *Harry L. Crosby*

Will dated June 27, 1977
Will signed at Los Angeles, California

John Lennon

DATE AND PLACE OF BIRTH
October 9, 1940
Liverpool, England

DATE AND PLACE OF DEATH
December 8, 1980
The Dakota, 1 West 72nd Street
New York, New York

Strawberry Fields Forever

Senselessly murdered by a deranged drifter at the street entrance to his home in New York City, Beatle John Lennon left a legacy of music, lyrics, and wit that changed the world. The Beatles' rise from tough-club obscurity to being the objects of "Beatlemania" sweeping the world was quite meteoric and could have turned calmer heads. And Lennon was no calm head to begin with. His experimentations with a variety of mind-altering techniques including meditation, hallucinogenic drugs, cannabis, heroin, and yoga have all widely been reported and only add to the mystical aura surrounding Lennon.

Lennon's devotion to his Japanese-born wife, Yoko Ono, has been called one cause of the breakup of the Beatles in 1970. In that same year, Lennon dedicated a solo album entitled *Plastic Ono Band* to Yoko. In that album, Lennon describes his relationship with God and Yoko as follows: "God is a concept by which we measure our pain." He then lists those things he does *not* believe in: magic, I-Ching, Bible, tarot, Hitler, Jesus, Kennedy, Buddha, mantra, Gita, yoga, kings, Elvis, Zimmerman, or Beatles. "I just believe in me, Yoko and me, and that's reality."

The November 1979 Will that Lennon signed is unusually vague and unstructured for a person with the enormous wealth and copyright considerations that Lennon would have had. Yoko is the only named beneficiary. She received one-half of Lennon's enormous estate outright, and for the other half, the Will states:

> I give, devise and bequeath all the rest, residue and remainder of my estate, wheresoever situate, to the Trustees under a Trust Agreement dated November 12, 1979, which I signed with my wife, YOKO ONO, and ELI GARBER as Trustees . . .

After John's death, Yoko was in complete control of John's wealth.

As a result of the sheer volume of Beatles albums sold and royalties received for his compositions, Lennon was a very wealthy man. The income from principal alone was a significant sum. Yoko Ono was known to be the business manager in the family, with John assuming the role of "house husband" and primarily rearing his son Sean, who was around five years old when his father was killed.

Without knowing the provisions of the private trust referred to in the Will, we can only wonder whether Lennon made any provisions for his beloved son Sean, older son Julian from his first marriage to Cynthia Powers, or any of the other people in Lennon's life.

As one would expect, the Will contains the following provision regarding Lennon's designation of executor:

> I hereby nominate, constitute and appoint my beloved wife YOKO ONO, to act as the Executor of this my Last Will and Testament. In the event that my beloved wife

YOKO ONO shall predecease me or chooses not to act
for any reason, I nominate and appoint ELI GARBER,
DAVID WARMFLASH and CHARLES PETTIT, in the order named, to act in her place and stead.

Garber was the Lennons' accountant and Warmflash
was both Lennons' attorney and had prepared John's
Will.

It is somewhat unusual and totally unnecessary for a
husband to appoint his wife as the guardian of their children, but that is exactly what Lennon did in the following
clause in his Will:

I nominate, constitute and appoint my wife YOKO ONO,
as the Gurdian [sic] of the person and property of any
children of the marriage who may survive me. In the
event that she predeceases me, or for any reason she
chooses not to act in that capacity, I nominate, constitute and appoint SAM GREEN to act in her place and
stead.

Sam Green was an intimate employee of the Lennons
who had a good rapport with Sean and was obviously
trusted by John.

At the end of the Will, there is an unusual *in terrorem*
clause that reads as follows:

If any legatee or beneficiary under this Will or the trust
agreement between myself as Grantor and YOKO ONO
LENNON and ELI GARBER as Trustees, dated November 12, 1979 shall interpose objections to the probate
of this Will, or institute or prosecute or be in any way
interested or instrumental in the institution or prosecu-

tion of any action or proceeding for the purpose of setting aside or invalidating this Will, then and in each
such case, I direct that such legatee or beneficiary shall
receive nothing whatsoever under this Will or the
aforementioned Trust.

This is certainly a strange provision to include because
the only direct beneficiary in the Will was Yoko Ono, and
it would be patently clear that she would have no objection to the Will.

Lennon's unusually short Will concludes as follows:

IN WITNESS WHEREOF, I have subscribed and sealed
and do publish and declare these presents as and for
my Last Will and Testament, this 12th day of November,
1979.

/s/ J Lennon
_____

THE FOREGOING INSTRUMENT consisting of four (4)
typewritten pages, including this page, was on the 12th
day of November, 1979, signed, sealed, published and
declared by JOHN WINSTON ONO LENNON, the Testator therein named, as and for his Last Will and Testament, in the present [sic] of us, who at his request, and
in his presence, and in the presence of each other, have
hereunto set our names as witnesses.

That sounds like a lot of presents, considering no one
but Yoko got anything under the Will.

It is sadly ironic that Lennon signed this Will at the
Dakota, "One West 72nd Street, New York, New York," the
same address and only a few hundred feet from the spot

where he was fatally shot on a cold December night returning from the recording studio. In the 1970s, Lennon had vigorously resisted deportation from the United States and won a legal victory in 1976 that allowed him to remain at his home in New York.

The preamble to Lennon's Will reads, "I, JOHN WINSTON ONO LENNON, a resident of the County of New York, State of New York, which I declare to be my domicile . . ." The lad from Liverpool was enjoying living in New York, but tragically, it was on the mean streets of New York where John Lennon fought to remain that he died a tragic and untimely death.

One of the ways in which Yoko Ono commemorated her husband's death was by donating funds to New York City to replant and relandscape a section of Central Park near the Lennons' apartment and naming it Strawberry Fields, "where nothing is real." Unfortunately for Lennon, and the world, the streets of New York were all too real.

/s/ *John Lennon*
_____

Will dated November 12, 1979

Samuel Barber

DATE AND PLACE OF BIRTH
March 9, 1910
West Chester, Pennsylvania

DATE AND PLACE OF DEATH
January 23, 1981
Fifth Avenue
New York, New York

A Different Drummer

Pulitzer Prize winning American composer Samuel Barber achieved international success early in his career, and he knew it. He was a musical prodigy born near Philadelphia, and at the age of 14 he entered the renowned Curtis Institute of Music. Awards, honors and prizes were heaped on him for the rest of his life. His most well known work was the neo-romantic operatic essay entitled, "Vanessa", the words to which were composed by Mr. Barber's "friend", Gian-Carlo Menotti. Mr. Menotti and Mr. Barber were professional collaborators and personal co-habitators for over thirty years. In Mount Kisco, New York they lived in a house they called "Capricorn" during the summer. The provisions of Barber's Will reveal a deep love for the spiritual bond with Menotti. One does not normally find such sensitive consideration given in the Wills of a husband and wife.

With regard to the arrangments for his burial, Barber's Will provides:

1. If my friend, GIAN-CARLO MENOTTI, shall have predeceased me and shall have been buried in a place other than the plot that I own at the Oaklands Ceme-

tery, in the Town of West Chester, Pennsylvania, which plot is located adjacent to the Barber family plot, I wish to be buried in the Barber family plot at the Oaklands Cemetery, next to my mother. In this event, I further wish that a small tombstone to be erected on the plot that I own at the Oaklands Cemetery, which tombstone shall bear only the following inscription: "To the memory of two friends."

If you can follow that convoluted legalese, then perhaps you should be working at the fancy Park Avenue law firm that drafted the language. It gets a little clearer, with the score provided by Barber:

2. If my friend, GIAN-CARLO MENOTTI, shall have predeceased me and shall have been buried in the plot that I own at the Oaklands Cemetery or if he shall not have predeceased me, I wish to be buried in the plot that I own at the Oaklands Cemetery.

C. I DIRECT that my grave shall be marked by a simple tombstone bearing only the following inscription:

SAMUEL BARBER
March 9, 1910—[the date of my death]

D. If I die in the United States, I REQUEST (but I do not direct) my Executors to carry out the following arrangements for my funeral:

1. I wish my funeral to take place at the First Presbyterian Church in the Town of West Chester, Pennsylvania.

2. The funeral service should be a simple one, with the coffin kept closed throughout. I request but do not direct that the music played at my funeral included (a) the Twelfth Madrigal from "The Unicorn" by Gian-

Carlo Menotti, or such part or parts thereof (preferably including the concluding portion) as my Executors shall determine; (b) the following Bach chorales
(the chorale should be played first, followed by the
choral prelude; page references are to the Barenreiter
edition now located in the library at my apartment in
New York, New York: "Das alte Jahr vergangen ist" (p.
49); "Christe, Du Lamm Gottes" (pp. 66-67); "O Men-
sch, bewein dein Suende Gross" (p. 75); "Ich ruf zu
dir, Herr Jesu Christ" (p. 119); and (c) such other work
or works of music, if any as my Executors shall choose.
I also direct that the following prayer from the Episcopal prayer book be read at an appropriate place in the
service:

> We seem to give him back to Thee, dear Lord,
> who gavest him to us. Yet as Thou didst not lose
> him in giving, so we have not lost him by his re-
> turn. Not as the world givest, givest Thou, O
> Lover of Souls. For what is Thine is ours, always
> if we are Thine. What Thou givest Thou Takest
> not away. And life is eternal; and love is im-
> mortal; and death is only a horizon, and the
> horizon is nothing save the limit of one's sight.
> Lift us up, O God, that we may see further;
> cleanse our eyes that we see more clearly; draw
> us closer to Thyself, that we may know our-
> selves closer to our beloved who are with Thee;
> and grant that where they are, and Thou art,
> we too, may one day be. Through Jesus Christ,
> our Lord. Amen.

This entire Section D of the Will assumes that Barber
would die in the United States. Can you imagine the in-

structions if Barber had died in Italy, France or Germany? At least the Germans would know what was being sung. That must have been some funeral.

At the time of his death, Barber also owned a beautifully furnished home in the Province of Bolzano in Italy. To his servant and friend, Valentin Herranz, Barber gave the right to select three (3) pieces of furniture from the Italian house. To Gian-Carlo Menotti Barber gave the right to occupy and inhabit the house situated in Santa Cristina, Val Gardena, in the Province of Bolzano for the rest of Menotti's life. Upon Menotti's death, the property passes to Barber's other "friend", Agnese Bonechi.

Barber's Will also includes detailed provisions for the disposition of his musical legacy. The Will states:

A. I GIVE my musical manuscript of "The Lovers" to my friend, VALENTIN HERRANZ.

B. I GIVE all of my musical manuscripts not otherwise herein effectively disposed of to the LIBRARY OF CONGRESS, MUSIC DIVISION, Washington, D.C.

C. I GIVE all of my books of every nature and my musical collection (consisting of records, tapes, memorabilia and other tangible personal property relating to my musical career and/or to the general field of music other than my manuscripts of my musical compositions, including lyrics, and my manuscripts of other literary and musical works) to my friend, GIAN-CARLO MENOTTI, if he shall survive me. . . .

D. I GIVE my Marino Marini statue, my small painting of a bird on glass by Audrey Sheldon and my John Helliker drawing of myself to the METROPOLITAN MUSEUM OF ART, New York, New York.

One must wonder whether the Metropolitan Museum was as excited to receive the portrait of Barber as he was to give it to the museum.

After making cash bequests to several friends and relatives, the Will places the residuary estate, including all income from future royalties, in trust for the benefit of Gian-Carlo Menotti, Valentin Herranz and two of Barber's nephews. Upon the death of all the trust beneficiaries, the remaining property is left to the New York Public Library, Music Division of the Lincoln Center Library of the Performing Arts.

It seems fitting that after providing for those whom he cared for during their lives, the master American composer Barber would leave the last share of his estate to assist the performing arts.

/s/ Samuel Barber

Will dated October 5, 1978

Count Basie

DATE AND PLACE OF BIRTH
August 21, 1904
Red Bank, New Jersey

DATE AND PLACE OF DEATH
April 26, 1984
Doctors' Hospital
Hollywood, Florida

Out for the Count

A king of swing, a jazz great, and one of the leading bandleaders of the century, William Basie was an only son born into a poor black family in New Jersey. Despite racial barriers, by his incredible musical talents, charm, and wit, young William joined the ranks of other musical nobility such as "Duke" Ellington and "Earl" Hines and was dubbed "Count" early in his career.

When he died of the bigger C (cancer) at the age of seventy-nine, Basie was living in Freeport in the Grand Bahamas. Basie's wife, Catherine, had died in 1983, and he was survived by his only daughter, Diane Basie, also of Freeport. In his Will, Basie places his entire estate in trust for his daughter's benefit. If she had not survived, then the Basie estate was to be divided three ways. As the Will states:

> I give, bequeath and devise all the rest, residue and remainder of my property . . . to the following individuals, who are then surviving, in equal shares: LAMONT GILMORE, ROSEMARIE MATTHEWS, and AARON WOODWARD, <u>all of whom I have sometimes affectionately referred to as my children, although none are my</u>

<u>natural children nor legally adopted by me.</u> [emphasis added]

Although his permanent home was in the Grand Bahamas, Basie requests under the first article of his Will that he be cremated and "my ashes buried in Pine Lawn Mausoleum, located in Farmingdale, Long Island." When the Count finally laid down his baton, he apparently felt more comfortable in northern soil than in a tropical paradise.

/s/ *William J. Basie*

Will dated February 13, 1984

Ricky Nelson

DATE AND PLACE OF BIRTH
May 8, 1940
Teaneck, New Jersey

DATE AND PLACE OF DEATH
December 31, 1985
De Kalb, Texas

"The Miss Adventures of Ricky Nelson"

Eric ("Ricky") Hilliard Nelson was the younger son of Ozzie and Harriet Nelson of Teaneck, New Jersey. During the 1940s, 1950s, and 1960s, the Nelson family entertained in living rooms all across America until "The Adventures of Ozzie and Harriet" ended in 1966. After that, Ricky Nelson continued a successful career in music.

It was on the way to a New Year's Eve concert when Nelson's own DC-3 airplane crashed and burned in De Kalb, Texas, approximately thirty-five miles from Texarkana, Texas. Aboard the plane with Ricky was his twenty-seven-year-old fiancée, Helen Blair, who also died in the crash together with five others. Nelson signed this Will less than five months before his death.

Nelson's Will does not mince any words when describing his marital history and family relationships.

> SECOND: I hereby declare that I am not married at this time and was divorced from KRISTIN NELSON in 1982 and specifically and intentionally fail to provide for her herein.

THIRD: I hereby declare that I have four children of said aforementioned marriage, specifically: TRACY NELSON, GUNNAR NELSON, MATTHEW NELSON and SAM NELSON. I hereby give, devise and bequeath all the rest, residue and remainder of my estate . . . to said four beloved children, in equal shares, share and share alike. . . .

It gets rougher as under the eighth article of the Will, Nelson expressly disinherits a named child: "I specifically fail to provide herein for a minor, ERIC CREWE as I dispute the paternity of said minor child."

Next the Will makes the following two statements about the two most important women in Nelson's life at that time:

SEVENTH: I have specifically failed to provide for my mother HARRIET NELSON as she is well taken-care of and comfortable at this time.

NINTH: I specifically fail to provide herein for HELEN BLAIR as that is our wishes.

The fact that Nelson failed to provide in his Will for his fiancée, Helen Blair, obviously did not make any difference, as she died with him in the plane crash.

Nelson named his brother, David Nelson, as the executor of his Will. Ricky's personal manager, Greg McDonald, is named as a successor executor and also given the following authority:

I further direct that my personal manager and good friend, GREG McDONALD retain full control over the management of all my show business properties, past present and future including all publishing rights and decisions of MATRA-GUN/NELSON MUSIC. He shall also have full power and control to make all creative decisions for the use of my name, likeness and biography in perpetuity. In compensation for his services, GREG McDONALD shall be paid the usual fee of 15% of all gross revenues from said ventures. The remaining funds generated therefrom shall be divided evenly between my four children as hereinbefore provided. The revenues from my family television show, "The Adventures of Ozzie and Harriet" are specifically excluded from this paragraph, as to McDonald.

Nelson's Will also includes the following patently incorrect *in terrorem* clause:

I have intentionally and with full knowledge thereof, omitted to provide for any heirs or other individuals I may leave surviving. In the event that any such person should contest this Will, then in such event, I give, devise and bequeath to said person the sum of $1.00 (one dollar) and no more.

Nelson's Will is *not* a model of "artful draftsmanship" by the attorney who prepared it. For example, in the *in terrorem* clause above, it is hard to believe that Nelson would not have realized that his four children, to whom he gave his entire residuary estate, were exactly his "heirs." Perhaps the Will was intended to read "any *other* heirs.

After reading this Will, it is not surprising to learn from the papers filed with the Los Angeles County Superior Court that the original Will, which had apparently been left with the drafting attorney, was never located. A copy of Nelson's Will was finally admitted to probate. The adventures of Ricky Nelson had finally ended.

/s/ *Eric H. Nelson*

Will dated August 22, 1985
Signed at Encino, California

Vladimir Horowitz

DATE AND PLACE OF BIRTH
October 1, 1903
Kiev, Russia

DATE AND PLACE OF DEATH
November 5, 1989
14 East 94th Street
New York, New York

Strings Attached

His death certificate states simply that his "usual occupation" was as "pianist," and that his "business" was "music," but Vladimir Horowitz had few peers as a virtuoso at the piano. Horowitz was also known for his high-strung disposition and for his idiosyncratic interpretations of great musical compositions.

Horowitz was born to the cultured and wealthy Gorowitz family in Kiev, Russia. In 1925, young Vladimir left the Soviet Union on a student visa and then proceeded to take Europe by musical storm. For his Berlin debut in 1926, he changed his name from Gorowitz to Horowitz. Horowitz made his American debut in 1928. It was in 1933 that Horowitz met Wanda Toscanini, the daughter of famous conductor Arturo Toscanini. Wanda and Vladimir were married that same year. For the rest of the maestro's life, Wanda took charge of Horowitz's personal and professional affairs. In 1940, the couple settled permanently in New York. The magical Wanda was the one who made sure that Vladimir's favorite piano was moved to recitals, that special foods were prepared, and even that the hotel rooms Horowitz used be redecorated so that he would not be rattled by the change in his personal surroundings. The couple had a daughter, Sonya, in 1934, but she died in 1975.

Horowitz's Will manifests his devotion to his wife and his dedication to music. At the time of his death, Horowitz had amassed an estate worth between $6 million and $8 million, according to papers filed with the Surrogate's Court of New York. The bulk of that went to his surviving spouse, Wanda Toscanini Horowitz, outright, but there are also the following preresiduary bequests of interest:

I hereby give, bequeath and devise to Yale University School of Music, New Haven, Connecticut, for inclusion in and subject to the terms of, the Horowitz Archive established pursuant to an Agreement dated August 14, 1987, all of my memorabilia, musical scores, correspondence, recital transcriptions, photographs, awards and trophies, programs and similar items relating to my musical career, all of which are presently contained in the library and other rooms of my residence at 14 East 94th Street.

Over the course of Vladimir's prolonged and prolific career, no doubt there was a lot of "memorabilia."

There was also a $200,000 outright bequest to Horowitz's "friend and companion, GIULIANA B. LOPES of Queens, New York." Ms. Lopes was described as a longtime employee of the Horowitzes'. If wife Wanda had not survived, then Ms. Lopes was to get an additional $300,000 outright.

In his Will, Horowitz also made the following unusual conditional bequest to the famous New York music school, Juilliard:

> To the Juilliard School of Music, New York, New York, the sum of Three Hundred Thousand ($300,000) dollars, such sum to be used for one or more scholarships for promising piano students who shall have the need for such financial assistance in order to continue their artistic training, <u>provided that</u> such institution acknowledges that, by accepting such bequest, <u>it agrees never to hold any piano or other musical competition in my name or honor.</u> [emphasis added]

An unusual bequest by one of musical history's most eccentric virtuosos.

If wife Wanda had not survived, then Juilliard was to receive an additional $200,000 "subject to the conditions and proviso set forth." The balance of the estate was to be left to the Columbia Presbyterian Medical Center Fund, Inc., "for use in carrying out research to prevent, treat or cure Cancer, Acquired Immune Deficiency Syndrome, Alzheimer's Disease or Mental Illness." Horowitz's sensitive charitable bequest never vested because Wanda survived. As might be expected, Horowitz appointed Wanda and his manager to act as the executors of his Will.

Though the Will is silent on the issue of burial, Horowitz reportedly left instructions that he wanted to be buried in the Toscanini family plot in the Cimitero Monumentale in Milan, Italy.

/s/ *Vladimir Horowitz*

Will dated November 1, 1988
Signed at 14 East 94th Street, New York, New York

Kate Smith

———

DATE AND PLACE OF BIRTH
May 1, 1909
Greenville, Virginia

DATE AND PLACE OF DEATH
June 17, 1986
Raleigh Community Hospital
Raleigh, North Carolina

God Bless Kate Smith

Best known for her vibrant rendition of Irving Berlin's composition "God Bless America", Kate Smith recorded almost 3000 songs and was one of America's most beloved singers. Smith made her debut on the radio at the age of 22 and sang her trademark song, "When the Moon Comes Over the Mountain". It was in 1938 that she first sang the song which Irving Berlin wrote expressly for her—"God Bless America." The song became America's unofficial national anthem. Both Berlin and Smith waived their royalties from the song with all proceeds going to the Boy Scouts and Girl Scouts of America.

Smith was born in Virginia, but grew up in Washington, D.C. Reportedly, she did not begin speaking until she was 4 years old, but began singing soon thereafter. In this case, she sang before she could run. It appears that Smith did not run too much at all. She was a large woman, weighing close to 250 pounds most of her life. She never married and had no children. As she states in her Will:

I have not married during my lifetime. My sister and nieces are my sole blood relatives, have received gifts from me during my lifetime. I have taken this into consideration in making the bequests hereinafter set forth.

Smith made bequests of $15,000 to each of her nieces, several smaller bequests to various friends and $25,000 bequests to certain charitable organizations and "To my dear friend HIS EMINENCE TERRANCE CARDINAL COOKE, Archdiocese of New York . . . to use as he sees fit."

Smith gave all of her "trophies, placques, awards, photographs, sound films, recordings, clippings (bound and unbound) and scripts in leather bound volumes and all my professional memorabilia" to Boston University "to do with as they see fit."

Besides her patriotism, Smith was also known to be a deeply religious person. In 1965 she was baptized as a Roman Catholic at a church in Lake Placid, New York where she maintained a summer home for over 40 years. Smith's Will evidences her religious beliefs as she left her substantial residuary estate in equal shares to the St. Agnes Catholic Church and Uihlein Mercy Center, both of Lake Placid.

Perhaps most interesting about Smith's Will are the elaborate provisions pertaining to her funeral and burial. The Will states:

It is my desire to be buried in the Catholic Cemetery of St. Agnes, in the Village of Lake Placid, Essex County, New York. I direct that my remains be interred in a hermetically sealed bronze casket in a mausoleum, sufficient to contain my remains alone, of natural granite construction. It is my preference that pink or rose granite be used, but the choice of the granite shall be made by my Executors hereinafter named. . . .

If my demise shall take place in Lake Placid, New York, it is my desire that Father Albert Salmon of Glenfield, New York, officiate at the mass and interment.

If my demise shall not take place in Lake Placid, it is my desire that His Eminence Terrance Cardinal Cooke of the Archdiocese of New York, officiate at the mass.

Terrence Cardinal Cooke predeceased Smith so of course he was unable to officiate at her mass.

For the last ten years of her life Smith was in poor health, stemming from brain damage suffered as a result of a diabetic coma. Six months before she died, her right leg was amputated, and one month before she died she had a mastectomy. She died in Raleigh, North Carolina, but was buried in Lake Placid, New York in a "hermetically sealed bronze casket" in a mausoleum of either pink or rose granite as she had pointedly requested in her Will.

/s/ *Kathryn E. Smith*

Will dated July 12, 1973
Codicil dated October 26, 1979

Jascha Heifitz

DATE AND PLACE OF BIRTH
February 2, 1901
Vilna, Lithuania

DATE AND PLACE OF DEATH
December 10, 1987
Cedars-Sinai Medical Center
Los Angeles, California

High-Strung

When he died at age 86, Jascha Heifitz was generally acclaimed to have been the greatest violinist of the century, with an elegance and purity of phrasing that was without rival. He began to play the violin at age 3, graduated from the Royal School of Music conservatory at the age of 8, and gave a commanding performance with the Berlin Philharmonic at the age of 10. At the age of 16, Heifitz made his United States musical debut at Carnegie Hall in New York and continued his peripatetic career giving violin performances world-wide for almost seventy more years. It was estimated that Heifitz traveled more than two million miles to give concert performances during his lifetime. Heifitz continued to play the violin until arthritis crippled him during his last years.

Whereas his friend and counterpart on the piano, Vladimir Horowitz, loved the limelight, Heifitz shunned showmanship, shied away from publicity, and guarded his privacy closely. He was a perfectionist at his craft and always strove to improve his skills. He once stated that he agreed with Liszt that "If I don't practice one day, I know it; two days, the critics know it; three days, the public knows it."

In 1929 he married the silent film star named Florence Vidor. They had two children, Joseph and Robert, before the couple was divorced in 1945. In 1947 Heifitz married Frances Spiegelberg and they had a son, Joseph, also known as Jay. Heifitz divorced his second wife in 1963 and never remarried.

In his two-page handwritten Will which he wrote on his Beverly Hills stationary, Heifitz seems to deliberately leave nothing to any of his three children. The Will begins, "I am aware I have 3 children—Joseph, Robert and Jay", but then they are not mentioned again. Heifitz gives his house in Malibu and a $60,000 bequest to Ann Neblett who was Heifitz' personal secretary for over twenty-five years. He gives to Sherry Kloss "my Tononi Violin, and one of my 4 good bows." To the De Young Museum in San Francisco, Heifitz bequeathed his Guarnerius Violin with the instruction that it was "to be used by playing it on Special Occasions—by Worthy Performers." The balance of Heifitz estate was left to Ann Neblett, Tamara Charozo and Marvin Gross with the vague instruction that they should "decide where and to whom it should go." Ms. Neblett was named as the Executor of the Will.

The Will concludes with the following "P.P.S.":

I direct that my body be cremated—and the ashes scattered from a plane, over the ocean as close as possible to Malibu Beach (near my House)

True to form, Heifitz did not want to make a big splash, even after his death, and wanted to come to rest near his home on the coast of California, a musical lifetime away from his birthplace in Lithuania.

The Heifitz Will is amended by two later Codicils which

give his Malibu house, its contents, and $60,000 in cash to Ann Neblett, and $15,000 in cash to his friend, Ayke Agus.

Needless to say, the three children of Heifitz were not pleased by their father's estate plan leaving them nothing, and that may have been the sourest note that Heifitz ever played.

/s/ *Jascha Heifitz*
_____

Will dated October 31, 1980
Will signed at 1520 Gilcrest Drive, Beverly Hills, California
First Codicil dated June 21, 1983
Second Codicil dated December 15, 1983

Oct. 31, 1980 (1)

1.—I revoke all my prior Wills—

1a.—I am aware I have 3 children—Joseph, Robert and Jay.

2.—On my death, I give the following:

a. The Malibu House and $60,000.00 cash to <u>Ann Neblett</u>—if she does not survive me—then to my Estate.

b. To <u>Sherry Kloss</u> my Tononi Violin, and one of my 4 good bows—if she does not survive me—then to my Estate.

c. To <u>Ayke Agus</u>—$15,000 in cash—and from my desk: (1) Prism glass (2) Gold Holder (of Scissors and letter opener, with magnifying glass) and (3) Desk clock (she got for me).

d. To the "de Young Museum"—in San Francisco, Calif. my Guarnerius Violin—to be used by playing it on Special Occasions—by worthy Performers—

c. The rest of my Estate, to Ann Neblett, Tamara Charozo and Martin Gross, allowing them to decide where and to whom it should go.

3.—I name as Executor, Ann Neblett, alternate, Marvin Gross, to serve without Bond—

/s/ Jascha Heifitz
_____

(Continued)

Oct. 31, 1980 (2)

P.S. Don't forget Jack Pfeiffer, the Chazoros, Myra Livington, Claire Hodgkins, and the like—

/s/ Jascha Heifitz
_____

P.P.S. I direct that my body be cremated—and the ashes scattered, from a plane, over the ocean as close as possible to Malibu Beach (near my House)

/s/ Jascha Heifitz
_____

The Comedians

Last Laughs

PHIL HARTMAN
From Saturday Night Live to Thursday Morning Dead
MAY 28, 1998

W. C. FIELDS
Last Call for Alcohol
DECEMBER 25, 1946

JACK BENNY
Not 39 Anymore
DECEMBER 26, 1974

HENNY YOUNGMAN
"Take My Life, Please."
FEBRUARY 24, 1998

PAUL LYNDE
Hollywood Box
JANUARY 9, 1982

PHIL SILVERS
Do-It-Yourself Special
NOVEMBER 1, 1985

JOHN BELUSHI
Singing the Blues
MARCH 5, 1982

GROUCHO MARX
"You Bet Your Life"
AUGUST 19, 1977

JACKIE GLEASON
"And Away We Go. . . ."
JUNE 24, 1987

Phil Hartman

DATE AND PLACE OF BIRTH

September 24, 1948

Ontario, Canada

DATE AND PLACE OF DEATH

May 28, 1998

5065 Encino Avenue

Encino, California

From Saturday Night Live to Thursday Morning Dead

Despite the fact that a murderer normally cannot inherit from the estate of his or her murder victim, the family of Brynn Hartman took legal control of her late husband's estate and their minor children. There is little doubt about the chronology of events surrounding the murder/suicide of Phil/Brynn Hartman on May 28, 1998. First, 40 year old Brynn shot her 49 year old husband in their Encino, California home. Within four hours of the murder, she went to a friend's house, confessed, returned to the scene of the crime, and then locked herself in the bathroom and shot and killed herself with the same gun as the one with which she killed her husband. The coroner's report found a .12 percent blood alcohol level, and also the presence of cocaine and an "anti-depressant" drug called Zoloft in Brynn's blood.

Page one of the Will of "PHILIP EDWARD HARTMAN, formerly known as PHILIP EDWARD HARTMANN, a resident of the County of Los Angeles, State of California . . ." includes the following "Statement Concerning Family:"

I am married to BRYNN HARTMAN, formerly known as
VICKI JO HARTMAN, and all references in this Will to
"my Spouse" are to her. My Spouse and I are both
United States citizens. I have two (2) children now living, namely, SEAN EDWARD HARTMAN, born June 17,
1988, and BIRGEN ANIKA HARTMAN, born February
8, 1992, and all references in this Will to "my children"
are to them. I have no other children, living or deceased.

Immediately following the statement concerning family, Hartman's Will provides the following instructions for
cremation:

I direct cremation of my bodily remains with my ashes
to be scattered at Emerald Bay, California.

In view of the macabre way in which he died at the
hands of his wife, it is certainly good that Hartman's Will
provided for his ashes to be scattered over Emerald Bay,
and did not direct that his body be buried in a grave next
to his wife's so that this troubled couple could remain together for eternity.

Hartman's forty-eight (48) page Will dated March 11,
1996 left his entire estate primarily to his wife Brynn, if
she survived him. Included in the Hartman's bequest to
his Spouse were "all of my clothing, jewelry, and personal
effects, and all of my interest in our automobiles, boats,
airplanes, household furniture, furnishings and equipment, china, silver, glassware, books, and other items of
domestic, household or personal use."

Although she did survive him, it was only for a few
hours, and she would have been barred from inheriting

from the estate of her murder victim and also because under California law an heir must survive by at least 120 hours in order to inherit. Instead, both Brynn's and Phil's estates passed to their two minor children subject to the terms of the trusts under the Will until each child reached the age of 35. The Will provides that if none of the children survived them, the estate was to be divided into thirteen (13) lucky shares with 2/13ths going to Phil's parents, Doris and Rupert Hartmann (with Rupert having predeceased Phil) and 2/13ths going to Brynn's parents, Constance and Donald Omdahl; and one-thirteenth (1/13) to each of Phil's sisters, Nancy Hartmann McCoy, Mary C. Hartmann, Barbara J. Hartmann, and Martha Hartman Willey; Phil's brothers, John R. Hartmann and Paul A. Hartmann; Brynn's sisters, Katherine K. Wright and Debra F. Borreson; and to Brynn's brother, Gregory C. Omdahl.

Hartman named his wife Brynn as sole Executor, "Literary Executor", Trustee and "Literary Trustee". In the event that she could not serve as Executor or Trustee, which of course, she could not, then Brynn's brother, GREGORY C. OMDAHL, of Fargo, North Dakota was named as successor Executor and successor Trustee. If Brynn did not act in the "Literary" role, then Hartman's agent Carol Yumkas was named as a back-up. For a comedian, Hartman was certainly unusually concerned about his literary legacy.

If Brynn's brother, Gregory, were unable or unwilling to serve or to continue to serve as Executor or Trustee, then Brynn's sister, KATHARINE K. WRIGHT, of Eau Claire, Wisconsin, was named as the back-up Executor and Trustee. Sister Katharine was named as the Guardian of the couple's two minor children, and if she could not act, then Brynn's sister Sandra Kay Hapka was named as the back-up Guardian. The Will includes the following unusual provision with respect to the compensation of the Guardian:

> The Trustee shall distribute the sum of Fifty Thousand Dollars ($50,000) to the first Guardian who consents to serve. This gift is made in gratitude for the Guardian's willingness to disrupt her life by serving as Guardian and in recognition of the fact that there may be expenses incurred by the Guardian for which she may elect not to bill the Trust.

Talk about trust, as shown by his choices, Phil Hartman seemed very comfortable with Brynn's family handling his personal and legal affairs after his death. Nonetheless, we have to wonder if he would have felt the same way had he known about the tragic end which Phil'd him to the Brynn.

Phil Hartman's lengthy Will is revealing both about Phil Hartman, and his lawyers. Not only does Phil's Will have a Table of Contents which is called an "Index", but at the bottom of the first page we are advised that the "NEXT PAGE IS -2-". In the inordinately lengthy "Powers of Trustee" section, the Will states truisms such as, "In exercising discretion under this instrument, the Trustee shall at all times act in a fiduciary capacity." At the bottom of each page is a legend stating "Will of Philip Edward Hartman" and the top of almost every page has the law firm's computer program location cite stating "CLIENTS\HARTMAN.P\PHILIP.WIL." Each of the unnecessarily lengthy Wills of Phil and Brynn is a good example of legal "overkill".

The untimely and tragic deaths of comedian and "News Radio" Phil Hartman and his beautiful third wife Brynn showed the sometime ugly side of life in the Hollywood fast lane. Although Phil must have been aware of the demons his wife battled at the time he signed his Will, Hartman still made the decision to allow her, or her family, to assume total control of his estate and of his young children after his death. We can only hope that the fresher air of Eau Claire, Wisconsin, where the named Guardian lives, will allow the Hartman children to cope with their tragic loss.

/s/ *Philip Edward Hartman*

Will dated March 11, 1996.
Will signed in Beverly Hills, California

W. C. Fields

DATE AND PLACE OF BIRTH
January 29, 1880
Philadelphia, Pennsylvania

DATE AND PLACE OF DEATH
December 25, 1946
Pasadena, California

Last Call for Alcohol

Commonly reported to have requested that his tombstone bear the inscription "I would rather be here than in Philadelphia" (the city of his birth), W. C. Fields, one of the great comic actors of all time, left a Will that includes no such instruction. The Will does, however, include the following fascinating provisions regarding Fields's directions for his own funeral:

> I direct my executors immediately upon the certificate of my death being signed to have my body placed in an inexpensive coffin and taken to a cemetery and cremated, and since I do not wish to cause my friends undue inconvenience or expense I direct my executors not to have any funeral or other ceremony or to permit anyone to view my remains, except as is necessary to furnish satisfactory proof of my death.

Fields, who died with an estate reportedly worth close to $800,000 in 1946, expressly requested that he be buried in an "inexpensive coffin" and that he be cremated as soon as possible.

Fields was named William Claude Dukenfield at his birth in Philadelphia. Apparently Fields put down his "Dukes" along the way because his Will begins, "I, WILLIAM C. FIELDS, also known as W. C. FIELDS, also known as BILL FIELDS, residing at 2015 DeMille Drive, Los Angeles . . ." In the end, Fields signs his Will with his trademark initials "W. C." and last name.

Perhaps most fascinating about the disposition of Fields's estate are the provisions in the letter that he signed on the same day he signed his Will, which follows this piece. This detailed description of Fields's personal property illustrates many things about him, especially his love for things alcoholic. Fields died of cirrhosis of the liver, among other maladies, while he was in a sanitarium in Pasadena, California.

With a meticulous inventory such as that, it seems that Fields did not want to omit any articles of his property, including his treasured bottles of Shalimar perfume, which were apparently kept in the closet.

In his Will, Fields clearly favors two of his four siblings. He gave bequests of $5,000 to both his sister Adel C. Smith and his brother Walter Dukenfield, "also known as Walter Fields," and they are also both beneficiaries of a residuary trust, receiving weekly allowances of $60 and $75 respectively. As for his sister Elsie May and brother LeRoy Russell Dukenfield, Fields appears to have lost touch with them because the Will recites their "last known" addresses and he gave them each only token $500 bequests.

Upon the deaths of Adel, Walter, and Fields's friend and "nursemaid" Carlotta Monti, the property remaining in the trust was to be distributed as follows:

> I direct that my executors procure the organization of a membership or other approved corporation under the name W.C. FIELDS COLLEGE for orphan white boys and girls, where no religion of any sort is to be preached. Harmony is the purpose of this thought . . .

If "harmony" were truly the purpose of this thought, one wonders why it was restricted to white orphans. Ultimately, no orphans got any money because Fields's estranged wife, Harriet (aka Hattie), whom Fields had married in 1900 and never divorced, contested the Will and won. It is interesting that Fields does make the following bequest in his Will for his wife and son, but does not refer to them as such:

> To Hattie Fields and W. Claude Fields, now residing at 123½ North Gale Drive, Beverly Hills, California, the sum of Twenty Thousand Dollars to be divided equally.

In an attempt to deter any contest of the Will, Fields included the following provision: "I wish to disinherit anyone who in any way tries to confuse or break this Will or who contributes in any way to break this Will." In light of the ultimate victory of his wife and son over his estate, Fields looks like the sucker, and his wife and son got the break.

/s/ *W. C. Fields*

Will dated April 28, 1943
Will signed at Los Angeles, California

2015 DeMille Drive,
Hollywood, California

To my Executor, Magda Michael:

In subparagraph 16 of the Third Paragraph of my last will and testament, executed today, I bequeath to you in trust the following articles of furniture and personal effects, for delivery to the following persons:

To Charles Buyer: My desk, chair, chest, waste basket, desk, knick-knacks, side table for telephone, one open book case, revolving book case, two wood baskets by fireplace, Executone set, large steel cabinet and contents, camera (he gave me) one-third liquor, golf bag and clubs, one-third ties, square trunk in basement containing books of press notices and programs, also all the books of press notices and programs upstairs, garden furniture, station wagon, decanter set, 3 birdcage stands, 2 ladders, ice chest, champagne bucket.

To Carlotta Monti: One typewriter, red Taylor Trunk, large Webster's Unabridged Dictionary, my small dictionary and Roget's Thesaurus, Packard Bell radio, with recording equipment, one open book case, Encyclopedia Brittanica, electric clock, secret filing cabinet ("Secretaire") rubber mattress, picture of me in Honolulu, one set of gold dishes in closet, one set of gold lamps in closet, blue Angora knit robe, smaller steel cabinet in office, secretary's desk and chair, two bottles Shalimar in closet, large pair field glasses (Zephyr 7-35) share silverware in trunk and kitchenware with Adele Clines, Frigidaire, water softener fireless cooker, 1 croquet set, 1 umbrella, records, 1 foot heater, electric steam table, large safe, rubbing table, also my 16-cylinder Cadillac limousine.

To Brother Walter Fields: General Electric portable radio, traveling clock, one-half remaining trunks in basement, one-third neckties (first choice) all of my clothes, shoes, underwear, shirts, one third of my liquor, one rubbing table, 2 car trunks, 2 auto robes, billiard table & chairs, ping pong table.

To Sister Adel Smith: Waterbury ships clock, one-half of the remaining trunks in basement, 2 bottles of Shalimar.

To Magda Michael: One typewriter, large dictaphone, 1 croquet set, 1 umbrella, 1 food heater.

To Gregory LaCava: revolvers, one third liquor, large electric fan, pictures taken in Soboba, one set of gold dishes in closet, one set gold lamps in closet, electric refrigerator on wheels.

To Adele Vallery Clines: All the glasses upstairs and down, washing machine (Bendix) silverware in trunk and kitchen ware (share with Carlotta Monti) bottle of Shalimar, square glass ash tray, ash stands, 2 fly catchers, adjustable square tables in office.

To Bob Murphy: Pictures in rubbing room, ½ Decker pictures

To Hershal Crockett: Double pen set on my desk and brown pencil to match.

To Frank Clines: Paint spray gun and equipment, all paints, big jack, carpenter tools, etc.

To Gene Fowler: Howard heating cabinet, all my pens and pencils except those before mentioned, also my small dictaphone, small leather trunk and contents.

To Dave Chasen: ½ Decker pictures.

To Bob Howard: 2 wooden chairs in office, rocking chair, bar chairs and fixtures.

To all my friends, herein mentioned: Distribute the wooden paper holders I had made.

To George Moran: My jewelry, cuff links, tie clips and chains.

If lease of house cannot be broken, my brother Walter, or sister Adel Smith or Carlotta Monti or Magda Michael may occupy it until end of first year.

Dated this 28 day of April, 1943.

/s/ *W.C. Fields*

Jack Benny

DATE AND PLACE OF BIRTH
February 14, 1894
Chicago, Illinois

DATE AND PLACE OF DEATH
December 26, 1974
Beverly Hills, California

Not Thirty-nine Anymore

Originally named Benjamin Kubelsky, Jack Benny was given his first violin at age eight. For the rest of Benny's seventy-year-plus career, the violin became his signature prop, which he used more as an instrument to evoke laughter than to create music. Jack Benny's success with the violin led him to collect at least two valuable violins, a Stradivarius and a Presenda, about which Benny's Will states:

> I declare that I have heretofore made a gift of my Presenda and Stradivarius violins during my lifetime to the Los Angeles Philharmonic Orchestra, reserving only a life interest therein, and I direct my executors to deliver said violins to the aforesaid donee thereof.

By arranging to have Benny reserve only a life interest in the violins, Benny's attorney may have been able to avoid having that valuable property taxed to his estate. In a similar tax-saving vein, the Will continues,

> My wife and I have similarly made an inter vivos gift of two paintings owned by us, namely, "La Charette de

Paille, Montfouchault" by Camille Pissarro and "Mont-
martre et Sacre Coeur" by Maurice Utrillo to the Los
Angeles County Museum of Art, reserving a life interest therein for our joint lifetimes. If I survive my wife, I
direct my Executor to deliver said paintings to said Museum.

Of course, one could not conceive of Jack Benny ever
uttering such words, but his lawyers were paid to put
them in his mouth.

Perennially claiming to be only thirty-nine years old,
Jack Benny's humor depended upon people's common
concerns and faults, including lying about their age and
penny-pinching. Apparently his penny-pinching paid off,
as Jack died with an estate reported to be worth over $4
million, according to papers filed with the court. Benny's
Will contains a bequest of $20,000 to his sister, Florence
Fenchal, and a relatively modest bequest of $10,000 to the
Motion Picture and Television Fund. The bulk of his estate
was to be held in trust for the benefit of his surviving
widow, Mary Benny, and to a lesser degree for the benefit
of his sister, daughter, and grandchildren. Mary Benny
was named as co-executor of the Will to act with Benny's
attorney.

Perhaps wanting to "die up to" his reputation for
penny-pinching, Benny includes a one-dollar *in terrorem*
clause in his Will, which concludes as follows:

If any heir-at-law, next of kin, or devisee, legatee or
beneficiary under this Will shall contest it or any of its
parts or provisions, any share or interest given to that
person shall be revoked and become void, and in that

event, I bequeath to any such person the sum of ONE DOLLAR ($1.00) only.

Maybe the penny-pinching Jack Benny believed that even "ONE DOLLAR" was too much.

/s/ *Jack Benny*

Will dated June 26, 1974
Will signed Beverly Hills, California

Henny Youngman

DATE AND PLACE OF BIRTH
March 16, 1906
London, England

DATE AND PLACE OF DEATH
February 24, 1998
Mount Sinai Medical Center
New York, New York

"Take My Life, Please"

Despite his youthful name, Henny Youngman had a seventy-three year career in show business, and worked almost non-stop until he died at the age of 91. Youngman had been performing two shows a night in San Francisco during the holiday season at the end of 1997, caught a bay area cold, which developed into the pneumonia that caused his death in a New York hospital. As Youngman himself once observed, "death is nature's way of telling a man to slow down." That appears to be the case with the peripatetic, schtickaholic whose name at his birth in 1906 was Henry Youngman.

The Will of the "King of One Liners" did not have any last laughs, one-liners or punch lines in it. One of Youngman's most famous bits involves the reading of a Will as follows:

A rich old garment manufacturer died, and his family met in the lawyer's office for the reading of his will. He left $300,000 to his wife, $100,000 to his brothers, and $10,000 each to his sisters. Then the Will read, "to my nephew Irving, who always wanted to be mentioned in my Will, 'Hello Irving.'"

There is no "Hello" to Irving in Youngman's Will. There are no bequests of his "Stradivaricose" violin or his trademark "Diamond Pins" (i.e. a safety pin with a dime attached to it). There is no bequest of a sun lamp to "my brother-in-law, who always insisted that health is better than wealth."

In view of the number of times that Youngman had requested publicly that we should "Take My Wife, Please!", it is not surprising that Youngman's wife of 58 years, Sadie, was finally taken from him, dying in 1987. Although Sadie was the butt of so many of her husband's jokes, they reportedly had a very close and supportive marriage.

Youngman was survived by his daughter, Marilyn Kelly, and his son, Gary Youngman. His simple three (3) page Will divides Youngman's estate "in equal shares to my beloved children MARILYN KELLY and GARY YOUNGMAN . . ." If either of them predeceased their father, his or her share was to be given to his or her "lawful issue." One has to wonder what Youngman might have to say about "unlawful" issue as the case might be. In fact, at his death, Youngman was survived by two "lawful" grandchildren.

Both daughter Marilyn and son Gary are named as the "Personal Representatives" of their father's Will, which is the term that the state of Florida uses instead of "Executor". Despite the recitation at the start of his Will of Dade County, Florida, as his residence, Youngman did not venture far from the Broadway theaters that he first knew. On the probate papers filed for his estate his legal domicile address is listed as 77 West 55th Street, New York, New York.

Another of Youngman's famous bits about death goes as follows:

Old man Krastenfeld lay on his deathbed for months and finally passed away. Two weeks later, the relatives gathered like vulture to hear the reading of the will. The lawyer tore open an envelope, drew out a piece of paper and read: "Being of sound mind, I spent every dime before I died."

Youngman did not take that advice and leave nothing to his heirs, but the probate papers filed for his estate reflect a gross testamentary estate of less than $400,000. Whether that is a low-ball figure used only for publicly filed papers, we do not know. However, after Youngman's seven decade career as a comedian and a "household name", and frugal lifestyle married to one woman, one has to wonder whether Youngman paid the theaters, instead of the theaters paying him, for the right to perform his beloved shtick whenever and wherever he wanted.

Youngman told a joke about a woman who asked that her ashes be spread over Bloomingdales so that she would be assured that her daughter would visit her at least twice a week. We do not know where Henny's daughter or son like to shop, but we do know that the King of the One-Liners was buried at the Mt. Carmel cemetery located in Queens, New York. Finally, the 91 year old Youngman had to slow down.

/s/ *Henny Youngman*

Will dated July 30, 1991
Will signed at 502 Park Avenue, New York, New York

LAST WILL AND TESTAMENT
OF HENNY YOUNGMAN

I, HENNY YOUNGMAN, of the County of Dade, State of Florida, being of sound and disposing mind and memory, do hereby revoke all Wills and Codicils, as well as all other instruments of a testamentary nature heretofore made by me, and do hereby make, publish and declare this to be my Last Will and Testament in manner and form following:

FIRST:

I direct that all of my debts and funeral and testamentary expenses shall be paid as soon after my death as can conveniently be done.

SECOND:

I give, devise and bequeath all of my estate, real, personal and mixed and wheresoever situate of which I may die seized or possessed or to which I may be entitled at the time of my death in equal shares to my beloved children MARILYN KELLY and GARY YOUNGMAN, but if either of them shall predecease me his or her share is hereby given, devised or bequeathed to his or her lawful issue per stirpes.

THIRD:

I nominate, constitute and appoint my children MARILYN KELLY and GARY YOUNGMAN as Personal Representatives under this Will, but in the event that either of them shall fail to qualify or cease to serve, the other shall serve alone. I direct that neither of my Personal Representatives shall be required to furnish any bond or other security for faithful performance hereunder.

FOURTH:

I hereby grant and give to my Personal Representatives and their successor or successors the power to sell or exchange or otherwise dispose of any and all property, both real and personal, of which I may die seized or possessed, at such time and for such prices, for cash or upon credit, or partly for cash or partly upon credit, and upon such terms as my Personal Representatives shall deem proper and to execute and deliver good and sufficient deeds of conveyance therefor; the discretion of my Personal Representatives shall be absolute and not subject to any person or persons so long as she, or they, as the case may be, shall properly account for the said property of my estate. I further give and grant to my Personal Representatives the power to do all such acts, take all such proceedings and to exercise all such rights and privileges although not specifically mentioned hereinbefore with relation to any and all such property as if the absolute owner thereof.

IN WITNESS WHEREOF, I have hereunto set my hand and seal to this my Last Will and Testament consisting of three typewritten pages, this 30th day of July, 1991.

/s/ *Henny Youngman*

Signed, sealed, published and declared by HENNY YOUNGMAN, the Testator above named, as and for his Last Will and Testament in the presence of us and each of us, and we at his request, in his presence and in the presence of each other, have hereunto subscribed our names as witnesses thereto the day and year last above written.

STATE OF NEW YORK
COUNTY OF NEW YORK ss.:

The within GAIL N. ROGERS and ALBERT I. DA SILVA, being duly sworn depose and say:

That they witnessed the execution of the within Will by the aforementioned Testator HENNY YOUNG-MAN; that said Testator subscribed said Will and de-clared it to be his Last Will and Testament in the presence of them, who were both present at the same time at 502 Park Avenue, New York, NY 10022 on July 30th, 1991; that they thereafter subscribed the same as witnesses thereto in the presence of said Testator, HENNY YOUNGMAN at his request and in the presence of each other, that the execution of said Will was super-vised by a lawyer, namely Bruce Lazarus; that said Tes-tator at the time of the execution of said Will was known to them to be the said HENNY YOUNGMAN and appeared to them to be of sound and disposing mind and memory and competent in every respect to make a will and not under any restraint; that they make this Af-fidavit at the request of said Testator who has exam-ined the within Will, to which this Affidavit is attached.

Paul Lynde

DATE AND PLACE OF BIRTH
June 13, 1926
Mount Vernon, Ohio

DATE AND PLACE OF DEATH
January 9, 1982
Los Angeles, California

Hollywood Box

Best known as the somewhat effeminate and effusive star of television's long running game show, "The Hollywood Squares", Paul Lynde died at his home in Los Angeles, California at age 55.

Mr. Lynde was unmarried and had no children. He was survived by his sister, Helen Lynde, who has a favored role in the 1965 Will he signed seventeen (17) years before his death in 1982. Part of sister Helen's booty included the following items near and dear to Paul: "all of my art collection, my furniture and my dog, to dispose of as she wishes. . . ." To his brother-in-law, Lynde gave "all of my clothing and personal effects, including my jewelry.

Mr. Lynde also appeared on Broadway in "Bye, Bye Birdie" and in light-hearted films including "Son of Flubber," "The Glass Bottom Boat" and "Under the Yum Yum Tree." For a brief period he had his own show on television and regularly appeared on the variety and talk show circuit.

Once asked the question on "Hollywood Squares", "In what state was Abraham Lincoln born?", Mr. Lynde replied, "The same state as every baby—naked and crying." Mr. Lynde's own hysterical laughter usually added to the amusement of the studio and home audience.

Article NINTH of Lynde's Will directs that he be cremated and that "I be buried with my mother and father at their burial place in Amity, Ohio."

/s/ *Paul Lynde*
_____

Will dated October 6, 1965
Will signed in Beverly Hills, California

Phil Silvers

DATE AND PLACE OF BIRTH
1912
Brooklyn, New York

DATE AND PLACE OF DEATH
November 1, 1985
Los Angeles, California

Do-it-yourself Special

Comedian Phil Silvers was best known for his role as the conniving and scheming Sergeant Ernie Bilko on "The Phil Silvers Show," a popular 1950s television series. With his overbearing yet winning personality, Silvers could make his villainous characters lovable. In his last years, Silvers appeared regularly on the variety and talk-show circuit.

What follows is an exact transcription of Phil Silvers' Will and codicil in toto, which were handwritten and obviously prepared without the assistance of an attorney. Despite inconsistencies and misspellings in the Will and codicil, they were admitted to probate by the Los Angeles County Superior Court. Letters testamentary were issued to Phil's eldest daughter, Tracey, and attorney David Flynn. The Will speaks for itself, but one noteworthy bequest is for $5,000 to his "nurse and constant companion" for her consideration during his long illness. Phil had had a stroke 1973, and he himself described his medical condition as "shaky."

Silvers's Will concludes: "I go to my God knowing at least as a comedian I was one of a kind." So was his Will.

/s/ *Phil*
_____

Will dated July 4, 1984

1

Phil Silvers

(July 4th 1984)

This handwritten document
will serve as my last will and testament

I request for David Flynn of the firm of Traubner &
Flynn to share the duties of Executor with my eldest
daughter Tracey

For carrying out my requests they are to receive
and share the sum of Five thousand dollars $2500 each

Excluding the following bequests I leave my entire
fortune to be shares equally by my five daughters
namely Tracey, Nancey, Cathy, Candace and Laury. This
legacy includes my ownership of all Stock and Bodns,
Bank accounts, securities and monies in banks and possible partial ownership such as the television series
"Gilligan Island" - My many awards and documents,
photos, and memophilia should be shared equally by
my five above mentioned daughters, this is to be supervised by my eldest child Tracey

My further requests

To my sister Mrs Pearl Sabin of 200 W 54th St New York
City 10014 the sum of Fifteen Thousand dollars
$15,000

To my brother Bob Silver 1120 Brighter Beach Ave-
Brooklyn, N.Y.11235 Fifteen thousand dollars $1500
In the event both the above my Brother and Sister are

not alive to accept this legacy both Sums $30,000 Thirty thousand in Total should be awarded my Nephew Saul Silver, 390 First Ave, New York City, N.Y. 10010

Pg 2

Phil Silvers

To my friend Leo de Lyon 13147 Hartland Dr. No Hollywood, CA 91605 To Leo I bequest the Sum of Five Thousand dollars $5000 and with this sum my deep respect and love - To my nurse and constant companion

> Mrs. Jean Edward
> 109348 Eucaplyus
> Apt. E
> Hawthorne
> CA 90250
> Phone no. 978-8989

I bequeth to Mrs Edwards the sum of Five Thousand Dollars $5000 small payment for her many considerations during my long illness

I have made no reference to my ex wife Evelyn Patrick early in our marriage there were some years and there are five children will attest however for reasons best to the both of us I leave her nothing material in my also no bitterness At this writing she is doing very well in her well prepared profession and I wish her well

Any reference to the validity of my mental alertness can be attested by my Doctor of many years

Clarence M. Agress 553-2021 he kept me going when my physical condition was shaky following a stroke in 1973

I request my daughter Tracey to inform the media of my passing and to arrange my funeral in Forest Lawn

I want a simple coffin and a small headstone inscribed Phil Silvers Comedian

3
Phil Silvers

I expect David Flynn and TRACY to inform the media and if possible I would appreciate a small Eulogue delivered by my friend of many years Milton Berle. I request my funeral arrangments coffin and head stone not to exceed the sum of Ten thousand dollars $10,000

Good by I go to my rest willingly

The last years were painful but were made bearable by friends I made through the years especially Ed Traubner who smmothed out many a curve

I go to my God knowing at least as a comedian I was only one of a kind

Shalom

Phil

John Belushi

DATE AND PLACE OF BIRTH
January 24, 1949
Wheaton, Illinois

DATE AND PLACE OF DEATH
March 5, 1982
Chateau Marmont
Hollywood, California

Singing the Blues

Manic comic John Belushi had married high school girlfriend, Judith Jacklin, on New Year's Eve in 1976. The couple had no children at the time of Belushi's death six years later. Pursuant to the second article of his Will, Belushi's entire estate was left to Judith, if she survived him, which she did.

If Judith had not survived her husband, the estate was to be divided into eleven equal parts with shares given outright, or in trust, to the following relatives of Belushi and his wife: Belushi's father, Adam; mother, Agnes; sister, Marion; brother, James; brother, William; nephew, Adam; father-in-law, Robert L. Jacklin; mother-in-law, Jean Jacklin; brother-in-law, Robert B. Jacklin; sister-in-law, Pamela Jacklin; and sister-in-law, Patricia Brewster.

Because Judith Jacklin Belushi survived her husband, none of these surviving relatives inherited anything from Belushi's estate. Belushi's Will also contained a comprehensive *in terrorem* clause, but with the entire estate passing to his wife, there would be no one who could realistically contest his Will. Dying at a young age, Belushi's twenty-two page, detailed Will seems eerily unnecessary.

After his death from a drug overdose in Hollywood's infamous Chateau Marmont Hotel, Belushi was buried in Abel's Hill Cemetery on Martha's Vineyard near the home Belushi and his wife owned. Leading the funeral procession in black leather on a motorcycle was Belushi's close friend Dan Aykroyd, who was singing the blues with Blues Brother Belushi.

/s/ *John A. Belushi*

Will dated March 23, 1979
Residing at 60 Morton Street, New York, New York

Groucho Marx

DATE AND PLACE OF BIRTH
October 2, 1890
East 93rd Street
New York, New York

DATE AND PLACE OF DEATH
August 19, 1977
Cedars Sinai Medical Center
Los Angeles, California

"You Bet Your Life"

As his Will makes evident, comedian Groucho (a/k/a Julius) Marx was the self-appointed victim of three ex-wives. The second article of Groucho's Will states:

> I declare that I am not married; that I have had three former wives, to-wit, RUTH GARRITY (formerly RUTH MARX), CATHERINE MARIE MARX (also known as KAY MARIE MARX), and EDNA MARIE MARX (formerly known as EDNA MARIE HIGGINS and also as EDEN HARTFORD), from whom I have been divorced by final decree. I have three children, namely, my son, ARTHUR J. MARX, my daughter, MIRIAM RUTH MARX, and my daughter, MELINDA MARX. . . . Except as above specified, I have never been married and have no children.

Later in the Will, Marx reiterates, "I have, except as otherwise stated in this will, intentionally and with full knowledge omitted to provide for my heirs living at the time of my decease. Moreover, except for the trust established in Article SIXTH, I expressly disinherit my ex-wives." The trust referred to was $25,000 placed in trust for the benefit of his ex-wife Catherine Marie Marx and provides for the payment to her of the grand sum of $100 per week.

Groucho married his first wife, Ruth Johnson, in 1920, and his son, Arthur, and daughter Miriam were the issue of that marriage, which ended in divorce in 1942. In 1945, Groucho married Catherine Gorcey. That marriage produced his daughter Melinda before ending in divorce in 1950. Groucho's third marriage was to twenty-four-year-old model Eden Hartford in 1953 when Groucho was on the other side of sixty. That marriage ended in 1969 as Eden was hitting forty, and Groucho was looking at eighty.

After three strikes, Groucho never remarried. However, in 1972 he began publicly appearing with his attractive "secretary-companion," Erin Fleming. In Groucho's twilight years, his mental competence came into question, and he became the object of a messy conservatorship proceeding involving Miss Fleming and Groucho's family. Ultimately, Groucho's grandson, Andrew, was named Groucho's permanent conservator until Groucho's death.

Groucho's Will makes the following interesting provisions for the disposition of some his personal property:

A. I give and bequeath to the Smithsonian Institution, Washington, D.C. all of my memorabilia, including items such as scrapbooks, still pictures, scripts and film materials (but not the intangible property rights therein), my Academy Award statuette, my French medal, and such other items as ERIN FLEMING determines to constitute the collection of memorabilia; provided, however, that prior to the gift to the Smithsonian Institution, subject to approval of ERIN FLEMING, each of my children may select from among the memorabilia such items as each desires, and I hereby give to each of them the items so selected, as tokens of my affection.

B. I give to ERIN FLEMING . . . the Boutonnière of the Commander des Arts et Lettres presented to me by the French government.

C. I give to GODDARD LIEBERSON, if he survives me, that painting in my home depicting myself and my brothers, painted by John Decker.

D. I direct my executors to sell as soon as reasonably convenient all remaining items of jewelry, books, pictures, paintings, works of art, furniture, furnishings, fixtures and personal effects, together with my home at 1083 Hillcrest Road, Beverly Hills, California . . .

Despite the foregoing bequests and a cash bequest to Miss Fleming of $150,000, she filed a claim against the estate for approximately $75,000, according to papers filed with the court. The Bank of America National Trust and Savings Association, which was named as the sole executor of the Groucho Marx estate, rejected Miss Fleming's claim. There was additional legal skirmishing over the estate between Marx's children and Miss Fleming, which was widely reported by the press.

Marx was generous with others named in his Will. He gave $50,000 to each of his brothers who survived him (only Zeppo), and $5,000 to each of his grandchildren living at the time of his death. He rewarded a cousin of one of his ex-wives with a bequest in the amount of $3,500 "because she has been so kind to my daughter Melinda."

Despite his apparent generosity, Marx's Will also utilizes the feared *in terrorem* clause. Pursuant to the provisions of the Will, if a bequest were forfeited by any beneficiary, it was to be paid instead to the Jewish Federation Council of Greater Los Angeles.

Finally, for the man who once remarked that he would not want to be a member of any club that would accept him as a member, Groucho specifically bequeaths his membership in the Hillcrest Country Club to his son, Arthur. According to papers filed by the estate with the Los Angeles County court, that Hillcrest Country Club membership had an appraised value of $20,000 in Marx's estate, which had a reported value of almost $2 million. Apparently, Groucho said the magic words many times.

/s/ *Julius H. Marx*

/s/ *Groucho Marx*

Will dated September 24, 1974
Signed in Beverly Hills, California

Jackie Gleason

DATE AND PLACE OF BIRTH
February 26, 1916
Brooklyn, New York

DATE AND PLACE OF DEATH
June 24, 1987
Fort Lauderdale, Florida

"And Away We Go . . ."

Born in Brooklyn, New York, he was named Herbert John Gleason. His father, an insurance clerk, abandoned the family when "Jackie" was eight years old. Gleason's mother supported her son by working as a subway-booth attendant until she died in 1932 when Jackie was sixteen. Gleason's show business career rose steadily from his winning amateur talent contests, to working as a "barker" in carnivals, to small parts in films, to acting on Broadway, and ultimately entering the medium of television in its infancy in 1949. Gleason was one of television's most popular entertainers and had a prolonged honeymoon with the American public.

Jackie Gleason was best known as the scheming and bumbling bus driver, Ralph Kramden, in "The Honeymooners." Gleason had a reputation for being a big eater and big drinker, and it showed; his weight was reported to be in excess of 280 pounds at one time. His gregarious manners and larger-than-life ego gave him an inimitable comic style.

At the time of his death from cancer at the age of seventy-one, Gleason was survived by his third wife, Marilyn, and two daughters, Geraldine and Linda, from his first marriage. His thirty-five-year first marriage had ended in divorce in 1971 when he married Beverly McKittrick, a former secretary. That marriage lasted until 1974, when he was divorced from Ms. McKittrick and subsequently married Marilyn Taylor Horwich.

Most interesting about Jackie Gleason's Will is not the Will itself but the codicil, dated June 23, 1987, Gleason increased the bequest to "my longtime secretary SYDELL SPEAR" from $25,000 to $100,000. However, due to his debilitating illness, Gleason was not able to sign his own name on the codicil; he directed another to sign his name for him in the presence of two witnesses.

The balance of Gleason's estate was divided among Gleason's wife and two daughters.

For the comedian who often referred to himself as "the Great One," it is not surprising that in the first section of his Will he authorizes his "personal representatives" (the name for executors under Florida law) to spend as much as they want on "funeral expenses, the acquisition of a burial site, the erection of a suitable headstone or monument over my grave . . . without regard to any provision of law limiting such expenditures." It seems that the Great One did not want to go unnoticed, even in the cemetery.

/s/ *Herbert John Gleason*

Will dated April 11, 1985
Will signed at 3425 Willow Wood Road, Lauderhill, Florida
Codicil dated June 23, 1987

The Showmen

The Show Must Go On

SAMMY DAVIS, JR.
The Candy Man Can't
MAY 16, 1990

DANNY KAYE
The Secret Life of Danny Kaye
MARCH 3, 1987

LIBERACE
Flame Buoyant
FEBRUARY 4, 1987

HARRY HOUDINI
No Escape
OCTOBER 31, 1926

GEORGE M. COHAN
Born on the 4th of July, Dead on the 5th
NOVEMBER 5, 1942

BOB FOSSE
Dinner's On Me
SEPTEMBER 23, 1987

FRED ASTAIRE
Last Dance
JUNE 22, 1987

RUDOLF NUREYEV
"I Will Keep Dancing Till The Last Moment"
JANUARY 6, 1993

Sammy Davis Jr.

DATE AND PLACE OF BIRTH
December 8, 1925
Harlem, New York

DATE AND PLACE OF DEATH
May 16, 1990
Los Angeles, California

The Candy Man Can't

Sammy Davis Jr., the son of vaudevillian parents, had a career as a singer, dancer and actor which began at age 3 and spanned over sixty years, until his death at age 64. Sammy Davis was one of the most versatile showmen of his day. He tap-danced his way onto Broadway, starring in hit musicals such as "Mr. Wonderful" and "Golden Boy," and soft-shoed onto the silver screen in films such as "Porgy and Bess" and the more recent "Tap." He also had numerous hit songs, among them such signature tunes as "What Kind of Fool Am I?" and "Mr. Bojangles," and "Candy Man."

Davis is also as notorious for his health problems and life style as he is for his success as a star of stage, screen and song. He lost his left eye in a 1954 automobile accident, and was the subject of many spurious jokes and idle gossip concerning his glass eye. Mr. Davis also converted from Baptism to Judaism after his death-defying recovery from his car crash, garnering him still more attention. Unfortunately, the "Candy Man" also battled cocaine and alcohol addiction throughout his life, but whether he got high with a little (or a lot of) help from his friends, fellow "rat pack" members, Dean Martin and Frank Sinatra, is another story.

The often bejewelled Mr. Bojangles made certain in his Will, which was executed approximately two months before his death, that several of his friends would have a little token of his "Samminess" to remember him by. For example, Davis made the following bequests of jewelry to his friends:

> I give to my dear friend FORTUNATUS RICARD, my pinky ring;
>
> I give to my dear friend JOHN R. CLIMACO my brown diamond ring;
>
> I give to my dear friend SHIRLEY RHODES the sum of Twenty-Five Thousand Dollars ($25,000.00) to be used as "fun money", along with my large diamond ring.

It should be noted that brown diamond rings, while certainly unusual, do not appear to be more valuable than, say, gold diamond rings, and that calling a bequest "fun money" does not require the beneficiary to spend that money frivolously or even festively (although, in a sense, all monetary bequests under a Will are fun because they are tax-free). Regardless of the value of brown diamonds and the meaning of "fun money," Mr. Climaco and Ms. Rhodes were entitled to receive some "serious money" for their services, as they were named as co-Executors of Sammy Davis Jr.'s Will.

Not known for his affinity for firearms, Mr. Davis made three specific bequests of guns in his Will, including the following:

> I give to my friend CLINT EASTWOOD my 'Gary Cooper' gun;

I give to the GENE AUTRY WESTERN MUSEUM all remaining pieces of my Western gun collection; and

I give to my dear friend BRIAN DELLOW my personal Chrysler automobile and my non-Western gun collection

In his Will, Mr. Davis made many charitable bequests. Though he never went to school, Davis made several gifts to institutions of higher learning, including the following:

I give to MOREHOUSE TEACHERS COLLEGE, in Atlanta, Georgia, the sum of One Hundred Thousand Dollars ($100,000) to be used as a scholarship fund; and

I give to my beloved wife, ALTOVISE, and my beloved children the right to select and divide amongst themselves, for their ownership, my papers, memorabilia, musical arrangements, photographs, awards and other items of sentimentality. Those not selected by my wife or any of my children shall be directed one half (½) to WILBERFORCE COLLEGE in Ohio and one half (½) to HOWARD UNIVERSITY in Washington D.C., equally;

Although he was charitable, Davis was not as generous towards his fellow "brat packers" and former wives. Each of Messrs. Sinatra and Martin, and Mr. Davis's former wives, May Britt and Loray White, are absent from his Will.

Davis surrounded himself with friends and family during his lifetime, and in his Will he made many bequests to his friends and family members. Of his family, Sammy wrote the following:

I am married to ALTOVISE GORE DAVIS and all references in this Will to "my wife" are to her. I have no natural born children of this marriage; however, I recently adopted a young son. I have children and grandchildren of a previous marriage. I have made, other than in this Will, provisions for each of my beloved children from my previous marriage.

The bulk of his estate went to his wife, the dancer Altovise Gore Davis. For example, Davis made the following gifts and bequests to his wife:

I give, devise and bequeath to my dear wife, ALTOVISE, real property, consisting of our marital home located at 1151 Summit Drive, Beverly Hills, California, to be hers absolutely.

All of the rest and residue of my estate I give to my dear wife, ALTOVISE, in whatever form or wherever place located, to be hers absolutely.

Unfortunately, it is unclear if Altovise received anything pursuant to this bequest, as Sammy reportedly was broke at the time of his death and owed around $6,000,000 in debts.

Davis was able to make the following bequest of his motion picture films:

I give to my beloved wife, ALTOVISE, all my motion picture films. All films which my dearest wife chooses not to retain, I give to the NEGRO FILM SOCIETY in Oakland, California.

The consummate showman, Sammy signed his Will with a flourish, as the "S" of his first name reaches well up into the text of his Will. In fact, Davis signed *every page* of his Will with his full name, another uniquely expressive gesture!

During his lifetime, Sammy Davis Jr. exclaimed his individuality in his showstopping song "I've Gotta Be Me." In much the same way, his Will stands as a testament to the exuberant and generous person that he was.

/s/ *Sammy Davis Jr.*

Will dated March 12, 1990

LAST WILL AND TESTAMENT
OF
SAMMY DAVIS, JR.

I, SAMMY DAVIS, JR., a resident of Los Angeles, California, declare that this is my Last Will and Testament, and I revoke all wills and codicils that I have previously made.

ARTICLE I
DECLARATIONS

1.1 FAMILY DECLARATIONS. I am married to AL-TOVISE GORE DAVIS and all references in this Will to "my wife" are to her. I have no natural born children of this marriage; however, I recently adopted a young son. I have children and grandchildren of a previous marriage. I have made, other than in this Will, provisions for each of my beloved children from my previous marriage.

1.2 PROPERTY DISPOSED OF BY WILL. I confirm to my beloved wife, ALTOVISE, her interest in our community property. I intend by this Will to dispose of all property that I am entitled to dispose of by Will, including my one-half interest in our community property. I do not intend by this Will to exercise any testamentary powers of appointment that I may hold at the time of my death.

1.3 NO CONTRACT TO MAKE WILLS. My beloved wife, ALTOVISE, and I have not entered into either a contract to make wills or a contract not to revoke wills.

ARTICLE 2
TESTAMENTARY GIFTS

2.1 GIFTS OF PERSONAL PROPERTY. I make the following gifts of certain of my tangible personal property. The gifts to named individuals are on the condition they survive me. If they do not survive me, the gifts shall fail and pass with the residue of my estate as later provided for.

1) I give to my beloved mother, ELVERA DAVIS, the sum of Fifty Thousand Dollars ($50,000.00);

2) I gave to my dearest sister, RAMONA JAMES, the sum of Seventy-Five Thousand Dollars ($75,000.00);

3) I hereby give my son, MANNY, the sum of Fifty Thousand Dollars ($50,000.00);

4) I give to my dear friend SHIRLEY RHODES the sum of Twenty-Five Thousand Dollars ($25,000,00) to be used as "fun money", along with my large diamond ring;

5) I give to my dear friend MURPHY BEN-NETT the sum of One Hundred Thousand Dollars ($100,000.00);

6) I give to my housekeeper, LESSIE LEE,

the sum of One Hundred Thousand Dollars ($100,000.00);

7) I give to WALLACE WILSON the sum of Twenty-Five Thousand Dollars ($25,000.00);

8) I give to EDDIE PETERSON the sum of Seventy-Five Thousand Dollars ($75,000.00);

9) I give to MOREHOUSE TEACHERS COLLEGE, in Atlanta, Georgia, the sum of One Hundred Thousand Dollars ($100,000.00) to be used as a scholarship fund;

10) I give to my dear friend JOHN R. CLIMACO my brown diamond ring;

11) I give to my dear friend FORTUNATUS RICARD, my pinky ring;

12) I give to my friend CLINT EASTWOOD my "Gary Cooper" gun;

13) I give to the GENE AUTRY WESTERN MUSEUM all remaining pieces of my Western gun collection;

14) I give to my dear friend BRIAN DELLOW my personal Chrysler automobile and my non-Western gun collection;

15) I give my personal and professional wardrobe to a fund for needy children, for their best use and discretion, including auction or sale under their auspices for fund raising;

16) I give to my beloved wife, ALTOVISE, and my beloved children the right to select and divide amongst themselves, for their ownership, my papers, memorabilia, musical arrangements, photographs, awards, and other items of sentimentality. Those not selected by my wife or any of my children shall be directed one-half (1/2) to WILBERFORCE COLLEGE in

Ohio and one-half (1/2) to HOWARD UNIVERSITY in Washington, D.C., equally;

        17) I give to my beloved wife, ALTOVISE, all my video tapes. Any video tapes she chooses not to retain, I give to my dear friend JACK HALEY;

        18) I give to my beloved wife, ALTOVISE, all my motion picture films. Any films that my dearest wife chooses not to retain, I give to the NEGRO FILM SOCIETY located in Oakland, California; and

        19) All the rest, residue and remainder of my tangible personal property, including jewelry, furniture, fixtures, cameras, video equipment, art work, etc., located at my residence, or that personally owned by me and located wherever, not specifically hereinbefore bequeathed, I give to my beloved wife, ALTOVISE, absolutely.

In the event there are not sufficient assets in the form of personal property in my estate to fund the cash gifts indicated above to the specifically named individuals and institutions, I direct my Executors to eliminate the institutions and to fund such cash gifts proportionately, to the individuals named, as my funds will allow.

2.2 GIFT OF REAL PROPERTY. I give, devise and bequeath to my dearest wife, ALTOVISE, real property, consisting of our marital home located at 1151 Summit Drive, Beverly Hills, California, to be hers absolutely.

2.3 GIFT OF RESIDUE. All of the rest and residue of my estate I give to my dear wife, ALTOVISE, in whatever form or wherever place it may be located, to be hers absolutely.

2.4 ALLOCATION OF DEATH TAXES. Under the terms of this Will, as executed on this date, my Executors are either authorized or directed to pay from the residue of my estate any and all death taxes. However, my Executors shall charge and recover any such death tax payments from persons interested and/or receiving from my estate, whether receiving property under this Will, insurance or otherwise by contract, and my Executors shall make such claims in accordance with applicable federal and state laws and proration statutes.

ARTICLE 3
EXECUTOR PROVISIONS

3.1 NOMINATION OF EXECUTORS. I hereby nominate my dear friend, SHIRLEY RHODES, and my dear friend and attorney, JOHN R. CLIMACO, to serve as Co-Executors of this Will. In the event SHIRLEY RHODES or JOHN R. CLIMACO are unable, unwilling, or cease to act as Co-Executors hereof, then the remaining one shall act as the successor Executor and serve as the sole Executor of this Will. I request that no bond be required of any person named as Executor of this Will, whether that person is acting jointly or individually as Executor. The term "my Executor" as used in this Will shall include any personal represesntative of my estate acting under this Will.

3.2 INDEPENDENT ADMINISTRATION. I authorize my Executors to administer my estate with full authority under the California Independent Administration of Estates Act.

3.3 ADDITIONAL POWERS OF EXECUTOR. My Executors shall have the powers conferred on executors by law, including all powers granted by the Independent Administration of Estates Act: (1) to sell assets of my estate at public or private sale, for cash or on credit terms, as my Executors consider necessary for the proper administration and distribution of my estate; (2) to lease assets of my estate on such terms as my Executors consider proper, without restriction as to duration; (3) to invest and reinvest any surplus money of my estate as my Executors consider advisable in any kind of real or personal property and in any kind of investment; and (4) to retain any property of my estate for as long as my Executors consider appropriate, without liability for any resulting losses.

3.4 EXECUTORS' DISTRIBUTION POWERS. In selecting assets to be distributed in satisfaction of any gift under this Will, my Executors shall have absolute discretion to determine what assets are to be allocated to the gift or share to be distributed. Whenever distribution is being made to more than one beneficiary, my Executors shall have the discretion to distribute assets among them on a pro rata or no-pro rata basis, with the assets valued by my Executors as of the date of distribution. My Executors are authorized to distribute any assets otherwise distributable to a minor beneficiary under this Will by distributing the assets (1) to the court appointed guardian of the minor's estate, (2) to any adult person with whom the minor resides and who is responsible for the care, custody and control of the minor, or (3) to a custodian serving on behalf of the minor under the Uniform Gifts to Minors Act or Uniform Transfers to Minors Act of any state.

3.5 TAX DECISIONS AND ELECTIONS. My Executors shall have the power to make any tax decision or election that my Executors are authorized to make under state or federal law. I authorize my Executors to make these decisions and elections in my Executors' discretion as my Executors consider appropriate, regardless of the resulting effect on any person interested in my estate or the amount of any taxes imposed on my estate. No person adversely affected by any of these decisions or elections shall be entitled to any reimbursement or adjustment.

ARTICLE 4
GENERAL PROVISIONS

4.1 NON-CONTEST CLAUSE. If any beneficiary under this Will, in any manner, directly or indirectly, contests or attacks this Will or any of its provisions in any legal proceeding designed to thwart my intentions as expressed in this Will, any share or interest in my estate given to that contesting beneficiary under this Will is hereby revoked and shall be disposed of in the same manner provided herein as if that contesting beneficiary had predeceased me without surviving descendants.

4.2 DEATH TAXES DEFINED. The term "death taxes" as used in this Will includes all estate, inheritance, and other death taxes, including interest and penalties, except for generation-skipping and special use valuation recapture taxes.

4.3 GENDER AND NUMBER. In this Will, masculine, feminine, and neuter pronouns, and singular and plural words, shall each include the others whenever the context so indicates.

4.4 CONSTRUCTION OF HEADINGS. The headings of the Articles and paragraphs of this Will are for convenient reference only and are not intended to be fully descriptive of the contents. In no event shall the headings be relied upon in interpreting this Will.

SIGNATURE OF TESTATOR

I subscribe my name to this Will on this 12th day of March, 1990, at Los Angeles, California.

/s/ Sammy Davis, Jr.

STATEMENT OF WITNESSES

On the date written below, SAMMY DAVIS, JR., the Testator, declared to us, the undersigned, that this instrument, consisting of ten (10) pages, including the page signed by us as witnesses, was his Last Will and Testament, and requested us to act as witnesses to it. He then signed this Last Will and Testament in our presence, all of us being present at the same time. We now, at his request, in his presence, and in the presence of each other, sign our names below as witnesses.

We declare that the testator appears to be of sound mind and is under no duress, fraud or undue influence.

We declare under penalty of perjury under the laws of the State of California that the foregoing is true and correct and that this declaration was executed on the 12th day of March, 1990.

Danny Kaye

DATE AND PLACE OF BIRTH
January 18, 1913
Brooklyn, New York

DATE AND PLACE OF DEATH
March 3, 1987
Cedars-Sinai Medical Center
Los Angeles, California

The Secret Life of Danny Kaye

Born in Brooklyn and named David Daniel Kaminski, Danny Kaye quickly found that humor helped the world seem brighter and happier. As a dancer, mock orchestra leader, singer and joker, Kaye charmed audiences around the world, particularly children. Kaye performed on the stage and in Hollywood with his most memorable roles including Walter Mitty in the film version of James Thurber's "Secret Life of Walter Mitty", Hans Christian Andersen in the film with that name, and as Noah in the biblical Broadway musical "Two by Two." Besides his acting career, Kaye was involved with several charitable causes including Unicef and the Symphony Musicians Pension Fund. He was also a part owner of the Seattle Mariners baseball team.

In 1940 Kaye married a young lady from Brooklyn who was a pianist, composer, and lyricist. For the next 47 years, Kaye's wife Sylvia would be closely involved with his career in some capacity including composing songs for him, coaching or critiquing his performance.

At the outset of his Will, Kaye states, "I declare that I am married to SYLVIA FINE KAYE and that I have one child now living, namely my daughter DENA KAYE."

To his wife, Kaye gave "all household furniture and furnishings, clothing, automobiles, silverware, books, paintings and other works of art, personal effects and other articles of similar kind and nature, as well as my entire interest in all club memberships. . . ." Kaye's residuary estate was paid to an *inter vivos* trust which he and his wife had previously established. Kaye named his wife as the Executor of his Will.

There are no dispositive provisions for Kaye's daughter, Dena, in his Will. There is also a rather harsh *In Terrorem* clause and the following article:

INTENTIONAL OMISSION: I have, except as otherwise specified in this Will, intentionally and with full knowledge omitted to provide for my heirs, expressly including, but not limited to, any person now living or hereafter born who is, or claims to be my spouse, my child or the issue of a deceased child of mine.

With such a clause included in the Will, one wonders whether Kaye might have had a secret life of his own.

/s/ *Danny Kaye*

Will dated August 18, 1983
Will signed at Los Angeles, California
Residing at 1103 San Ysidro Drive
Beverly Hills, California

LAST WILL

OF

DANNY KAYE

I, DANNY KAYE, a resident of the County of Los Angeles, State of California, declare this to be my Last Will and revoke all former Wills and Codicils.

ARTICLE I

DECLARATION: I declare that I am married to SYLVIA FINE KAYE and that I have one child now living, namely my daughter DENA KAYE. I have no other children or issue of a deceased child.

ARTICLE II

INTENTION AND ELECTION: It is my intention to dispose of my share of the community property of my wife and myself and of my separate property, if any; provided, however, it is not my intention to exercise any power of appointment which I may have under the Declaration of Trust referred to in Article IV below.

I further urge and request my wife to either make a proper and timely election under California Probate Code Section 202(b) to have her community one-half interest in all our community property (except for her community one-half interest in the property described in Article III below) administered under Division 3 of the California Probate Code or to transfer her community one-half interest in all our community property (except for her community one-half interest in the property described in Articles III below) to the then acting Trustee under the Declaration of Trust referred to in Article IV below.

ARTICLE III

DISPOSITION OF TANGIBLE PERSONAL PROPERTY: I give to my wife, SYLVIA FINE KAYE, if she survives the date of my death by sixty (60) days, my entire interest in all household furniture and furnishings, clothing, automobiles, silverware, books, paintings and other works of art, personal effects and other articles of similar kind and nature, as well as my entire interest in all club memberships. This gift is limited to items held for the personal use and enjoyment of my family and myself and shall not include similar items, if any, held primarily for use in a trade or business or for the production of income. If my wife fails to survive the date of my death by sixty (60) days, then I give such of said items to my daughter DENA KAYE as she may select and I direct that the Executor dispose of the balance thereof, either with or without consideration, as said Executor deems best, the proceeds of sale, if any, to form part of the residue of my estate.

ARTICLE IV

<u>DISPOSITION OF RESIDUE:</u> I give the entire residue of my estate, of whatsoever kind and nature, wherever situated, to the then acting Trustee under that certain document entitled "DECLARATION OF TRUST" heretofore executed on the date this Will is executed, in which I and my wife, SYLVIA FINE KAYE, are referred to as Trustors and as Trustees, to be added to and form part of the assets subject to said trust and to thereupon be divided, held, administered and distributed in accordance with the terms and conditions thereof, including any amendments thereto hereafter made during my lifetime.

If for any reason the foregoing trust should not be in existence at the date of my death, or should it be finally determined for any other reason that the gift due to the Trustee of the foregoing inter vivos trust is inef-

fective, then in that event I give, devise and bequeath
the entire residue of my estate to my wife, SYLVIA FINE
KAYE, IN TRUST, to be held, administered and distributed in accordance with the terms of that certain document entitled "DECLARATION OF TRUST" heretofore
executed on the date this Will is executed in which I
and my wife, SYLVIA FINE KAYE, are referred to as
Trustors and as Trustees, which are valid and effective,
and I do hereby incorporate herein by this reference
said document and the terms of the trusts as created
therein and direct that said residue be held as a testamentary trust according to the terms and conditions of
said instrument.

ARTICLE V

INTENTIONAL OMISSION: I have, except as otherwise specified in this Will, intentionally and with full
knowledge omitted to provide, for my heirs, expressly
including, but not limited to, any person now living or
hereafter born who is, or claims to be my spouse, my
child or the issue of a deceased child of mine.

ARTICLE VI

WILL CONTEST: If any devisee, legatee, or beneficiary under this Will or any legal heir of mine, or person
claiming under any of them, shall contest this Will
and/or the inter vivos trust described in Article IV or attack or seek to impair or invalidate any of the provisions
of this Will and/or said trust, or conspire with or voluntarily assist anyone attempting to do any of those
things, in that event I specifically disinherit each such
person and all legacies, bequests, devises and interests
given under this Will and/or said trust to that person
shall be forfeited and shall augment proportionately the
shares of my estate going under this Will to or in trust

for such of my devisees, legatees and beneficiaries as shall not have participated in such acts or proceedings.

ARTICLE VII

<u>PAYMENT OF DEATH TAXES:</u> I direct that all estate, inheritance and succession taxes, and all other death duties by whatever name they may be called, chargeable against any property disposed of during my life or at my death, either by this Will or by any other means, or chargeable against my probate estate by reason of any such gift, devise, bequest or other conveyance or disposition, shall be paid out of the residue of my probate estate as a whole, or in the joint discretion of my Executor and the Trustee under that certain Declaration of Trust referred to in Article IV above, paid in whole or in part from the assets subject to said Declaration of Trust which are includable in my gross estate for Federal Estate Tax purposes; provided that should said assets be comprised in whole or in part of obligations of the United States which are redeemable at par in payment of Federal Estate Tax, my Executor and Trustee are mandatorily directed to apply such obligations in payment of said tax up to the whole thereof, and if said tax exceeds the face amount of such obligations then my Executor is mandatorily directed to apply any such obligations contained in the probate estate in payment of such taxes. No reimbursement or collection shall be sought or obtained from any person receiving property from me by any of the above means, and the property to which the beneficiaries of the trusts under said Declaration of Trust are entitled shall be determined after payment of all such taxes.

ARTICLE VIII

<u>APPOINTMENT OF EXECUTOR:</u> I appoint my wife,

SYLVIA FINE KAYE as Executor of this Will, and should she be dead or unable or unwilling so to act, or should she fail to complete the administration of my estate, then I appoint as Executor such person or institution as SYLVIA FINE KAYE may have designated in writing and should she fail to so designate or should the designee fail or refuse to act then I apppoint as Co-Executors LEO ZIFFREN and SECURITY PACIFIC NATIONAL BANK and should either be dead, unable or unwilling so to act, or should either also fail to complete the administration of my estate than I appoint the other as sole Executor.

No bond shall be required of any Executor acting hereunder, and any Executor acting hereunder shall have full power and authority to lease, sell, exchange or encumber the whole or any part of my estate, at public or private sale, with or without notice, subject only to such confirmation of court as may be required by law; shall have full power and authority to continue to operate any business or other enterprise in which my estate has an interest, the profits and losses therefrom to inure to and be chargeable against my estate as a whole; and shall have full power and authority to distribute the assets of my estate in cash or in kind, allocating assets among the beneficiaries and following such procedure as said Executor deems reasonable.

Any Executor acting hereunder is further empowered to invest and reinvest surplus moneys of this estate in such types of investments, both real and personal, as may be selected in the discretion of such Executor including corporate obligations of every kind, preferred or common stocks and common trust funds, (including if a corporation shall ever act as Executor any common trust fund of that corporate Executor), subject only to such authorization of court as may be required by law.

My Executor is hereby directed to elect for Federal Estate Tax purposes to have property, in which my wife, SYLVIA FINE KAYE is receiving a qualifying income interest for life as a result of my death, qualify for a marital deduction.

My Executor is specifically authorized to employ as their legal counsel any law [sic] with which any Executor is associated, in whatever capacity, and in such event the usual fees shall be paid to said law [sic] and the usual compensation shall also be paid to such Executor in the same manner as if he were not so associated, regardless of whether or not, under any arrangements between them, all or a part of such Executor's compensation is to be paid over to such law firm.

IN WITNESS WHEREOF, I have hereunto set my hand this 18 day of August, 1983.

/s/ *Danny Kaye*
DANNY KAYE

On the date written below, DANNY KAYE declared to us, the undersigned, that this instrument, consisting of 5 pages including the page signed by us as witnesses, was his Will and requested us to act as witnesses to it. He thereupon signed this Will in our presence, all of us being present at the same time.

At this time DANNY KAYE is over eighteen years of age and appears to be of sound mind. We have no knowledge of any facts indicating that this instrument, or any part of it, was procured by duress, menace, fraud or undue influence. Each of us is now over eighteen years of age. We now, in his presence and in the presence of each other, subscribe our names as witnesses.

Executed on August 18, 1983, at Los Angeles, California.

We declare under penalty of perjury that the foregoing is true and correct.

Liberace

DATE AND PLACE OF BIRTH
May 16, 1919
635 51st Street
West Allis, Wisconsin

DATE AND PLACE OF DEATH
February 4, 1987
Riverside County
Palm Springs, California

Flame Buoyant

I, LIBERACE, also sometimes known as WALTER VALENTINO LIBERACE, LEE LIBERACE, and WLADSIU VALENTINO LIBERACE, domiciled, in Las Vegas Nevada, being of sound and disposing mind and memory, do hereby make, publish and declare this to be my LAST WILL AND TESTAMENT.

Flamboyant, glitzy, happy-go-lucky, and gay pianist Liberace had a decidedly dry Will. The Will begins with the following sentence under the seemingly inappropriate heading "Marital and Family Status": "I declare that I am unmarried and have no living issue." Anybody who had ever seen Liberace "perform" could probably have told you that. Liberace was never married in a formal sense, although his liaisons with a host of male companions have been widely reported. In 1982, Scott Thorson, who had been Liberace's companion, chauffeur, and "bodyguard," sued the guarded body for over $100 million. According to published reports, that suit was settled for $95,000, or less than one-tenth of one percent of the total amount originally sought.

According to his Will, which was signed thirteen days

before he died, Liberace transferred his entire estate "to JOEL R. STROTE, as Trustee, or any successor Trustee of the trust designated as "THE LIBERACE REVOCABLE TRUST" established earlier this day, of which I am the Grantor and he is the original Trustee." Mr. Strote, who was Liberace's attorney, has stated that most of the Liberace estate will pass to the Liberace Foundation for the Performing and Creative Arts. Undoubtedly, Liberace's estate was quite substantial, as he had earned over $5 million per year for over twenty-five years, according to newspaper reports. That equals at least $125 million in lifetime earnings.

When he died, Liberace was survived by his sister, Ann Liberace Farrell, of Las Vegas, Nevada, niece Ina Mae Liberace, and nephews Lester Lee Liberace, Rudolph V. Liberace, and Harry Henry Liberace. Whether these Liberace relatives were beneficiaries of the trust established by Liberace about two weeks before he died only Joel R. Strote and a few others know for sure.

The cause of Liberace's death was officially termed "cardiac arrest due to congestive heart failure brought on by subacute encephalopathy . . . a contributing cause was aplastic anemia." After the flamboyant entertainer's death the Riverside County, California, coroner said that that was just an oblique way of saying that the death stemmed from AIDS, but that has repeatedly been denied by many of those closest to Liberace. Having lived a lifetime of fantasy and illusion, Liberace himself may not have wanted the specter of a dreaded disease to tarnish his gilded image.

/s/ *Liberace*

Will dated January 22, 1987

Harry Houdini

DATE AND PLACE OF BIRTH
April 6, 1874
Brooklyn, New York

DATE AND PLACE OF DEATH
October 31, 1926
(Halloween)
Detroit, Michigan

No Escape

The world-famous magician and great escape artist known simply as Houdini was originally named Ehrich Weiss at birth and was the son of a rabbi. At the age of nine, Houdini joined a traveling circus as a contortionist and trapeze performer, and the rest is mystery.

At a young age, Houdini became a celebrated figure throughout America and earned large sums of money for performing in vaudeville acts and winning bets. His most famous escape was from his own self-styled torture chamber, in which he was shackled head down in a tank full of water. Contrary to popular belief, Houdini did not die in one of those chambers but in a hospital in Detroit, as the result of complications resulting from an appendix operation. The appendicitis was the result of a hard blow to Houdini's appendix delivered by a college student whom Houdini had just lectured on spiritualistic tricks and Houdini's own physical prowess.

During his lifetime Houdini collected an extensive library devoted to magic, spiritualism, and the black arts. When he died in 1926, that book collection was valued at $500,000, according to *The New York Times*. Under his Will, Houdini bequeaths his library relating to "spiritualism, occultism and psychical research to the Congressional Library at Washington" and his "collection of books, pamphlets, letters and the like related to spiritualism, occultism and psychical research" to the "American Society for Psychical Research."

However, in the hastily drawn codicil to his Will, Houdini revokes the bequest to the Society as follows:

> I . . . wish to cancel the codicil giving my Spiritualistic library to the American Society of Psychic Research, the entire collection is to go with my Magical Library to the Congressional Library in Washington. The reason I object giving my Spiritualistic library to the American Society of Psychical Research is because I object to a dishonorable person like J. Malcolm Bird being connected with any reputable organization.

Obviously, Houdini believed J. Malcolm to be a strange bird.

Perhaps most interesting about Harry Houdini's Will is the consideration that he gives to his own burial. During his life he had always said that if there were any way to come back from the dead he would, so his burial arrangements required special consideration. Under the nineteenth article of his Will, Houdini directs that upon his death his body

> be embalmed and buried in the same manner in which my beloved mother was buried upon her death, and that my grave be construed in a vault in the same manner as my beloved mother's last resting place was constructed for her burial; and I also direct that I shall be buried in the grave immediately alongside of that of my dear departed mother. . . .

What a field day Sigmund Freud would have had with that one.

Houdini also provided that "the bronze bust of me, made by Cassidy of Manchester, England, shall be put on the exedra erected by me in said cemetery in the place provided for it on such exedra." An "exedra" is a porch or portico adjacent to the grave; apparently, Houdini wanted to be sure that his returning spirit found the right tomb.

Despite Houdini's magical powers, there appears to have been significant domestic strife within the Weiss family. In one section of his Will, Houdini expressly disinherits a woman named Sadie Glantz Weiss, "the divorced wife of my brother Nathan Joseph Weiss and the present wife of my brother, Dr. Leopold David Weiss."

Houdini bequeathed all of his "household effects, furniture, trophies, silverware, ornaments, jewelry, diamonds and personal effects, including my oil paintings" and one-sixth of his residuary estate to his wife, Wilhelmina Rahner Houdini. He also appointed his wife to be the executor of his Will. Bankers Trust Company was named as a successor executor.

As was appropriate for the doyen of magicians, in his Will Houdini made a bequest of $1,000 to the Society of American Magicians.

/s/ *Harry Houdini*
formerly Ehrich Weiss

Will dated July 30, 1924
Residing at 278 West 113th Street, New York, New York
Codicil dated May 6, 1925

George M. Cohan

DATE AND PLACE OF BIRTH
July 4, 1878
Providence, Rhode Island

DATE AND PLACE OF DEATH
November 5, 1942
993 Fifth Avenue
New York, New York

Born on the 4th of July, Dead on the 5th

America's favorite Yankee-Doodle Dandy of the stage, George M. Cohan once stated, "I can write better plays than any living dancer and dance better than any living playwright."

Cohan seemed to have had American patriotism in his stars, as he was, in fact, born on the 4th of July to Helen and Jeremiah Cohan, who worked the vaudeville circuit. For a while, the family performed as "the Four Cohans," including George's sister Josephine. During the "gay nineties," Cohan was best remembered for his nightly farewell on stage: "My mother thanks you, my father thanks you, my sister thanks you, and I thank you."

Cohan's first wife was named Ethel Levey and was his dancing partner after sister Josephine danced off to get married. George and Ethel had one daughter, named Georgette. In 1907 that marriage ended. On his birthday in 1908, Cohan married Agnes Mary Nolan Cohan, who was by his bedside when he died thirty-four years later. Together, George and Agnes had three children: Helen Frances, Mary Helen, and George Michael Cohan, Jr.

In his Will, Cohan provides equally for his four children and his wife, Agnes. Each got 5 percent of his substantial estate outright, and each was the beneficiary of a trust holding the remaining 75 percent of the estate. Cohan takes pains to defend the equal gift to Mrs. Cohan with the following paragraph in his Will:

> Because of my beloved wife having registered in our joint names, with the right of survivorship, a substantial amount of my securities which will become her property in the event of my dying before her, I respectfully request that she accept the provisions that I herein make for her in lieu of her right to elect her statutory rights against the provisions of this will.

According to papers filed with the surrogate's court, Mrs. Cohan complied with her husband's "respectful" request.

Cohan appointed "my friend and legal counselor of many years, DENNIS F. O'BRIEN," as executor of his Will and co-trustee of the residuary trust. Cohan, who was known to be quite shrewd about protecting the value of his copyrights, also provided the following in his Will:

> (a) It is my intention to convey to a corporation that I plan to organize in the near future title to all of the literary compositions, dramatic compositions, dramatico-musical compositions, musical compositions and songs and all copyrights that I may own in connection with such compositions . . .
>
> (b) I respectfully request those persons who are authorized to renew copyrights of any of my literary compositions, dramatic compositions, dramatico-musical

compositions, musical compositions and songs pursuant to the rights of renewal of such copyrights, to procure such renewals of copyrights . . .

(c) I respectfully request that such moneys as may be payable to me from the American Society of Composers, Authors and Publishers be paid to the executor of my estate . . .

One doesn't hear too much about "dramatico-musical compositions" these days, but Cohan did not want to miss a beat, or a royalty.

Toward its conclusion, the Will states Cohan's "wish" that title to the copyrights of all his compositions be retained and never sold. Cohan points out that the request is "based upon my experience of many years in dealing with the licenses to use and turn to account the literary compositions, dramatic compositions, dramatico-musical compositions, musical compositions and songs that I have originated, written and composed."

After a prolific songwriting career spanning over fifty years, Cohan certainly had quite a lot of copyright to protect. Now that's the spirit of a dandy Yankee!

/s/ *George M. Cohan*

Will dated March 2, 1939
Codicil dated October 23, 1941

Bob Fosse

DATE AND PLACE OF BIRTH
June 23, 1927
Chicago, Illinois

DATE AND PLACE OF DEATH
September 23, 1987
Washington University Hospital
Washington, D.C.

Dinner's On Me

In 1973, Bob Fosse was the first person to win entertainment's triple crown, winning an Oscar as the director of the film *Cabaret*, a Tony Award for his direction of the play *Pippin* on Broadway, and an Emmy Award for his direction of the television special "Liza with a 'Z.'"

Known for his nonstop work habits and chain-smoking, Fosse's personal life was also a whirlwind affair. Fosse was married three times and was romantically linked with many women. Fosse's three wives were dancers and performers, Mary Ann Niles, Joan McCracken, and Gwen Verdon, and his girlfriends included actresses Jessica Lange and Ann Reinking.

Throughout his career Fosse worked with a variety of performers, and through his Will, Fosse remembers many of those with whom he worked, and played. Most unusual about the Will of Bob Fosse is the following bequest:

I give and bequeath the sum of Twenty-Five Thousand ($25,000) Dollars to my Executor, to be distributed by him to the friends of mine listed, and in the amounts set forth, in a letter of instructions which I have delivered to him. <u>I have made this provision so that when</u>

<u>my friends receive this bequest they will go out and</u> <u>have dinner on me.</u> [emphasis added] They all have at one time or other during my life been very kind to me. I thank them.

Among the sixty-six people remembered by Fosse were the following well-known names from film and theater: actors Dustin Hoffman, Roy Scheider (who portrayed the Fosse character in *All That Jazz*), Ben Gazzara, and Ben Vereen; actresses Liza Minnelli, Ann Reinking, Melanie Griffith, Julie Hagerty, Janet Leigh, and Jessica Lange; writers E. L. Doctorow, Neil Simon, and Elia Kazan; and comedian Buddy Hackett. After the $25,000 bequest was equally divided among the sixty-six designated recipients, each one received the odd figure of $378.79 to "go out and have dinner on" Fosse. Even at the pricey restaurants that Fosse often frequented, that sum was enough to assure that no one on the list would go hungry.

In addition to the dinner allowances, Fosse made the following more substantial devises and bequests to certain people from his past and to two charitable causes of special interest to him:

A. To my friend and agent, SAMUEL COHN, if he shall survive me, all of my right, title and interest in and to the restaurant known as The Laundry and located in East Hampton, New York, in whatever form my interest in this business entity may take.

B. To my sister, MARIANNE DIMOS, if she shall survive me, the sum of Twenty Thousand ($20,000) Dollars.

C. To the HEART FUND, New York City Chapter, the sum of Fifteen Thousand ($15,000) Dollars.

D. To the POSTGRADUATE CENTER FOR MENTAL HEALTH, the sum of Fifteen Thousand ($15,000) Dollars.

E. To my assistant, CATHY NICOLAS [sic, "Nicholas"], if she shall survive me, the sum of Fifteen Thousand ($15,000) Dollars.

F. To my friend, HERB GARDNER, if he shall survive me, the sum of Fifteen Thousand ($15,000) Dollars.

G. To my former wife, MARY ANN NILES, if she shall survive me, the sum of Fifteen Thousand ($15,000) Dollars.

After Fosse survived a near-fatal heart attack in 1967, one can well understand the motivation behind his gift to the Heart Fund of New York. It is also heartwarming to see a gift to Fosse's first wife, Mary Ann Niles, whom he had divorced in 1951 but with whom he was still close. Coincidentally, Niles died a few days after Fosse did.

In addition to those specific bequests, Fosse established a $100,000 trust fund designated as the "Bob Fosse Theatre Scholarship," which was to provide financial assistance for the education and training in the theatrical arts for "deserving individuals." In his Will Fosse states, "I have been motivated to establish this fund because my life has been devoted to the American theatre and its continued well-being and improvement are of great importance to me." Fosse named Gwen Verdon and his daughter, Nicole, as the trustees of this trust.

The final curtain for Bob Fosse came at approximately the same time as the curtain was going up on the opening night of the revival of his 1966 hit *Sweet Charity* at the National Theatre in Washington. Prior to the opening, Fosse collapsed from another heart attack in his room at the Willard Hotel in Washington and was pronounced dead at the George Washington University Hospital shortly thereafter. At his side when he died was his third wife and artistic collaborator, Gwen Verdon. The cast of the show was not informed of Fosse's death until the curtain went down at the end of the show after a thunderous standing ovation from the audience. True to the spirit of Bob Fosse, the show went on.

At the time of his death, Fosse's estate was reportedly worth close to $4 million and was divided equally between his wife, Gwen Verdon, and daughter, Nicole. The last act of Fosse's successful career was his Will, which included "sweet charity" and rewarded many of the people through whose lives Bob Fosse had danced.

/s/ Robert Fosse

Will dated March 28, 1985
Residing at 58 West 58th Street, New York, New York

Fred Astaire

DATE AND PLACE OF BIRTH
May 10, 1899
Omaha, Nebraska

DATE AND PLACE OF DEATH
June 22, 1987
Century City Hospital
Los Angeles, California

Last Dance

Born Frederick Austerlitz, in Omaha, Nebraska, Fred Astaire, "the Ultimate Dancer," appeared in vaudeville, on stage, screen, and television, and starred in over thirty musical films between 1933 and 1968. Offscreen, Astaire shunned the debonair top-hat-and-tails look that became his trademark. He was known as an affable and ordinary man, blessed with an extraordinary talent.

Astaire's first wife was Phyllis Livingston Potter, whom he married in 1933. The couple had two children together and she had one from a previous marriage. Phyllis died in 1954. Astaire's second wife, Robyn Smith, was more than forty-five years younger than Astaire when he married her in 1980 at the age of eighty one. Mrs. Smith was a jockey, and Astaire met her through his own interest in horses and his ownership of a stable. Seems like Fred wanted a new filly in his personal stable.

In his 1986 Will, Astaire describes his family relationships as follows:

My family includes my wife, ROBYN ASTAIRE, and my adult children by my first wife, PHYLLIS ASTAIRE, who died many years ago. The names of my children are

FRED ASTAIRE, JR. and PHYLLIS AVA ASTAIRE McKENZIE. My stepson, ELIPHALET NOTT POTTER, is the son of my deceased wife PHYLLIS by a former marriage. Aside from the foregoing, all references in this Will are to ROBYN ASTAIRE.

Astaire named his son, Fred Astaire, Jr., stepson Eliphalet Nott Potter, Jr., and an attorney as executors of his Will, and as trustees of a trust that he had established with his first wife in 1942. In addition to that 1942 trust, Astaire created another *inter vivos* trust in 1985 that received his residuary estate upon his death. In the event that two or all of the named executors were not able to act, Astaire named his daughter, Phyllis Ava Astaire McKenzie, to act as a successor executrix. In deference to his wife, who was not named as an executrix, the Will states:

> I request that my acting Executors consult with my wife ROBYN and obtain her approval prior to any disposition proposed for my interest in Ava Productions, Inc., or any of its assets, or my interests or royalties in special television properties which form part of my estate.

The last article of Astaire's Will succinctly states, "I direct that my funeral be private and that there be no memorial service." Without wanting any fanfare, dancer extraordinaire Fred Astaire danced into the dark at the age of eighty-eight.

/s/ *Fred Astaire*

Will dated January 16, 1986
Signed in Los Angeles, California

Rudolf Nureyev

DATE AND PLACE OF BIRTH
March 17, 1938
Siberia, Russia

DATE AND PLACE OF DEATH
January 6, 1993
Hospital Notre Dame
Du Perpetual Secours
Levallois-Perret, France

"I Will Keep Dancing Till the Last Moment"

When world famous ballet dancer Rudolph Nureyev defected from the Soviet Union at age 23, he did not have more than the clothes on his back in the Paris airport on that day in 1961. But when he died 32 years later, Nureyev died a remarkably wealthy man, with numerous homes around the world, including a villa in Monte Carlo, an estate outside of London, a cooperative apartment in New York's fabled Dakota apartment house, a large farm in Virginia, and even his own private island. The tangible personal property which Nureyev amassed was sold for almost $8,000,000 at Christie's auction house in New York.

How did this defector, who was born on a train in Siberia, amass such substantial wealth? First, his legs which were insured by Lloyd's of London, propelled him to ballet engagements all over the world, for which he demanded record-setting payments, in advance, in cash. Second, Nureyev shrewdly invested that cash in real estate around the world and filled his homes with valuable objects. Finally, it has been said that Nureyev had an "impediment of the reach" and rarely, if ever, picked up the check or bill for anything. Perhaps it was the combination of the strong legs, smart investments and weak reach that made Rudolph Nureyev the wealthiest man in his profession, leaving a substantial fortune around the world at his death at the young age of 54.

During his lifetime, Nureyev never married and had no children. At his death, Rudolf Nureyev (a/k/a Rudolf Noureev) was survived by two sisters, Rosa Noureeva of Monaco and Rezida Evgrafova of Russia, and a niece named Alfia Rafikova-Yagudina. Alfia was the daughter of another sister of Nureyev's who had died before he did. Sister Rosa petitioned the New York County Surrogate's Court to be appointed the co-administrator of her brother Rudy's estate, together with one of New York's finest, cutting edge estate attorneys, Joshua Rubenstein of the Rosenman Colin law firm. Although they were appointed as administrator's of Nureyev's estate by the New York Court, it was only a Pyrrhic victory for the reasons described below.

The purported American Will of Rudolph Nureyev is dated April 28, 1992, and is reproduced here in full.

The first paragraph of Nureyev's purported Will states that "I, Rudolf Nureyev, citizen of Austria, being of sound and disposing mind, do make, publish and declare this to be my Will." The balance of the Will bequeaths and devises "all my tangible property, intangible property including my shares in the Dakota, Inc. and all my real estate which are located in the United States, which I own at my death, to the Rudolf Nureyev Dance Foundation, an Illinois Not-For-Profit Corporation." That Foundation was incorporated and established only shortly before Nureyev signed his purported last Will.

The purported Will, which appears on "Tully & Weinstein" law firm stationary, is only six short paragraphs long. In one of those paragraphs, Nureyev appoints his attorney Barry L. Weinstein as Executor of his Will. Although the Will is quite short, and no successor Executor to Mr. Weinstein is named, the purported Will does expressly provide that "I direct that no Executor shall be required to give bond or surety."

Nureyev's purported Will was purportedly signed in New York under the supervision of attorney Barry Weinstein, who chose not to act as one of the three witnesses to the Will, the execution of which he was supervising. According to court papers filed on his behalf, Mr. Weinstein had been Nureyev's legal advisor for over twenty years.

The term "purported" is used repeatedly above to describe "the paper writing dated April 28, 1992" because that writing was never actually offered for probate in New York, or any other jurisdiction, and therefore cannot technically be referred to as Nureyev's "Will" because no Court has ever determined that it was indeed a valid Will. You cannot contest a Will that has not been offered for probate, and there is no strict requirement in New York, or most other jurisdictions, that a Will must be offered for probate.

Prior to his death, with the able assistance of Barry Weinstein, and others, Nureyev had legally transferred all, or close to all, of his United States assets to the recently formed Rudolf Nureyev Dance Foundation headed by Mr. Weinstein. Because there were no assets to pass under his purported Will, or even by intestacy, there is no need to offer the Will for probate, nor is there anything for an administrator to administer. Despite the high-powered legal efforts of Joshua Rubenstein, Esq. and Gerald Rosenberg, Esq., Barry Weinstein's estate planning (and fancy footwork) prior to Nureyev's death appeared to carry the day.

Dead at 54 after a long battle with AIDS and late nights at Studios 54 around the globe, Rudolf Nureyev danced across the world stage from East to West and North to South, and lifted himself and the art form of dance to dazzling and intoxicating new elevations.

/s/ *Rudolf Nureyev*

Paper writing dated April 28, 1992

WILL OF RUDOLF NUREYEV

I, Rudolf Nureyev, citizen of Austria, being of sound and disposing mind and memory, do make, publish and declare this to be my Will.

My executor shall pay debts and costs of administration, including ancillary costs of safeguarding and delivering bequests.

I give and bequeath all my tangible property, intangible property including my shares in the Dakota, Inc. and all my real estate which are located in the United States, which I own at my death, to the Rudolf Nureyev Dance Foundation, an Illinois Not-For-Profit Corporation.

I give and bequeath the rest, residue and remainder of my estate located in the United States, of all kinds, real and personal to the Rudolf Nureyev Dance Foundation, an Illinois Not-For-Profit Corporation.

I appoint Barry L. Weinstein as Executor of this

Will; I direct that no Executor shall be required to give bond or surety.

In Witness, whereof, I have signed this Will consisting of three pages, this 28 day of April, 1992.

/s/ *Rudolf Nureyev*

SIGNED, SEALED, PUBLISHED AND DECLARED by the above-named Testator, Rudolf Nureyev, as and for his Last Will and Testament, this 28 day of April, 1992, in the presence of us, the undersigned, who were all together with him at such time and thereupon, we, at his request and in his presence and in the presence of each other, did sign our names as attesting witnesses thereto, and we do severally hereby certify that, at the time of the occurrences aforesaid, we, and each of us, were acquainted with the said Testator, and knew of our own knowledge that he was of sound and disposing mind, memory, and understanding, that he was under no coercion or restraint, and that he was in all respects fully competent to make a will.

AFFIDAVIT OF EXECUTION

State of New York)
County of New York)

In the County of New York, State of New York, on the 28 day of April, 1992, then and there personally appeared the within named Robert Tracy, Neil Boyd, and Jane P. Hermann, who being severally duly sworn depose and say that they witnessed the execution of the within Last Will and Testament of the within named Testator, Rudolf Nureyev, that said Testator subscribed said Last Will and Testament in their presence; that they thereafter subscribed the same as witnesses in the presence of said Testator and in the presence of each other and at the request of said Testator; that the said Testator at the time of the execution of said Last Will and Testament appeared to them of full age and of sound mind, memory and understanding not under any restraint or in any respect incompetent to make a will, could read, write and converse in the English language and was suffering from no defect of sight, hearing or speech, or from any other physical or mental impairment which would affect his capacity to make a valid will; that said Last Will and Testament was executed as a single, original instrument and was not executed in counterparts; that they make this affidavit at the request of said Testator; and that Barry L. Weinstein, an attorney-at-law admitted to practice in the State of Illinois, supervised the execution of said instrument in accordance with the statutory requirements of the Estates, Powers and Trusts Law.

The Presidents

All the Presidents' Ends

RICHARD NIXON
We Don't Have Dick to Kick Anymore
APRIL 22, 1994

CALVIN COOLIDGE
Short, and to the Point
JANUARY 5, 1933

FRANKLIN ROOSEVELT
Warm Springs Eternal
APRIL 12, 1945

HARRY TRUMAN
The Buck Stopped in Independence
DECEMBER 26, 1972

GEORGE WASHINGTON
Father of No One but our Country
DECEMBER 14, 1799

THOMAS JEFFERSON
Declaration of Dependents
JULY 4, 1826

JOHN F. KENNEDY
"Mindful of the Uncertainty of Life"
NOVEMBER 22, 1963

Richard Nixon

———

DATE AND PLACE OF BIRTH
January 9, 1913
Yorba Linda, California

DATE AND PLACE OF DEATH
April 22, 1994
New York Hospital
New York, New York

We Don't Have Dick to Kick Anymore

The 37th President of the United States and the only one ever to resign from office before his term was completed, Richard Milhous Nixon had a lengthy political career that took him from the bottom to the top back to the bottom again. Nixon's Will, which was signed about two months before he died, reflects the mind of a unusually calculating person. The unusual provisions of his Will also indicate that Nixon may have continued to harbor a grudge against the country that had elected him as its President in 1972 with one of the largest victory margins in presidential history, but then clamored for his resignation or impeachment in the Watergate wake two years later.

Most unusual about Nixon's Will was its direct citation of the case, _Richard Nixon v. United States of America._ On the first page of his Will under "Article One", Nixon makes a bequest to "**THE RICHARD NIXON LIBRARY AND BIRTHPLACE** (hereinafter sometimes referred to as the "Library") of an amount of money that equals

(i) the amount due or paid to me and/or my estate under the judgment entered following the decision of the United States Court of Appeals for the District of Columbia Circuit in the case of <u>Richard Nixon v. United States of America</u>, decided on November 17, 1992, and/or concurrent or subsequent proceedings relating or pertaining thereto, and any related or subsequent case, provided that any such amounts paid during my life shall only be included as adjusted proceeds to the extent such amounts as of the date of my death are held or invested in a segregated and traceable account or accounts over

(ii) the sum of (a) the amount of all attorneys' fees and other costs or expenses, whether previously paid or unpaid, associated with or incurred in connection with such proceedings or any case similar to or relating thereto and all other attorneys' fees from 1974 on, which my estate or I have paid or which are outstanding, excluding, however, any attorneys' fees paid to the firm of which William E. Griffin has been a member, and (b) One Million Four Hundred Fifty Thousand Dollars, the amount equal to my contribution to the Library made in 1992. The amounts under (a) and (b) of this subparagraph (ii) shall be part of my residuary estate. It is my intention, by this bequest, to make a charitable gift of any "windfall" received under the lawsuits referred to above, and to first make my family whole by recovering all of the legal expenses I have incurred or my estate is to incur because of these and other lawsuits.

Once a lawyer, always a lawyer. Once a politician, always a politician. A person who is both a lawyer and a politician should be watched carefully. In fairness to former President Nixon, the litigation involving his presidential papers was ground-breaking and the Court ultimately held that the Presidential Recordings and Materials Preservation Act, passed by Congress in 1974, severely restricted Nixon's rights to his presidential papers and, therefore, constituted a *per se* taking of his property under the Takings Clause of the Fifth Amendment. In its decision the Court found that "the Constitution requires compensation even where the conversion of private property is based on a weighty public issue."

Perhaps in order to avoid any other "takings", in his Will Nixon carefully directs the disposition of his personal property. There is a bequest to the Library of all his tangible personal property relating to his or his late wife Pat's official or personal life, excluding Nixon's "personal diaries." Those private diaries are expressly bequeathed to Nixon's two daughters, Julie Nixon Eisenhower and Patricia Nixon Cox, if they survived him. Those diaries must have had some personally revealing entries because Nixon's Will expressly provided:

"If neither of my daughters survives me, I direct my executors to collect and destroy my 'personal diaries.' Notwithstanding any other provisions of this Will, if neither of my daughters survives me, the property constituting my 'personal diaries' shall be subject to the following restrictions: At no time shall my executors be allowed to make public, publish, sell, or make available to any individual other than my executor (or except as required for Federal tax purposes) the contents or any part or all of my 'personal diaries' and,

provided further, that my executors shall, within one
year from the date of my death or, if reasonably necessary, upon the later receipt of a closing estate tax
letter from the Internal Revenue Service, destroy all
of my 'personal diaries.'

Just so there is no mistaking what Nixon's "personal
diaries" included, his Will defines the terms broadly as
follows:

"My 'personal diaries' shall be defined as any notes,
tapes, transcribed notes, folders, binders, or books labeled as Richard Nixon's Diaries, Diary Notes, or labeled just by dates, that may contain my daily, weekly
or monthly activities, thoughts or plans. The determination of my executors as to what property is included in this bequest shall be conclusive and binding
upon all parties interested in my estate; however, it is
my wish that my executors consult with my surviving
daughters and/or my office staff in making this determination."

In view of the infamous Watergate tapes, it is interesting that Nixon defines "personal diaries" to include
"tapes."

Each of daughters Julie and Patricia, commonly referred to as "Tricia", are given the right to pick from father Dick's "awards, plaques, works of art of all kinds,
medals, membership or achievement certificates, commemorative stamps and coins, religious items, commemorative and personal photographs and all
correspondence, documents, notes memoranda, letters
and all other writings that I own at my death," "pro-

vided that under no circumstances shall the amount of such property taken by my daughters exceed in value three (3%) of the total value of all such property . . ." We have to wonder where in the world tricky Dick came up with the one and one-half percent (1.5%) limitation for each of his daughters.

All other tangible personal property, other than the items mentioned above, was bequeathed in equal shares to Nixon's two daughters, Julie and Tricia.

Although he was disbarred as an attorney, Nixon's Will specifically directs his executors to continue any pending lawsuit or lawsuits regarding the ownership of his tangible personal property "for as long as they, in their discretion, deem it appropriate to do so, knowing my wishes in this matter."

Nixon's Will also includes the following disproportionate bequests to his three grandchildren:

(A) $70,000 to his granddaughter, Melanie Eisenhower.

(B) $30,000 to his grandson, Alexander Richard Eisenhower.

(C) $10,000 to his grandson, Christopher Cox.

The consummate politician to the end, Nixon explains why the bequests are disproportionate as follows:

"The specific bequests to my grandchildren named above are made to equalize the gifts made to all of my grandchildren during my life. The disparity in amounts, or lack of a bequest, is not intended and should not be interpreted as a sign of favoritism for one grandchild over another."

From his "residuary estate", Nixon's Will provides for an additional fifty thousand dollars ($50,000) bequest to each of his surviving three grandchildren, and the balance of his residuary estate was given "to my issue, per stirpes." We all know that Nixon had many issues during his lifetime, but he was survived by his two daughters, and they shared his estate equally. If Nixon had died with no issue, which does not seem possible, his residuary estate was directed to pass to his beloved Library, for which no public funding was provided.

As the co-Executors of his Will, Nixon named "my friends, WILLIAM E. GRIFFIN and JOHN H. TAYLOR." Because his friend Mr. Griffin was also an attorney, attorney Nixon provided, "The appointment of my attorney, WILLIAM E. GRIFFIN, as a co-executor is made with my knowledge and approval of his receipt of commissions as provided by law, and his law firm's receipt of compensation for legal services rendered to my estate." It is noteworthy that attorney Griffin was also one of the three witnesses to Nixon's Will. Although either or both of his daughters could have acted as Executors of his Will, Nixon named two trusted friends instead. Nixon's former Vice President, Spiro Agnew, who also resigned from office, was not available.

Perhaps the most indefatigable politician of our times, Richard Nixon was ultimately undone by a "third rate burglary" of the Democratic headquarters into a much larger scandal known simply as "Watergate". His legacy of great foreign policy initiatives and successes will survive him, and the Nixon Library located in the town of his birth which figures so prominently in his Will represents the monument to himself that America would never build.

/s/ *Richard M. Nixon*

Will signed on dated February 24, 1994
Will signed at Woodcliff Lake, New Jersey

Calvin Coolidge

DATE AND PLACE OF BIRTH

July 4, 1872

Plymouth, Vermont

DATE AND PLACE OF DEATH

January 5, 1933

Northampton, Massachusetts

Short, and to the Point

Known for his taciturn nature and brevity, Calvin Coolidge had a one-line Will, which is the shortest of any of the presidents', or almost anyone else's. And Coolidge was trained as a lawyer besides!

When he died in 1933, John Calvin Coolidge (as he was named at birth) was survived by his wife, Grace Goodhue Coolidge, and his son, John. As his Will, which he signed in the White House in the middle of his first full term, states:

> Not unmindful of my son John, I give all my estate both real and personal to my wife Grace Coolidge, in fee simple—Home at Washington, District of Columbia this twentieth day of December, A.D. nineteen hundred and twenty six.

By expressly mentioning son John in his Will, Coolidge evidenced that he did not forget to include his son, but purposely intended to leave his entire estate to his wife. We can only speculate as to why Coolidge deliberately disinherited John. Mrs. Coolidge lived until July 8, 1957.

Also known for being thrifty, Coolidge died with an estate reportedly worth more than \$500,000, which was in part derived from his \$75,000 annual salary as president.

/s/ Calvin Coolidge

Will dated December 20, 1926
Will signed at the White House, Washington, D.C.

Franklin D. Roosevelt

DATE AND PLACE OF BIRTH
January 30, 1882
Hyde Park, New York

DATE AND PLACE OF DEATH
April 12, 1945
"Little White House"
Warm Springs, Georgia

Warm Springs Eternal

When he died during his unprecedented fourth term as president of the United States, Franklin Roosevelt was survived by five adult children and his wife, Eleanor Roosevelt. Eleanor Roosevelt survived her husband by another seventeen years, dying in 1962.

Roosevelt's Will makes meticulous provisions for the disposition of his tangible personal property among his wife and descendants. For example, there is the following provision pertaining to Eleanor's use of certain tangible property:

> If my wife, ANNA ELEANOR ROOSEVELT shall survive me, I direct that she shall have the right to use during her lifetime, at such place or places as she may wish, all or any part of the jewelry, books, paintings, pictures, works of art, statuary, silver, plate, china, glass, ornaments, rugs, tapestry, automobiles and boats and their equipment, household furniture and equipment and other tangible personal property of a similar kind of nature which I may own at the time of my death and wherever located, except such personal property bequeathed to Georgia Warm Springs Foundation under

Article FIFTH of this Will; PROVIDED, HOWEVER, that my said wife shall select the articles of personal property to be used by her as aforesaid and shall notify my Executors in writing of the articles so selected by her within six (6) months after my death. Upon the receipt of such written notification by my Executors, my said wife may take possession of the articles of personal property so selected by her.

The Will provides lengthy and detailed mechanisms for the selection of various articles of tangible personal property by other Roosevelt family members after Eleanor's death.

The natural mineral springs and property located in Warm Springs, Georgia, were used by Roosevelt to give him some relief from his affliction by the crippling disease polio. In 1927, Roosevelt had incorporated the Georgia Warm Springs Foundation as a not-for-profit medical and healing foundation. Under his Will, Roosevelt devised and bequeathed to the Georgia Warm Springs Foundation all of the real estate, buildings, and personal property owned by him in Meriwether County, Georgia.

The bulk of Roosevelt's substantial estate was directed to be held in trust for the benefit of his wife, Eleanor, and to a lesser degree for the benefit of his secretary, Marguerite A. Le Hand. Roosevelt's son James and two attorneys were named as the executors and trustees of his Will.

The Will directs that Roosevelt's executors "erect a simple stone over the grave of my wife and myself to be located in the garden of my property in the Town of Hyde Park, County of Dutchess and State of New York." Furthermore, Roosevelt made a $5,000 bequest to the rector, wardens, and vestry of St. James Church in Hyde Park "to be added to the Cemetery Fund and used for the upkeep of the Roosevelt family burial lots, the grave of my wife and myself, and for general cemetery upkeep purposes."

Finally, as is appropriate for the man who introduced the New Deal to America, Roosevelt provides the following bequests:

> I give and bequeath to each of the persons who are my employees or servants at the time of my death and whose salaries or wages are at that time being paid by me personally the sum of One Hundred Dollars ($100.00).

It is important that the Will limited payment to employees whose salaries were personally paid by Roosevelt; otherwise, all United States government workers might have asserted claims as $100 beneficiaries of their deceased leader's estate.

/s/ *Franklin D. Roosevelt*

Will dated November 12, 1941

Harry Truman

DATE AND PLACE OF BIRTH
May 8, 1884
Lamar, Missouri

DATE AND PLACE OF DEATH
December 26, 1972
Independence, Missouri

The Buck Stopped in Independence

When he died at the age of eighty-eight, Harry Truman was survived by his wife, Elizabeth "Bess" Truman, who was then eighty-seven years old, his daughter, Margaret, and four grandsons. Harry Truman was also survived by his eighty-three-year-old unmarried sister, Miss Mary Jane Truman, who was a patient in the same hospital as her brother on the night he died.

During his life and in his Will, Truman showed an extraordinary concern with the disposition of his presidential papers and other historical materials. His Will and subsequent codicils indicate Truman's obsession with this issue, as shown by the following brief excerpts from Truman's unusually verbose Will:

> I have from time to time during my life given and transferred to the United States of America all of my right, title and interest in, and the possession of, certain papers, historical materials and other property, to be kept in the Harry S. Truman Library in Independence, Missouri, on certain conditions enumerated in correspon-

dence between me and the Administrator of General Services of the United States and the Archivist of the United States.

II. All of my remaining historical materials, which shall, for the purposes of this Will, include all cartoons, books, portraits, statues, objets d'art, models, pictures and miscellaneous objects or materials having historical or commemorative values, other than those thereof (a) which shall be located at the time of my death in my private residence in Independence, Missouri or in any other private residence which I or my daughter may have at such time, or (b) which shall contain a label or other indication showing a reservation of title in me, or (c) which shall be determined by my Executors in their sole and absolute discretion to be related in whole or in part of the business or personal affairs of myself or any of the members of my family.

In deference to his wife and daughter, Truman also made the following bequests:

I bequeath all of my papers and historical materials not bequeathed to the United States of America pursuant to the provisions of part B of Article THIRD hereof (a) to my wife and daughter, in equal shares.

TENTH: If my wife shall survive me, and if any (or all) of my daughter and her issue shall also survive me, I devise and bequeath to my wife one-half of the Balance of my Remaining Estate. I direct that said one-half of the Balance of my Remaining Estate shall include the following property:

A. All of my jewelry, clothing and personal effects.

B. Any automobiles which I shall own at the time of my death.

C. All of the household furniture, furnishings and equipment, rugs, silverware, plated ware, china, glassware, linens, books, paintings, pictures and objets d'art which I shall own at the time of my death, other than the property referred to in part B of Article THIRD hereof and in Article SIXTH hereof.

D. All farm machinery and equipment, <u>gardeners', mechanics' and other tools and domestic animals which I shall own at the time of my death.</u> [emphasis added]

Truman also remembered his local lodge mates with the following devise of real property that he owned:

I devise to Grandview Lodge No. 618, A.F. & A.M., as a site for a Lodge Hall, the southerly one hundred and ten feet of Lots 9 and 10 in Sheltons Addition to Grandview, Missouri.

A number of Bess and Harry Truman's nieces and nephews received bequests of amounts ranging from $5 to $1,000 under Truman's Will:

In addition to the specific bequests made by me in my Will and as above made to the nephews and nieces of myself and Mrs. Bess Wallace Truman, I give and devise to the following greatnephews and greatnieces of myself and my wife the sum of Five Hundred Dollars ($500.00) to each, except to John Ross Truman, I give the sum of Five Dollars ($5.00). They are as follows:

Children of John Curtis Truman:

John Ross Truman	$5.00
Mary Martha Truman	500.00
Rita Marie Truman	500.00
Loretta Ann Truman	500.00
Gilbert Higbee Truman	500.00
Jean Ellen Truman	500.00

It might appear that Truman's grandnephew, John Ross Truman, was disliked by the late president because he receives only a minimal $5 bequest rather than the $500 bequests received by his siblings. It has been reported that this small bequest was attributable to the fact that John Ross Truman was planning to become a Catholic priest in an order that necessitated a vow of poverty. Apparently, practical and thrifty testator Truman determined that it would be pointless to give that particular grandnephew a gift that he would not be able to enjoy directly, but nonetheless remembers him in his Will with a token amount.

Truman's Will also provides the following detailed instructions regarding his burial, gravesite, the "slab over the graves" and the suggested obelisk:

It is my will and desire, and I direct that my Executrix or Executor arrange and cause my remains to be laid to rest in the center of the plaza South of my office on the premises of THE HARRY S. TRUMAN LIBRARY, in Independence, Missouri. . . . If it is desired that an obelisk should be put at the head of the graves, and the Executrix or Executor shall so decide. It is my desire that a slab be placed over the graves, whether the obelisk is set up or not.

I would suggest that the slab over the graves, which will lie flat, have the following inscriptions:

HARRY S. TRUMAN
Born May 8, 1884
Lamar, Missouri
Married June 28, 1919
Daughter Born February 17, 1924
County Judge Eastern District
Jackson County
January 1, 1925
Presiding Judge, Jackson County
January 1, 1927–January 1, 1935
United States Senator, Missouri
January 3, 1935–January 12, 1945
Vice-President, United States
January 20, to April 12, 1945
President, United States
April 12, 1945–January 20, 1953

Truman's lengthy Will is unusual in including the text of suggested epitaphs for himself and his wife. Pursuant to his wishes, Truman's funeral was privately held in his hometown of Independence, Missouri, and he was buried on the grounds of his beloved Harry S. Truman Library. Harry's buck finally stopped in Independence, Missouri.

/s/ *Harry S. Truman*

Will dated January 14, 1959
First Codicil dated October 23, 1961
Second Codicil dated November 4, 1967

George Washington

DATE AND PLACE OF BIRTH
February 22, 1732
Pope's Creek, Virginia

DATE AND PLACE OF DEATH
December 14, 1799
Mount Vernon, Virginia

Father of No One but Our Country

When he died in 1799, George Washington was reported to be one of the wealthiest men in the young nation. He owned more than 33,000 acres of land, including over 23,000 in Virginia, 5,000 in Kentucky, and large tracts in Maryland, New York, and the Northwest Territory. He owned coporate stocks worth over $25,000, and his livestock consisted of 640 sheep, 329 cows, horses, and mules.

Washington also owned hundreds of slaves. In the second item of his Will Washington reveals his personal thoughts on the slavery question. The Will states:

> Upon the decease of my wife, it is my Will & desire that all Slaves which I hold in <u>my own right</u>, shall receive their freedom. . . . And whereas among those who will receive freedom according to this devise, there may be some, who from old age or bodily infirmities, and others who on account of their infancy, that will be unable to support themselves; it is my Will and desire that all . . . shall be comfortably cloathed & fed by my heirs while

they live. . . . And I do expressly forbid the Sale, or trans-
portation out of the said Commonwealth of Virginia, of
any Slave I may die possessed of, under any pretence
whosoever. . . . And to my Mulatto man William (calling
himself William Lee) I give immediate freedom; or if he
should prefer it (on account of the accidents which have
befallen him, and which have rendered him incapable of
walking or of any active employment) to remain in the
situation he now is. . . . This I give him as a testimony of
my sense of his attachment to me, and for his faithful
services during the Revolutionary War.

At the age of twenty-seven, George Washington had
married Martha Dandridge Curtis, a wealthy Virginia
widow who had two children from her prior marriage.
Martha Washington outlived her husband, dying in 1802,
and she is his primary beneficiary under his Will. Under
item one of the Will he gives her a life interest in almost
his entire estate as well as outright gifts, including the
"liquors and groceries" that were on hand at the time of
his decease.

George Washington died without having any natural
children. Nonetheless he treated his nephews and nieces
and wife's prior children with paternal affection. Under
the third article of his Will Washington states:

And whereas it has always been my intention, since my
expectation of having issue has ceased, to consider the
Grand children of my wife in the same light as I do my
own relations . . . more especially by the two whom we
have reared from their earliest infancy . . . I give & bequeath . . . the residue of my Mount Vernon Estate, not
already devised to my Nephew Bushrod Washington.

In addition to Martha, George provided for many relatives and friends under his Will. He left his famous home, Mount Vernon, to his nephew Bushrod Washington. Other bequests include the following:

Item To my Nephew Bushrod Washington, I give and bequeath all the Papers in my possession, which relate to my Civel and Military Administration of the affairs of this Country;—I leave to him also, such of my private Papers as are worth preserving.

Item To my brother Charles Washington I give & bequeath the gold headed Cane left me by Doctr. Franklin in his Will.

. . . To General de la Fayette I give a pair of finely wrought steel Pistols, taken from the enemy in the Revolutionary War.

The bulk of Washington's land-rich estate was to be sold, with the proceeds to be divided among twenty-three friends and relatives. Washington named his ailing wife, Martha, and five male members of his family—William Augustine Washington, George Steptoe Washington, Samuel Washington, Lawrence Lewis, and the ubiquitous Bushrod—to be his executors. After naming his executors, Washington cautioned that "having endeavored to be plain, and explicit in all the Devises—even at the expense of prolixity, perhaps of tautology, I hope, and trust, that no disputes will arise concerning them." Despite this admonition Washington's Will provides a mechanism for any disputes to be arbitrated by three "impartial and intelligent men, known for their probity and good understanding."

Regarding the plans for his burial and funeral, Washington's Will states:

The family Vault at Mount Vernon requiring repairs, and being improperly situated besides, I desire that a new one of Brick, and upon a larger Scale may be built . . . And it is my express desire that my Corpse may be Interred in a private manner, without—parade, or funeral Oration.

Perhaps one secret to Washington's great leadership ability was his modesty and lack of ostentation.

Washington signed his Will in the summer before his death in 1799. The date he wrote at the end of the Will incorrectly omits the word *nine* and that explains the inconsistency with his final remark that the Will was being signed in the twenty-fourth year from the date of United States independence in 1776. Perhaps Washington was tired at the end of his illustrious and incomparable career, and after having written the thirty-page Will by hand.

/s/ *G. Washington*

Will dated July 9, 1790 [*sic*, "1799"]
Will signed at Mount Vernon, Virginia

Thomas Jefferson

DATE AND PLACE OF BIRTH
April 13, 1743
Shadwell, Virginia

DATE AND PLACE OF DEATH
July 4, 1826
Monticello, Virginia

Declaration of Dependents

When he died on the fiftieth anniversary of the signing of the Declaration of Independence, which he had drafted at the age of thirty-three, Thomas Jefferson was a debt-ridden man. Jefferson was known to have an extravagant lifestyle and to be quite generous with those who sought his assistance.

The following excerpts from the Will and codicil were signed only a few months before Jefferson's death at the age of eighty-three. Jefferson had been a widower for more than forty years. Only one of his six children survived him. At the time of this Will and codicil his immediate family was composed of one daughter, a bankrupt son-in-law, and grandchildren. Jefferson, who was trained as a lawyer, drafted a Will that provided his residuary estate be held in trust for the benefit of his daughter and descendants during the life of his son-in-law.

> Considering the insolvent state of the affairs of my friend & son in law Thomas Mann Randolph, and that what will remain of my property will be the only resource against the want in which his family would otherwise be left, it must be his wish, as it is my duty, to

guard that resource against all liability for his debts.
. . . I do hereby devise and bequeath all the residue of
my property . . . in trust . . . for the sole and separate
use of my dear daughter Martha Randolph and her
heirs . . . Jefferson was aware that the legal effect of
placing the property in trust would be to shield it from
his son-in-law's many creditors. However, this legal
protection was ultimately futile as Jefferson's own in-
solvent estate was subject to his creditors' claims.

In 1814, facing mounting debts, Jefferson was forced
to sell part of his incomparable library to Congress for
$23,950, and those books can be found in the Library of
Congress today. Jefferson's bequest of his remaining collection of books to the University of Virginia helped establish that institution as one of the premier learning
centers in the nation. Jefferson dispensed with a formal
inventory of his property for the following reasons: "In
consequence of the variety and undescribableness of the
articles of property within the house at Monticello, and
the difficulty of inventorying and appraising them sepa-
rately and specifically, and its inutility, I dispense with
having them inventoried and appraised . . ."

Jefferson appointed his grandson, Thomas Jefferson
Randolph, as executor of his Will. To his grandson Jefferson gave "my silver watch in preference to the golden
one, because of it's superior excellence, my papers of business going of course to him, as my executor, all others of
a literary or other character I give to him as of his own
property."

Perhaps most touching in Jefferson's Will is his gift of
his gold-mounted walking staff of animal horn to his
friend and successor president James Madison, as "token

of the cordial and affectionate friendship which for nearly now an half century has united us in the same principles and pursuits of what we have deemed for the greatest good of our country."

/s/ *Thomas Jefferson*

Will dated March 16, 1826
Codicil undated
Signed at Monticello in Albemarle County, Virginia

John F. Kennedy

DATE AND PLACE OF BIRTH
May 29, 1917
Brookline, Massachusetts

DATE AND PLACE OF DEATH
November 22, 1963
Dallas, Texas

"Mindful of the Uncertainty of Life"

In 1954, the year he signed his last Will and testament, thirty-seven-year-old John F. Kennedy was serving in his first term as a United States senator from Massachusetts. Six years later, the youngest U.S. president would be succeeding the oldest, and Kennedy would be moving his wife, Jacqueline, and young children, Caroline and John, Jr., into the White House. Unfortunately, the Kennedy family's stay in the White House would be short-lived as a result of the tragic assassination of JFK in November 1963. Ironically, the preamble to Kennedy's Will is archaic yet prophetic by his reference to being "mindful of the uncertainty of life."

Kennedy signed this Will before either of his children were born (or the infant death of a third child while in the White House) and certainly before any thought had been given to the disposition of "presidential papers." The Will established trust vehicles to provide primarily for his wife, Jackie, and for any future descendants. In addition, there is the following cash and specific bequest for Jackie:

I give and bequeath unto my wife, JACQUELINE B. KENNEDY, if she survives me, the sum of Twenty-Five Thousand ($25,000.00) Dollars, together with all of my personal effects, furniture, furnishings, silverware, dishes, china, glassware and linens, which I may own at the time of my death.

As president, Kennedy received an annual salary of $100,000, in addition to a $50,000 expense account. Furthermore, Kennedy was independently wealthy, being the beneficiary of a significant trust fund (reportedly generating annual income in excess of $500,000 per year) from the substantial estate of his father, Joseph P. Kennedy, with the fortune made through shrewd investments and allegedly from bootlegging during Prohibition.

Early in the Will there is a reference to the charitable foundation established in memory of Kennedy's predeceased brother, Joseph P. Kennedy, Jr., who had been young John's primary rival for family and political attention. The provision does not make any gift, but merely refers to prior gifts made. What a politician Kennedy was, even in his Will:

During my life, I have made substantial contributions to divers charities, causes and institutions of all faiths, both individually and through The Joseph P. Kennedy Jr. Foundation, which was established in honor of my late beloved brother. I am certain that the contributions which I and other members of my family have made to the Foundation will be applied after my death without bias or discrimination to the fulfillment of the Foundation's eleemosynary purposes.

Kennedy names his wife and brothers, Robert F. Kennedy and Edward M. Kennedy, to be the executors of his Will. If any of them were unable to serve as an executor, then the vacancy was to be filled by Kennedy's sisters, Eunice K. Shriver, Patricia Lawford, and Jean Kennedy, *in the order named* according to the Will.

It strikes one as unusual that Kennedy did not update his Will after becoming president and entering the White House. His failure to address presidential issues such as establishing archives for his presidential papers left this issue open for his family and various governmental entities to determine. Nonetheless, the Kennedy legacy has been great, as evidenced by monuments all over the world to the president who won America's heart.

/s/ *John F. Kennedy*

Will dated June 18, 1954
Will signed in Washington, D.C.

The Writers

Last Writes

CARLOS CASTANEDA
This Don Juan Will Not Return
APRIL 27, 1998

ALLEN GINSBERG
And the Beat Does Not Go On
APRIL 5, 1997

JAMES THURBER
"Talk of the Town"
NOVEMBER 2, 1961

AYN RAND
You Can't Take It With You
MARCH 6, 1982

MARK TWAIN
"The Reports of my death are greatly exaggerated"
APRIL 21, 1910

F. SCOTT FITZGERALD
The Other Side of Paradise
DECEMBER 21, 1940

THORNTON WILDER
Heaven's My Destination
DECEMBER 7, 1975

WILLIAM FAULKNER
As He Lay Dying
JULY 6, 1962

CARL SANDBURG
"Death comes once, let it be easy."
JULY 22, 1967

TENNESSEE WILLIAMS
Here Today, Iguana Tomorrow
FEBRUARY 25, 1983

JOHN STEINBECK
The Best Laid Plans of Mice and Men
DECEMBER 20, 1968

TRUMAN CAPOTE
Unfinished Prayers
AUGUST 25, 1984

LILLIAN HELLMAN
Banned in Boston, Dead in the Vineyard
JUNE 30, 1984

JAMES BEARD
Just Desserts
JANUARY 23, 1985

Carlos Castaneda

DATE AND PLACE OF BIRTH

December 25, 1923

Cajmarca, Peru

DATE AND PLACE OF DEATH

April 27, 1998

1672 Pandora Avenue

Los Angeles, California

This Don Juan Will Not Return

The Will of the high-flying metaphysical writer, Carlos Castaneda, was signed just four days before he died and is direct and to the point. There are no bequests of any of Castaneda's tangible personal property, perishable or not, to Don Juan or any other figments of Castaneda's vivid imagination or from his separate reality.

On page 1 of his Will, Castaneda states his marital and parental status in the blunt manner reproduced on the following pages.

Despite the fact that the name of Carlos Aranha Castaneda is listed as "father" on Carlton Jeremy Castaneda's birth certificate, it is generally accepted that Carlos was not Carlton's biological father. In her book entitled, *A Magical Journey with Carlos Castaneda*, Castaneda's former wife, Margaret Runyan Castaneda, writes, "I was certain the marriage would never work. We had been together just six month and already he was lost for the weekends on his field trips, unable or unwilling to talk about exactly what he was doing. Having met a slender blond businessman named Adrian Gerritsen, I pressed Carlos for a divorce. . . . A couple of years later, Carlos hit me with the news: we weren't really divorced after all. . . . Sitting there with me, Carlos explained that we were still legally married and, furthermore, claimed the boy as his own. . . . It was weeks before I grasped it and months before the three of us—Carlos and Adrian Gerristen and I—reached any kind of understanding of the situation." Thus, Margaret Castaneda confirms her former husband's non-paternity of "C.J.", and if anyone should know, she would. Although Castaneda "once treated him as if he were my son", the Will makes no provision whatsoever for the son of Castaneda's former wife, known both as "C.J. Castaneda" and Adrian Vashon. Tough love, indeed. No wonder that C.J. commenced a lawsuit against his purported father's estate. He had nothing more to lose.

Pursuant to his Will, Castaneda's entire estate passed to an entity called "The Eagle's Trust" which was created on the same day that he signed his Will. It appears that after his death Carlos wanted certain people to fly high on the wings of an "Eagle" of his own creation.

Although the terms of the Eagle's Trust are not known, it is public information that the Eagle's Trust had numerous beneficiaries, including Castaneda's adopted daughter, Nuri Alexander. In all, there are twenty listed beneficiaries of The Eagle's Trust, including six people who listed Castaneda's home at 1672 Pandora Avenue as their legal address. Why does it seem so right for Carlos Castaneda to have lived and died on a street named "Pandora". In any case, Castaneda's box could probably hold its own against Pandora's. Several beneficiaries of The Eagle's Trust are listed in the probate papers as "Toltec Artists" and many of them lived together at two other houses in Los Angeles. With all those mouths to feed, we can only hope that Castaneda's copyright and royalty income are flowing through the Eagle's Trust to its passengers.

As the Executor of his Will, Castaneda named his attorney, Deborah Drooz. If Ms. Drooz did not act, which she has, the Will provided that the successor Executor would be a Toltec Artist named Julius Renard, or if he did not act then another Toltec Artist named Fabricio Magaldi was designated to lead the bandwagon left behind by one of the most colorful and controversial writers of the late twentieth century.

/s/ *Carlos Castaneda*

Will dated April 23, 1998
Will signed in Los Angeles, California

LAST WILL AND TESTAMENT
OF
CARLOS CASTANEDA

I, CARLOS CASTANEDA, a resident of the County of Los Angeles, State of California, make, publish and declare this to be my Last Will and Testament, and do hereby revoke all prior Will and Codicils to Wills made by me. I direct my Executor to pay my funeral expenses, the expenses of my last illness and the expenses of administering my estate.

ARTICLE I

I am not currently married. I was previously married to MARGARET RUNYON CASTANEDA, which marriage was terminated by dissolution. Although I once treated him as if he were my son, ADRIAN VASHON, also known as C.J. CASTANEDA, is not my son, natural or adopted. I have legally adopted NURI ALEXANDER as my daughter. I have no other issue.

ARTICLE II

I give, devise and bequeath all my property and estate of every kind and nature and wherever situated, both real and personal, to the Trustee of THE EAGLE'S TRUST (the "Trust"), established pursuant to that certain Declaration of Trust executed on the date on which this Will is executed, by me as Trustor and Deborah Drooz as Trustee, to be added to and become a part of the corpus of the trust estate thereunder and to be held, administered, and distributed according to the terms and provisions thereof, including any amendments thereto made prior to the date of my death. To the extent permitted by law, it is not my intent to create a separate trust by this Will or to subject the Trust or the property added to it by this Will to the jurisdiction of the probate court.

If the foregoing disposition to the said Trustee under the Trust is not operative or is invalid for any reason, or if the Trust fails or has been revoked, then I hereby incorporate by this reference the terms of the Trust executed on this date, without giving effect to any amendments made subsequently, and I give my said property and estate to the Trustee named therein, to be held, administered and distributed as provided in this instrument after incorporating herein the terms of the Trust.

ARTICLE III

The Trust provides for the payment from a portion of the assets held thereunder of all taxes incurred or payable by reason of my death, whether or not such taxes are attributable to assets held in that portion of the Trust, or to other assets subject to tax upon my death. If and to the extent that the assets held under the Trust and available for the payment of such taxes shall be insufficient therefor, I direct that all estate, inheritance and succession taxes imposed by the federal government or by any country, state, district or territory and occasioned and payable by reason of my death, whether or not attributable to property subject to probate administration, shall be chargeable to and paid out of the residue of my estate provided for under the terms of Article II, above, without apportionment, deduction or reimbursement therefor, and without adjustment thereof among any of the beneficiaries of my estate.

ARTICLE IV

Except as otherwise provided in this Will, I have intentionally and with full knowledge omitted to provide for my heirs.

ARTICLE V

If any devisee, legatee or beneficiary named in this Will, or any person who would be entitled to share in my estate through intestate succession, shall in any manner whatsoever, either directly or indirectly, oppose, contest, or attack this Will or the distribution of my estate hereunder, or seek to impair, invalidate or set aside any of the provisions of this Will, or shall aid in doing any of the above acts, then in that event I specifically disinherit each such person and all legacies, bequests, devises and interests passing under this Will to that person shall lapse and be forfeited and shall be disposed of as if such person (together with anyone claiming through such person under any anti-lapse law) had predeceased me.

ARTICLE VI

If any provision of this Will is unenforceable, the remaining provisions shall nevertheless be carried into effect.

ARTICLE VII

I nominate and appoint DEBORAH DROOZ as Executor of this Will, and if she is unable or unwilling to serve as Executor, then I nominate and appoint JULIUS RENARD to serve as Executor in her stead and if he is unwilling or unable to serve, then I nominate and appoint FABRICIO MAGALDI to serve as Executor. No bond shall be required of my Executor.

My Executor shall have full power and authority to sell any property of my estate at public or private sale, with or without notice; to lease, exchange, or encumber the whole or any part of my estate, with or without notice; to own and manage any property and to operate any business belonging to my estate, at the risk of my estate and not at the risk of my Executor, the profits and losses therefrom to inure to and to be chargeable to my estate as a whole; to invest and reinvest surplus monies of my estate in such types of investments, both real and personal, as said Executor in his, her or their discretion may select, including corporate obligations of every kind, preferred or common stocks, common trust funds, improved or unimproved real properties, interests in joint ventures and partnerships and interests in ownership and/or operation of a business. I further authorize my Executor to administer my estate with full authority pursuant to the Independent Administration of Estates Act, as amended from time to time.

My Executor shall be empowered to retain professional financial counsel and to charge the expense of such counsel to my estate as a whole.

IN WITNESS WHEREOF, I have hereunto subscribed my name this 23rd day of April, 1998, at Los Angeles, California.

/s/ Carlos Castaneda
_____

CARLOS CASTANEDA

On the date written above, CARLOS CASTANEDA declared to us, the undersigned, that this instrument, consisting of six (6) pages, including the page signed by us as witnesses, was his Will and requested us to act as witnesses to it. He thereupon signed this Will in our presence, all of us being present at the same time.

At this time, CARLOS CASTANEDA is over eighteen (18) years of age and appears to be of sound mind. We have no knowledge of any facts indicating that this instrument, or any part of it, was procured by duress, menace, fraud, or undue influence. Each of us is now over eighteen (18) years of age. We now, in his presence and in the presence of each other, subscribe our names as witnesses.

EXECUTED on April 23, 1998, at Los Angeles, California.

We declare under penalty of perjury under the laws of the State of California that the foregoing is true and correct.

Allen Ginsberg

DATE AND PLACE OF BIRTH
June 3, 1926
Newark, New Jersey

DATE AND PLACE OF DEATH
April 5, 1997
405 East 13th Street
New York, New York

And the Beat Does Not Go On

The last surviving voice of the generation of writers labeled "Beat", Allen Ginsberg died in his apartment in the East Village of New York City at the age of 70. Among his intimate friends he counted such cultural icons and writers as Jack Kerouac, Neal Cassady, Herbert Huncke, William S. Burroughs, William Carlos Williams, and Philip Glass. After all, how many people could count on Philip Glass and William S. Burroughs to act as witnesses to his Will or Codicil, as Allen Ginsberg did.

Most interesting about Ginsberg's Will is its thoughtful attention to the specific directions surrounding "my funeral and disposition of my physical body. . . ." Ginsberg was a devoted Buddhist and the following reproduction of the specific directions on the first page of his Will, edited by him at the time he was signing his Will, illustrates his concerns despite the involvement of "the Office of Three Yana Studies of the Vajradhatu Buddhist Church":

ARTICLE III

Upon my death I direct my Executors shall arrange for my funeral and disposition of my physical body in accordance with the rites, practices, and teachings of the

Buddhist religion, as were taught and practiced by the Venerable Chogyam Trungpa, Rinpoche who was my spiritual friend and teacher, and by the Vajradhatu Buddhist Church and Association of Buddhist Churches with its headquarters in Halifax, Nova Scotia.

I direct my Executors to select an ordained Buddhist clergyman ~~of the Vajradhatu Buddhist Church~~ to conduct my funeral and arrange for the disposition of my physical body. If helpful to my Executors, the selection of the clergyman may be made with the assistance of the Office of Three Yana Studies of the Vajradhatu Buddhist Church, and my good friend Gelek Rinrocke.

I direct that if local laws allow, my physical body not to be embalmed upon my death.

My direction under this Article is one of the strongest possible nature and shall be observed under all circumstances.

As the Executors of his Will, Ginsberg named his long-time secretary, confidante and friend, Bob Rosenthal, and his literary agent, Andrew Wylie. Always one to recognize the talents of others, Ginsberg requests in his Will that his Executors "call upon the following persons to assist and advise them in the area in which they are experts: Gordon Ball, Bill Morgan, Raymond Foye, Barry Miles, Ira Lowe, Harvey Silvergate." The Will provides further that "those persons assisting and advising my Executors shall be paid a reasonable fee for their services." That direction is not surprising for a man whose mother was a Marxist. In his generosity and equanimity, Ginsberg also nominates and appoints "Ira M. Lowe with the law firm of Lowe & Mahon to act as attorney for my estate." Despite his good intentions, and his attorney's foresight, such an appointment is not legally binding or even effective, in most states. The Executors are allowed to select the attorney they want to assist them, or get them out of trouble, if necessary. Despite Mr. Ginsberg's expressed preference Mr. Lowe did not in fact file the probate papers on behalf of the Executors of the Will of Allen Ginsberg.

Although Allen Ginsberg achieved international fame as a writer, prophet, poet, "social bandit", Guru, philosopher, and cultural icon, he does not appear to have died a wealthy man. The probate papers filed with the Court show a "gross testamentary estate" of less than $20,000. That small value might also be explained by the existence of a trust established by Ginsberg prior to his death. The value of that trust is not in the public record, but it is known that Ginsberg transferred the following assets to the trust when it was established:

1. All my cash, bank and investment accounts, whether checking, savings, retirement, etc. and any other sources of funds or similar monetary interests of any kind and in any location owned by me.

2. All my personal effects, works of art, personal property, household goods, appurtenances, and the like;

3. All monies, notes, bonds and other obligations and interests which are due me;

4. All my interest in the San Juan Association and its property on San Juan Ridge;

5. All my poetic, artistic and literary creations and all of my interest in poetic, artistic and literary works created jointly with others;

6. All my archival materials, whether created by me or which have been given to me by others;

7. All my statutory and common law copyrights, copyright renewals, publicity rights, and similar rights and interests owned by me, and all royalties, income and entitlements therefrom; and

8. All other property, rights or interests of any kind which I now own and which are not specifically enumerated above.

The Allen Ginsberg Living Trust had numerous beneficiaries including several nieces and nephews and friends, including a blast from Ginsberg's past, the convicted killer Lucien Carr, Peter Hale, and his long-time companion Peter Orlovsky.

By an amendment to that trust September 12, 1996, Ginsberg again displays his generosity, thoughtfulness, and community spirit by directing that:

The condominium unit at 404E. 14th St. a/k/a 405 E. 13th St. in the city and county of New York, state of New York, described as unit 5N titled in the name of Allen Ginsberg, Trustee of the Allen Ginsberg Trust dated July 20, 1991; upon my demise, I give, devise and bequeath to Bob Rosenthal with a life estate in Peter Orlovsky to live in and enjoy the premises with a provision that Andrew Wylie shall determine, with the advice of physicians and social workers, his competency to reside there.

It is my wish that Bob Rosenthal shall make usage of the premises for my estate's continuing business activities and for the perpetuation of what he knows to be my interests and concerns.

Although his Certificate of Death listed his "usual occupation" as "Poet", Allen Ginsberg was an integral part of the Beat which would allow a new generation of literary social activists to reinvent America's consciousness of itself.

In the end, the Guru of the Beatniks died without a howl as he took his own advice, "Don't Grow Old", and succumbed to cancer at the last gasp of middle age. The poet himself said it best with this excerpt from his 1959 poem "Kaddish".

"And how Death is that remedy all
singers dream of, sing,
remember, prophesy as in the
Hebrew Anthem, or the
Buddhist Book of Answers—
and my own imagination of a
withered leaf-at dawn-
Dreaming back thru life, Your time
—and mine accelerating
toward Apocalypse,
the final moment"

/s/ *Allen Ginsberg*

Will dated July 20, 1991
First Codicil dated July 26, 1991

LAST WILL AND TESTAMENT
OF
ALLEN GINSBERG

I, Allen Ginsberg, domiciled and residing in the City, County, and State of New York, do make, publish and declare this to be my Will and Testament, hereby revoking all Wills and Codicils heretofore made by me.

ARTICLE I

I direct that all my enforceable debts, funeral, and administration expenses be paid, as soon as may be practicable, from my general estate, without apportionment. Notwithstanding the foregoing, any such debt which is secured by a mortgage, lien or similar encumbrance on any property which is owned by me shall be charged on the property encumbered.

ARTICLE II

I direct that all inheritance, estate and other taxes (including any interest and penalties thereon) imposed by any jurisdiction whatsoever with respect to any property includible in my estate for the purposes of any such taxes, or upon or with respect to any person receiving any such property, whether such property shall pass under or shall have passed outside the provisions of this Will, be paid out of the residue of my estate as an expense of the administration thereof without apportionment.

ARTICLE III

Upon my death I direct my Executors shall arrange for my funeral and disposition of my physical body in accordance with the rites, practices, and teachings of the Buddhist religion, as were taught and practiced by the Venerable Chogyam Trungpa, Rinpoche who was my spiritual friend and teacher, and by the Vajradhatu Buddhist Church and Association of Buddhist Churches with its headquarters in Halifax, Nova Scotia.

I direct my Executors to select an ordained Buddhist clergyman ~~of the Vajradhatu Buddhist Church~~ to conduct my funeral and arrange for the disposition of my physical body. If helpful to my Executors, the selection of the clergyman may be made with the assistance of the Office of Three Yana Studies of the Vajradhatu Buddhist Church, and my good friend Gelek Rinpoche.

I direct that if local laws allow, my physical body not to be embalmed upon my death.

My direction under this Article is one of the strongest possible nature and shall be observed under all circumstances.

ARTICLE IV

I give, devise and bequeath my entire estate, both personal and real, of whatsoever kind and wheresoever situated, to those Successor Trustees under the Trust Agreement executed by me on July 20, 1991.

This gift, devise and bequest is to be added to the property then held in that Trust and shall become part of the corpus thereof. It is to be held in accordance with the terms and conditions of that Trust as now written and as hereafter amended, and to that end, I direct this gift, devise and bequest to be interpreted by reference to that Trust instrument.

If for any reason that Trust is not in full force and effect at the time of my death, or if this gift, devise and bequest to the Successor Trustees of that Trust is held invalid, then I direct that this gift, devise and bequest shall be held and managed in exactly the manner described in the instrument of Trust as now written and as hereafter amended, and by the same Successor

Trustees, and for that purpose only. I hereby incorporate that Trust Agreement by reference to this my Last Will and Testament.

ARTICLE V

I nominate and appoint Bob Rosenthal and Andrew Wylie, or the survivor, as co-Executors of this my Last Will and Testament with the request that they call upon the following persons to assist and advise them in the area in which they are experts:

Gordon Ball

Bill Morgan

Raymond Foye

Barry Miles

Ira Lowe

Harvey Silverglate

Those persons assisting and advising my Executors shall be paid a reasonable fee for their services.

I nominate and appoint Ira M. Lowe with the law firm Lowe & Mahon to act as attorney for my estate.

If it becomes necessary to have ancillary administration of my estate in any jurisdiction where my Executors are unable to act as ancillary legal representatives, I appoint as such ancillary legal representative such individual as my Executors shall designate, in writing. I direct that any balance of my property remaining after such ancillary administration be delivered, to the extent permitted by law, to my Executors for disposition in accordance with the terms of this Will. I direct that all of the powers and discretion granted to my Executors hereunder shall also apply to any such ancillary legal representative.

I direct that no bond or other security shall be required of any Executor or ancillary legal representative hereunder, in any jurisdiction where any of them may qualify or act.

ARTICLE VI

My Executors are authorized and empowered to exercise from time to time in their discretion and without prior judicial authority all powers conferred upon them by law and all powers granted to them in this Will, including, but not limited to, those listed below (all powers including the following to be construed in the broadest possible manner):

A. To sell any estate property at either public or private sale, through brokers, dealers, agents or otherwise, for cash or on credit of any duration, to exchange any such property and to grant options for the purchases of any such property.

B. To invest and reinvest in property of any character, real or personal, foreign or domestic, including, without limitation, bonds, notes, debentures, mortgages, certificates of deposit, common and preferred stocks, shares or interest in investment trusts and participations in common Trust funds, without regard to the proportion which such property or property of a similar character, so held, may bear to the entire amount of my estate, whether or not such property is of the class in which Executors are authorized by law or any rule of court to invest estate and Trust funds.

[sic] individually, or others, upon such terms, with or without security, as they in their discretion may determine and to pledge or mortgage any such property as security.

D. To appoint and compensate agents to act on their behalf and to delegate to such agents discretionary powers.

E. To extend the time of payment of any obligation at any time owing by or to him or my estate and to compromise, settle or submit to arbitration upon such terms as they may deem advisable, or to release, with or without consideration, any claim in favor of or against my estate.

F. In satisfying any general legacy or in deviding or distributing my estate under this Will, or any part thereof, to make partition, division or distribution of property in kind and, for any such purpose, to determine the value of any such property so far as permitted by law.

G. To employ accountants, brokers, investment advisors, banks, trust companies, fiduciaries, agents, experts in the field of art, appraisers, and any other persons, whenever deemed expedient, and to determine and to pay to them reasonable compensation.

H. To obtain or effect fire, title, liability, casualty, rent, or any other insurance coverage of such nature and in such forms and amounts, if any, as may be determined.

I. To select any valuation date permitted by the applicable law for estate tax purposes; and to elect as permitted by law whether to claim any expenses of administration of my estate, in whole or in part, as a deduction in computing estate tax or income tax as in their discretion they shall deem to be advisable, irrespective of the effect any such decision would have upon any beneficiary or the value of any legacy, bequest or trust and without any adjustment being made as between any beneficiaries under my Will upon any accounting or otherwise by reason of such election or selection and without liability to any person for the making of such election or selection, it being intended hereby that the foregoing provision shall govern notwithstanding any contrary provisions of any law.

J. To hold and retain all or any part of my estate or any trust created hereby, in the form in which the same may be at the time of my decease, as long as they may deem advisable.

K. To do all such acts, take all such proceedings and exercise all such rights and privileges, although not herein specifically mentioned, with respect to any such property, as if the absolute owner thereof.

ARTICLE VII

No money or property payable or distributable under this Will, whether income or principal, shall be pledged, assigned, transferred, sold, or in any manner whatsoever anticipated, charged, or encumbered by any beneficiary hereunder, nor shall the Trustee be in any manner liable for the debts, contracts, obligations, or engagements of any beneficiary hereunder, for any claims, legal or equitable, against any such beneficiary.

IN WITNESS WHEREOF, I sign, seal, publish and declare this as my Last Will and Testament, in the presence of the persons witnessing it at my request, this 20 day of July, 1991, and for better identification I have initialled each of the six pages of this my Last Will and Testament.

/s/ *Allen Ginsberg*
Allen Ginsberg

Second of two identical copies

The foregoing instrument was on this day signed, sealed, published and declared by the Testator, Allen Ginsberg, as his Last Will and Testament in our presence, and we, at his request, in his presence, and in the presence of each other, subscribed our names as witnesses, all of us, including the Testator, being present together throughout the execution and attestation of the Will.

CODICIL

OF

ALLEN GINSBERG

I, Allen Ginsberg, domiciled and residing in the City, County, and State of New York, do make, publish and declare this as the First Codicil to my Last Will and Testament dated the 25th day of July, 1991.

<u>FIRST</u>:

I hereby delete the two lines of text at the top of page 4 in their entirety and replace those two lines with the following language:

> C. To make loans and borrow money for any purpose, including, without limitation, for the payment of any taxes payable by my estate, upon such terms, with or without security, as they in their discretion may determine and to pledge or mortgage any such property as security.

<u>SECOND</u>:

In all other respects I hereby ratify, confirm and republish my aforesaid Last Will and Testament.

IN WITNESS WHEREOF, I sign, seal, publish and declare this as my First Codicil to my aforesaid Last Will and Testament, in the presence of the persons witnessing it at my request, this 26 day of July, 1991.

/s/ *Allen Ginsberg*
_____
Allen Ginsberg

/s/ *William S. Burroughs*
_____
William S. Burroughs

The foregoing instrument was on the 26 day of July, 1991, signed, sealed, published and declared by the Testator, Allen Ginsberg, as his First Codicil to his Last Will and Testament in our presence, and we, at his request, in his presence, and in the presence of each other, subscribed our names as witnesses, all of us, including the Testator, being present together throughout the execution and attestation of the Codicil.

/s/ *Philip Glass*

Philip Glass

James Thurber

DATE AND PLACE OF BIRTH
December 8, 1894
Columbus, Ohio

DATE AND PLACE OF DEATH
November 2, 1961
Doctors Hospital
New York, New York

Talk of the Town

Prolific writer and humorist, James Thurber has been called one of the great comic artists of our times. His simple but expressive line drawings with biting and satirical captions were an immediate success when they first appeared in the *New Yorker* magazine. Sadly, Thurber was totally blind when he died. He had had the use of only one eye for most of his life as a result of being "inadvertently" shot by an arrow in his left eye by his brother when he was 6 years old. Thurber often joked that he would entitle his memoirs, "Long Time, No See."

Thurber's most well known literary work is his "Secret Life of Walter Mitty" about a little man who is a legend in his own mind. The book about Mitty was turned into a movie starring Danny Kaye as the ordinary man with extraordinary dreams. A few of Mitty's other well-known books include: "Is Sex Necessary?", "The Owl in the Attic and Other Perplexities," and "The Seal in the Bedroom and Other Predicaments". Thurber's work also appeared on the stage in the guise of "The Male Animal" in 1940.

Thurber's personal life appears to have first been urban and turbulent and then more settled and bucolic. Thurber divorced his first wife in 1935 after having had a daughter named Rosemary together. With his second wife, Thurber lived in a large house on a 65-acre tract of land in West Cornwall, Connecticut. He and his second wife did not have any children together.

In his Will Thurber leaves the bulk of his estate to his wife, Helen, and $15,000 to be divided equally among his daughter Rosemary and two brothers, William and Robert. If Helen had not survived her husband, then one-half of his residuary estate was to be left to his daughter, Rosemary, and one-fourth to each of his brothers. The Will also includes a bequest of "all stock owned by me at the time of my death in the *New Yorker* magazine, Inc. or in Bermudian Publishing Co. Inc." to Thurber's wife.

Thurber named his wife and literary advisor Harriet Pilpel as the Executrices of his Will. It is interesting to note that in the section pertaining to the powers of his executrices, the Will states: "I hereby clothe my Executrices with full power, discretion and authority . . ." One wonders whether Thurber or his lawyer would "clothe" his Executors if they had been men.

For such a colorful and creative writer, Thurber left a relatively mundane Will. The provocative writer of the *New Yorker*'s popular "Talk of the Town" column, James "Mitty" Thurber did not leave much to talk about in his last written words.

/s/ *James Thurber*

Will dated November 12, 1956

Ayn Rand

DATE AND PLACE OF BIRTH
February 2, 1905
St. Petersburg (Leningrad)
Russia

DATE AND PLACE OF DEATH
March 6, 1982
120 East 34th Street
New York, New York

You Can't Take It With You

Born in Russia, writer Ayn (rhymes with "pine") Rand graduated from the University of Leningrad, came to America at the age of 21 and went to Hollywood to work as a movie extra and screenwriter. She met and married an artist named Charles Francis O'Connor in 1929 and the couple moved to New York. Rand's real name was Alice O'Connor, but she adopted the *nom de plume* of Ayn Rand. Frank O'Connor died in 1979. The O'Connors had no children.

In her writings Rand became the leading exponent of the doctrine of "rational selfishness" and a champion of unbridled capitalism. She was best known for her books "The Fountainhead" and "Atlas Shrugged" which were published in 1943 and 1957, respectively. In "The Fountainhead", the protagonist, an architect loosely based on Frank Lloyd Wright, ultimately blows up a building after realizing that his original architectural plans had been altered.

Selfish Ayn Rand died with an estate in excess of $500,000, which she left entirely to a friend, Leonard

Peikoff. According to papers filed with the court, "Alice O'Connor aka Ayn Rand" had a surviving sister whose name and address were unknown.

/s/ Alice O'Connor
_____

Will dated November 17, 1981

Mark Twain

DATE AND PLACE OF BIRTH
November 30, 1835
Florida, Missouri

DATE AND PLACE OF DEATH
April 21, 1910
Stormfield
Redding, Connecticut

"The Reports of My Death Are Greatly Exaggerated"

Named Samuel Langhorne Clemens at his birth in Missouri, he took his nom de plume of "Mark Twain" from the expression used by Mississippi River boatmen to describe a certain depth of the water. With his pen name picked, Twain wrote about life on the Mississippi or on other bodies of water, as in his first famous book, *Innocents Abroad,* about his adventures on a steamship bound for the Holy Land.

It was on this trip to the Holy Land that Clemens met Judge Jervis J. Langdon of Elmira, New York, and his daughter Lizzie, who would subsequently become Clemens's wife. Together Clemens and his wife had three daughters and one son. The son died in infancy and one daughter died in her teens. Clemens's wife died during their marriage, and Clemens never remarried. In the year before he died, Clemens's daughter Miss Jean Clemens drowned in the bathtub in her father's house in Redding, Connecticut, on Christmas morning. Despondent over the loss of his daughter, Clemens's own health deteriorated rapidly after her death.

Clemens signed his Will on August 17, 1909, before his daughter Jean died, and he never updated his Will to reflect her death. The Will provides that his daughters Jean and Clara were each to receive 5 percent "of any and all moneys which at the time of my death may be on deposit to my credit, and subject to withdrawal on demand in any bank or trust company, or in any banking institution." The balance of his estate was to be held in trust for his two daughters and their descendants. Since daughter Jean died without any descendants, the entire estate was inherited by Clara, who was married to a man named Ossip Gabrilowitsch.

For his executors and trustees, Clemens named his nephew, Jervis Langdon, and two other "friends" from the city of New York. "Reposing confidence in their integrity," Clemens directed that they should not be required to furnish any bond. Clemens was well aware of the value of his tremendous literary output and included the following provision in his Will related to that:

As I have expressed to my daughter, CLARA LANGDON CLEMENS, and to my associate, ALBERT BIGELOW PAINE, my ideas and desires regarding the administration of my literary productions, and as they are especially familiar with my wishes in that respect, I request that my executors and trustees above named confer and advise with my said daughter CLARA LANGDON CLEMENS, and the said ALBERT BIGELOW PAINE, as to all matters relating in any way to the control, management and disposition of my literary productions, published and unpublished, and all my literary articles and memoranda of every kind and description, and generally as to all matters which pertain to copyrights and such other literary property as I may leave at the time of my decease. The foregoing suggestion as to consultation is, however, made subject to my contract dated July 24th, 1909, with ALBERT BIGELOW PAINE for the preparation of my letters for publication, and in full recognition thereof, and subject also to the contract dated August 27th, 1906, made by and between the said ALBERT BIGELOW PAINE and HARPER & BROTHERS, as I have appointed the said ALBERT BIGELOW PAINE as my biographer, and have ratified and approved his said contract relating to the publication thereof.

Obviously, Paine was someone whom Clemens trusted and was also one of the witnesses to Clemens's Will.

A prankster for much of his life, Clemens had once arranged for his obituary to be printed in New York newspapers. After the article had appeared Clemens cabled from London the following famous line: "The reports of my death are greatly exaggerated." When he did finally succumb to death in his seventh-fifth year, Clemens is reported to have died quietly while in an unconscious state and the State of Connecticut. Earlier that afternoon Clemens had written a note to his nurses—"Give me my glasses"—because he had been too weak to speak. On the bed when he died was one book he had particularly admired and was rereading—Thomas Carlyle's *French Revolution*. At his bedside watching the great writer slip out of this world were his daughter, Clara, her husband Ossip, and Twain's designated biographer, Albert Bigelow Paine. The reports of Samuel Clemens's/Mark Twain's death in 1910 in newspapers all across America were detailed, but not exaggerated.

/s/ *Samuel L. Clemens*

Will dated August 17, 1909

F. Scott Fitzgerald

DATE AND PLACE OF BIRTH
September 24, 1896
St. Paul, Minnesota

DATE AND PLACE OF DEATH
December 21, 1940
Hollywood, California

The Other Side of Paradise

Fatally stricken by a heart attack at the age of forty-four, F. Scott Fitzgerald was one of America's leading literary voices during the roaring twenties. He began his first novel, *This Side of Paradise,* in 1916 while still an undergraduate at Princeton University. In 1917 he left Princeton, ostensibly to join the Army and fight for his country, but also as a result of failing grades. While stationed in Alabama, he met and married Zelda Sayre, who has been called "the brilliant counterpart" of the heroines in his novels. In 1921, F. Scott and Zelda had their only child, Frances Scott Fitzgerald. F. Scott published his most famous novel, *The Great Gatsby,* in 1925 "at a time when gin was the national drink and sex the national obsession," according to his obituary in *The New York Times*. During the last years of his life, Fitzgerald's literary output was minimal, and many have claimed that his early promise of a brilliant career was never fulfilled as a result of alcoholism and other personal problems.

Fitzgerald's handwritten Will appears to have been written without the assistance of an attorney, while Fitzgerald was in North Carolina "drying out" late in his life. It is interesting to note the unusual preamble to the Will, which speaks of "the uncertainty of life *and the certainty of death*" [emphasis added].

Three years after signing the Will, Fitzgerald made some revealing changes to it pertaining to his own burial. On November 10, 1940, less than two months before his death, Fitzgerald made the following change:

> ITEM ONE: I will and direct that at my death my executors to be hereinafter named shall provide for me ~~a suitable~~ the cheapest funeral and burial ~~in keeping with my station in life and in due regard to the bequests hereinafter made,~~ the same to be without any undue ostentation and unnecessary expense.
>
> F. Scott Fitzgerald, Nov. 10th, 1940

Perhaps most unusual about this Will are Fitzgerald's repeated references to his wife's, Zelda's, insanity. Early in the Will, Fitzgerald states that Zelda is "non Compos Mentis" (Latin for "not sound of mind; insane"). Subsequently, the Will provides:

> ITEM SIX: I give, devise and bequeath unto my wife, Zelda Fitzgerald in the event she shall regain her sanity all of my household and kitchen furniture to be used and controlled by her as she may desire . . .
> ITEM SEVEN: In the event that my wife has not regained her sanity at my death, I give, devise and bequeath unto my said daughter, Frances Scott Fitzgerald, the above designated household and kitchen furniture to be held by her for Zelda Fitzgerald during her lifetime or until she shall regain her sanity. . . .

ITEM EIGHT: I give, devise and bequeath unto my daughter, Frances Scott Fitzgerald all my family silverware, portraits, pictures, and all special and valuable books, short stories or other writings which I may have written, or all books of value which I may have collected or purchased to be used and controlled by her until my wife Zelda Fitzgerald shall regain her sanity . . .

It is revealing that Fitzgerald's Will never provides who would make the determination whether Zelda had regained her sanity or not. Perhaps that omission is an indication that Fitzgerald did not believe that his wife would ever regain her sanity.

Fitzgerald's only daughter, Frances, was attending Vassar College when he died in 1940. Zelda Fitzgerald lived eight years more and died on March 11, 1948. Upon Zelda's death, the balance of the estate, including all Fitzgerald's literary-property interests, passed entirely to the Fitzgerald's only child, Frances.

/s/ *F. Scott Fitzgerald*

Will dated June 17, 1937
Place of will signing at Polk County, North Carolina
Will changes dated November 10, 1940

Thornton Wilder

DATE AND PLACE OF BIRTH
April 17, 1897
Madison, Wisconsin

DATE AND PLACE OF DEATH
December 7, 1975
50 Deepwood Drive
Hamden, Connecticut

"Heaven's My Destination"

Winner of three Pulitzer Prizes, Thornton Wilder was not a particularly prolific writer, but obviously a great one. During his over fifty years of writing, Wilder's major works included only seven novels and two dramatic plays. His most well known work was his play "Our Town" which won the Pulitzer Prize in 1938. Other books by Wilder include "Heaven's My Destination" and "The Eighth Day", both of which had Biblical undertones.

Besides writing, Wilder also taught at institutions of higher learning such as Harvard and the University of Chicago. He had a reputation of never being too busy to help students wanting to speak with him, and he once remarked, "On my grave they will write: 'Here lies a man who tried to be obliging'". Wilder never married during his lifetime and once said that he had "just skipped" marriage because he was too involved with his work.

As evidenced by the terms of his Will, Wilder remained close with his three sisters and one brother. He appears to have been closest with his sister, Isabel, who resided with him in his house in Hamden, Connecticut. His sister Charlotte was "an incapable person" and lived at the "Brattleboro Retreat" in Vermont according to papers filed with the court. Sister Janet was a zoologist and conservationist and lived in Amherst, Massachusetts. Wilder's older brother Amos was a Reverend and lived in Cambridge, Massachusetts. Perhaps it was an amalgam of all these New England towns which led Wilder to create the fictitious Grover's Corners, New Hampshire in "Our Town".

To his sister Isabel, Wilder gave all of his tangible personal property "including but not limited to all my furniture, books, pictures, rugs, china, silverware, furnishings, household effects, wearing apparel, jewelry, automobiles, and all letters to me from my sisters Isabel Wilder, Janet W. Dakin, and Charlotte Wilder, my brother Amos N. Wilder, and either of my parents and all letters to any of them from me." In addition, Wilder devised to his sister Isabel any real estate which he owned, including his house in Hamden, Connecticut. Wilder also made the following cash bequests in his Will which might have been attempt to equalize the treatment of his siblings: $25,000 to Isabel and $50,000 to each of sister Janet and brother Amos. There is no bequest to sister Charlotte presumably because she was not capable of handling funds, but there is a $300,000 trust established primarily for her benefit later in the Will. There are several other bequests, ranging from $5,000 to $25,000, to various other relatives and friends. Finally, there is an additional bequest of $25,000 to sister Isabel, with the "expectation that my said sister will make payments out of said sum. . . . in accordance with the suggestions which I may make to her. . . ." Living in Thornton's house, Isabel was obviously subject to brother Thornton's suggestions.

To Yale University in New Haven, Connecticut, where he had studied during College, Wilder bequeathed:

. . . all of my personal papers, notes, records, manuscripts of my published works, and all of my letters except those bequeathed to my sister Isabel. . . . In addition, I give and bequeath to Yale University the sum of Fifteen Thousand Dollars ($15,000), the income or principal of which is to be used for the purposes of preserving, cataloguing and maintaining the items bequeathed by this Article. . . . The person acting as the curator of the Yale Collection of American Literature at the time of my death . . . shall have full authority, discretion, and responsibility with respect to the use and publication of any such letters, personal papers, notes, and records and the selection of a biographer or biographers and the materials to which they may have access.

Wilder left his residuary estate in equal one-third shares to Oberlin College, in Oberlin, Ohio; to Berea College, in Berea, Kentucky; and to the MacDowell Colony located in Peterborough, New Hampshire. Undoubtedly, the royalties generated by Wilder's much dramatized plays and films have provided significant income to each of those institutions over the years.

As Executor of the Will and Trustee of the family trust, Wilder appointed The Union & New Haven Trust Company, of New Haven, Connecticut. However, the Executor was directed to "take no action concerning my books, novels, stories, plays, articles, scenarios, or other writings, published or unpublished, including but not limited to the granting of publication and production rights, subsidiary rights, licenses, permissions, copyrights and similar matters, or with respect to the making of said matters, without the written instructions of said Donald C. Gallup . . ." Gallup was the curator of the

American Collection at Yale's Beinecke Library whose judgement was obviously trusted by Wilder.

Wilder died in his sleep at home in Hamden, Connecticut after suffering a heart attack at the age of 78. Alluding to his literary goals, Wilder once said, "I am interested in those things that repeat and repeat and repeat in the lives of millions." No doubt the great literary works of Thornton Wilder will continue to repeat and repeat and repeat in the minds of millions.

/s/ *Thornton Wilder*

Will dated November 3, 1967

William Faulkner

DATE AND PLACE OF BIRTH
September 25, 1897
New Albany, Mississippi

DATE AND PLACE OF DEATH
July 6, 1962
Oxford, Mississippi

As He Lay Dying

Born and bred in Mississippi, Nobel and Pulitzer Prize-winning author William Faulkner introduced the entire world to *his* world of fictional Yoknapatawpha County, Mississippi. According to Faulkner, "Yoknapatawpha" was a Chickasaw Indian term meaning "water passes slowly through the flatlands," and the fictional place in his novels was modeled on his own home count of Lafayette, Mississippi.

Besides his literary brilliance, Faulkner was an indefatigable horseman and a bona fide bourbon-sipping southern gentleman. One day while riding on his farm in old Miss, a horse bucked him, and that buck indirectly led to his death. Nonetheless, he was drinking his bourbon "as a painkiller" until shortly before his end. A painkiller it was, indeed.

In his Will, Faulkner ("being the same person as William Falkner, of Charlottesville, Virginia") named his daughter, Jill Faulkner Summers, as his sole executor and trustee of the trust for the benefit of his wife, Estelle Oldham Faulkner, whom Faulkner had married in 1929. Mrs. Faulkner receives approximately one-half of her husband's estate in trust, with the balance of the estate being paid outright to Faulkner's daughter, Jill.

Faulkner makes two $5,000 bequests, to a niece and a nephew, but for the most part, his Will is rather technical and dry, and disappointing for anyone hoping to see Faulkner's vernacular style showing through. There is no reference of any kind to Faulkner's tremendous literary output.

For several years before his death Faulkner was an enigmatic presence on the University of Virginia campus. In a codicil signed in December of 1960, Faulkner gives to The William Faulkner Foundation, Charlottesville, Virginia, "all of my manuscripts and other tangible personal property deposited at the Alderman Library of the University of Virginia."

/s/ *William Faulkner*

Will dated June 1, 1960
Codicil dated December 28, 1960
Residing in Charlottesville, Virginia

Carl Sandburg

DATE AND PLACE OF BIRTH
January 6, 1878
Galesburg, Illinois

DATE AND PLACE OF DEATH
July 22, 1967
Flat Rock, North Carolina

"Death comes once, let it be easy"

"Finish" by Carl Sandburg

Pulitzer Prize winning author for both poetry and prose, Carl Sandburg is best known for his monumental biography of (Will-less) Abraham Lincoln. In a tribute at the time of Sandburg's death, then President Lyndon Johnson stated, "Carl Sandburg was more than the voice of America, more than the poet of its strength and genius, he was America. We knew and cherished him as the bard of democracy, the echo of the people, our conscience and chronicler of truth and beauty and purpose."

Despite the reference to democracy, young Sandburg also had socialist affiliations earlier in his life. It was at the Social Democratic headquarters in Milwaukee where Sandburg met another party member named Lilian Paula Steichen. Miss Steichen, who was the sister of acclaimed photographer Edward Steichen, became Carl Sandburg's wife on June 15, 1908. Together Lilian and Carl had three daughters.

During their marriage the couple lived throughout

America, spending much time in the City of Chicago that Sandburg characterized as the "Hog Butcher for the World/ Tool Maker, Stacker of Wheat/ Player with Rail-roads and the/ Nation's Freight Handler/ Stormy, husky, brawling, City of the Big Shoulders."

For the last 22 years of his life, Sandburg lived with his wife and children on a 240 acre goat farm and ranch in Flat Rock, North Carolina. Sandburg's Will, which he signed about four years before he died is relatively simple and straightforward, like the man himself:

FIRST: I give and bequeath all of the clothing, jewelry, furniture and furnishings, and other personal and household effects owned by me at my death to my wife, LILIAN STEICHEN SANDBURG, if she survives me and if she does not survive me, to such of my children as survive me, to be divided among them by my Executor in shares of substantially equal value.

SECOND: I give, devise and bequeath all the rest, residue and remainder of the property owned by me at my death, or to which I shall then be entitled in any way, to the Trustee of a certain trust heretofore created this date under a certain trust agreement executed this date by and between myself, as Grantor, and my wife, LILIAN STEICHEN SANDBURG, as Trustee, to be held, administered and distributed pursuant to the provisions of said agreement as it shall exist at my death.

THIRD: I name my wife, LILIAN STEICHEN SAND-BURG, Executor of this, my Last Will and Testament, and if she fails to qualify or having qualified, ceases to act as such Executor for any reason, I name FRANK M. PARKER, of Asheville, North Carolina, and HARRY GOLDEN, of Charlotte, North Carolina, jointly. . . .

Sandburg's Will appears to be the dull product of a North Carolina country lawyer, and not truly reflective of the thoughts of one of America's deepest writers and poets. The terms of the trust referred to in the Will are private, but we do know that Sandburg died with an estate consisting of "personal" property valued at $37,398.00 and real estate worth $20,615.00 according to papers filed with the court.

The former socialist had given much away during his lifetime. But there would be no end to the legacy of prose and poetry that Carl Sandburg left to the English speaking world.

/s/ *Carl Sandburg*

Will dated April 29, 1963

Tennessee Williams

DATE AND PLACE OF BIRTH
March 26, 1911
Columbus, Mississippi

DATE AND PLACE OF DEATH
February 25, 1983
Hotel Élysée
New York, New York

Here Today, Iguana Tomorrow

Playwright Tennessee Williams's prodigious output created some of the English-speaking theater's most riveting dramas, including *Cat on a Hot Tin Roof, A Streetcar Named Desire,* and *The Night of the Iguana.* Despite his repeated critical successes, Williams was known to be sensitive about criticism of, or changes to, his writings. In his Will, Williams gives explicit directions that none of his literary works should be altered, stating:

> It is my wish that no play which I shall have written shall, for the purpose of presenting it as a first-class attraction on the English-speaking stage, be changed in any manner, whether such change shall be by way of completing it, or adding to it, or deleting from it, or in any other way revising it, except for the customary type of stage directions. It is also my wish and will that no poem or literary work of mine be changed in any manner, whether such change shall be by way of completing any such work or adding to it or deleting from it or in any other way revising it, except that any complete poem or other literary work of mine may be translated into a foreign language or dramatized for stage, screen or televi-

sion. I expressly direct that neither my Executors nor my Trustees make or authorize the making of any changes prohibited in this Article. To the extent that I can legally do so, no party who shall acquire any rights in any play, poem or literary work of mine shall have the right to make or authorize the making of any changes in any play, poem or literary work of mine prohibited in this Article.

When he was born in Mississippi, Williams was named Thomas Lanier Williams. Apparently his childhood was an unhappy one; his father, Cornelius Coffin Williams, was reported to be a violent and brutish traveling salesman. Williams had an older sister named Rose, who had mental problems, and after the failure of a frontal lobotomy operation, Rose spent most of the rest of her life in mental institutions.

After taking nine years to complete his college education, at the age of twenty-eight Williams left home for New Orleans and invented a new name for himself—"Tennessee." It was while living in New Orleans that Williams wrote *A Streetcar Named Desire*. At the time of his death, Williams reportedly still maintained an apartment in the French Quarter of New Orleans in addition to his home in Key West, Florida, and a suite at the Hotel Élysée in New York.

At the time he signed his Will in 1980, Williams was working on a play tentatively titled *Two Character Play*. The name of that play was finally changed to *Out Cry*. Under the first article of his Will Williams gives all the royalties and other proceeds from that play to "my good friend, LADY MARIA ST. JUST of London, England." Unfortunately for Lady Just, this Williams play has not been a commercial success.

In his 1980 Will, Williams directed that many of his personal journals, diaries, and other literary properties should either be sold or given to the University of the South. However, in a codicil to his Will, which Williams signed in 1982, he changed the recipient of his valuable papers from the University of the South to Harvard University.

Most of Williams's estate was placed in trust for the benefit of his mentally deranged sister, Rose, who lived at the Stony Lodge Sanitarium in Ossining, New York. Expressing the wish that the trustees provide liberally for his sister, Williams's Will states:

> In addition to the payment of the normal expenses of maintenance of said Institution, my Trustees shall pay . . . such amounts as they deem necessary or advisable for medical and dental expenses, clothing and her usual customary pleasures as she now enjoys, including shopping trips to New York City, personal spending money, it being my intention that said Trustees shall provide liberally for her, not only for her needs but also for her comfort and pleasures.

In addition to providing for his sister, Williams's Will provides that his brother, Walter Dakin Williams, is to receive a lump-sum payment of $25,000 upon Rose's death. "I have intentionally made no other provision for my said brother as he is well provided for."

The rest of the property remaining after Rose's death was originally to be paid to the University of the South, but that bequest was also changed to Harvard University. Williams directs that that property is to be held in a separate fund called the "WALTER E. DAKIN MEMORIAL

FUND" to be used for "the purposes of encouraging creative writing and creative writers in need of financial assistance to pursue their vocation whose work is progressive, original and preferably of an experimental nature."

It was in his suite at the Hotel Élysée that Tennessee Williams was found dead on the morning of February 25, 1983, by his secretary. According to the chief medical examiner's report, Williams choked to death on a bottle cap that had become lodged in his larynx. Williams's inability to gag and expel the object lodged in his throat was possibly attributable to impaired response caused by the presence of drugs and/or alcohol. According to police reports, an empty bottle of wine and several types of medication were found in the room where Williams died. Mr. Williams's history with alcohol and drugs was well-known and may have been the silent cause of his death. Choking to death on a bottle cap, brilliant playwright Tennessee Williams unbottled human emotions and expressed those emotions by words uttered by characters of his imagination.

/s/ *Tennessee Williams*

Will dated September 11, 1980
Codicil dated December 1982

John Steinbeck

DATE AND PLACE OF BIRTH
February 27, 1902
Salinas, California

DATE AND PLACE OF DEATH
December 20, 1968
190 East 72nd Street
New York, New York

The Best Laid Plans of Mice and Men . . .

Evidencing his reputation as a private family man, John Steinbeck's Will makes a $25,000 bequest to his sister Elizabeth of Pacific Grove, California, $50,000 bequests in trust for each of his two sons, John Steinbeck IV and Thom Steinbeck, with the balance of his estate left outright to his third wife, Elaine. There is one other bequest of $5,000 to a woman who worked in the Steinbeck home, which is an example of Steinbeck's lifelong concern with the plight of the worker.

Steinbeck's most well-known book, "The Grapes of Wrath", was published in 1939 and examined the plight of a depression ravaged family from Oklahoma that was forced to migrate from the dust bowl of the midwest to the exploitive labor camps of California. Steinbeck takes a depressingly realistic view of his individual characters and a larger biological view of mankind, in which man is forced to adapt to his environment in order to survive. Furthermore, in the novel the historical American ideal of rugged individualism is sacrificed to the notion that in order to survive in a hostile economic or natural environment, man has to cooperate with his neighbors to achieve greater strength.

The "Grapes" earned national fame for the author and the book was subsequently made into a powerful film starring Henry Fonda. Other well known books by Steinbeck include "Of Mice and Men", which was adapted for the theater and film, "Tortilla Flats", "East of Eden" and "Cannery Row." Throughout his literary life, Steinbeck examined the effects of a capitalist society on the working class and many believed that he was espousing communist views in his writings.

Steinbeck was born John Ernest Steinbeck Jr. in the working class town of Salinas, California. His mother was a school teacher and his father was a miller. Young Steinbeck was a voracious reader and entered Stanford University, but dropped out before he obtained a college degree. His sense of adventure took him to New York where he worked briefly as a reporter and construction worker. Early written works attracted the attention of The San Francisco News which hired Steinbeck to write about California's migrant labor camps where the seeds for "The Grapes" were planted.

Steinbeck's first wife divorced him in 1942 and reportedly received a $220,000 settlement. In 1943, Steinbeck married Gwyndolen Conger and together they had two sons, John and Thom. That marriage ended in divorce in 1948. In 1950 Steinbeck married Elaine Scott and they stayed married until Steinbeck's death in 1968. Towards the end of his life, Steinbeck became even more reclusive, staying either at his ranch house in California, summer home in Sag Harbor, Long Island or townhouse in New York City. Steinbeck died in the New York townhouse of severe heart disease. It seems ironic that the American writer most known for his heartfelt compassion for the working class and the weak should have died from a broken heart.

/s/ *John Ernest Steinbeck*

Will dated August 5, 1968

Truman Capote

DATE AND PLACE OF BIRTH
September 30, 1924
New Orleans, Louisiana

DATE AND PLACE OF DEATH
August 25, 1984
Bel Air, California
(Joanna Carson's home)

Unfinished Prayers

Truman Capote, a self-proclaimed homosexual, provided in his Will primarily for his longtime companion, "my friend, JOHN PAUL DUNPHY." Under the Will, Dunphy was to receive all real estate owned by Capote at his death. At the time of his death, Capote owned an apartment at the United Nations Plaza in New York and an apartment in Verbier, Switzerland.

To dispose of Capote's tangible personal property, the Will provides under the first article:

> I give so much of my tangible personal property to such persons (including himself) as my Executor [Alan U. Schwartz] determines that I would wish to receive such property. I give the balance of my tangible personal property to my friend, JOHN PAUL DUNPHY, if he survives me.

This provision gave Capote's attorney, Alan U. Schwartz, unusually broad discretion to dispose of Capote's most personal property, including manuscripts, books, objects of art collected by Capote, and other items of potentially significant value. Rather than making the decisions pertaining to the disposition of this property himself, Capote shifted those decisions to Schwartz. The ultimate disposition of this property is not a matter of public record, and we can only wonder what John Paul Dunphy's (and other Capote friends') share of the property was.

According to papers filed with the New York Surrogate's Court, Capote's estate was worth well in excess of $2 million when he died. The bulk of the estate was to be placed in trust for the benefit of John Paul Dunphy until his death. Upon the death of Dunphy, the property remaining in the trust is to be held by a charitable trust with the following purpose:

> My Trustee shall pay the income from the trust to a college or university located in the United States that will agree to establish a prize or prizes to be awarded annually for excellence in literary criticism. The prize shall be known as the <u>Truman Capote award for Literary Criticism in memory of Newton Arvin</u>. My trustee is authorized to allow a reasonable portion of the funds to be used by the college or university to administer the award. The prizes shall be awarded on a competitive basis in a manner similar to awarding of the Pulitzer Prize . . . I authorize my trustee to pay the trust income annually or more frequently to one or more colleges or universities located in the United States to provide scholarships for promising writers.

Newton Arvin, in whose memory the Capote award for literary criticism is established, was one of Capote's most influential lovers and his literary mentor. Arvin was a professor of English literature at the all-women Smith College when Capote met him in the summer of '46. A most learned man, Arvin read French, German, Italian, Latin, and of course, Greek. Besides their sexual/romantic liaisons, Arvin became the college professor that the self-taught and somewhat provincial Truman Capote never had. Arvin died of cancer in 1963. His impact on Capote was crucial to Capote's literary development. It seems fitting that in the Will Capote signed almost twenty years after Arvin's death, he would honor his former lover, mentor, and literary Virgil by naming the award for literary criticism in his memory.

Named Truman Streckfus Persons at his birth in New Orleans, Louisiana, Truman later adopted the surname of his mother's second husband, Joe Capote. His mother was an alcoholic and eventually committed suicide. Capote's younger years were spent being shuttled among relatives throughout the South. Capote later worked at *The New Yorker* and displayed great precociousness as a writer; his first published book, *Other Voices, Other Rooms,* appearing when he was twenty-three, established him as a young writer whose star was rising. Capote wrote intermittently throughout the 1950s, 1960s, and 1970s, including the popular *Breakfast at Tiffany's.* However, it was his searing "nonfiction novel," *In Cold Blood,* about the cold-blooded murder of the Herbert Clutter family in rural Kansas and the mentality, trial, and execution of the Clutter killers, that shocked and captivated America.

Capote continued writing until his death, but much of it was gossip about the celebrities whom he had courted. He became addicted to alcohol and drugs and proclaimed to the world in a 1980 interview, "I'm an alcoholic. I'm a drug addict. I'm homosexual. I'm a genius. Of course, I could be all four of those dubious things and still be a saint." At the time of his alleged overdose from sleeping pills in the home of Joanna Carson, Capote was working on "his masterwork," entitled *Answered Prayers*. For Truman Capote, those prayers were never finished.

/s/ *Truman Capote*

Will dated May 4, 1981
Signed at Apt 22G, U.N. Plaza, N.Y.—Capote's apartment

Lillian Hellman

DATE AND PLACE OF BIRTH
June 20, 1905
New Orleans, Louisiana

DATE AND PLACE OF DEATH
June 30, 1984
Martha's Vineyard
Massachusetts

Banned in Boston, Dead in the Vineyard

Best known for her scandalous 1934 play entitled *The Children's Hour,* which was banned in Boston, Chicago, and other cities, Lillian Hellman was controversial throughout her life until her death at the age of seventy-nine.

Her most well-known alliance was to writer Dashiell Hammett, with whom she lived off and on for over thirty years until his death in 1960. In her 1984 Will Hellman makes several references to her former lover Hammett, including the following bequest:

I give and bequeath all my right, title and interest in and to the works of Dashiell Hammett or works based upon his writings (including, but not limited to, books, stories, plays, scripts and theatrical, radio, movie or television productions) to the fiduciaries hereinafter named, IN TRUST . . . I further request that the fiduciaries in making such selections shall be guided by the political, social and economic beliefs which, of course, were radical, of the late Dashiell Hammett who was a believer in the doctrines of Karl Marx.

As trustees of the Dashiell Hammett Fund, Hellman named John Hersey, Jules Feiffer, Ephraim London, Howard Bay, and Isadore Englander.

As for her own literary property, Hellman gave all her "original writings, manuscripts, papers, notes, memoranda and other literary property," excluding a manuscript to be selected by her friend Mike Nichols, to the University of Texas in Austin.

At the time of her death, Ms. Hellman was not married and had no children. However, she did have quite a collection of friends and admirers (despite some harsh critics) and had also collected many objects of sentimental value, which she designated for particular friends. The following list of bequests reads like a literary who's who and gives a good indication of Hellman's various relationships.

I give and bequeath the following articles of my tangible personal property except cash, wherever located, to such of the persons hereinafter named as shall survive me:

(1) to BLAIR CLARK, the English or American Hiboy chest in the bedroom of my New York apartment and any photographs of me he may choose, except the one effectively bequeathed in item "(12)" hereof.

(2) to MIKE NICHOLS, the Toulouse Lautrec poster in the hall of my New York apartment, any of the manuscripts in my possession and the Italian sconces in the hall of my apartment.

(3) to ANNABEL NICHOLS, my diamond necklace recently made from a bracelet.

(4) to RITA WADE, any and all coats she may choose; my gold watch and large platinum diamond pin, feather design; the Betamax in the study of my New York apartment and any other object she may choose, except as otherwise designated;

(5) to BARBARA HERSEY and JOH HERSEY, or to BROOK HERSEY, the Queen Anne table in the living room of my Martha's Vineyard house; to BARBARA HERSEY, the platinum flower diamond pin; and any other piece of furniture and any and all paintings or pictures that JOHN HERSEY may choose from either my Martha's Vineyard house or my New York apartment, except as otherwise designated.

(6) to SELMA WOLFMAN, the pallet pin which Dashiell Hammett gave to me.

(7) to MAX PALEVSKY, the Spanish table presently in the study of my New York apartment; . . . the framed Russian altar cloth presently over the fireplace in the living room, given to me by Pudovkin, the movie director, as it was executed by a member of his family in 1796; any pictures or statues of art work that he may choose, except as otherwise designated; and the two chairs against the wall near the sofa in the living room of my New York apartment, made by unknown cabinet makers in Bohemia or possibly France and exchanged by these amateurs one to the other in the early nineteenth century; and any other object he may choose, except as otherwise designated.

(8) to RICHARD POIRIER, any and all books he may choose; the three-step library ladder in the study of my New York apartment; the three (3) Russian china doves,

the French secretary and two electrified brass lamps with tulip bulbs in the living room of my New York apartment; and the rare 18th century Bibilo bookcase in the bedroom of my New York apartment.

(9) to DR. GEORGE GERO, all the Russian icons he may choose, except as otherwise designated.

(10) to HOWARD BAY, the Forain drawing and the wooden birdcage hanging from the ceiling in the living room of my New York apartment.

(11) to RICHARD De COMBRAY, the small empire French loveseat and the four Empire arm chairs in the living room of my New York apartment; the four-pronged French candlesticks on my bedroom fireplace; and the English wall sconces near the fireplace on my living room wall and the chandeliers in my bedroom.

(12) to DR. MARTIN WEXLER (of Los Angeles, California), the Ben Shahn portrait of Albert Einstein and the enlarged photograph of me as a child with nurse, and the two (2) pictures depicting the ages of man, and any other object he may choose, except as otherwise designated.

(13) to JOHN MARQUAND, the small blue dial Cartier clock that was given to me by his wife, Sue Marquand.

(14) to MILDRED LOFTUS, the 18th century silver set with pistol handle knives, forks, spoons, etc. from Chichton in London.

(15) to JOSEPH WEINSTEIN and MRS. JOSEPH (``BOBBIE'') WEINSTEIN, the special bound gift copies of my plays and books given me by Arthur Thornhill.

(16) to WILLIAM ABRAHAMS, the box in the guest bathroom of my New York apartment that has the little foxes on it; and any other object he may choose, except as otherwise designated.

(17) to EPHRAIM LONDON, the Rouault in the living room of my New York apartment; and any other object he may choose except as otherwise designated.

(18) The balance of my tangible personal property including any items not hereinbefore effectively disposed of, shall be dealt with and disposed of as follows:

> a) to PETER FEIBLEMAN, any ten (10) items thereof that he may choose; and fifty (50%) percent of all royalties due or to become due for my literary work only, and upon his death, all royalties shall be paid to the Lillian Hellman Fund.

> b) The remainder of such balance in as nearly equal shares as practicable to JACK H. KLEIN, LORD VICTOR PRITCHETT and LADY DOROTHY PRITCHETT, JOHN MELBY, FRED GARDNER, RUTH FIELD, JASON EPSTEIN, WILLIAM ABRAHAMS and ANNABEL NICHOLS.

At the time of her death Hellman was romantically linked with Peter Feibleman. In addition to the bequest mentioned above, Feibleman received $100,000 outright, the right to use and occupy Hellman's property in Vineyard Haven on Martha's Vineyard for the rest of his life, and the option to buy her New York apartment on Park Avenue at its appraised value. The Will also makes monetary bequests to other friends, including a $35,000 bequest to each of the grandchildren of Dashiell Hammett "to be designated as a gift from Dashiell Hammett."

The rest of Hellman's substantial estate, including her interest in Hammett's estate, was to be held in trust in two separate funds: "The Lillian Hellman Fund" and "The Dashiell Hammett Fund." The Hellman fund was to make grants or gifts "to any person to assist him or her in engaging in writing in any field or upon any subject, or in scientific research, anywhere in the world . . . gifts or grants shall be made from the general public, with preference given to person showing distinction or promise in writing, but without regard to race, creed, national origin, age, sex or political beliefs." The Hammett fund was intended to "make gifts or grants for the promotion and advancement of political, social and economic equality, civil rights and civil liberties to any person, cause or organization, anywhere in the world, but preferably here in the United States. . . . I further request that the fiduciaries in making such selections shall be guided by the political, social and economic beliefs which, of course, were radical, of the late Dashiell Hammett who was a believer in the doctrines of Karl Marx." One wonders whether in 1984, twenty-four years after his death, the "late" Dashiell Hammett would still have been a believer in the political ideology of Karl Marx.

In her Will, Hellman also made a $2,500 bequest to Temple Israel of New York City as a fund for the perpetual care of the cemetery plot of her parents in Hastings-on-Hudson, New York. For her own burial, she provided that her executors purchase a cemetery plot and "suitable tombstone" and that she be buried in the Chilmark section of Martha's Vineyard. One month and five days after she signed her Will, Lillian Hellman died of a cardiac arrest in her summer home in Martha's Vineyard.

Even after her death, Hellman was the source of controversy. Her Will, though seemingly carefully prepared by her attorneys, was seriously flawed. For one thing, she named certain persons as her "literary property fiduciaries," but never established any literary property trust under the Will. As New York County Surrogate Marie Lambert wrote in her decision in the construction proceeding brought to interpret the Will, "while [Lillian Hellman's] literary works can be characterized as creative genius, her Will cannot."

/s/ Lillian Hellman

Will dated May 25, 1984

James Beard

DATE AND PLACE OF BIRTH
May 5, 1903
Portland, Oregon

DATE AND PLACE OF DEATH
January 23, 1985
New York Hospital
New York, New York

Just Desserts

Chef and prolific cookbook writer James Andrew Beard's own physical appearance betrayed his fascination with food; he reportedly weighed over 275 pounds throughout most of his adult life. In an obituary in *The New York Times,* fellow food connoisseur Craig Clairborne described Beard as "a giant panda, Santa Claus and the Jolly Green Giant rolled into one" and added that Beard "wore his rotundity with dignity and grace."

At the outset, Beard's Will proclaims, "I declare that I am not married and have no children." The bulk of his estate, including the New York town house/cooking school that he owned at 167 West 12th Street, New York, New York, Beard left in trust for his "good friend, GINO CO-FACCI." Upon Cofacci's death the remaining property in the trust was to pass to Beard's alma mater, Reed College in Portland. In addition, the royalties accruing from Beard's numerous cookbooks, including *Beard on Bread, How to Eat Better for Less Money,* and Beard's tour de force, *The Complete Book of Outdoor Cookery,* was to be paid to two named friends for their lifetimes and upon their deaths would revert to Reed College.

Beard died of a cardiac arrest at the age of eighty-one. At the time of his death he was working on another cookbook, entitled *Menus and Memories*. Considering how well and how much he ate and drank during his lifetime, Beard must have had many epicurean memories indeed.

/s/ *James A. Beard*
_____

Will dated August 13, 1976
Codicil dated June 4, 1983

The Producers and Directors

No More Lights, No More Cameras, No More Action

DAVID SUSSKIND
Not Too Kind
FEBRUARY 22, 1987

LEE STRASBERG
Madness in Monroe's Method
FEBRUARY 17, 1982

VINCENTE MINNELLI
Just a Matter of Time
JULY 25, 1986

JOHN CASSAVETES
A Man under the Influence
FEBRUARY 3, 1989

ORSON WELLES
Raising Kane
OCTOBER 10, 1985

WALT DISNEY
A Mickey Mouse Operation
DECEMBER 15, 1966

ALFRED HITCHCOCK
The Master of Suspense Until the End
APRIL 29, 1980

David Susskind

DATE AND PLACE OF BIRTH
December 19, 1920
New York, New York

DATE AND PLACE OF DEATH
February 22, 1987
Wyndham Hotel
New York, New York

Not Too Kind

Combative and provocative talk-show host David Susskind left a Will which indicated a disintegrated relationship with his second wife, the former Joyce Davidson. The Will which was signed in 1985 was never updated to reflect Susskind's 1986 divorce from his estranged wife. The Will provides for the minimum amount payable to a spouse under applicable New York law. Furthermore, the Will states:

> My executors shall pay in due course my funeral expenses, any expenses of my last illness, the expenses of administering my estate, and my debts; <u>provided however, my executors shall not pay or prepay the mortgage loan on the cooperative apartment occupied by my wife, JOYCE SUSSKIND (hereinafter called my wife), except and unless they are obligated to do so other than under the provisions of my will</u>. (emphasis added).

Clearly, Susskind was not inclined to give his then spouse any breaks, including any contribution towards the maintenance of their cooperative apartment.

Susskind had one son, Andrew Susskind, and three daughters, Pamela Schaenen, Diana Laptook and Samantha Susskind. Susskind named his son and two of his three daughters, excluding Samantha, as executors and Trustees of his Will.

To his son Andrew, Susskind left "all automobiles and men's jewelry I own at the time of my death." Excluding those items, Susskind gave

> my clothing, and other jewelry and other articles of personal use or adornment, and all books, furniture, objects of art and other articles of household use or ornament, to such of my children as shall survive me, in as nearly equal shares as shall be practicable.

That seems like quite a lot of "adornment" and "ornament", but the Harvard educated Susskind was known to have an overly inflated opinion of his urbane, sophisticated self.

During his nearly thirty years of continuous television broadcasts, Susskind aggressively interviewed thousands of guests ranging from Richard Nixon to Nikita S. Khrushchev to princes and paupers. His interviewing style was blunt and to the point, much like his Will. On his television shows "Open End" and "The David Susskind Show", he liked to instigate the clash of ideas and address controversial issues in a no-holds-barred manner. His defenders were staunch and his critics harsh; one could not be neutral about David Susskind.

Susskind's television show had finally been taken off the air the year before he died. On the day that he was found dead in his hotel suite at the Wyndham Hotel in New York, Susskind had reportedly been scheduled to enter Lenox Hill Hospital for treatment of a heart ailment. Dead at the age of 66, David Susskind finally stopped talking.

/s/ *David Susskind*

Will dated February 5, 1985

Lee Strasberg

DATE AND PLACE OF BIRTH
November 17, 1901
Budzanow, Poland

DATE AND PLACE OF DEATH
February 17, 1982
New York, New York

Madness in Monroe's Method

When he was born in a town in Poland that is now part of Russia, Strasberg was named Israel Strassberg. When he was seven his family moved to the United States, where Strassberg subsequently Americanized his name to I. Lee Strasberg, and later dropped the "I." As a legendary acting teacher, Lee Strasberg opened the eyes of a generation of American actors, including Marlon Brando, Robert DeNiro, and Marilyn Monroe. Commenting on Strasberg's "method" of acting, Tennessee Williams once said that Strasberg-trained actors are more intense and honest: "They act from the inside out. They communicate emotions they really feel. They give you a sense of life."

During his life, Strasberg apparently had a profound impact on Marilyn Monroe around the time she signed her last Will in 1961. In her Will, Monroe gave Strasberg 75 percent of her residuary estate and all her tangible personal property to dispose of as he deemed appropriate. Ironically, when Strasberg himself died in 1982, he left his entire estate, including his substantial interest in Monroe's estate, to this third wife, Anna. Sixty-seven-year-old Strasberg had married then thirty-one-year-old Anna

Mizrahi in 1968, six years after Monroe's death. One wonders whether Monroe would really have wanted Strasberg's third and final wife to inherit the substantial continuing income from her estate.

Strasberg's first two wives died while married to him. He was survived by his third wife, Anna, and four children—"ADAM and DAVID STRASBERG, sons of my present marriage, and JOHN STRASBERG and SUSAN STRASBERG, children of my first marriage." As mentioned earlier, Strasberg left his entire estate to Anna, but if she had not survived him, the estate was to be left to his two sons from his third marriage, Adam and David. Perhaps Strasberg believed he had already adequately provided for his two older children. It is interesting to note that his daughter, Susan Strasberg, is named as a successor guardian for her stepbrothers, Adam and David, if Anna had not survived.

Ultimately, it would not matter because the then forty-five-year-old Anna survived her eighty-year-old husband and inherited his entire estate, valued at over one and one-half million dollars, plus the lion's share of the Marilyn Monroe legacy as well. Widow Anna Strasberg was subsequently appointed the sole administrator of the Monroe estate by the New York court. With Monroe's estate still generating enormous annual income, Monroe might feel mad that she took some expensive acting lessons from a master of the method.

/s/ *Lee Strasberg*

Will dated April 24, 1981
Residing at 135 Central Park West, New York, New York

Vincente Minnelli

DATE AND PLACE OF BIRTH
February 28, 1903
Chicago, Illinois

DATE AND PLACE OF DEATH
July 25, 1986
812 North Crescent Drive
Beverly Hills, California

Just a Matter of Time

Best known for his deft direction of grand and roman-tic Hollywood song-and-dance productions, Vincente Minnelli wrote in his autobiography entitled *I Remember It Well,* "I work to please myself. I'm still not sure if movies are an art form. And if they're not, then let them inscribe on my tombstone what they could about any craftsman who loves his job, 'Here lies Vincente Minnelli. He died of hard work.'"

Minnelli married the talented and volatile actress Judy Garland in 1946, shortly after she had completed her star-ring role in a movie being directed by Minnelli called *Meet Me in St. Louis.* Five years later, in 1951, Garland filed for divorce, claiming in part that Minnelli "secluded himself and wouldn't explain why he would be away and leave me alone so much." During their marriage, they had one daughter, Liza. Referring to his former wife Judy, who had died in 1969, and his Academy Award-winning daughter, Liza, Minnelli wrote, "How many men can lay claim to being loved by the most extraordinary talents of not one, but two generations? And who loved, not always wisely, in return? But love is what life is all about. Love of wife, love of family, love of work."

Besides Liza and Judy, Vincente found the time to love his second and third wives, Georgette Magnani and Denise Gigante. Unfortunately, both of those marriages also ended in divorce. During his second marriage, Minnelli had a second daughter, named Christiane Nina. At the time of his death, Minnelli was married to his fourth wife, formerly Lee Anderson. As succinctly stated in his 1982 Will:

I declare that I am married to LEE ANDERSON MIN-NELLI, formerly known as LEE ANDERSON, and that all references to "my wife" in this Codicil [sic] and here-after, shall be to her. I have two (2) children, namely, LIZA MINNELLI GERO, and CHRISTIANE NINA MIN-NELLI MIRO. I have no deceased children.

In his Will, Minnelli refers to an "Antenuptial Agreement between myself and my wife, then LEE ANDERSON, dated March 6, 1980, which Agreement is incorporated herein by reference." Perhaps due to or in spite of that antenuptial agreement, Minnelli makes a $50,000 bequest to his wife, Lee. He also makes a $5,000 bequest to his second daughter Christiane Nina. Referring to the $5,000 bequest to his second daughter, the Will states, "The amount of this gift is with the recognition that my daughter, CHRISTIANE NINA MINNELLI MIRO, is financially well provided for al-ready."

Despite the reference to one daughter's financial well-being, Minnelli gives "all my tangible property, including my household furnishings, jewelry, memorabilia, works of art and any automobiles to which I hold title" and his entire residuary estate to his other daughter, Liza, who was not exactly a pauper herself. In addition, Minnelli made the following devise to Liza:

> I give my real property situated in Los Angeles County, California, and commonly known as 812 North Crescent Drive, Beverly Hills, California, together with any insurance on the property, to my daughter, LIZA MINNELLI GERO, if she survives me. . . .

In deference to his wife, Minnelli includes the following "wish" in the article giving the real property outright to Liza:

> . . . it is my wish that my wife, LEE ANDERSON MINNELLI, be permitted to continue to occupy the house on this real property, furnished substantially as it is at my death, during her life time, without payment of costs and maintenance of the home (excluding food, daily supplies and the like). In the event my daughter, LIZA MINNELLI GERO or her issue decide it is necessary to sell or occupy this real property, then it is my wish that a suitable apartment or other place of residence be provided on the same terms as above stated.

Liza was clearly being designated to "wear the pants" after father was somewhere over the rainbow with her mother. However, not taking any chances that his estate's disposition would be contested, Minnelli's Will also included the basic *in terrorem* clause.

In a codicil that he signed a year after his Will, Minnelli increased the bequest to his wife from $50,000 to $100,000.

Despite his often climactic endings on the silver

screen, Minnelli wanted his own exit to be quiet and inconspicuous. His Will simply states:

> This will confirm my previously stated desire that upon my death my remains be cremated, and that there be no funeral services.

As one might have guessed, Minnelli appointed his daughter Liza as the sole executor of his Will. It is ironic that, like Henry Fonda, Minnelli died shortly after completing a film starring his daughter, entitled *A Matter of Time*.

/s/ *Vincente Minnelli*

Will dated March 25, 1982
Codicil dated June 23, 1983
Signed at Beverly Hills, California

John Cassavetes

DATE AND PLACE OF BIRTH
December 9, 1929
New York, New York

DATE AND PLACE OF DEATH
February 3, 1989
Los Angeles, California

A Man Under the Influence

Like many of his films, the one-page, handwritten will of director and actor John Cassavetes is an example of his truthful and direct style. Cassavetes's Will bluntly and simply states:

> I leave all and everything I own or will own to my beloved wife, Gena Rowlands Cassavetes.
>
> I leave nothing to any one else, whomsoever, they may be.
>
> I owe no one any debt or obligation, other than usual and ordinary bills.
>
> No one has done me a special service that I feel obligated to.
>
> I hereby appoint my wife, Gena Executor of this Will . . .

Cassavetes had been married to Gena Rowlands for over thirty years. She had appeared in several of her husband's films and won an award at the 1980 Venice Film Festival for her role in the film *Gloria*.

Besides his wife, Cassavetes was survived by his three children—Nicholas, Alexandra, and Zoe. It is a good thing that Cassavetes's wife survived him because there were no provisions for the guardians of his children or a successor executor if she had not. From this bare-bones Will, it is clear that Cassavetes's calling was as a filmmaker, not as a Will drafter.

/s/ *John Cassavetes*

Will dated June 3, 1988
Will signed at 7917 Woodrow Wilson Drive
Los Angeles, California

Orson Welles

DATE AND PLACE OF BIRTH
May 6, 1915
Kenosha, Wisconsin

DATE AND PLACE OF DEATH
October 10, 1985
1717 N. Stanley Avenue
Los Angeles, California

Raising Kane

Radio broadcaster, actor, and film director Orson Welles was a source of controversy from the time of his faked broadcast of a Martian invasion of New Jersey in 1938 through his tour de force film *Citizen Kane* and until the day he died. Welles's Will was also controversial because it included substantial gifts to a woman who was not Welles's wife.

In his 1982 Will, Welles makes the following bequests and devise of real property to a woman who had been his companion for several years:

> I hereby give to Olga Palinkas (also known as Oja Kodar), whose address is Post Restante Primosten, Republic of Yugoslavia, the house located at 1717 North Stanley Avenue, Los Angeles, California . . . and all of the improvements and household furniture, furnishings, pictures, books, silver, paintings, works of art and other personal effects therein. . . . All taxes attributable to this bequest shall be paid from the residue of my Estate.

Welles left his residuary estate to his third wife, the Italian actress Paolo Mori Welles, whom he had married in 1955. If Mrs. Welles had not survived her husband, then Welles's residuary estate was to be left entirely to Olga Palinkas.

To each of his three daughters, Rebecca, Christopher, and Beatrice, Welles made a $10,000 bequest. Daughter Christopher was the issue of his first marriage, to Virginia Nicholson. Daughter Rebecca was Welles's child with his second wife, Rita Hayworth. And daughter Beatrice was Welles's child with his third and final wife, Paola. Although Welles had been divorced from his first two wives, he treated all his daughters equally under his Will.

As the executor of his Will, Welles named producer Greg Garrison, whom Welles had first met in 1946 and with whom Welles collaborated often in his later years. Apparently, Welles felt that neither his wife Paola nor friend Olga were appropriate for the role of his executor.

Finally, the Will contains this unusual section excerpted from the *in terrorem* clause:

> If any beneficiary under this Will is any manner directly or indirectly contests or attacks this Will or any of its provisions, including paragraph B or Article FOURTH hereof giving the entire house to Olga Palinkas, any share or interest in my Estate given to such beneficiary under this Will is revoked and shall be disposed of in the same manner provided herein as if such beneficiary had predeceased me leaving no living lawful descendants.

By specifically referring to the gift to his companion Olga, Welles obviously wanted to prevent his wife from contesting the gift of his California home to his beautiful companion. Although Welles maintained a home in

Los Angeles, California, he was a legal resident of
Nevada when he died. It was, however, in his Los Angeles home that Welles suffered the fatal heart attack that
killed him.

/s/ *Orson Welles*

Will dated January 15, 1982

Walt Disney

DATE AND PLACE OF BIRTH
December 5, 1901
Chicago, Illinois

DATE AND PLACE OF DEATH
December 15, 1966
St. Joseph's Hospital
Los Angeles, California

A Mickey Mouse Operation

Walter Elias Disney was raised on a farm. That might partially explain his fascination with mice, ducks, dogs, deer, crickets, pigs, and just about every other kind of animal real or imagined. In his creations of Mickey and Minnie, Donald and Daffy, Pluto, Bambi, Jiminy, and three little pigs, it has been said that Disney was the first person to give animals a soul and imbue them with distinct personalities.

About his most famous international star, known as Topolino in Italy, Michel Souris in France, Miki Kuchi in Japan, Miguel Ratoncito in Spain, and Mikki Maus in Russia, Disney once said, "Sometimes I've tried to figure out why Mickey appealed to the whole world. . . . He's a pretty nice fellow who never does anybody any harm, who gets into scraps through no fault of his own, but always manages to come up grinning. Why, Mickey's even been faithful to one girl, Minnie, all his life. Mickey is so simple and uncomplicated, so easy to understand that you can't help liking him."

Like his favorite character Mickey Mouse, Walt himself was married to one girl all his life. He married the woman who had been the maid of honor at his brother Roy's wedding on April 7, 1925. Lillian Bounds was from Idaho and had been working as an inker and painter at the Disney Studios. On July 13, 1925, Walt married Lillian in her uncle's living room in Idaho. After their marriage, Lillian worked at the studio in times of need and was with her husband over forty years later until the night before he died. Together, they had two daughters, Diane and Sharon. As Walt's 1966 Will states:

> I declare that I am married to LILLIAN B. DISNEY and that I have only two children, namely, DIANE DAISEY MILLER and SHARON DISNEY BROWN.

To Lillian, Disney gave "all of my tangible personal property and personal effects, including without limitation, all my household furniture, furnishings, silverware, books, paintings, works of art, automobiles, clothing, jewelry, miniatures, awards and all other similar items." In addition, Lillian was the beneficiary and a trustee of a family trust consisting of 45 percent of Disney's residuary estate, which was quite substantial and continues to receive royalty payments from the many Disney creations. Another 45 percent of the residuary trust was distributed to the Disney charitable foundation, which contributed part of its funds toward the completion of Disney's esteemed California Institute of the Arts ("Cal Arts") campus. The remaining 10 percent of the residuary estate was held in trust for a group of Disney relatives.

In his Will, Disney appointed his wife, Lillian, his attorney, Herbert F. Sturdy, and the United California

Bank as his executors. The Will was prepared by one of Los Angeles's most expensive law firms and is quite detailed.

There is also the standard *in terrorem* clause and the following:

> Except as otherwise provided in this Will, I have intentionally and with full knowledge omitted to provide for my heirs, including any persons who may claim to be an issue of mine.

Perhaps Walt was concerned that there might be some others claiming to be little Disney mice scampering around.

Conspicuously absent from Disney's Will are any instructions or provisions for his funeral or burial. It has been reported that Disney was intrigued by the possibilities of cryogenesis. (Cryogenesis is the scientific technique whereby a person may be chemically frozen or preserved until a cure for the particular fatal ailment has been discovered.) It has long been rumored that Disney himself opted to avail himself of cryogenesis. However, papers filed with the court indicate a payment made by Disney's estate to the Forest Lawn Memorial Park Association in Glendale, California, in an amount exceeding $40,000 "for the interment property, a memorial tablet, Endowment Care Fund deposit and state and city sales taxes." It is noteworthy that the interment property was not selected until September 19, 1967, almost a year after Disney's death. It may have been this delay that has fueled the speculation of Walt Disney on ice.

Seeming to whistle while he worked throughout his

productive career, Walt Disney left a legacy of happiness, dopiness, grumpiness, bashfulness, and sheer joyfulness. All around the world, countless wishes have been made on his stars.

/s/ *Walter E. Disney*

Will dated March 18, 1966

Alfred Hitchcock

DATE AND PLACE OF BIRTH
August 13, 1899
London, England

DATE AND PLACE OF DEATH
April 29, 1980
10957 Bellagio Road
Los Angeles, California

The Master of Suspense Until the End

An undisputed master of suspense, Alfred Hitchcock often turned the world upside down or inside out in his movies. But despite plots filled with international intrigue, suspicion, violence, or sexual obsession, Hitchcock himself appears to have had a stable and serene personal life, especially by Hollywood standards. He married his assistant Alma Reville in 1926, and they remained married for the next fifty-four years until the day he died. Alma worked on many of his films as his general assistant or as a writer. The couple had one child, Patricia, who appeared in several of Hitchcock's films and on his television shows, "Alfred Hitchcock Presents" and the "Alfred Hitchcock Hour," broadcast during the late 1950s and early 1960s.

Like the intricately woven plots that deliberately and methodically unfold in his films, Hitchcock signed his Will in 1963, and then proceeded to make six sets of changes to that Will during the next seventeen years. The last codicil was signed only one month before he died. The signature on that final codicil shows the serious effects that his arthritis had on Hitchcock's ability to sign his name.

Compared to the richness of his cinematic imagery, Hitchcock's twenty-five-page Will is rather dry. Despite the lengthy legal verbiage, there is little of Hitchcock's personality showing through. Not one of his great films is mentioned, nor any particular items from his large collection of art or other memorabilia. Essentially, the entire estate is left to his wife, outright and in trust, with the remainder passing to his daughter and then grandchildren.

Hitchcock's Will is also unusual in that the *in terrorem* clauses appear on page one, rather than being more discreetly placed in the "boilerplate" clauses later in the Will. Despite the prominent placement of this clause in his Will, one wonders whether Hitchcock might have enjoyed a battle royal over his estate.

Also unusual about the Hitchcock Will is that his long-time wife, Alma, signed a "waiver" that was attached to the Will and also admitted to probate. This unusual waiver states in part:

I, ALMA REVILLE HITCHCOCK, wife of ALFRED J. HITCHCOCK, have read the foregoing Will of my husband. . . . I am fully convinced of the reasonableness and wisdom of the provisions of this Will, and I hereby elect to accept and acquiesce in the provisions of his Will, waiving all claims to my share of any community property and all other claims that I may have upon any of the property disposed of by his Will . . .

Draw your own conclusions of Hitchcockian intrigue on that one.

As mentioned above, Hitchcock made six subsequent changes to his 1963 Will. Some of these codicils change the changes made in prior codicils, and one wonders why a new Will was not prepared. Perhaps Hitchcock wanted people to see how his thinking had changed over the years. The most significant and startling change is the one he made in the final codicil he signed about one month before he died. In that final codicil, Hitchcock removed his wife, Alma, his friend and previous agent Lew Wasserman, who was then the chairman and chief executive officer of Universal Studios, and an attorney named Citron as his executors and trustees. He retained his longtime attorney Samuel Taylor and added his daughter, Patricia, as a co-executor and co-trustee with Hitch's Taylor. We can only speculate about the reasons for this radical change shortly before Hitchcock died at the age of eighty.

/s/ *Alfred Hitchcock*

Will dated August 8, 1963

Alma Hitchcock's waiver dated August 8, 1963

First Codicil dated December 7, 1965

Second Codicil dated January 30, 1967

Third Codicil dated July 3, 1969

Fourth Codicil dated November 17, 1971

Fifth Codicil dated August 3, 1977

Sixth Codicil dated March 25, 1980

The Artists

Art Is Long, Life Is Short

WILLEM DE KOONING
The Man of Women
MARCH 19, 1997

MARK ROTHKO
Art "Appreciation"
FEBRUARY 25, 1970

NORMAN ROCKWELL
No More Rock in Stock
NOVEMBER 8, 1978

GEORGIA O'KEEFFE
Above New York and Below New Mexico
MARCH 6, 1986

ANDY WARHOL
"Death Means a Lot of Money, Honey"
FEBRUARY 22, 1987

LOUISE NEVELSON
Mother Knows Best
APRIL 17, 1988

ROBERT MAPPLETHORPE
Lights Out
MARCH 9, 1989

Willem de Kooning

DATE AND PLACE OF BIRTH
April 24, 1904
Rotterdam, Holland

DATE AND PLACE OF DEATH
March 19, 1997
182 Woodbine Drive
East Hampton, New York

The Man of Women

For the 20th Century abstract expressionist artist whose most famous paintings were depictions of women, it is not surprising that his Will is filled with women. In his bold and expressive paintings, de Kooning illustrated his view of women ranging from sex symbols to fertility goddesses to Edvard Munch-like witchy women. It is not for us to determine which women in his life represented each of those character types, but it is noteworthy that de Kooning's sole surviving legal heir was his daughter, Lisa, who was born from her father's relationship with a woman who was not his wife.

It seems that daughter Lisa was the apple of her father's eye as he named her a co-Executor of his Will and bequeathed to her under Article SECOND, "all jewelry, clothing, and other articles of personal use or adornment, and my studio and its contents, except for works of art, and land at 182 Woodbine Drive, East Hampton, N.Y."

As for his long-time companion and Lisa's mother, Joan Ward, de Kooning's Will provides the following:

THIRD: I give and bequeath to JOAN WARD, if she shall survive me, any and all automobiles and their accessories and equipment which may be owned by me at the time of my death.

One of de Kooning's most famous paintings is entitled "Woman and Bicycle" (1953), but there is no bequest of any bikes in his Will.

De Kooning provided for Miss Ward further by directing the establishment of a life estate for her in "the house owned by me at Acabonac Road [sic], Springs, East Hampton, New York, and all household furniture and other articles of household use or adornment (but not including works of art)." If Miss Ward had not survived, which she did, then that property was to pass to their daughter Lisa.

Finally, de Kooning also provided for a $200,000 trust fund for Miss Ward, which was to be payable to Miss Ward at the rate of $20,000 per year with any remaining balance at the time of her death, passing to Lisa.

At the time that he signed his Will in 1981, Willem de Kooning was married to Elaine de Kooning. Together, they had no children. Although Elaine predeceased her husband, dying eight years before he did on February 1, 1989, his Will was never updated to reflect her death. For wife Elaine, the Will provides for one-half of the residuary estate (i.e. the property remaining in the estate, including artworks, after the foregoing bequests and devises) to be held in trust for her life, with the other one-half to be held in trust for daughter Lisa until she reached the age of thirty-five (35). Since Elaine did not survive her husband, the entire residuary estate passed to Lisa. If both Elaine and Lisa had not survived, the residuary estate was to be distributed to a charitable foundation selected by the Executors.

As for the Executors of his Will, de Kooning named

Elaine, Lisa and his attorney, John L. Eastman. The Will provided further that if any of the three of them did not act, then his or her replacement was to be Lee V. Eastman (the father of John, and also an attorney). As the elder Mr. Eastman also predeceased the artist, only Lisa de Kooning and John L. Eastman qualified as the Executors of his Will. It is worth noting that John L. Eastman was also the co-Executor of the Will of his famous sister, Linda Eastman McCartney, and that the Eastman family name was originally "Epstein".

In view of de Kooning's relationships with both Elaine and Joan, the Will includes these unusual survivorship clauses which provide as follows:

TENTH: If either ELAINE deKOONING or JOAN WARD and I shall die under circumstances that it is doubtful which of us died first then the provisions of this Will shall take effect in like manner as if such beneficiary had predeceased me.

ELEVENTH: If my daughter LISA deKOONING and I shall die under circumstances that it is doubtful which of us died first, then the provisions of this Will shall take effect in like manner as if such beneficiary had survived me.

It is noteworthy that throughout the Will, the "de Kooning" name is not punctuated in the manner in which the artist himself wrote it. In fact, the initials "W de K" appear on each page of the Last Will and Testament.

Having made his mark as one of the greatest painters of his time, Willem de Kooning left a Will which highlighted his complicated and complex relationships with the women in his life. The Will does not mention any of the specific artworks which helped to make the house painter turned fine artist from Rotterdam, Holland into a towering figure of the post World War II art world.

/s/ *Willem de Kooning*

Will dated March 1, 1981

Mark Rothko

DATE AND PLACE OF BIRTH
September 25, 1903
Dvinsk, Russia

DATE AND PLACE OF DEATH
February 25, 1970
157 East 69th Street
New York, New York

Art "Appreciation"

The painter whose life and death changed the course of art and artists' estates was named Marcus Rothkovich at his birth in the Latvian region of Russia, but the world knew him simply as "Rothko." It was during the 1940s and 1950s that Rothko became a leader of a loosely knit group of artists labeled "abstract expressionists" (a label he disdained) in New York.

Rothko's large-scale paintings dating from the late 1940s until his suicide in 1970 were outpourings of human emotions ranging from tragedy to ecstasy. Rothko's earliest abstract works were greeted with skepticism by many in the postwar art world. For the painter and his much younger second wife (he had been married first to Edith Sacher in the early 1930s and divorced from her in the 1940s), Mary Alice ("Mell") Beistle, those were years of struggle and sacrifice. But in the early 1950s, a new artistic consciousness arose among some in the art world who began to take notice of an emerging cadre of "abstract expressionists."

Increasingly critically acclaimed, in 1958 Rothko was commissioned by the wealthy Bronfman family of the Seagram company to paint a series of murals to hang in modern architecture's monolith on New York's Park Avenue bearing the family name. The Seagram Building was being designed by Mies van der Rohe and Philip Johnson. The Rothko paintings were to hang in the The Four Seasons restaurant, which, since its opening, has for over one hundred seasons catered to the tastes of the most wealthy and powerful people in New York. For reasons that are not fully documented, Rothko himself allegedly canceled the prestigious Seagram commission, withdrew the completed paintings, and reportedly returned $14,000 that he had already received of the total commission of $35,000.

As Rothko's Will makes evident, these Four Seasons paintings had special significance for Rothko. The second article of his Will bequeaths to "the Tate Gallery, London, England, five (5) paintings of their choice of those paintings which were created by me for the Seagram Building, New York in 1959." In this one respect, the artist's wishes were honored, as these paintings, and others by Rothko, can be found today in special rooms devoted to Rothko's work in London's Tate Gallery.

With failing health leading to increased alcoholism and depression, Rothko's twenty-five-year marriage to Mell showed strain, and the two were separated in the fall of 1968. It was around that time that Rothko signed his last Will, dated September 13, 1968.

In that last Will, Rothgo gives Mell the 118 East 95th Street town house he owned, "together with all of the contents thereof" (including all the paintings therein, as subsequently determined in a "construction proceeding" brought in the New York Surrogate's Court) and a $250,000 bequest. The Will provided further that if his wife did not survive him, then that property was to be equally divided between his two children, Kate and

Christopher. The balance of his estate, including hundreds of paintings worth millions of dollars, was left to the not-yet-formed "MARK ROTHKO FOUNDATION," whose charitable purposes were not defined in his Will. In the Will, the foundation was vaguely described as "a nonprofit organization, incorporated under the laws of the State of New York." The value of Rothko's estate was reportedly $30 million when he died, and $50 million by the time the precedent-setting case of *Matter of Rothko* had concluded.

Rothko's two-page Will was prepared by his longtime accountant, Bernard J. Reis. Reis and two other friends of Rothko's, painter Theodoros Stamos and anthropologist/professor Morton Levine, were named as the executors of Rothko's Will.

To control the undefined multimillion-dollar foundation, the Will states: "The Directors of the Foundation are to be: William Rubin [Museum of Modern Art curator], ROBERT GOLDWATER [Rothko's designated biographer], BERNARD J. REIS, THEODOROS STAMOS and MORTON LEVINE." It is ironic that Reis's secretary, who typed the Will, left William Rubin's name in lowercase letters and put the other names in all capital letters because Rubin would be dropped as a director of the foundation before Rothko's death.

The vibrations caused by *Matter of Rothko* have had a major impact upon the art world. The problems arose from a poorly conceived and drafted Will. Besides the divided royalties and conflicts of interest rife within the Rothko estate, the purpose of the "MARK ROTHKO FOUNDATION" was nowhere defined. The executors ostensibly wanted to give grants to aging artists in need (which would also allow them to liquidate the estate's assets, thereby "earning" substantial commissions for themselves). On the other side was daughter Kate Rothko, who claimed that her father always wanted his paintings kept in groups and hung in the proper environments. The Will itself demonstrates Rothko's concern with the issue of keeping certain paintings together, as shown by the initial bequest of five paintings to the Tate Gallery.

When Surrogate Millard L. Miconick handed down his opinion in 1977, Kate Rothko, her brother, Christopher, and the art-loving public won hands down. The Surrogate decreed that all three executors were to be removed and replaced by Kate Rothko as the sole administrator of the estate. The contracts with the Marlborough Gallery were voided in toto, and the three executors were assessed surcharges, fines, and damages amounting to over $9 million. All the Rothko artworks that had not been removed by the Marlborough Gallery were ordered returned to the estate. Half of those artworks were given equally to the two Rothko children (Mell Rothko died only six months after her husband's death), and the other half were given to the Mark Rothko Foundation to be distributed to art museums and other institutions as the newly constituted Foundation Board deemed appropriate. After protracted appeals, the New York Court of Appeals upheld Surrogate Midonick's decision in 1977, finally ending the litigation over the artist's estate seven years after his death.

The Rothko Foundation wound up the core of its activities in 1986, sixteen years after the death of the artist. The artworks were distributed to approximately thirty museums in the United States and abroad, with most of them going to the National Gallery of Art in Washington.

Rothko's daughter, Kate, is now a doctor, is married, and has two children. Christopher Rothko was graduated from Yale University and is pursuing an interest in music. Those who find themselves staring into the depths of Mark Rothko's magnificent paintings may briefly forget the disconcerting relationships between great art and money that often lie beneath the surface.

/s/ Mark Rothko

Will dated September 13, 1968

Norman Rockwell

DATE AND PLACE OF BIRTH
February 3, 1894
New York, New York

DATE AND PLACE OF DEATH
November 8, 1978
Stockbridge, Massachusetts

No More Rock in Stock

One of the most popular American artists of his times, Norman Rockwell was best known for his memorable cover illustrations of *The Saturday Evening Post*. The subject matter was invariably wholesome and usually in a country setting, but later in his career, Rockwell created pictures addressing pressing social issues. He may have had his artistic detractors for being an "illustrator" and not an artist, but there can be no doubt that Norman Rockwell's art has touched the hearts of millions of people.

Rockwell was married three times. His first marriage, to Irene O'Connor, lasted from 1916 until ending in divorce in 1928. Two years later, Rockwell married a California teacher named Mary Rhodes Barstow. Together, Norman and Mary had three sons—Jarvis, Thomas, and Peter. The Rockwells first lived in Vermont, but later settled into a carriage house with a studio in Stockbridge, Massachusetts. Mary Rockwell died in 1959. In 1961, Rockwell married his third and final wife, Mary L. Punderson.

In his Will Rockwell leaves all of his tangible property

and his residential property, exclusing his studio and the contents thereof, to his wife, Mary. For the studio of the great draftsman and painter, the Will provides in "CLAUSE FIRST":

> I give, devise and bequeath to the NORMAN ROCK-WELL ART COLLECTION TRUST . . . the building which I have used as my studio together with the contents thereof at the time of my death, including but not limited to any works of art done by me or others . . .

This provision was supplemented by a second codicil to Rockwell's Will which he signed shakily a few months before his death, which provides:

> I hereby add the following sentence to CLAUSE FIRST: Notwithstanding the foregoing, this bequest is conditioned upon the payments by Old Corner House, Inc., a charitable corporation located in said Stockbridge, of all expenses of removing said studio from said real estate and regrading and relandscaping said real estate so as to restore the same to an attractive and aesthetically appealing condition following such removal, and of any other costs in any way connected with or related to the fulfillment of this bequest, and if such condition is not satisfied, this bequest shall lapse . . .

Such a conditional bequest was a clever way to be sure that the work would be done properly and that the cost would be borne by the recipient of this artistic gold mine. Today, Rockwell's studio is not open to the public, but it will become a part of the new Norman Rockwell Museum scheduled to be opened in Stockbridge in 1993.

Under his Will Rockwell established a $500,000 trust for the benefit of his wife. The balance of Rockwell's estate was to be divided into equal shares for each of his three sons and held in trust for them for their lives. Income could also be paid to any widowed daughters-in-law until such time as she might remarry, and the remainder was left for his grandchildren. Rockwell took a trustworthy approach when dividing his estate.

In his Will Rockwell named his wife, Mary L. Punderson Rockwell, and one of his three sons, Thomas Rhodes Rockwell, as his executors. However, in a later codicil to that Will Rockwell added the Berkshire Bank and Trust Company as a coexecutor with his wife and son.

As trustees, Rockwell named his wife, son Thomas, and the Berkshire Bank. If Thomas could not act, then Rockwell designated his son Peter to act, of if he could not act, he named his son Jarvis. However, in the first codicil to his Will Rockwell changed the successor executor designation to provide that if either his wife or son could not act, that no successor executor needed to be added. Regarding his trustees, Rockwell's codicil continued:

> In the event no one of my said three sons shall be able
> or willing to serve or to continue to serve, I direct that
> the oldest adult grandchild of mine who is willing and
> able to serve as Trustee hereunder . . . shall serve as a
> successor Trustee together with said bank . . .

Apparently, Rockwell believed that one of the trustees of his wife's or sons' trusts should always be a family member, in addition to the bank.

The great sensitivity to family relationships depicted

in Norman Rockwell's art shows itself in the artist's own Will. It is often said that art imitates life, but in Norman Rockwell's case, life also imitated art.

/s/ *Norman Rockwell*

Will dated December 9, 1976
First Codicil dated June 17, 1977
Second Codicil dated May 29, 1978

Georgia O'Keeffe

DATE AND PLACE OF BIRTH
November 15, 1887
Sun Prairie, Wisconsin

DATE AND PLACE OF DEATH
March 6, 1986
St. Vincent's Hospital
Santa Fe, New Mexico

Above New York and Below New Mexico

Georgia O'Keeffe was one of the unique artistic forces of the twentieth century. In 1916 she had a one-woman exhibition of her paintings at famed photographer Alfred Stieglitz's legendary "291" Fifth Avenue gallery in New York. That show established O'Keeffe as an important emerging artist; she continued to delight critics until her death seventy years later at the age of ninety-eight.

O'Keeffe's relationship with Stieglitz was more than merely professional. They were married in 1924 and collaborated personally and professionally until Stieglitz's death twenty-one years later. After Stieglitz's death, O'Keeffe left the urban sprawl of New York and went to live in the starkly contrasting desert of New Mexico. With the change of landscape, O'Keeffe's art continued to express a deeply individualistic spirit.

After O'Keeffe had settled in her studio in an Abiquiu, New Mexico, ranch a new man appeared in her life. A young potter named "Juan" (not Don) Hamilton appeared at O'Keeffe's door one day looking for work and never left. Hamilton certainly won the trust and love of an opinionated and often brusque woman. He assisted O'Keeffe with the production of a book about her and a documentary film and attended to all the other things that a nonagenarian might want and need from a man in his thirties.

In her 1979 Will, made when she was ninety-one years old, O'Keeffe gives:

> all my right, title and interest to my ranch, consisting of a house and acreage located outside of Abiquiu, in the County of Rio Arriba and State of New Mexico, which was formerly part of the "Ghost Ranch" . . . together with the furnishings therein . . . to my friend, JOHN BRUCE HAMILTON, or if he does not survive me, to THE UNITED PRESBYTERIAN CHURCH IN THE UNITED STATES OF AMERICA, located at 475 Riverside Drive, New York, New York, for its general purposes.

In addition, Mr. Hamilton was allowed to select any six of O'Keeffe's paintings on canvas and any fifteen works from among O'Keeffe's drawings, watercolors, or pastels not otherwise disposed of in the Will.

O'Keeffe specifically bequeathed certain paintings to each of eight museums expressly named in her Will: The Art Institute of Chicago, Boston's Museum of Fine Arts, New York's Modern, Metropolitan, and Brooklyn museums, the Cleveland Museum of Art, the Philadelphia Museum of Art, and The National Gallery of Art received "all photographs of me taken by my late husband, ALFRED STIEGLITZ, which are presently on loan to said institution." She gave all her "letters, personal correspondence and clippings to YALE UNIVERSITY." All the rest of "my writings and papers, together with all copyrights thereon and rights of publication thereto," she gave to "my friend, JOHN BRUCE HAMILTON."

As one might have expected, O'Keeffe appointed Mr. Hamilton as the sole excecutor of her Will. In a 1983 codicil, his fee for acting as executor is limited to a not-so-mere $200,000. We need not be concerned about the plight of Mr. Hamilton because in a 1984 second codicil to her Will, O'Keeffe gives her entire residuary estate to "my friend, JOHN BRUCE HAMILTON." If Hamilton failed to survive her, O'Keeffe's estate would pass as *he* would appoint under his own Will. The changes made by this last codicil are even more incredible as that clause concludes, "In default of [John Bruce Hamilton's] effective exercise of this power of appointment, my residuary estate shall instead be distributed among the heirs of John Bruce Hamilton as if he had died intestate." The ninety-six-year-old's signature on that final codicil is very shaky. It is interesting to note that on the probate petition submitted with the Will and codicils, the "John Bruce Hamilton" mentioned repeatedly in the Will signed his name as "Juan Hamilton." Let's hope that at least O'Keeffe had the right man in mind.

That same codicil giving O'Keeffe's entire residuary estate to Hamilton also includes a one-dollar *in terrorem* clause just in case anyone was considering contesting the disposition of her estate. O'Keeffe was survived by a sister named Catherine Klernet. Sister Catherline lived in Portage, Wisconsin, and is not mentioned in sister Georgia's Will.

Finally, the Will makes no mention of O'Keeffe's burial, funeral, or cremation provisions. O'Keeffe's attorney said that she had been cremated and her ashes would be scattered in New Mexico, but he would not reveal where or when. "Ashes to ashes, dust to dust"; it seems fitting that the last remains of Georgia O'Keeffe should be spread on the desert lands that she had loved.

/s/ *Georgia O'Keeffe*

Will dated August 22, 1979
First Codicil dated November 2, 1983
Second Codicil dated August 8, 1984

Andy Warhol

DATE AND PLACE OF BIRTH
August 6, 1928 (?)
Pittsburgh, Pennsylvania

DATE AND PLACE OF DEATH
February 22, 1987
New York Hospital
New York, New York

"Death Means a Lot of Money, Honey"

The pop of Pop, Andy Warhol, died with a multifaceted estate worth in excess of $500 million. Yet under his Will he bequeathed $750,000 (less than 1 percent of the total value) to only three people—his two brothers, John and Paul, and "my friend, FREDERICK HUGHES," the man who gave him life-saving mouth-to-mouth resuscitation after Warhol's near fatal shooting in 1968. Warhol also named Mr. Hughes as his sole executor. Many have said that after Warhol's death, Hughes actually exercised more power than Warhol ever did. Hughes quickly sold Warhol's nonWarhol art and collectibles, netting over $25 million for the estate, and later sold *Interview Magazine* for a reported sum of $14 million.

Even in Warhol's bequest to his two brothers, Warhol gave Hughes unusually broad discretion. The third article of the Will states:

I give such portion of my residuary estate as my friend, FREDERICK HUGHES (or, if my said friend shall not survive m, my friend, VINCENT FREEMONT), shall validly appoint in equal shares, to such of my brothers,

JOHN WARHOL [sic] and PAUL WARHOL [sic], as shall survive me, by the exercise of a power of appointment over such portion of my residuary estate contained in an instrument in writing duly signed and acknowledged by my said friend and delivered to my Executor within six (6) months after the issuance of Letters Testamentary to my Executor; provided, however, that such portion of my residuary estate shall not exceed the sum of Five Hundred Thousand ($500,000) Dollars. . . .

One has to wonder what kind of consideration was given to allow one person the option to give Warhol's own two brothers (whose names are misspelled in the Will) nothing from his vast estate. As it turned out, each of Warhol's brothers received the maximum possible bequest under the Will—$250,000, the same as Fred Hughes himself. However, as executor and director of the Foundation for Visual Arts (discussed below), Hughes also stood to make millions of dollars in commissions.

With Warhol's gargantuan collection of cookie jars, bronzes, Fiesta ware, cigar-store Indians, watches, funeral urns, toys, jewelry, furniture, and other collectibles, seminal modern-art collection, and an estate holding separate parcels of real estate in New York, Montauk, and Colorado, one wonders whether Warhol ever considered the possibilities of establishing the Pop Art Museum or doing something more thoughtful with his estate. Instead, Warhol left the vast portion of his estate to a nebulous foundation, "THE FOUNDATION FOR VISUAL ARTS," which had not even been incorporated at the time of Warhol's death.

One of three sons of immigrant parents from Czechoslovakia, Andrew Warhola got a degree in pictorial design from Carnegie Institute of Technology (now Carnegie-Mellon University) and headed for New York in 1950. He dropped the *a* in Warhola and became a successful women's shoe (among other items) illustrator. In 1962, Warhol hit his mark and began to mirror American's consumer and voyeuristic society back at itself by exhibiting larger-than-life icons such as the Campbell's soup can, a Brillo box, or the late Marilyn Monroe.

Later, a darker side emerged in Warhol's art as he depicted images of death and disasters, including his arresting sequential images of the assassination of President Kennedy, an empty and waiting electric chair, or the scene of a fatal car crash. It has been observed that lurking beneath almost all of Warhol's paintings is the color black.

An assassination attempt by a disgruntled former Factory worker in 1968 turned Warhol even more inward. Themes of death played an important part throughout Warhol's entire artistic oeuvre as his late works include a series of skull paintings strangely reminiscent of the *memento mori* (or reminders of death) in Renaissance paintings.

In the late 1970s, Warhol emerged from his artistic shell and became a court painter for the rich and famous. At a minimum of $25,000 per portrait, Warhol was able to generate enough cash to support his many infamous film projects and a periodical that served to institutionalize Pop Culture—*Interview Magazine*.

Warhol was notoriously afraid of going to the doctor and hospitals. (He also attended church religiously.) In light of Warhol's concerns about medical care, it is ironic that his death from a heart attack, after his condition was termed "stable" following an elective gall bladder operation, occurred at five-thirty a.m. when Warhold was left alone in his room in one of New York's best hospitals.

Warhol's death came at a time in his life when he had been rejuvenated by the friendships and collaborations with a younger generation of artists, particularly Jean-Michel Basquiat. Basquiat's own drug-overdose death a year and a half later in the Great Jones Street studio, which he had rented from Warhol and then from Warhol's estate, was said to be indirectly related to Warhol's death. In artists such as Basquiat, Keith Haring, Kenny Scharf, and Ronnie Cutrone, Warhol saw a new breed of 1980s-style Pop artists with graffiti-art roots and whose friendships meant much to Warhol. It is noteworthy that Cutrone, who worked as one of Warhol's assistants, was also one of the witnesses to his Will when it was signed in 1982, at 860 Broadway, one of the Factory sites. Evidently, Warhol did not want to go to his fancy Park Avenue lawyers' office to sign a Will, so an associate from that prestigious law firm was apparently hastily dispatched* to supervise the Will's execution.

In light of the radical and drastic changes wrought on Warhol's estate after his death, one wonders whether the proper attention was directed toward estate planning for the unusual Andy Warhol. Shortly before he died, Warhold could not have been more correct when he prophetically stated in a videotape, "Death means a lot of money, honey."

/s/ *Andy Warhol*

---

*Will dated March 11, 1982. (The Will had apparently first been prepared in 1981, but that year was crossed out in five places on the Will and witnesses' affidavit and the year 1982 was inserted.)

Louise Nevelson

DATE AND PLACE OF BIRTH
September 23, 1899
Kiev, Russia

DATE AND PLACE OF DEATH
April 17, 1988
29 Spring Street
New York, New York

Mother Knows Best

One of the leading sculptors of the twentieth century, Louise Nevelson created monumental works that were often moody and mysterious. After a major retrospective of her works at the Museum of Modern Art in 1967, Nevelson's sculptures were quite valuable by the time she died. Her estate was reportedly worth almost $100 million. Not bad for the daughter of Russian immigrants—named Isaac and Minna Berliawsky—who had first settled at the age of five in the unlikely town of Rockland, Maine.

In her autobiography, called *Dawns and Dusks,* Nevelson says that she had always wanted to be an artist. About Rockland, Maine, Nevelson said, "I never made friends because I didn't intend to stay in Rockland, and I didn't want anything to tie me down." In 1920 she married Charles Nevelson and they moved to New York City, which would be Nevelson's home until the day she died. In 1922, the Nevelsons' only child, named Myron, was born. Eight years later, the marriage was disintegrating, and young Myron was reportedly tossed back and forth from father to mother and back to father again. Eventually, son Myron, who used the name Mike, left town on a merchant ship during World War II and was married three times by the time of his mother's death.

Nevelson's 1974 Will is about as simple and straight-forward as they come. She leaves her entire estate to "my son, Mike Nevelson"; if Mike did not survive her, then to Mike's "issue surviving me in equal shares per stirpes" (which is a contradiction in legal terms). The property was to be held in trust for any of her issue who might inherit property and be under the age of twenty-one. It is note-worthy that Nevelson herself had gained her own inde-pendence around the age of twenty-one.

Son Mike was the only person individually named in his mother's Will, other than his mother. Mike is named as the sole executor of the Will. The Will did include the following thirty-day survivorship provision:

> In the event that any beneficiary hereunder shall sur-vive me, but shall die within thirty (30) days after the date of my death, then all the provisions of this Will shall take effect in like manner as if said beneficiary had predeceased me.

Presumably, Mike looked both ways when crossing the street for at least thirty days after his mother's death. He met the thirty-day survivorship requirement and inher-ited his mother's entire estate. Mike Nevelson also met Di-ana Mackowan.

Reportedly for the last twenty-five years of her life, Nevelson had been attended to and assisted by a woman named Diana Mackowan. Mackowan claimed that she had been given many of Nevelson's sculptures over the years. Furthermore, Mackowan claimed that she was enti-tled to compensation amounting to $325,000 for her many years of service. Son and executor Mike rejected her claim for any compensation, attempted to evict her from the building that she had occupied for many years, and withheld the sculptures allegedly belonging to Miss Mackowan. The feud between the two has been unusually vitriolic and has divided Nevelson's art-world friends.

The battle over the estate is still being fought, but the question must be asked why Nevelson never updated her rather skimpy 1974 Will to make provision for her friend Diana Mackowan, if that is what she wanted to do. From Mike Nevelson's perspective, mother knew best.

/s/ *Louise Nevelson*

Will dated May 3, 1974

Robert Mapplethorpe

DATE AND PLACE OF BIRTH
November 4, 1946
Floral Park, New York

DATE AND PLACE OF DEATH
March 9, 1989
New England Deaconess Hospital
Boston, Massachusetts

Lights Out

According to personal accounts, handsome photographer Robert Mapplethorpe was as much a participant as a voyeur hiding behind his camera. Tragically, Mapplethorpe died from complications of acquired immune deficiency syndrome (AIDS). One of the most important influences in Mapplethorpe's life had been his companion, major art collector, and patron, Sam Wagstaff. Before he died of AIDS himself in 1987, Wagstaff had assembled one of the greatest photography collections ever, reportedly valued at $20 million, which he eventually sold to the Getty Museum. Wagstaff named his younger friend Robert Mapplethorpe as the primary beneficiary and executor of his estate. In that regard, Mapplethorpe's own Will provides:

> In the event that at the time of my death the administration of the Estate of Samuel J. Wagstaff, Jr., in which I have a substantial interest, has not been completed, I direct my executor to apply for letters of administration C.T.A. with respect to said estate and to complete the administration of said estate.

("C.T.A." describes the administration of an estate by a person not named in the Will, but who has been appointed to act *cum testamento annexo,* Latin for "with the Will annexed.")

Mapplethorpe is very generous to many friends named in his Will. He makes bequests ranging from $100,000 to $2,500 to almost twenty different people. One of the recipients of a $100,000 bequest is Mapplethorpe's former girlfriend, rock star Patti Smith. Mapplethorpe also establishes a $230,000 trust fund for the benefit of his friend Jack Walls. One other friend is the legatee of a "Fang wood reliquary figure from Gabon."

Mapplethorpe was survived by his father, mother, two brothers, and two sisters. His parents are not mentioned in his Will. One of his sisters gets a $10,000 bequest. To his brother Edward, who aided him during his last illness, Mapplethorpe made the following bequest:

> I give the sum of $100,000 and such of my photographic equipment as he shall select to my brother, ED-WARD MAPPLETHORPE, if he survives me.

Brother Ed survived and is using some of his late brother's photographic equipment today and operating under the nom de camera of Edward Maxey (which was mother Mapplethorpe's maiden name).

The bulk of Mapplethorpe's estate was left to The Robert Mapplethorpe Foundation, Inc., which he had established before he died. That foundation was established for the purposes of medical research, especially AIDS research, and for the visual arts, especially photography. Photography and AIDS—the two things that Mapplethorpe had lived for and died of respectively.

As his executor, Mapplethorpe appoints his attorney and trusted adviser, Michael Ward Stout. It appears that Stout had advised his client of the significant executor's commissions and fees he would earn as an executor of an estate of such size and property. But Mapplethorpe did not seem to mind, as in his Will he states:

> I am presently serving as executor of a substantial estate [Sam Wagstaff's] and am fully familiar with the duties of an executor and the compensation to which an executor is entitled to receive under the law of New York. I anticipate that the administration of my estate will be very time consuming and will require considerable skill and I direct that my executor and my trustee shall receive full statutory commissions.

Later, it gets thicker, as the Will states:

> I have appointed as fiduciaries persons with whom I presently have business associations. Michael Ward Stout, my designated executor and trustee, has served me as my attorney for more than five years, under difficult circumstances, and has served with great distinction. He is far more familiar than any other individual with my business activities and with my wishes with respect to the disposition of works of art which I have created as well as with respect to works created by others which I have collected. He is a specialist in the law of intellectual and artistic properties as well as a close and trusted personal friend.

With language such as that, it is not surprising that mom and pop Mapplethorpe chose not to contest the

Will. They would have been their wealthy son's only heirs if he had not had a Will.

Two days before he died a slow and painful death from AIDS in a Boston hospital, Mapplethorpe made additional bequests of either $2,500 or $5,000 to three other people. His attorney wisely chose to make this change by a codicil to the Will rather than by preparing a new Will with Mapplethorpe already so close to death. In that way, the Will itself would be less subject to attack as that of a seriously debilitated man; only the last codicil would be at risk. That last codicil was admitted to probate and those three individuals received their bequests.

Mapplethorpe's signature on the codicil is a jagged example of the signature of the photographer. In life, he had lived on the edge, and he fell over the edge at the age of forty-two, after leaving a legacy of controversy and photography that history and society would never forget.

/s/ Robert Mapplethorpe

Will dated June 23, 1988
Codicil dated March 7, 1989

One of a Kind

The One

ALBERT EINSTEIN
Personal Theories of Relativity
APRIL 19, 1955

Albert Einstein

DATE AND PLACE OF BIRTH
March 14, 1879
Württemberg, Germany

DATE AND PLACE OF DEATH
April 19, 1955
Princeton Hospital
Princeton, New Jersey

Personal Theories of Relativity

When he died in his sleep at the age of seventy-six, brilliant scientist, physicist, and pacifist Albert Einstein left a legacy of revolutionary scientific concepts that changed the world's view of itself.

For all his great achievements, Einstein had an inauspicious start, with his often-cited poor grades in school and then as an unknown clerk in a Swiss patent office. In 1901, Einstein married a Swiss student named Mileva Marec. Together, they had two sons—Albert Einstein, Jr., and Eduard Einstein. Subsequently, that marriage ended in divorce. In 1919, Einstein married his second cousin, Elsa Einstein, a widow with two daughters. She remained married to Einstein until her death in 1936 in Princeton, New Jersey. Einstein never again married before his own death almost twenty years later. However, Einstein did have a "secretary-housekeeper" named Helena Dukas for many years. Einstein's Will, which he signed in 1950, makes it quite clear that Helena Dukas was his top priority above and beyond Einstein's own relatives. Apparently, Einstein maintained certain personal theories of relativity.

Under his Will, Einstein gives to "my secretary, Helena Dukas . . . all of my personal clothing and personal effects, except my violin . . ." Einstein also established a trust to hold "all of my manuscripts, copyrights, publication rights, royalties and royalty agreements, and all other literary property and rights, of any and every kind or nature whatsoever." The income from that trust was to be paid to secretary Helena Dukas and then upon her death to stepdaughter Margot Einstein. Upon the death of both Margot and Helena, the property was to be delivered to the Hebrew University in Israel. In this article creating this trust for his manuscripts, Einstein states:

> In the interpretation of this provision of my will, it is to be borne in mind that my primary object is to make further provision for the care, comfort and welfare of my said secretary, HELENA DUKAS, during her lifetime; my secondary object is to make such further provision for the care, comfort and welfare of my said stepdaughter, MARGOT EINSTEIN, during her lifetime; and my final object is that any such property which may then remain (whether it consist of original manuscripts, or literary rights or property still owned by my estate, or the proceeds from the disposition of any such property or rights) shall to the extent that the same shall not have been distributed or paid over to my said secretary and my said step-daughter, pass to HEBREW UNIVERSITY and become its property absolutely, to be thereafter retained or disposed of by it as it may deem to be in its best interests . . .

To his stepdaughter Margot Einstein, who lived in Einstein's Princeton home with Albert and Miss Dukas, Einstein bequeathed "all of my furniture and household goods, chattels and effects, of every kind or nature." The parameters of "every kind or nature" to the mind of Albert Einstein must be left open to speculation.

Einstein made the following cash bequests under his Will: $20,000 each to stepdaughter Margot and secretary Helena, $15,000 to son Eduard, $10,000 to son Albert Einstein, Jr., or if he predeceased Einstein, to Einstein's favorite grandchild, Bernhard Caesar Einstein. A $10,000 trust was also established for the benefit of Albert's sister, Marie Winteler.

Einstein's violin was bequeathed to his grandson, Bernhard Caesar Einstein, with the provision that "if he shall not be of legal age, then I authorize and empower my Executors to deliver the same to his father, my son Albert Einstein, Jr., in his behalf, to be turned over to my said grandson when he shall attain majority." It seems to have been quite important to Einstein that his grandson be able to fiddle around with his beloved violin.

Einstein gave the remaining portion of his estate to his stepdaughter Margot, or if she did not survive him, to his son Albert Einstein, Jr. The Will provides that "without limitation of the absolute nature of the bequest of my residuary estate," if his sister, Marie Winteler, survived him and the $10,000 trust fund established for her was exhausted, then he requested that his said son or stepdaughter make other or further provisions "for the care, comfort and welfare of my said sister, as long as she shall live."

Einstein's Will does not contain any provisions regarding his funeral or burial. It was reported that shortly after his death Einstein's body was cremated—but not before his vital organs, including his brain, were removed from his body for the purpose of scientific study. Einstein's brain was certainly a worthy specimen.

/s/ Albert Einstein

Will dated March 18, 1950

The Sporting Life

Out of the Ballpark

JOE DIMAGGIO
"Where Have You Gone, Joe DiMaggio?"
MARCH 9, 1999

ARTHUR ASHE
Love 40-9
FEBRUARY 6, 1993

BABE RUTH
No More "Better Years"
AUGUST 16, 1948

Joe DiMaggio

DATE AND PLACE OF BIRTH
November 25, 1914
Martinez, California

DATE AND PLACE OF DEATH
March 8, 1999
Hollywood, Florida

"Where Have You Gone, Joe DiMaggio?"

The thirty-two (32) page Last Will and Testament of "JOSEPH P. DIMAGGIO, of the City of Hollywood, County of Broward and State of Florida, being of sound and disposing mind and memory. . . ." is signed by the great one himself on each and every page. In fact, on the signature page, where most mortals sign their Will only once, the great DiMaggio signed his exuberant signature twice, both before and after the witnesses' signatures. By the way the Will is printed on the stationery of the law firm in which DiMaggio's designated Personal Representative is a name partner. That good publicity may have been Mr. Coffee's last pitch.

Married to Marilyn Monroe at the height of her stardom and prowess, Joe DiMaggio captured the hearts, and other parts, of almost everybody in America. Whether it was his wholesome All-American good looks, or the sweet stroke of his bat in game after game and in nine World Series Championships, DiMaggio is on everyone's list of all-time sports greats and American icons. There was never anyone quite like Joe DiMaggio, and his Will reveals much about how the "Yankee Clipper" wanted his legal affairs handled after he brewed his last cup of coffee.

Article I on page one of the Will begins with a short "Statement of Family Members" as follows:

> I am not married and I have one adult child and two (2) grandchildren, to wit: my son, JOSEPH PAUL DIMAG-GIO, JR., and my grandchildren, KATHERINE MARIE DIMAGGIO and PAULA SUE DIMAGGIO, both of whom are adopted children of my said son.

In addition to the son and granddaughters mentioned above, Joe was also survived by four (4) great-grandchildren.

In his Will Joe provides for each of his relatives mentioned above in very different ways which is quite revealing about his personal feelings about each of them. For example, Joe gives all of his tangible personal property, including "household furnishings, silverware, china or linens, automobiles and jewelry together with all prepaid insurance policies on the above items" only to his granddaughter, Paula Sue DiMaggio. If she did not survive, that valuable property was to go to her children (i.e. DiMaggio's great-grandchildren), If Paula had had no children, then granddaughter Katherine Marie DiMaggio would step up to the plate for the china and linens, etc. It is hard to believe that the son of immigrant parents born in a poor California town was overly concerned with the disposition of his china and linens, but he must have had a careful attorney who was. Of course, conspicuously absent from the bequest of tangible personal property is Joe's son, from whom he was estranged at his death, for reasons which only the two of them will ever truly know.

The Will directs the establishment of a $250,000 trust fund for the benefit of each of Joe's great-granddaughter Kendahl R. Stein and for his great-grandson, Mitchell J. Stein. There are then $500,000 trust funds established for the benefit of each of Joe's great-granddaughters, Valerie F. Hamra and Vanessa S. Hamra. For those who need help on the arithmetic, that is a $250,000 differential between certain grandchildren. Despite that dramatic differential, the terms of the trusts were the same and each of those trusts continued until the great-grandchild reached the age 40, with principal payments also directed at ages 30 and 35.

From the balance of Joe's residuary estate, forty-five percent (45%) was to be placed in trust for the life of Joe's son, Joseph Paul DiMaggio Jr. The terms of that trust provide for payments of no more than $20,000 per year to Joe Jr. from the income of the trust, and the principal of the trust could be distributed to Joe Jr. only at the Trustee's discretion. Upon the death of Joe Jr., the property passes as he appointed to the extent of "his personal legal obligations owing at his death." To the extent that the power of appointment was not exercised, the remaining property passed 30% to the Katherine Marie DiMaggio trust and 70% to the Paula Sue DiMaggio trust.

Fifteen percent (15%) of the residuary estate was bequeathed to the Katherine Marie DiMaggio trust, and forty percent (40%) was given to the Paula Sue DiMaggio trust. Based on the various percentages in his Will, DiMaggio really knew how to make some seemingly cold-hearted decisions.

In his Will, DiMaggio appoints "my dear friend and attorney, MORRIS ENGELBERG, ESQ., as the Personal Representative of my estate." Engelberg is also appointed Trustee of the trusts, and is appointed attorney for the estate. The appointment of Engelberg as attorney is not only legally ineffective, but entirely unnecessary because who else would Morris Engelberg, as Personal Representative, hire to be his attorney. It is noteworthy that there is no one named as a back-up to Engelberg if he did not act. Perhaps Joe did not trust anyone else, but in view of Joe's many friendships throughout his lifetime, that seems unlikely. Furthermore, Engelberg had the right to name an individual or a bank or a trust company as his co-Personal Representative and co-Trustee and/or successor; Attorney Engelberg also had the right to revoke any such appointments. That unusually broad authority gives attorney Engelberg unrestricted and essentially absolute control of the Yankee Clipper's estate.

The Will expressly provides, "I further waive compliance with any other law now or hereinafter enacted in effect requiring qualification, registration, administration or filing of the accounting by my Trustee to any court." Needless to say, there was no requirement that Mr. Engelberg post any bond or other security in any jurisdiction. Besides, with the substantial fees that Mr. Engelberg would make as Trustee of the various trusts under the Will and as attorney for the estate, there is no reason to ever think that he might need to steal from the estate in any type of surreptitious or under the table way.

Much of DiMaggio's Will is thick "legalese" which is overly verbose and often nonsensical. For example, the Will provides that any successor corporate Trustee must be a bank or trust company "having a capital and surplus of not less than Five Million Dollars ($5,000,000)." These days, that amount is a drop in the bucket for a bank; even the Bowery Savings Bank, which Joe used to promote, had much more than that.

Near the end of the Will is an unusual clause pertaining to the "Services of Outside Representative" and provides:

My attorney and friend, MORRIS ENGELBERG, ESQ., or his designated representative as so appointed by him, in writing prior to his death, shall act at the representative of my estate and all trusts created hereunder in connection with the licensing and/or used of any [sic] name, photo, likeness, image and facsimile signature or memorabilia items to include, but not limited to, baseballs, T-shirts, photographs, mugs, jerseys, bats, baseball gloves and other memorabilia type merchandise together with all existing contracts in effect at the time of my death.

In view of the his place in America's collective consciousness, we can hope only that the "mugs" and "T-shirts" mentioned in his Will do justice to the image of the great DiMaggio, and portray him in a way that our cherished memories of Joltin' Joe will never go away.

/s/ *Joseph P. DiMaggio*

Will dated May 21, 1996
Will signed in Broward County, Florida

LAST WILL AND TESTAMENT
OF
JOSEPH P. DIMAGGIO
I, JOSEPH P. DIMAGGIO, of the City of Hollywood, County of Broward and State of Florida, being of sound and disposing mind and memory do hereby make, pub-

lish and declare this to be my Last Will and Testament hereby revoking any and all Wills and Codicils by me heretofore made.

ARTICLE I
STATEMENT ON FAMILY MEMBERS

I am not married and I have one adult child and two (2) grandchildren, to wit: my son, JOSEPH PAUL DIMAGGIO, JR., and my grandchildren, KATHERINE MARIE DIMAGGIO and PAULA SUE DIMAGGIO, both of whom are adopted children of my said son.

ARTICLE II
PAYMENT OF DEBTS, TAXES AND COSTS
OF ADMINISTRATION

I direct that all estate, inheritance, succession and other death taxes of any nature, together with any interest and penalties thereon, which may be levied or assessed by reason of my death by the laws of any state or of the United States with respect to property passing under this Will or any other property shall be considered a cost of administration of my estate, and that such taxes, together with all debts which I am legally obligated to pay at the time of my death, my last illness and funeral expenses and other costs of administration of my estate, shall be paid out of my residuary estate. In the event my residuary estate is insufficient to pay such debts, expenses, costs and taxes, I direct that the amount thereof in excess of my residuary estate shall be paid from other assets in the order provided by law. I authorize my Personal Representative to pay any and all of my debts which it feels, in its sole judgment and discretion, to be just and reasonable without the necessity of a formal claim being filed in the court by the creditor; provided, however, that my Personal Representative shall file its sworn statement with the court as to such debts paid within the prescribed time provided by law.

I authorize my Personal Representative to spend such sums for funeral expenses, the acquisition of a burial site, the erection of a suitable headstone or monument over my grave and for the perpetual care of my grave as he may think proper, without regard to any provisions of law limiting such expenditures.

ARTICLE III
CASH BEQUESTS

I hereby give and bequeath the sum of One Hundred Thousand Dollars ($100,000) to my nephew, JOSEPH DIMAGGIO (son of my deceased brother, MIKE DIMAGGIO).

ARTICLE IV
BEQUEST OF TANGIBLE PERSONAL PROPERTY

A. I hereby give and bequeath to my granddaughter, PAULA SUE DIMAGGIO, outright, if living, any and all tangible personal property excluding cash, stocks, bonds and real estate) which I may own at the time of my death. This bequest includes, but is not limited to, household furnishings, silverware, china or linens, automobiles and jewelry together with all prepaid insurance policies on the above items. If PAULA SUE DIMAGGIO shall not survive me, then I give, devise and bequeath to her surviving issue, in equal shares per stirpes, all of my tangible personal property (excluding cash, stocks, bonds and real estate) which I may own at the time of my death. This bequest includes, but is not limited to, household furnishings, silverware, china or linens, automobiles and jewelry together with all prepare insurance policies on he above items.

B. <u>Alternate Bequest</u>. If there is no living issue of PAULA SUE DIMAGGIO, then I bequeath any and all of my tangible personal property to my granddaughter, KATHERINE MARIE DIMAGGIO, outright, if living, if not, then to her issue, in equal shares, per stirpes. My granddaughter's issue shall divide such property among themselves amicably if able to do so; otherwise, my Personal Representative shall make the division in any manner deemed advisable, and the decisions of my Personal Representative shall be final and binding on all concerned.

If any beneficiary should be under the age of eighteen (18) years at the time distribution is required to be made to him or her under this Article of my Last Will and Testament, my Personal Representative is authorized to distribute such beneficiary's portion of this property to any suitable person selected by them, to be free of trust, for distribution to such beneficiary when he or she reaches his or her majority, and a receipt of such person shall constitute a complete acquittance to my Personal Representative.

C. Any property that is not distributed under this Article because the named beneficiary does not survive me, shall pass under and be distributed as part of my residuary estate.

/s/ *Joseph P. DiMaggio*

Arthur Ashe

DATE AND PLACE OF BIRTH
July 10, 1943
Richmond, Virginia

DATE AND PLACE OF DEATH
February 6, 1993
New York, New York

Love 40-9

Tennis great and humanitarian Arthur Ashe died from AIDS in February of 1993 at the age of 49, and was survived by his wife, Jeanne Moutoussamy and their 6 year old daughter named Camera. (Her name was a reference to the career as a photographer of Mrs. Ashe).

Ashe's 1990 Will specifically bequeathed all of his trophies, of which there were many, to his daughter Camera. However, that bequest specifically excluded all of the solid "gold tennis balls" owned by Ashe at the time of his death. Court records indicate that Ashe's multi-million dollar estate included gold bullion worth over $110,000.

The balance of Ashe's tangible property was bequeathed as follows:

I give and bequeath the balance of the tangible personal property owned by me at my death, and not effectively disposed of pursuant to the provisions of sub-paragraph A(1) of this Article II, including, but not limited to, household effects (such as furniture, furnishings, silver and objects of art), clothing, jewelry, books, camera, sporting equipment, automobiles and all other articles of personal or household use or ornament, together with any insurance thereon, to my wife, JEANNE MARIE MOUTOUSSAMY (herein referred to as "my wife"), if my wife survives me. If my wife does not survive me, I give and bequeath one-half (½) of such tangible personal property (either in kind or after sale and conversion into cash, as my Executors may determine) to my daughter, if she survives me, and I give and bequeath one-half (½) such tangible personal property (either in kind or after sale and conversion into cash, as my executors may determine) to such of my brothers and sister (namely, ROBERT K. ASHE, JOHNNIE E. ASHE and LORETTA ASHE HARRIS) as survive me, in such shares of substantially equal value as my Executors shall determine.

Arthur Ashe's Will also highlights what a sensitive and sensible person he was, and also how important education was to him. For example, in his Will, the terms of the trust for his daughter provides that certain payments to her were to be conditioned upon her obtaining a bachelor's degree from an accredited college or university. The Will was structured as follows so that Camera had a good reason to obtain her college degree as soon as possible:

My Trustees shall accumulate and add to the principal of such trust any balance of such net income not so paid or applied. When my daughter shall have attained the age of twenty-five (25) years, if she shall have earned a bachelor's degree from an accredited college or unversity (or if at the time property is to be disposed of under this paragraph C, my daughter shall have attained at lease such age, but not the age of thirty (30) years, and she shall have earned such a degree, then, at such time), my

Trustees shall pay over and distribute to my daughter, outright and free of trust, one-half (½) of the then-remaining principal and undistributed income, if and, of such trust. When my daughter shall have attained the age of thirty (30) years, if my daughter shall have earned a bachelor's degree from an accredited college or university, said trust shall terminate and my Trustees shall pay over and distribute to my daughter, outright and free of trust, all then-remaining principal and undistributed income, if any, of said trust. When my daughter shall have attained the age of thirty (30) years, if my daughter shall have earned a bachelor's degree from an accredited college or university, my Trustees shall pay over and distribute to my daughter, outright and free of trust, only one-half (1/2) of the then-remaining principal and undistributed income, if any, of said trust. At such time as my daughter shall have attained the age of thirty-five (35) years, said trust shall terminate, and my Trustees shall pay over and distribute to my daughter, outright and free of trust, all then-remaining principal and undistributed income, if any, of said trust.

The following family members were also important to Ashe and would have shared in his estate if his wife did not survive him:

ROBERT K. ASHE, Brother
LORETTA ASHE HARRIS, Sister
JOHNNIE E. ASHE, Brother
JOHN III MOUTOUSSAMY, Wife's nephew
DAVID MOUTOUSSAMY, Wife's nephew
ANGELLE MOUTOUSSAMY, Wife's niece
VERONICA MOUTOUSSAMY, Wife's niece

I appoint my wife, JEANNE MARIE MOUTOUSSAMY, to serve as sole Executor hereof. In the event that at any time and for any reason my wife fails to become or ceases to be Executor hereof, I appoint DONALD L. DELL, of Washington, D.C., to serve as substitute or successor sole Executor hereof.

Arthur Ashe's death states that his death was due to Acquired Immunodeficiency Syndrome as a consequence of "Blood Transfusion during coronary bypass surgery for Atherosclerotic Cardiovascular disease in 1983". It is ironic and tragic that an athlete with a very big heart died from an infection of that heart.

/s/ *Arthur Robert Ashe*

Will dated August 31, 1990

Babe Ruth

DATE AND PLACE OF BIRTH
February 6, 1895
Baltimore, Maryland

DATE AND PLACE OF DEATH
August 16, 1948
New York, New York

No More "Better Years"

George Herman Ruth, who was commonly known as "Il Bambino" or "Babe" Ruth, became one of the greatest sports icons in American history. At the height of his career Babe Ruth was reported to be the highest paid baseball player of his time. There was a period of time early in his career when Babe Ruth pursued an extravagant lifestyle and spent excessive amounts of money, however, later in life he apparently become a shrewd investor.

To the disappointment of his family, friends, and baseball fans across the nation, Babe Ruth succumbed to throat cancer at the age of fifty-three years. A week before his death, at the behest of then President Harry S. Truman, the White House had even inquired about Babe Ruth's condition at the hospital where he died. The Babe was survived by his wife, CLARA MAE RUTH, and two adopted daughters, DOROTHY RUTH SULLIVAN and JULIA RUTH FLANDERS, who were central figures in his life and his estate was primarily bequeathed to them accordingly. His will, which was executed just seven (7) days before his demise, provides for them as follows:

"I give and bequeath to my wife, CLARA MAE RUTH, if she shall survive me, all my household furniture, automobiles with the appurtenances thereto, paintings, works of art, books, china, glassware, silverware, linens, household furnishings and equipment of any kind, clothing, jewelry, articles of personal wear and adornment and personal effects, excepting however, souvenirs, mementoes, pictures, scrap-books, manuscripts, letters, athletic equipment and other personal property pertaining to baseball. In the event that my wife CLARA MAE RUTH shall not survive me, I direct my executors hereinafter named to divide the said property between my daughters, DOROTHY RUTH SULLIVAN and JULIA RUTH FLANDERS, as my said daughters may agree, or in the event they are unable to agree, to divide the said property between my said daughters as my Executors hereinafter named may, in their absolute discretion determine."

One can only guess whether his wife and daughters were not baseball fans or perhaps the prevailing generosity of Babe Ruth led him to bequeath all of his sports memorabilia as follows:

"I give and bequeath to my Executors hereinafter named or either of them who may qualify, all my souvenirs, mementoes, pictures, scrap-books, manuscripts, letters, athletic equipment and other personal property pertaining to baseball, and I request but do not direct my said Executors to divide the same among such persons, corporations and organizations as I may from time to time request or in such manner as they in their sole discretion may deem proper and fitting."

Under Babe Ruth's Will, his wife and daughters were also the beneficiaries of certain cash bequests, as well as Ruth's sister:

> "I give and bequeath to my wife, CLARA MAE RUTH, if she shall survive me, to my daughter, DOROTHY RUTH SULLIVAN, if she shall survive me, and to my daughter, JULIA RUTH FLANDERS, if she shall survive me, each the sum of Five Thousand ($5,000.) Dollars.
> I give and bequeath to my sister, MARY H. MOBERLY, now residing in Baltimore Maryland, if she shall survive me, the sum of Ten Thousand ($10,000.) Dollars."

Babe Ruth even graciously provided two former employees with cash sums pursuant to the terms of his Will:

> "I give and bequeath to FRANK DELANEY, providing he is in my employ at the time of my death, and to MARY REITH, providing she is in my employ at the time of my death, each the sum of Five hundred ($500.) Dollars."

Babe Ruth was a well-known sympathizer of the plight of underprivileged and sick children which was most likely the driving force for his establishment of a charitable organization, aptly named The Babe Ruth Foundation, Inc., in May of 1947. In fact, his charitable intent carried over at his death, as he bequeathed ten percent (10%) of his residuary estate, upon the death of his wife and termination of the testamentary trust set up for her, "to The Babe Ruth Foundation, Inc., a corporation organized under the Membership Corporations Law of the State of New York and dedicated to the interests of the kids of America."

Babe Ruth will always be remembered as one of the all-time greatest baseball players in history and his name lives on as a source of charity for needy children.

/s/ *George Herman Ruth*

Will dated August 9, 1948

The Super Rich

"*You Can't Take It With You*"

HARRY HELMSLEY
No More Rent
JANUARY 4, 1997

DORIS DUKE
From Poor Little Rich Girl
to Poor Tall Filthy Rich Woman
OCTOBER 28, 1993

MALCOLM FORBES
He Went Thataway . . .
FEBRUARY 24, 1990

JOHN JACOB ASTOR IV
Chivalry Is Dead
APRIL 15, 1912

NELSON A. ROCKEFELLER
Happy in Camp Rockefeller
JANUARY 26, 1979

J. PIERPONT MORGAN
No Guarantees
MARCH 31, 1913

HOWARD HUGHES
Summa, but Not Loud
APRIL 5, 1976

J. PAUL GETTY
Why Not to Marry a Billionaire
JUNE 6, 1976

CONRAD HILTON
No More Room Service
JANUARY 3, 1979

Harry Helmsley

DATE AND PLACE OF BIRTH
March 4, 1909
New York, New York

DATE AND PLACE OF DEATH
January 4, 1997
Scottsdale Memorial Hospital
Scottsdale, Arizona

No More Rent

Considering the substantial and unusual nature of his vast assets, including some of New York's most well-known buildings, the Will of Harry Helmsley is quite straight forward and seems almost too simple. For example, the following clauses in the Will of Harry Helmsley do not seem right:

ARTICLE SECOND: RESIDENCES

(A) I devise all residential real property and any interests in such real property (including condominiums), wherever situated, which I may own and maintain as a residence at the time of my death, together with all insurance policies thereon, to my wife, if she shall survive me.

(B) I devise and bequeath any interest which I may own at the time of my death in any cooperative apartment which I maintain as a residence, including, but without limitation, any securities of any cooperation owning the building in which such apartment is located and any lease or other agreement with such cooperation covering such apartment which I may own or hold at the time of my death, together with all insurance policies thereon, to my wife, if she shall survive me.

ARTICLE SIXTH RESIDUARY ESTATE

(A) If my wife survives me, I give my residuary estate to her.

Despite his wealth estimated at close to $2 billion dollars, Helmsley's Will makes a single bequest to his long-time secretary Cecil Fried:

<u>ARTICLE FOURTH: GENERAL LEGACIES</u> (A) I leave to my secretary, CECIL FRIED, if she shall survive me, the sum of TWENTY-FIVE THOUSAND DOLLARS ($25,000).

That represents an amount equal to approximately .0000125 of his estate.

There were two additional bequests in the Will of $250,000 each, but were conditioned upon the Queen not surviving the King.

<u>ARTICLE FOURTH: GENERAL LEGACIES</u> (B) If my wife does not survive me, I give to each of the individuals named below who survives me and who is employed at my death by me or by any corporation or partnership of which I am then a substantial owner, the sum set forth next to his name:

(1) To EDWARD BRADY, the sum of TWO HUNDRED FIFTY THOUSAND DOLLARS ($250,000).

(2) To BARBARA EVANS, the sum of TWO HUNDRED FIFTY THOUSAND DOLLARS ($250,000).

Unfortunately for Edward Brady, who was Head of Security for Helmsley, he was allegedly dismissed by Mrs. Helmsley about a year before Harry died. Despite the word "security" in his title, "job security" was not part of that in the Helmsley empire.

The clauses in Helmsley's Will pertaining to the choice

of successor Executors also manifests his dear wife's dominance and control. The Will states:

ARTICLE TENTH: FIDUCIARIES

(A) I appoint my wife, LEONA M. HELMSLEY, as the Executor of this Will. If my wife fails to qualify or ceases to act as Executor for any reason, the Executor shall be any one or more individuals or corporate fiduciaries, acting together or in succession, as my wife shall have appointed, whether before or after my death. Any such appointment shall be made by a written instrument signed by my wife in accordance with Section (C) of this Article or by my wife's Last Will and Testament.

Perhaps the most unusual clause in Harry's Will is this section from the very first paragraph of his Will:

"I direct that my remains be interred at the Helmsley Mausoleum at Woodlawn Cemetery, The Bronx, New York. I further direct that permission be granted as the need arises for the interment in the Helmsley Mausoleum of the remains of my wife, LEONA M. HELMSLEY ("my wife"), her brother, ALVIN ROSENTHAL, and her brother's wife, SUSAN ROSENTHAL, but for no other person".

That mausoleum was designed with stained glass depicting several of Helmsley's well-known buildings in the New York skyline. In view of his Queen's control of her King, it is not surprising that two or three of the four ultimate occupants of that mausoleum will not be Helmsleys at all, but his dear wife and in-laws. It is not known if Harry was wild about his in-laws moving in for eternity without paying any rent.

/s/ *Harry B. Helmsley*

Will dated January 25, 1994

Doris Duke

DATE AND PLACE OF BIRTH
November 22, 1912
New York, New York

DATE AND PLACE OF DEATH
October 28, 1993
Beverly Hills, California

From a Poor Little Rich Girl to a Poor Tall Filthy Rich Woman

When Doris Duke was 12 years old, her father died, and she inherited approximately fifty million dollars ($50,000,000) in the middle of the roaring twenties. Doris Duke continued to roar until her death at age 80. At the time of Doris Duke's death in 1993, her estate was worth approximately one billion two hundred million dollars ($1,200,000,000). From a family fortune grown from tobacco leaves, Duke's substantial assets included large homes like "Shangri La" in Kaalawai, Honolulu, Hawaii; "Falcon's Lair" in Beverly Hills, California; a Penthouse on Park Avenue in New York City; and her home called "Rough Point" in Newport, Rhode Island. Despite those exotic options, Duke's legal "domicile" (i.e. single primary legal residence) at the time of her death was her 2,700 acre estate in the great state of New Jersey. In view of the protracted and expensive legal machinations in the New York County Surrogate's Court, Duke's original estate attorneys might have been well-advised to probate Duke's Will in her local New Jersey court, rather than crossing the Hudson River to the Big Apple.

Doris Duke's aversion to publicity and reclusiveness during much of her life was well-known. It is therefore not surprising that the first paragraph of her Will states:

> ONE: A. I direct that there be no funeral service or memorial service of any kind for me and that I be buried at sea.

Even at her death, Duke wanted to be alone, and immersed in nature and surrounded by animals, as she was during life.

During her 80 years in the fast lane, Doris Duke must have seen it all. It is noteworthy that on page one of her lengthy Will, she provides:

> I give my eyes to THE EYE BANK FOR SIGHT RESTORATION INC., New York, New York, and I hereby ratify all that anyone theretofore may have done toward carrying out this gift.

We won't speculate as to what "anyone theretofore may have done toward carrying out" the gift of Doris' eyeballs.

Doris Duke not only had all the material possessions that a person could ever want, or even dream of wanting, but she had an extraordinarily rich life with fabled experiences all over the world. Duke was known as a peripatetic traveler, and truly seemed to relish her role as a provider and care giver to people less fortunate than she was (which included just about everybody). That generous spirit is evident from her Will.

Most of her vast estate was given to a variety of charities and private foundations of Duke's own creation, including the Doris Duke Foundation for the Preservation of New Jersey Farmland and Farm Animals; the Doris Duke Foundation for the Preservation of Endangered Wildlife; the Doris Duke Foundation for Southeast Asian Art and Culture; and, last but not least, the Doris Duke Foundation for Islamic Art. In the case of the Foundation for the Preservation of Endangered Wildlife, Duke directs that it use its resources to provide an enclosure "to protect endangered species of all kinds, both flora and fauna, from becoming extinct."

On the personal side, by her Will Doris Duke makes many major cash bequests and forgives (or does not forgive) various personal loans she had made to numerous friends (including a deposed dictator's wife), relatives and charities as follows:

FOUR: A. The following loans were owed to me as of August, 1991:

1. DR. ROBERT NIXON: Fifty-Eight Thousand Dollars ($58,000)

2. ELEANOR LAWSON: Sixteen Thousand Five Hundred Dollars ($16,500)

3. FRANCO ROSSELLINI: One Hundred Fifty-Eight Thousand Dollars ($158,000)

4. VERA CYCKMAN: Ten Thousand Dollars ($10,000)

5. EDWARD LEIATO: Thirty Thousand Dollars ($30,000)

6. RAPHAEL RECTO: One Hundred Thousand Dollars ($100,000).

I direct that, to the extent that these loans shall be outstanding at the time of my death, such loans shall be forgiven.

B. I direct that my Executors make reasonable arrangements with IMELDA MARCOS (or the legal representatives of her estate, if she shall not survive me) for the repayment of the Five Million Dollars ($5,000,000), plus accrued interest, that I loaned to her pursuant to a demand note dated March 6, 1990, such repayment to be made when Mrs. Marcos and the Philippines government settle their financial dispute or at such other time as my Executors shall deem appropriate in their absolute discretion.

C. I have made a loan in the current principal amount of Six Hundred Thousand Dollars ($600,000), plus accruing interest, to HEALTH MAINTENANCE PROGRAMS, INC., which loan is convertible to common stock in such corporation. I direct my Executors to convert such loan (as the same shall be outstanding at my death) into common stock and to add such stock to my residuary estate to be disposed of in accordance with the provisions of Article EIGHT hereof.

FIVE: A. I give and bequeath the following sums to the following organizations:

1. Ten Million Dollars ($10,000,000) to DUKE UNIVERSITY, Durham, North Carolina.

2. Five Hundred Thousand Dollars ($500,000) to the SELF-REALIZATION FELLOWSHIP, Los Angeles, California.

3. Ten Million Dollars ($10,000,000) to the METROPOLITAN MUSEUM OF ART, New York, New York.

4. One Million Dollars ($1,000,000) to the NEW YORK ZOOLOGICAL PARK operated by the New York Zoological Society, Bronx, New York.

B. I give and bequeath the following sums to such of the following persons as shall survive me:

1. Three Million Dollars ($3,000,000) to ELEANOR JOHNSON LAWSON.

2. One Million Dollars ($1,000,000) to DOROTHY MCCAWLEY.

3. One Million Dollars ($1,000,000) to ROSEANNA TODD.

4. Five Hundred Thousand Dollars ($500,000) to ANNA LUNDY LEWIS.

5. One Million Dollars ($1,000,000) to REVEREND LAWRENCE ROBERTS, in his individual capacity, whether or not he is, at the date of my death, affiliated with the First Baptist Church of Nutley, New Jersey.

6. Five Hundred Thousand Dollars ($500,000) to CONSTANCE PITTS SPEED.

7. Two Hundred Thousand Dollars ($200,000) to JOHN GOMEZ.

8. One Million Dollars ($1,000,000) to ANNA KENNESAY.

C. 1. The bequests to my employees under this Subdivision C are in gratitude for their past services rendered to me and my foundations. It is my hope and expectation that my Executors and Trustees and the foundations in which I am a member, director, trustee or officer at my death or which are to be created under this Will shall employ as many of these persons as reasonably possible in order to maintain my various properties and to operate these foundations after my death. The determination of my Executors as to the persons to receive a bequest under this Subdivision C and the amount of each such bequest shall be binding and conclusive on all interested persons.

But Duke's generosity was not limited to human be-
ings as there is the following provision for a $100,000
trust for her dog:

If I shall be survived by a dog owned by me and residing at my death at my residence known as Falcon's Lair,
in Beverly Hills, California, I give such dog to the caretaker of such property at my death or, if such caretaker
is at any time unwilling or unable to care for such dog,
to one of the foundations created under this Will or of
which I was a member, director, trustee or officer at my
death which is caring for other dogs of mine. If I shall
be survived by a dog owned by me and located at my
death at Falcon's Lair, I give and bequeath the sum of
One Hundred Thousand Dollars ($100,000) to my
Trustees, to be held by them in a separate trust for the
benefit of such dog, with the income and principal
thereof to be disposed of as follows:

a. My Trustees, at any time and from time to time, shall
apply such part or all or none of the net income and
principal of the trust for the benefit of such dog, at such
times and in such amounts as my Trustees, in their absolute discretion, shall deem necessary for the care,
feeding, comfort, maintenance and medical treatment
of such dog, even though any such application or appli-
cations may result in the termination of the trust. At
the end of each year of the trust, my Trustees shall accumulate and add to principal any net income not so
applied, any such capitalized income thereafter to be
disposed of as a part of such principal.

b. Upon the earlier to occur of (i) the death of such dog
and (ii) twenty-one (21) years after my death, the trust
shall terminate. Upon such termination, the principal of

the trust remaining at that time, and any accrued and undistributed income, shall be added to my residuary estate and disposed of in accordance with the provisions of Article EIGHT hereof.

For the record, even the trust for the benefit of the dog was the subject of litigation in the New York County Surrogate's Court. In that case, Surrogate Eve Preminger upheld the validity of the trust, finding in favor of Duke's Falcon's Lair caretaker, Mariano DeVelasco, and against the mighty U.S. Trust Company. In her decision Judge Preminger found that "by separating the legal ownership of the trust fund, which is vested in the United States Trust Company, and the legal ownership of the dog, which is vested in Mr. DeValasco, a valid trust is created of which Mr. DeVelasco is beneficiary." In layman's terms, the Judge decided that Duke's nine year old mutt named Minni had indeed resided at Falcon's Lair with Mr. DeVelasco, and that together they were entitled to the benefit of the $100,000 trust fund.

Duke's love of animals was well-known and her Will includes a bequest of "my two (2) camels, two (2) horses and donkey to the DORIS DUKE FOUNDATION FOR THE PRESERVATION OF WILDLIFE. That only her dog was awarded its own trust fund, could prove that it is indeed a dog's life, and that dogs truly are man's and woman's best friend.

Doris Duke was a sport even to the end as shown by this unusual clause included in her Will:

I direct my Executors not to seek a refund for the relinquishment of my memberships at the Newport Country Club and the Spouting Rock Beach Association.

Whether either of those clubs believe that the death of a member would be considered the "relinquishment" of a membership entitling the deceased member's estate to a refund, we do not know, but Doris was prepared to let her membership ride regardless of club policy.

During her long life Duke had two failed marriages which lasted a total of nine (9) years. She gave birth to one child, but he died within 24 hours of birth. Late in her life, at age 75, Duke adopted a 35 year old woman named Charlene ("Chandi") Gail Heffner, who was reportedly a former devotee of the Hare Krishna religious sect. Within a few years, the adoption went sour and Duke distanced herself from Heffner and expressly disinherited her in her Will as follows:

> TWENTY-ONE: As indicated in Article SEVEN, it is my intention that Chandi Heffner not be deemed to be my child for purposes of disposing of property under this my Will (or any Codicil thereto). Furthermore, it is not my intention, nor do I believe that it was ever my father's intention, that Chandi Heffner be deemed to be a child or lineal descendant of mine for purposes of disposing of the trust estate of the May 2, 1917 trust which my father established for my benefit or the Doris Duke Trust, dated December 11, 1924, which my father established for the benefit of me, certain other members of the Duke family and ultimately for charity.
>
> I am extremely troubled by the realization that Chandi Heffner may use my 1988 adoption of her (when she was 35 years old) to attempt to benefit financially under the terms of either of the trusts created by my father. After giving the matter prolonged and serious

consideration, I am convinced that I should not have adopted Chandi Heffner. I have come to the realization that her primary motive was financial gain. I firmly believe that, like me, my father would not have wanted her to have benefited [sic] under the trusts which he created, and similarly, I do not wish her to benefit from my estate.

Accordingly, I specifically authorize and direct my Executors to steadfastly take any and all actions and to expend such funds as my Executors in their sole discretion deem appropriate in order to prove the validity of this my will for the purpose of having it admitted to probate. I also specifically authorize and direct my Executors to steadfastly take any and all action and to expend such funds as my Executors in their sole discretion shall deem advisable in order to prove te effective exercise of the power of appointment described in Article SEVEN of this my will over the principal and income of the trust created by my father, J.B. Duke, as Grantor and Trustee, dated May 2, 1917.

Despite that emphatic and express language disinheriting Chandi Heffner, Chandi's attorneys commenced 20th century warfare known as litigation and were able to extract a settlement from the Duke estate of more than $65,000,000. Hare Krishna, Hare Rama indeed.

If ever there were a case where the butler may indeed have "done it", this may be the one. Bernard Lafferty, began as the butler, and proceeded to parlay his access to Miss Duke to becoming her closest confidante in the final years of her life. In fact, the semi-literate, profligate, imprudent Lafferty was named as the sole individual executor and he also was given the authority to select a corporate co-trustee to act together with him. That broad discretion may have led to the serious legal problems which plagued the Duke estate from the "let go."

Even the circumstances surrounding the death of Miss Duke in her Beverly Hills lair were the subject of legal inquiry. During the course of his "stewardship" of the Duke estate, Mr. Lafferty did things like have the estate buy a brand new Cadillac to replace the one that he himself had "totaled". He charged his zip code number personal credit card bills to the estate and he spared little expense. He renovated Doris Duke's bedroom into his own. The Surrogate's Court decisions involving him read almost like a criminal indictment, with allegations including: "Commingling of Estate and Personal Assets", "Self-Dealing", "Waste of Estate Assets", "Improvidence and Want of Understanding", "Substance Abuse." Ultimately, the legal, and capitalist, system worked. After protracted and expensive legal wrangling, Mr Lafferty was removed as co-Executor, surrendered his seat on the Duke Foundation Boards, but was awarded a substantial severance package in excess of five million dollars ($5,000,000). Unfortunately, things did not get better for Mr. Lafferty. Life in the fast lane caught up with him and he himself died on November 4, 1996 at the young age of 51. We don't know if former butler Lafferty had a chance to spend all of the Duke dough in the six months between the settlement and his death, but he certainly was a man who knew how to enjoy many of the finer things in life, and he may just have died trying.

In the end, Duke's billion dollar fortune that tobacco planted will be spent on a variety of good works and charitable causes. As New York County Surrogate Eve Preminger wrote in one decision in the case, "Ms. Duke intended that her assets create one of the largest vehicles for dispensing charity in the world. The Court has the responsibility to assure that decedent's determination to benefit the public be fulfilled and that the estate is administered without waste or mismanagement." The massive fortune that Doris Duke spent her whole life running from, and ultimately left behind will be used to preserve the endangered wildlife, flora and fauna that Doris Duke knew even all the money in the world couldn't buy.

/s/ Doris Duke

Will dated April 5, 1993.
Will signed at Falcon's Lair, Los Angeles, California

Malcolm Forbes

DATE AND PLACE OF BIRTH
August 19, 1919
Englewood, New Jersey

DATE AND PLACE OF DEATH
February 24, 1990
Timberfield
Far Hills, New Jersey

He Went Thataway . . .

M(B)illionaire Malcolm Forbes certainly knew how to live it up. He owned eight homes around the world ranging from his forty wooded acres and mansion in Far Hills, New Jersey, to his private island of Lauthala in the Fiji Islands. Forbes could travel to his various properties either on his 151-foot yacht called the *Highlander,* on his private 727 jet called *Capitalist Tool,* on any of his many motorbikes, or up, up, and away in one of his beautiful fleet of hot-air balloons. At home, Forbes could toy with one of his twelve Russian Imperial Fabergé eggs or his armies of tin soldiers or rare books and famous autographs. If it is true that "He who dies with the most toys, wins," then Malcolm Forbes had to be near the top of the heap. By the way, during business hours, Forbes ran a little magazine bearing his name. Somehow, despite a fortune variously estimated between $400,000 and $1.25 billion, his name managed to evade *Forbes* magazine's annual list of the richest four hundred. Editor in chief's prerogative.

Forbes's sixty-one-page Will lives up to his reputation for being a generous man with rich and eclectic tastes. Forbes proves his gastronomic and epicurean bent by making $1,000 bequests to each of the proprietors of nine of New York City's best restaurants "as a token of gratitude for the joy their skills and genius added to the lives of those who've been lucky and sensible enough to dine at their restaurants." The proprietors and restaurants making the Forbes favorite nine were the following: Paul C. Kovi and Tom G. Margittai of The Four Seasons, André Soltner of Lutèce, Giselle Masson and Charles Masson of La Grenouille, David and Karen Waltuck of Chanterelle, Sirio Maccioni of Le Cirque, Roberto Ruggeri of Bice, Nobuyoshi Kuraoka of Nippon, Rocky Akoi of Benihana, and Glenn Bernbaum of Mortimer's.

Following those gastronomic bequests, Forbes shifts gears and makes $1,000 bequests to almost thirty different "Motorcycle Clubs . . . whose Sunday runs provided so much pleasure and fellowship for me and so many other cycling enthusiasts." The names of these clubs ranged from Heavy Metal, of Newark, New Jersey, to the Blue Knights II, of the Bronx, New York. Forbes also made a $10,000 bequest to the American Motorcyclist Association, located in Westerville, Ohio.

In his Will Forbes rewards a few of his Far Hills, New Jersey, neighbors and "dear friends, as token compensation for the bridge (and other) lessons they've so generously, warmly and patiently given me over the years." One has to wonder what "other" types of lessons were so "warmly . . . given." Next Forbes makes two $10,000 bequests to two "treasured" friends, one of Washington, D.C., and the other, Countess Boul De Breteuil of Marrakech-Guleiz, Morocco. After those cash bequests to six friends, the Will section concludes:

> All other friends, family, employees and favored Causes
> (in most instances, they each are all of the foregoing)

I've taken care of either in life or by other means after my "cease-and-desisting."

If anyone out there can explain exactly what Forbes meant by his "cease-and-desisting," please let the author know.

In 1985, Forbes had been divorced from his wife of thirty-nine years, the former Roberta Remsen Laidlaw. Pursuant to a "Property Settlement Agreement" that the Forbeses signed in 1985, there is a $5-million bequest "to my former wife, Roberta L. Forbes." In addition she is entitled to payments from the Forbes estate of $4,000 per week. There is a $2-million bequest to Forbes's daughter, Moira F. Mumma (which would have been $5 million if former wife Roberta had not survived Forbes).

Forbes seemed to believe in the Anglo-Saxon tradition of primogeniture, in which the eldest son in a family received most if not all of his ancestor's estate. True to his Scottish form, Forbes made son Malcolm S. Forbes, Jr., the controlling heir by giving him a 51-percent voting interest in Forbes Inc. stock. The remaining stock is divided equally among the remaining Forbes children. After Forbes's death, the children appeared harmonious, so there must have been enough to keep everyone happy.

All the rest of Forbes's multivaried tangible property is divided among his five children. Forbes's residuary estate is devised and bequeathed to such of his descendants as survived him, "*per stirpes*, or, if none, in equal shares to such of the spouses of my deceased children as shall survive me." It is interesting that Forbes chose to mention the spouses of his children as possible residuary beneficiaries in the unlikely event that all of Forbes's descendants were deceased. Nonetheless, it is unusual to see spouses of children mentioned in that context. After all, Forbes could have chosen to name one of his favorite motorcycle clubs as the taker in the case of a Forbes family disaster.

In line with the concept of primogeniture, Forbes named his son Malcolm S. Forbes, Jr., as the sole executor of and trustee under his Will. If son Malcolm, Jr., ceased to act, then Timothy C., Christopher C., and Robert L., in the order named according to the Will, are designated as the successor to their brother. Youngest daughter Moira is not named as a fiduciary in the Will.

Despite his dramatic and high-flying lifestyle, Malcolm Forbes died mundanely—in his sleep in his bed in his primary home in Far Hills, New Jersey. Earlier that morning, Forbes had returned home from London aboard his private jet after playing in an international corporate bridge tournament. Forbes directed that he be cremated and that his ashes be buried on his private Fiji island, Lauthala. He further directed that the epitaph on his grave read simply, "WHILE ALIVE, HE LIVED." Dead at three score and ten, Malcolm Forbes had certainly led the richest of lives and definitely enjoyed himself before he experienced "life's only certainty."

/s/ *Malcolm S. Forbes*

Will dated July 8, 1988

John Jacob Astor IV

DATE AND PLACE OF BIRTH
July 13, 1864
Ferncliff, Rhinebeck-on-the-
Hudson, New York

DATE AND PLACE OF DEATH
April 15, 1912
Titanic
Atlantic Ocean

Chivalry Is Dead

One of America's richest men in the early 1900s, with a fortune reportedly close to $200 million, Colonel John Jacob Astor IV owned more hotels and high-rise buildings than any other New Yorker. It is ironic that Astor, who was such a devotee of ships, died on the maiden voyage of the newest, grandest ocean liner of them all—the "unsinkable" *Titanic*. Reportedly, as the *Titanic* was sinking, Astor chivalrously made sure that all the women and children were put in the lifeboats before himself. As his pregnant wife left the sinking ship, Astor reportedly coolly lit a cigarette and said to his wife, "Good-bye, dearie. I'll see you later." He never did; his chivalry led to his demise.

In his Will, Astor makes the following special provisions for an annual yacht trophy fund:

> I DIRECT that the Executors of this my will . . . in each year until my son William Vincent Astor shall attain the age of twenty-one years or sooner die, pay to the NEW YORK YACHT CLUB the sum of FIFTEEN HUN-DRED DOLLARS, to be used and applied by the said Club for the purchase of two silver cups as prizes, one

of such cups to cost One thousand dollars, to be sailed and competed for by the sloop yachts of the New York Yacht Club; and I DIRECT that such prizes shall be competed for at Newport, Rhode Island, on the cruise of said Yacht Club during the month of August in each year. . . .

Unfortunately, the Big A did not make the 1912 yacht race.

Born to a patrician family, Astor attended St. Paul's School in Concord, New Hampshire, and then attended Harvard College. He made a $30,000 bequest to St. Paul's, but Harvard was not mentioned in his Will.

In 1894, Astor married Miss Ava L. Willing, who was *very* willing. They had two children: William Vincent Astor, who was in his late teens when his father died, and a daughter, Alice, who was then ten. Apparently, the marriage was stormy; they were divorced in November of 1909. The divorce decree provided that father took son William and mother took daughter Alice. Ava reportedly received $50,000 a year as alimony and support payments.

In 1911, the forty-seven-year-old Astor was married to eighteen-year-old Miss Madeleine Talmage Force in Newport, Rhode Island. Astor had found a new port in which to dock. In his Will, which he signed one week after his marriage, Astor bequeaths his residiuary estate to his beloved son Vincent with the express intention of keeping certain assets in the Astors' place. William Vincent gets all the land in Rhinebeck, New York, and "all my jewelry, wearing apparel, personal effects, and all my yachts and boats." There go those boats again.

For his wife of one week, Astor provides:

THIRD: I GIVE AND DEVISE the plot of land situated at
the northeasterly corner of the Fifth Avenue and Sixty-
fifth Streete, in the Borough of Manhattan, City of New
York . . . with the dwellings and stable thereon, together
with the printed books, paintings, pictures, engravings,
marbles, bronzes, statuary and objects of art, plate and
silver plated ware, linen, china, glass, household furniture and effects, useful and ornamental, contained `
therein at the time of my death and not hereinbefore
otherwise disposed of, unto my wife, MADELEINE TAL-
MAGE FORCE ASTOR, to have and to hold the same
unto her for so long during her natural life as she shall
remain my widow, and upon her death or re-marriage,
whichever shall first happen, I GIVE, DEVISE AND BE-
QUEATH all of the property in this article mentioned
unto my son WILLIAM VINCENT ASTOR . . .

It should be noted that the Will provides that
Madeleine's life interest in the house and stables is revoked if Madeleine remarries. Madeleine did eventually
give it up for another man a few years later. Next, the Will
refers to "certain antenuptial settlements" that, even
then, were de rigueur for someone of Astor's background
and marital history.

FOURTH: Having by certain ante-nuptial settlements
made certain provisions for the benefit of my wife,
MADELEINE TALMAGE FORCE ASTOR, <u>I do make the
following further provision for her</u>:
I GIVE, DEVISE AND BEQUEATH to the <u>Executors</u> of
this my will the sum of FIVE MILLION DOLLARS . . . to
be had and holden by them and their successors in the
trust as trustees, IN TRUST. . . .

FIFTH: I GIVE AND BEQUEATH unto my said wife, MADELEINE TALMAGE FORCE ASTOR, the sum of ONE HUNDRED THOUSAND DOLLARS, payable immediately upon my death, all horses and other life-stock and all carriages and harness and stable furniture, and all automobiles, and all provisions and supplies which shall belong to me . . .

One has to wonder what she used all the horses and other livestock for after J.J.A. was with the fishes.

Astor also remembers various friends, relatives, and employees with "token" bequests ranging from $10,000 to $30,000.

In the end it seems as though young William takes the grand prize, inheriting most of Astor's place. "ALL THE REST, RESIDUE AND REMAINDER of my property and estate, real and personal, of whatsoever kind and wheresoever situated . . . I GIVE, DEVISE AND BEQUEATH absolutely and in fee simple, unto my son WILLIAM VINCENT ASTOR." However, after the date of the Will's execution, John Jacob Astor V was in the making and was born in August 1912, about four months after his father's death.

Astor names his brother-in-law James Roosevelt, friends Douglas Robinson and Nicholas Biddle, and also his son William Vincent Astor, upon his attaining the age of twenty-one years, to be his executors and trustees. After naming them, the Will states "I GIVE to each of them who shall qualify and act as such Executor the sum of THIRTY-FIVE THOUSAND DOLLARS in lieu of commissions upon the capital of my estate." It is interesting to note that Mr. Moneybags, John Jacob Astor IV, chose to limit the commissions that each of his executors would have earned executing his multiasseted estate. Perhaps Astor placed a value on the honor of their serving on his behalf.

When Astor's body was finally recovered from the Atlantic ten days after the *Titanic* went down for the count, Astor reportedly had about $2,500 in cash in his pockets. Perhaps it was the weight of the great Astor fortune and holdings that in part brought the *Titanic* down.

/s/ John Jacob Astor

Will dated September 18, 1911

Nelson A. Rockefeller

DATE AND PLACE OF BIRTH
July 8, 1908
Bar Harbour, Maine

DATE AND PLACE OF DEATH
January 26, 1979
13 W. 54th Street
New York, New York

Happy in Camp Rockefeller

A grandson of the founder of the Standard Oil Company, which created the vast family fortune, Nelson Aldrich Rockefeller used his immense family wealth to pursue a political career and later to collect and donate works of art worth hundreds of millions of dollars. After the Republican Party lost the White House in the 1976 elections, Rockefeller pulled out of politics and devoted himself to his personal affairs, especially those related to his many works of art. Many provisions of his Will demonstrate the great importance of art in Rockefeller's life, not only as investments, but as objects of beauty to be studied and enjoyed.

A few days after his being graduated from Dartmouth College, Rockefeller married Mary Todhunter Clark. After having five children together, Rockefeller was divorced from Mary in 1962. The divorce occurred shortly after one of the Rockefeller's five children, Michael, was lost on an anthropoligical expedition in the jungles of New Guinea and later declared dead after a massive search failed to find him. Despite this tragic loss, Rockefeller continued to collect primitive art.

In 1962, Rockefeller married Margaretta Fitler Murphy, nicknamed Happy, five weeks after her own divorce. Happy was nineteen years younger than Nelson, and apparently, she kept him happy. Together, they had two children, Nelson, Jr., who was born in 1964, and Mark, born in 1967. Regarding his second family, Rockefeller states in the preamble of his Will:

> In this Will I make my wife, Margaretta Fitler Rockefeller, my sons Nelson, Jr. and Mark and charity the primary beneficiaries of my estate. I make relatively small provision for my older children, Rodman, Ann, Steven and Mary. I do this because my older children have already been amply provided for by my father, John D. Rockefeller, Jr., and by gifts made by me during my lifetime. Nelson, Jr., and Mark were born after my father's death and do not benefit from his gifts to the same extent as do my older children. Although I have tried to make up for this during my lifetime, a discrepancy in the economic well-being of my two youngest children and my older children still exists. It is for this reason that I make greater provision in this Will for Nelson, Jr. and Mark than I do for my older children.

The Rockefeller family owned land and property all over the globe, and in his Will Nelson gives to his wife:

> 1) all real property owned by me at the time of my death on Mount Desert Island, County of Hancock, State of Maine, together with all buildings thereon and all rights and easements appurtenant to said real property . . .

2) the house designed by Junzo Yoshimura and all of my interest in the house known as the "Hawes" house both of which are located within the area known as the "Park" . . . in Pocantico Hills, County of Westchester, State of New York. . . .

3) the property known as "The Camp" located in Pocantico Hills, Westchester County, New York, which consists of approximately 147.025 acres of real property, together with all structures located on said real property, all rights and easements appurtenant to said structures and said real property and all policies of insurance relating thereto (hereinafter referred to as the "Camp property"). To guide my Executors and wife in the disposition of the Camp property, I am depositing with my Will a copy of a map which was prepared in May 1977 by Chas. H. Sells, Inc., which shows the Camp property and the division of said property into the parcels known as the "outer Camp property" and "inner Camp property".

Presumably, the "inner" and "outer" camps, the New York City cooperative apartment located at 812 Fifth Avenue, and other property left to Mrs. Rockefeller were enough to keep her happy.

But there was also the 4,180-acre Rockefeller-family estate in Westchester County, New York, left to Nelson and his brothers by their father, John D. Rockefeller, Jr. The disposition of this historic property required special consideration under Rockefeller's Will.

The Will makes detailed provisions for the disposition of Rockefeller's enormous art collection. From his primitive art collection, Rockefeller gave 1,610 items, which were all listed in the Will by their Rockefeller-collection catalogue number, to the Metropolitan Museum of Art in New York. This bequest was certainly fitting, as young Nelson had become a member of the Metropolitan Museum's Board of Directors the year he was graduated from college. Today, the Rockefeller collection of primitive art occupies an entire wing of that museum.

To the Museum of Modern Art, of which he had been the president in 1939, Rockefeller bequeathed many modern paintings, including important works by Picasso, Matisse, and Calder.

Rockefeller left his collection of oriental sculpture located on the property called Eyrie Garden, which he owned in Mount Desert Island, Maine, "to such one or more of the United States of America, any State or a political subdivision thereof, in all cases for exclusively public purposes." It seems oddly appropriate in the light of the later sale of Rockefeller Center to a Japanese company that the United States public should have been left "Rocky's" oriental sculpture collection.

After disposing of the larger art collections, the Will provides:

> All paintings, pieces of sculpture and other objects of art, all furniture, furnishings, rugs, pictures, books, silver, plate, linen, china, glassware, jewelry, wearing apparel, automobiles and their accessories, including antique automobiles, boats and their accessories, and all other household and personal goods and effects . . .

should be given to the charity taking the real properties where this tangible property was located, or to Mrs. Rockefeller, or to the two younger Rockefeller children if she did not survive. Other tangible property with a value not to exceed $25,000 (which was originally $100,000 in the Will) was to be selected by *each* of Rockefeller's six children and Happy's daughter from her prior marriage.

In addition to the real estate, artworks, Rockefeller's personal papers, and other tangible property left to Happy, she also received an amount equal to approximately one-half of Nelson's "adjusted gross estate," which was, of course, quite substantial.

There were no other gifts to individuals under the Will other than the following provision found under lucky article thirteen of the Will:

> I release and discharge each of Susan Cable Herter, Megan R. Marshack and Hugh Morrow from any indebtedness, including interest thereon, which he or she may owe to me at the time of my death, and I direct my Executors to cancel any promissory notes or other evidence of his or her indebtedness to me.

Morrow, Herter, and Marshack were all associates and friends of Rockefeller. The amount of Marshack's forgiven debt to Rockefeller was reportedly $45,000, which he had loaned her to purchase a cooperative apartment near the town house where she was with Rockefeller on the night he died.

It has widely been reported that the thirty-one-year-old Marshack was working with Rockefeller on a book about his art collection when he suffered a heart attack at approximately 10:15 p.m. on the night he died. The police reported that the first call for emergency help came in at 11:16 pm.; the delay in reporting the attack has never been explained. The first reports of Rockefeller's death stated that he was working at his Rockefeller Center office on the night he died. Later reports corrected that and placed him at the town house he owned at 13 West Fifty-fourth Street. Whether Rockefeller's death was attributable to low blood pressure—70 over 31—has long been a matter of ribald speculation. Family spokesman Hugh Morrow was quoted in *The New York Times* as saying about Rockefeller's death, "He was having a wonderful time with the whole art enterprise. He was 'having a ball,' as he put it."

When he died, Rockefeller was survived by two of his five siblings, David and Laurance. For his executors and trustees, Rockefeller named his brother Laurance and two longtime advisers, J. Richardson Dilworth and Donal C. O'Brien, Jr. Conspicuously absent from Nelson's nominated group of executors was his brother David, who was the chairman of the Chase Manhattan Bank. Perhaps Nelson did not want a banker on the team. But Nelson's own shrewdness is shown by the clause pertaining to executor's commissions requiring that brother Laurance waive all his executor's commissions due to him pursuant to New York law and that the other two named executors accept commissions in an amount agreed to with Laurance. The commissions to each executor of an estate the size of Rockefeller's would have been millions of dollars. Certainly brother Laurance did not need any more taxable income, and perhaps Nelson believed the money better spent by passing it to the next Rockefeller generation to inherit his philanthropic mantle.

/s/ Nelson A. Rockefeller

Will dated December 6, 1978

J. Pierpont Morgan

DATE AND PLACE OF BIRTH
April 17, 1837
26 Asylum Street
Hartford, Connecticut

DATE AND PLACE OF DEATH
March 31, 1913
The Grand Hotel
Rome, Italy

No Guarantees

When the Will of the monarch of Wall Street and one of the greatest financiers of his era, John Pierpont Morgan, was made public, people were surprised to see that the first article reflected a deeply religious man:

> I commit my soul into the hands of my Saviour, in full confidence that having redeemed it and washed it in His most precious blood He will present it faultless before the throne of my Heavenly Father; and I entreat my children to maintain and defend, at all hazard, and at any cost of personal sacrifice, the blessed doctrine of the complete atonement for sin through the blood of Jesus Christ, once offered, and through that alone.

Despite his great fortunes and successes, Morgan did not apparently necessarily believe that the success of one life could guarantee success in the next life. Hence, his commitment into the hands of his Saviour, in full confidence that . . . his soul would be presented "faultless." For J. P.'s sake, let's hope so.

Next, the Will states Morgan's wishes regarding his

burial, which reflected his close feelings for his family, particularly his father, Junius Spencer Morgan:

> It is my desire to be buried in the family burial place prepared by my father in Cedar Hill Cemetery, at Hartford, Connecticut, and I HEREBY DIRECT that my body be there interred on the west of the monument and opposite the place where my father's remains are interred.
>
> I wish that in all arrangements for my funeral the same general course be followed that was adopted in the case of my father, except that the service shall be held at St. George's Church in the City of New York, with the Bishops of New York, Connecticut and Massachusetts, and the Rector of St. George's officiating.

Morgan's wishes regarding his burial were respected by his family. Newspaper reports of his funeral state that after the service, held at St. George's Protestant Episcopal Church, a special train took Morgan's body from Grand Central Terminal in New York to Hartford, Connecticut, where the interment took place.

Morgan's Will, which was signed in January of the year he died, made the following provisions for Morgan's "beloved wife FRANCES," whom he had married in the same St. George's Church in 1865:

> . . . I MAKE THE FOLLOWING GIFTS AND PROVISIONS to and for the benefit of my beloved wife FRANCES LOUISA TRACY MORGAN.
>
> Section 1. I GIVE AND BEQUEATH unto my EXECUTORS and TRUSTEES the sum of ONE MILLION DOLLARS, IN TRUST . . .

Section 2. After my death my said wife will receive the income which will be produced by a certain trust fund now held by me as trustee under a deed of trust dated July 1st, 1867, made to me by my father Junius Spencer Morgan, which fund has been very largely increased during my lifetime.

Section 3. I GIVE, DEVISE AND BEQUEATH to my said wife for her own use during the term of her natural life, without impeachment of waste, my country place called "Cragston", in the Town of Highlands, in the County of Orange, in the State of New York . . .

AND I GIVE AND BEQUEATH unto my said wife absolutely for her own use all furniture, clothing, pictures (except family portraits) works of art, silver, plate, ornaments, bric-a-brac, household goods, or supplies, books, linen, china, glass, horses, carriages, automobiles, harness and stable furniture or equipment, and all implements, plants and tools, and all live stock, which may be in or upon my said country place at the time of my death or shall then be customarily used by me in connection therewith.

Section 4. I ALSO GIVE, DEVISE AND BEQUEATH to my said wife for her own use during the term of her natural life, without impeachment of waste, the lot of land in the Borough of Manhattan, City of New York, situated on the northeast corner of Madison Avenue and Thirty-sixth Street . . . together with all furniture, clothing, pictures (except family portraits) . . . (except wines) . . .

After forty-eight years of marriage, Mrs. Morgan might have felt too old to enjoy it all herself. During the first ten years of their marriage the Morgans had four children: Louisa, who later married Herbert Satterlee and was by her father's bed when he died; John Pierpont Morgan, Jr., who stepped into his father's shoes as head of the family business in 1913; Juliet Pierpont, who later married William P. Hamilton; and Anne Tracy, who never married.

For his children, Morgan makes the following gifts and obviously has the idea that women should receive property in trust rather than outright:

<u>Section 1</u>. I GIVE AND BEQUEATH unto my son JOHN PIERPONT MORGAN, Junior, if he shall survive me, the sum of THREE MILLIONS OF DOLLARS. . . .

<u>Section 3</u>. If my daughter LOUISA, wife of Herbert Livingston Satterlee, shall survive me, but not otherwise, I GIVE AND BEQUEATH unto my said executors and trustees the sum of THREE MILLIONS OF DOLLARS, IN TRUST. . . .

<u>Section 5</u>. If my daughter, ANNE TRACY MORGAN, shall survive me, but not otherwise, I GIVE AND BEQUEATH unto my said executors and trustees the sum of THREE MILLIONS OF DOLLARS IN TRUST. . . .

<u>Section 8</u>. I GIVE AND BEQUEATH unto my son-in-law WILLIAM PIERSON HAMILTON the sum of ONE MILLION DOLLARS.

There is also a provision for a million-dollar trust for the widow of his son, John, should he have predeceased his father.

Next, Morgan makes the following bequest of his prized wine collection to his son with the expectation that he would share the wine with sons-in-law and friends. Perhaps Morgan believed that his daughters should not be wine drinkers, but J. P. clearly wanted to keep the intoxicants in the Morgan family.

> I GIVE AND BEQUEATH all my wines unto my said son JOHN PIERPONT MORGAN, Junior, or if he shall not survive me, then unto his son JUNIUS SPENCER MOR-GAN, Junior, desiring, however, that the legatee thereof should divide such of them as he may think proper among my sons-in-law and my friends.

So that none of Morgan's other relatives got their noses out of joint, Morgan's Will includes the following:

> It is not from any lack of affection or regard for them that this will contains no provision for my sisters Sarah Spencer Morgan, Mary Lyman Burns and Juliet Pier-pont Morgan, but only because the property which they already have makes the same seem unnecessary.

Of course, another million or two would not have hurt. . . .

There were several other individual bequests in the Will, and every employee of J. P. Morgan & Co. was reportedly given an extra year's salary. Not bad for a bank job. There were also a $500,000 bequest to St. George's Church and $100,000 each to the Episcopal diocese and the House of Rest for Consumptives.

The balance of the estate, estimated at over $100 million, including the art collection, went entirely to J. P.'s son, John, who took over the helm of the great banking house. Compared to the other millionaires of his day such as Rockefeller, Carnegie, Mellon, or Frick, Morgan left a relatively modest estate. That has been attributed to his generosity during his life and the expensive collection of art he had amassed. A fragment of that collection can be seen today in the magnificent Morgan Library collection in Morgan's former home at Thirty-sixth street and Madison Avenue in New York.

/s/ *John Pierpont Morgan*

Will dated January 4, 1913

Howard Hughes

DATE AND PLACE OF BIRTH
December 24, 1905
Houston, Texas

DATE AND PLACE OF DEATH
April 5, 1976
In a Learjet flying over Texas

Summa, but Not Loud

Reclusive and mysterious Howard Hughes had an estate estimated to be worth in excess of $1.5 billion when he died in 1976. Hughes's great empire had rapidly grown from the time he began to direct his family's company, Hughes Tool Company, at the age of eighteen after his mother died. At his death, Hughes had parlayed the Hughes Tool Company into the billion-dollar-plus "Summa Corporation," which was Hughes's personal holding company controlling the bulk of his vast assets. Summa controlled his radio and television station, his architecture and design firm, his string of gold mines, and all the rest of Hughes's multifarious playthings.

Part of Hughes's vast fortune was accumulated through his ownership of the Hughes Aircraft Company. Later in his career, Hughes was the majority owner of Trans World Airlines, selling his interest for $566 million in the 1960s. Hughes was also associated with aircraft by the records he set flying planes. It is therefore ironic that it was ultimately on an airplane in flight from Acapulco to the Methodist Hospital in the city of his birth, Houston, on which the aviational phenomenon died from an illness that is still shrouded in mystery.

In addition to his aircraft-related investments, Hughes also owned substantial real estate and hotels in Las Vegas, Nevada, where he was domiciled when he died. In Las Vegas, Hughes was the owner of the Desert Inn, the Sands, the Silver Slipper, and the Castaway hotels, in addition to a huge range and a small airport. Earlier in his career, Hughes had dabbled in films and opened his own movie studio in Hollywood.

During the later part of his life, Hughes was reported to be obsessed with his privacy. He usually traveled in the dead of night and allowed himself to be seen only by a few of his closest advisers, preferring to shield himself behind telephone lines controlling his international business network.

Hughes had been divorced from his first wife, Ella Rice, in 1928 after four years of marriage. Hughes's second marriage, to Jean Peters, lasted from 1957 until ending in divorce in 1971. Besides his wives, only a few trusted advisers ever got close to the mystery man.

One close Hughes adviser described Hughes's concerns about the secrecy surrounding his Will as follows: "The industrialist had different secretaries type different pages and had several different versions typed. Then he could go in a closet, shuffle the papers together from different versions, and burn the pages he didn't want to use, and nobody would have the slightest idea what he wanted to do with his money." If Hughes intended to obfuscate his wishes regarding the distribution of his estate, he succeeded.

The legal controversy surrounding Howard Hughes's purported Last Will and Testament has probably never been rivaled. Over thirty different versions of Hughes's purported Will were submitted to the Nevada, California, and Texas probate courts, and all wanted a piece of the huge Hughes property pie. Following are only three of the purported Hughes Wills submitted to the courts, including the most famous, the "Melvin Dummar/Mormon Church" version.

The first purported Will was allegedly handwritten by Hughes. Under this Will the entire Hughes estate was left to the Howard Hughes Medical Institute (HHMI), which Hughes had established in 1953.

Jan. 11/72

This is my Last Will and Testament

(1) I hereby revoke all Wills and testamentary dispositions of every nature or kind whatsoever made by me before this date.

(2) I nominate, constitute, and appoint my counsel Chester C. Davis, sole executor and trustee of this, my Last Will and Testament. . . .

(3) I give, devise, and bequeath all my monies, holdings, property of every nature and kind, all of my possessions and any profits of the before mentioned to the Howard Hughes Medical Institute for the use of medical research and the betterment of medical and health standards around the world.

(4) I hereby direct my trustee Chester Davis and my assistants Nadine Henley and Frank Gay to continue in their positions and duties, and to also assume a controlling interest in management in the Medical Institute, to decide, direct and implement policies and funds for the proper uses of the Medical Institute in the areas of medical research

and the betterment of world health and medical standards.

(5) I hereby request that my trustee make known to any business associates, aides, or confidantes who wish to, or have undertaken a written documentation of any or all parts of my life, the terms of the Rosemont Enterprises agreement and possible infringements thereof—because of the conditions of that document.

(6) I hereby direct my trustee to instruct Rosemont Enterprises to complete all written, visual, and audio, documentation in the presentation of the factual representation of my life for public release two years to the day, after my death.

(7) I authorize my trustee to make funds available limited to one quarter of the total estate to a private agency of my trustee's choice, in the event of my death by unnatural or man-made cause; to apprehend such person or group of persons and to bring them within full prosecution of the law; the funds being made available for legal expenses and costs incurred on behalf of the trustee's appointed agency.

(8) I wish to make known to my trustee that I did not at any time enter into any contracts, agreements, or promises either oral or written, that transferred gave or bequeathed the bulk or any part of my estate to any person, persons, organizations or whatever other than the Howard Hughes Medical Institute. I sign this as my Last Will and Testament

/s/ *Howard R. Hughes*
_____
Jan. 11, 1972

Although the HHMI Will was not admitted to probate, we need not be concerned about the plight of the HHMI. Shortly after he established it in 1953, Hughes transferred all of his assets in the tremendous Hughes Aircraft Company in to the name of the HHMI. That gift made the HHMI one of the most well-endowed medical centers in the country, and it still is today.

According to this next purported Will, "Richard Robard Hughes, aka Joseph Michael Brown," was to inherit the entire estate:

LAST WILL AND TESTAMENT
OF
HOWARD ROBARD HUGHES JR.

I, Howard Robard Hughes, being of sound mind and body do hereby declare this my Last Will and Testament. I leave my entire estate to my son, Richard Robard Hughes, aka Joseph Michael Brown, born September 12th, 1945 in Fort Worth, Texas. At this time, I plan to make public my son's existence but in the event I am unable to do that, this will cancel and supercede any previous Wills that I have made in the past. By the time this would be read attorneys for Summa Corporation should have approached my son but in the event that has not been done my son should request a full accounting of all my holdings and should take full control thereof.

/s/ *Howard R. Hughes*
_____
April 11, 1975 Las Vegas, Nevada

Good luck, Joseph Michael Brown. It is of course highly unlikely that a man with the great resources and access to legal expertise of Howard Hughes would have resorted to such a crude Will as the foregoing. It is perhaps for that reason that this Will was never admitted to probate.

Finally, there is the famous "Melvin Dummar/Mormon Church" version of the Hughes last Will, which was portrayed in the film *Melvin and Howard*. The film starred Jason Robards as a very scraggly Howard Hughes, who is picked up after a motorcycle accident by a young trucker named Melvin Dummar, and the rest was mystery. According to this version of the Will, Dummar was to inherit one-sixteenth of the Hughes estate, valued at $156 million. Unfortunately for Melvin, that Will was not admitted to probate either. According to the move *Melvin and Howard*, Dummar was last seen driving a Coors beer delivery truck out west. In light of his experience, one wonders whether Dummar is still willing to pick up scraggly-looking hitchhikers.

I Howard R. Hughes being of sound and disposing mind and memory, not acting under duress, fraud or other undue influence of any person whomsoever, and being a resident of Las Vegas, Nevada declare that this is to be my last Will and revoke all other Wills previously made by me.

After my death my estate is to be divided as follows:

first: one fourth of all my assets to go to "Hughes Medical Institute of Miami.

second: one eight of assets to be divided among the University of Texas—Rice Institute of Technology of Houston—the University of Nevada and the University of Calif.

third: one sixteenth to Church of Jesus Christ of Latter-day Saints—David O. Makay

Fourth: one sixteenth to establish a home for Orphan Children

Fifth: one sixteenth of assets to go to Boy Scouts of America

sixth: one sixteenth to be divided among Jean Peters of Los Angeles and Ella Rice of Houston

seventh: one sixteenth of assets to William R. Loomis of Houston, Texas

eighth: one sixteenth to go to Melvin DuMar of Gabbs, Nevada

ninth: one sixteenth to be divided among my personal aids at the time of my death

tenth: one sixteenth to be used as school scholarship fund for entire country

the spruce goose is to be given to the City of Long Beach, Calif.

the remainder of My estate is to be divided among the key men of the companys I own at the time of my death

I appoint Noah Dietrich as the executor of this Will

signed the 19 day of march 1968

/s/ *Howard R. Hughes*

This last purported Will is not exactly a model of clarity, good grammar, or correct spelling. It does however make provisions for Hughes's famed airplane, the "Spruce Goose." Nonetheless, it is hard to imagine how anyone could expect a competent court to accept this as the worldly billionaire's last Will. Nonetheless, it was only after a lengthy court battle that this Will was finally rejected in the courts and Melvin went truckin' again, all his chips cashed in.

In the end, after lengthy trials and hearings none of the foregoing Wills or any of the other Wills submitted to the Nevada court were admitted to probate. The great Hughes estate passed by intestacy to various distant Hughes relatives with whom the reclusive billionaire had had little or no contact during his lifetime. By his failure to make and/or leave a valid Will, the Hughes estate passed to many "laughing heirs," and Uncle Sam was also able to reap more than a fair share. Perhaps the great brouhaha over his Will and estate would have made the litigious but secretive Hughes proud, but failing to leave his estate to medical research as he had often indicated as his desire cost his estate hundreds of millions of dollars in unnecessary taxes. That is enough to turn anyone over in his grave.

/s/ *Howard R. Hughes*

J. Paul Getty

DATE AND PLACE OF BIRTH
December 15, 1892
Minneapolis, Minnesota

DATE AND PLACE OF DEATH
June 6, 1976
Sutton Place
Surrey, England

Why Not to Marry a Billionaire

For many years described as "the richest man in the world," J. Paul Getty died in 1976 with an estate worth in excess of $2 billion. The bulk of his estate was the value of the over 12 million shares of the Getty Oil Company stock that he controlled through his personal ownership or by the Sarah Getty Trust, of which he was the sole beneficiary. Getty also owned a fabulous mansion called Sutton Place outside London, which was situated on over seven hundred acres of land, had its own private trout stream, and included over thirty cottages and lodges on the property. Sutton Place housed much of the great Getty art and furniture collection, which he had acquired over the course of many years with the shrewd advice of art and antique experts. Finally, there was the property located in Malibu, California, which was Getty's legal domicile at the time of his death. That property would later house the wealthiest art museum the world had ever known.

Throughout his life Getty had the reputation of being a womanizer who when he became bored with one playmate would move on to the next. He was married five times. In 1923 at the age of thirty, Getty married eighteen-year-old Jeannette Dumont. They had one child, George Franklin Getty II, and were then divorced in 1925. In 1926, Getty married the daughter of a Texas rancher, Allene Ashby, but they were divorced two years later. Next, Getty married a German fräulein named Adolphine Helmle, and together they had one son, Jean Ronald Getty, before getting divorced in 1932. That same year Getty married his fourth wife, the movie star Ann Rork, with whom he had two children. J. Paul Getty, Jr., and Gordon Peter Getty. J. P. divorced Ann three years later in 1935. Finally, Getty married a cabaret singer named Louise Dudley "Teddy" Lynch, with whom he had one son named Timothy Ware Getty. Timothy died at the age of twelve in 1958, the same year that his parents were divorced. After five strikes at marriage, Getty apparently gave up on matrimony, but not on women. It is interesting to note that only one of his five wives, Teddy, to whom he was wed the longest, is mentioned in his Will; her monthly support payment of $8,333 while Getty was alive was reduced in the Will to $4,583. However, many of Getty's girlfriends received bequests of Getty stock or monthly allowances under his Will. Apparently, a woman could do better financially by *not* marrying the billionaire.

Longtime Getty employees fared better than Getty's ex-wives, but not much. Most of them received bequests equal to a three- or six-month multiple of their respective salaries. One aide who was one of Getty's most trusted advisers received an extra six months pay under the Will, which was reportedly equal to approximately $36,000. Not an amount that someone who worked so closely with the world's richest man would want to write home about.

Getty signed his Will in Italy in 1958 after his last divorce and after the death of his son Timothy. The Getty Will ultimately admitted to probate is most unusual because it has twenty-one codicils, or subsequent amendments, to it. One wonders why a new Will was not prepared after 1958 that would incorporate the changes made up until then. One explanation for this extraordinary use of so many codicils is that Getty wanted people to know exactly when they had fallen out of his favor.

Getty was known to have stormy relationships with his sons. Their respective shares of his estate shift dramatically over the course of the many changes in the Will. At various points Getty's sons are removed or inserted as executors of the Will or their shares of Getty stock are increased or decreased. For example, in the fifth codicil to the Will, signed in 1963, Getty's youngest son, Gordon, is stripped of his right to share in his father's personal effects and receives a measly bequest of "the sum of Five Hundred Dollars ($500) and nothing else," while the shares of Getty stock given to his brothers George and Paul were doubled. Son Ronald's bequest was left the same. In the fourteenth codicil, signed in 1971, Getty son J. Paul Getty, Jr., joined his brother Gordon in the penalty box and also received only "the sum of Five Hundred Dollars ($500) and nothing else." In the nineteenth codicil, signed in 1975, son Gordon comes back into favor and becomes an executor and trustee of the Will with his brother Ronnie. Son Paul remained in the Getty penalty box.

Getty signed the twenty-first and last codicil to his Will in March of 1976, a few months before he died. In that last codicil, Getty turned control of the Getty Museum's Getty Oil Company stock over to the museum's board of trustees, which was not controlled by Getty-family members. By bequeathing most of his estate to the charitable museum, Getty was able to avoid huge estate taxes by virtue of the unlimited charitable deduction then in effect. Furthermore, Getty created an eternal monument to his name by creating the most richly endowed museum the world had ever known. By the time the Getty estate was distributed, the museum's endowment was greater than $1 billion. The annual income on that amount alone was significantly more than that available to any other museum in the world.

The Getty Museum in Malibu overlooking the Pacific Ocean was also intended to be Getty's final resting place. One of the first articles of Getty's 1958 Will states:

(a) I give and devise unto my Executors and Trustees . . . such portion of my ranch property located at 17985 Pacific Coast Highway, Pacific Palisades, California, not in excess of one (1) acre, as they, in their discretion, may deem appropriate for the erection thereon of a suitable small, marble mausoleum to receive my mortal remains and those of such of my sons and their respective wives and issue as shall choose to be interred therein, together with a right or easement of access thereto over or through the balance of my said ranch property.

(b) I give and bequeath to my said Executors and Trustees such sum, not in excess of Fifty Thousand Dollars ($50,000), as they in their discretion shall deem necessary or desirable for the purpose of erecting such mausoleum, and I direct that they cause such mausoleum to be so erected.

(c) I give and bequeath to my said Executors and Trustees the further sum of One Hundred Thousand Dollars ($100,000), IN TRUST . . . to apply the same and so much of the principal thereof as may be necessary to the perpetual maintenance and care of said mausoleum and the land upon which the same is erected.

Evidently, Getty's final resting place was important to him, but after his body was flown from England to California, it was discovered that none of Getty's expensive lawyers or anyone else had ever obtained the proper permits for Getty to be buried on his private property. Getty's body was kept embalmed and refrigerated at the Forest Lawn Memorial Park in Glendale for almost three years after his death until a variance in the California law could be obtained that would allow him to be buried on the property that he loved so dearly. Even the richest man in this world needed the proper paperwork before he could make his way to the next.

/s/ *Jean Paul Getty*

Will dated September 22, 1958
1st codicil June 18, 1960
2nd codicil November 4, 1962
3rd codicil December 20, 1962
4th codicil January 15, 1963
5th codicil March 6, 1963
6th codicil September 16, 1965
7th codicil March 11, 1966
8th codicil January 5, 1967
9th codicil November 3, 1967
10th codicil February 24, 1969

11th codicil March 28, 1969
12th codicil June 26, 1970
13th codicil March 8, 1971
14th codicil July 29, 1971
15th codicil March 20, 1973
16th codicil June 14, 1973
17th codicil October 9, 1973
18th codicil July 4, 1974
19th codicil January 21, 1975
20th codicil August 27, 1975
21st codicil March 11, 1976

Conrad Hilton

DATE AND PLACE OF BIRTH
December 25, 1887
Territory of New Mexico

DATE AND PLACE OF DEATH
January 3, 1979
St. John's Hospital
Santa Monica, California

No More Room Service

Hilton Hotel chain founder Conrad Nicholson Hilton came from humble beginnings when he was born on Christmas Day to a Norwegian immigrant family in the Territory of New Mexico. Hilton's father ran a $2.50-a-night boardinghouse in the little town where they lived. Conrad, who was the second of eight children, rose to be the chairman of the prestigious Hilton Hotel chain in nineteen countries around the world. Hilton was known to be a tireless worker, putting in six days a week well into his late eighties.

As evidenced by his Will, Hilton was also a profoundly religious man. Perhaps Hilton felt that because he was born on December 25, he also had a special mission to fulfill. As his Will states to the directors and trustees of the Conrad N. Hilton Foundation:

> I bequeath some cherished conclusions formed during a lifetime of observation, study and contemplation:
>
> There is a natural law, a Divine law, that obliges you and me to relieve the suffering, the distressed and the destitute. Charity is a supreme virtue, and the great channel through which the mercy of God is passed on

to mankind. It is the virtue that unites men and inspires their noblest efforts.

"Love one another, for that is the whole law"; so our fellowmen deserve to be loved and encouraged— never to be abandoned to wander alone in poverty and darkness. The practice of charity will bind us,—will bind all men in one great brotherhood.

As the funds you will expend have come from many places in the world, so let there be no territorial, religious, or color restrictions on your benefactions, but beware of organized, professional charities with high-salaried executives and a heavy ratio of expense.

Be ever watchful for the opportunity to shelter little children with the umbrella of your charity; be generous to their schools, their hospitals and their places of worship. For, as they must bear the burdens of our mistakes, so are they in their innocence the repositories of our hopes for the upward progress of humanity. Give aid to their protectors and defenders, the Sisters, who devote their love and life's work for the good of mankind for they appeal especially to me as being deserving of help from the FOUNDATION. I know the SISTERS OF LORETTO very well, as it was this order who first established educational institutions in my home state of New Mexico. I have had an opportunity of observing the fine work they do. The SISTERS OF THE SACRED HEART is another order that I have assisted in Chicago, but there are many deserving support in other fields, particularly hospitals. Deserving charities exist everywhere, but it is manifest that you cannot help all; so, it is my wish, without excluding others, to have the largest part of your benefactions dedicated to the Sisters in all parts of the world.

Besides having a soft spot for the Sisters, Conrad Hilton also had three wives. With his first wife, Mary Barron, he had three sons—William Barron Hilton, Eric Michael Hilton, and Conrad Nicholson, Jr. (Conrad "Nicky" Hilton, Jr., was once married to Elizabeth Taylor and died in 1969 at the age of forty-two.) After Conrad and Mary were divorced, Hilton married Zsa Zsa Gabor, with whom he had a daughter named Constance Francesca. After his divorce from Zsa Zsa (a/k/a Sari), Hilton married Frances Kelly when he was eighty-nine years old. The papers filed with the Los Angeles court state that Conrad Hilton and Frances Kelly had entered into a written antenuptial agreement "in contemplation of marriage" that provided for the lifetime support of Frances Kelly and in which she "relinquished, disclaimed, released and forever gave up any and all rights, claims or interest in or to" Hilton's property.

As a result of this antenuptial agreement, Hilton had no reason to change his 1973 Will after his 1976 marriage. In his 1973 Will Hilton described his family as follows:

FIRST: I declare that I am unmarried. I further declare that I have been duly and legally divorced from my last wife, SARI G. HILTON, and have fully discharged a final property settlement agreement entered into with her.

I have only three living children, namely WILLIAM BARRON HILTON, ERIC MICHAEL HILTON and CONSTANCE FRANCESCA HILTON. As will hereafter appear in this will, different and unequal bequests have been made to my several children, and I hereby declare this to be my deliberate intention and purpose.

To his two surviving sons, William Barron Hilton and Eric Michael Hilton, Conrad Hilton gave "all of my automobiles, jewelry and personal effects of every kind" to be divided by them as they should agree, or if they failed to agree, then as his executors (William Barron Hilton excluded) should decide. To his son William Barron, who was the president of the Hilton Hotels Corporation when his father died, Conrad gave "shares of stock in Hilton Hotels Corporation and Trans World Airlines, Inc., or both, in the combined aggregate value of Seven Hundred Fifty Thousand Dollars ($750,000.00)." To his son Eric, who was a divisional vice president of Hilton Inns, Inc. when his father died, Hilton gave "shares of stock in Hilton Hotels Corporation or Trans World Airlines, Inc., or both, in the combined aggregate value of Three Hundred Thousand Dollars ($300,000.00)." It is a good thing that Hilton pointed out at the start that bequests would not be so even among his children. But the bequests to children, employees, and other relatives get even more skewed, as follows:

SIXTH: I hereby make further gifts and bequests as follows . . .

A. (1) To my daughter, CONSTANCE FRANCESCA HILTON, the sum of One Hundred Thousand Dollars ($100,000.00).

(2) To my sister, HELEN BUCKLEY, of Little Compton, Rhode Island, the sum of Fifty Thousand Dollars ($50,000).

(3) To my sister ROSEMARY CARPENTER, of Little Compton, Rhode Island, the sum of Fifty Thousand Dollars ($50,000.00).

(16) To my valued friend and administrative assistant, OLIVE M. WAKEMAN, the sum of Seventy-five Thousand Dollars ($75,000.00).

(17) To my valued employee, HUGO MENTZ, the sum of Thirty Thousand Dollars ($30,000.00).

(18) To SISTER FRANCETTA BARBERIS, of Washington, D.C., my star sapphire ring.

(19) To THE CALIFORNIA PROVINCE OF THE SOCIETY OF JESUS . . . money or assets of the value of One Hundred Thousand Dollars ($100,000.00) in cash or in kind, or partly in cash and partly in kind.

I intentionally make no provision for my sister EVA LEWIS, as she is amply provided for by other means.

Hilton gave the rest of his entire estate, worth over $108 million, according to papers filed with the court, to the "CONRAD N. HILTON FOUNDATION, incorporated in the State of California on or about February 21, 1950 as a charitable corporation." To the directors of the Hilton Foundation, he also gave the words of religious wisdom quoted at the beginning of this subchapter.

For his executors, Hilton named his son William Barron Hilton and his trusted attorney and adviser James E. Bates. The Will states further, "By reason of the size and magnitude of my estate, my Executors . . . are authorized to appoint, upon such terms as they may fix, the BANK OF AMERICA NATIONAL TRUST AND SAVINGS ASSOCIATION . . . as a depository and as an agent or agents for Executors, to assist them in the administration and distribution of my estate." After all, somebody had to do all the paperwork.

As one might expect, there is an *in terrorem* clause in Hilton's Will, but it is unusual in stating that if all his heirs were to contest the Will, and lose, the ultimate beneficiary would be the State of California.

Finally, Hilton requested that he be buried next to his brother, August Harold Hilton, in Dallas, Texas. Hilton's first hotel successes had been in Texas, and it appears that he liked the Texas service.

/s/ *Conrad Nicholson Hilton*

Will dated October 31, 1973

End Notes

"Let's Choose Executors and Talk of Wills"
—SHAKESPEARE, *KING RICHARD II*

A *brief* bit of historical and legal background might be helpful here. The foreboding-sounding term *Last Will and Testament* is a creation of archaic legal scholars with names such as Blackstone, Kent, and Coke. During Anglo-Saxon times, the word *Will* applied to the disposition of only land, or "real" property, and the word *testament* applied to the disposition of only "personal" property, such as cattle, corporate stock, or cash. With the passage of the English Statute of Wills in 1837, the distinction between a Will and testament was formally abolished, and thereafter any and all property, real or personal, passed by one unified document, a decedent's "Last Will and Testament." Throughout this volume, we have taken twentieth-century license and referred to a "Last Will and Testament" simply as a "Will." Of course, all of the Wills excerpted within were the decedents' *last* Wills, as determined by the court where the Will was admitted to probate.

After a decedent's original Will (or a copy under certain circumstances if the original cannot be found, as was the case in the estate of Ricky Nelson) has been located, the person or institution named in the Will to execute the Will's directions (appropriately called the executor or executors) offers the Will to a "surrogate's court" or a "probate court" where the decedent had his domicile (i.e., his primary legal residence) for the Will to be "admitted to probate." If no one who has "standing" to object to the admission of the Will objects to its admission and wins, and the court accepts the validity of the Will, the propounded instrument is deemed by the court to be the legally binding Will of the decedent. After the Will has been admitted to probate, the court will issue "letters testamentary" to the person or institution designated as executor of the Will and who agrees to serve in that capacity. He, she, or it then becomes the legal representative of the estate and assumes a host of "fiduciary" duties.

To briefly and generally summarize the duties of an executor, after marshaling and valuing all of the decedent's assets, the executor pays all of the decedent's debts and liabilities. In addition, the executor must pay the taxes and estate administration expenses, including legal and accounting fees and executor's commissions, and the executor distributes the balance of the estate in accordance with the testator's directions.

A person metamorphoses into an "estate" upon his or her death. Usually, the estate is distributed and administered in accordance with the deceased person's directions as expressed in his or her Will and in accordance with applicable federal and state law.

After the Internal Revenue Service and the state taxing authorities have finally determined and accepted the tax payments made and a "closing" or "no tax" letter has been received by the executor, the estate can then be wound up or terminated. As simple as it may sound, an estate administration can continue for years, and many estates linger on forever and are never formally or finally wound up. Any trust established under a Will may continue long after the estate has been closed and be administered by the designated trustees in accordance with the terms of that particular trust. Many of the Wills contained in this volume include trust provisions for a surviving spouse, parents, children, grandchildren, or other friends or lovers.

The Terrorizing *in Terrorem Clause*

Many of the Wills excerpted here include the ultimate graveyard stick, an *in terrorem* clause. *In terrorem* is Latin for "in fright or terror" as a result of a threat. An *in terrorem* clause in a Will threatens the forfeiture of a beneficiary's bequest or interest under the Will should that beneficiary contest the validity of the Will—and lose. These terrorizing clauses are generally drawn quite broadly to apply to anyone who directly or indirectly contests the Will. An *in terrorem* clause is included in a Will when a problem with a beneficiary is foreseen. To be most effective as a threat, the person possibly raising any objections to the Will must have received something of some value under the Will, forcing him or her to think twice before "risking it all" to try for a larger pot of gold. The following rather comprehensive clause is excerpted from the Will of comedian Groucho Marx:

> If any devisee, legatee or beneficiary under this will, or any person claiming under or through any devisee, legatee or beneficiary, or any person who would be entitled to share in my estate through inheritance or intestate succession, <u>or any of my ex-wives</u> [emphasis added], their heirs, successors and assigns, shall, in any manner whatsoever, directly or indirectly, contest this will or attack, oppose or in any manner seek to impair or invalidate any provision hereof, or shall in any manner whatsoever conspire or cooperate with any person or persons attempting to do any of the acts or things aforesaid, or shall acquiesce in or fail to oppose such proceedings (all such persons being herein included within the word "contestant(s)") then in each of the

above mentioned cases, I hereby bequeath to such contestant or contestants the sum of $1.00 only, and no
more, in lieu of any other bequests, devises and interests given in this will or inuring to the benefit of such
contestant or contestants, and such devises, bequests
or interests shall instead be given to THE JEWISH FED-
ERATION COUNCIL OF GREATER LOS ANGELES. If as a
result of any attack or contest of this Will an intestacy
would otherwise result as to all or any portion of my estate, then, and in such event, with respect to any such
portion of my estate I hereby give, devise and bequeath
such portion of my estate to THE JEWISH FEDERATION
COUNCIL OF GREATER LOS ANGELES. For the purpose
of this Article, an action for declaratory relief or peti-
tion for instructions or any other action or proceeding
shall be deemed to constitute an attack upon this Will
where the purpose of the institution of such action or
proceeding would be to oppose, impair or invalidate
any provision hereof.

It is indeed ironic that the *in terrorem* clause appears
unusually frequently in the Wills of our group "The Comedians." Perhaps our funnymen saw the use of an *in terrorem* clause in their Wills as a way of getting the last
laugh on anyone who chose to question their wisdom after they were no longer around to personally defend
themselves.

Where There's No Will, There Was No Will . . .

When a person dies without a valid Will, he or she has
died "intestate." Despite the many important and emotional benefits derived from having an up-to-date Will,

many wealthy, well-educated, and famous people have died without having valid Wills.

The list of those dying intestate must be headed by President Abraham Lincoln. Lincoln's failure to have a Will is unforgivable because he was also one of the leading lawyers of his day. But doesn't "Honest" Abe, the lawyer from Illinois, deserve the benefit of the doubt on this one? Maybe his hiding place for his Will was *too* private and it was just never located. Lincoln is joined on the presidential intestacy parade by Ulysses S. Grant, James Garfield, and Andrew Johnson. Therefore, Bill, George, Ron, Jimmy and Jerry, if you are still out there, please be sure that your Wills are valid and can be located by your heirs.

Other well-known persons dying intestate include close-to-the-edge comics Lenny Bruce and Chris Farley, singer John Denver, singer-turned-Congressman Sonny Bono, actor Sal Mineo, actress Jayne Mansfield, designer Willi Smith (despite his first name), and artist Pablo Picasso. Songwriter George Gershwin died a very wealthy man, but with no Will. Gershwin's entire estate was inherited by his mother, Rose Gershwin. Perhaps that is what George wanted. Jazz great Duke Ellington was a Will-less widower, and his entire estate passed to his son, Mercer K. Ellington. Glamorous Hollywood pinup girl Rita Hayworth died without a valid Will. Her daughter, Princess Yasmin Aga Khan, was appointed administrator of her estate by the New York Surrogate's Court. Howard Hughes died intestate because none of his thirty purported Wills were deemed to be valid by the Texas, California, or Nevada courts.

The failure to make a Will may be a person's way of avoiding making binding and immutable decisions involving property, family, and friends, or may be a way of refusing to confront the inevitability of one's death. We have all heard Ben Franklin's often-quoted remark about the twin certainties in life—death and taxes. A Will is designed to address both of those unfortunate realities, but it is often unnerving for the person thinking of signing a Will to do so. In the case of perhaps the wealthiest artist who ever lived, Pablo Picasso (Picasso died with an estate estimated to be worth anywhere between $300 million and $1 billion), his failure to have prepared and signed a Will has been attributed to his superstition that signing his Will would hasten his demise. Perhaps there was something to that, as Picasso was painting until the night he died at the ripe old age of ninety-one. Likewise, one of the shining art stars of the eighties, Jean-Michel Basquiat, also died without a Will. But he was only twenty-seven, so he did not have as much time to contemplate the inevitable as Picasso did. Nonetheless, his Will-less multi-million-dollar estate has engendered nasty litigation that could have been avoided if Basquiat had prepared and signed a proper Will.

Besides all the practical reasons to have a Will, Wills also provide provocative and interesting reading for the curious of the present and future, as we hope has been the case with the 100 Wills assembled here.

Reproductions of
Telltale Signatures and
Interesting Wills

Georgia O'Keeffe
Robert Mapplethorpe
Alfred J. Hitchcock

The signatures of Georgia O'Keeffe, Robert Map-plethorpe, and Alfred J. Hitchcock reproduced here manifest the ravages of old age, AIDS, and other illness on these three great artists.

IN WITNESS WHEREOF, I have hereunto set my hand
this 2 day of August, 1979.

Georgia O'Keeffe
Georgia O'Keeffe

FOURTH: As thus amended, I hereby ratify, confirm,
redeclare and republish my said Will.

IN WITNESS WHEREOF, I, GEORGIA O'KEEFFE, have
hereunto subscribed my name and affixed my seal this 2
day of November, 1983.

Georgia O'Keeffe
Georgia O'Keeffe

TWELFTH: Except as hereinabove amended, I hereby ratify,
confirm and republish my aforesaid Last Will and Testament and
prior Codicils thereto.

IN WITNESS WHEREOF, I have hereunto set my hand this 8th
day of August, 1984.

Georgia O'Keeffe
GEORGIA O'KEEFFE

WE, the undersigned, do hereby certify that GEORGIA
O'KEEFFE, on the day of the date hereof, in our presence,
being in the presence of each other, signed, published and
declared the above instrument as and to be her Second Codicil to
her Last Will and Testament, and that we, on the same occasion,
at her request, in her presence, and in the presence of each
other, have hereunto signed our names as attesting witnesses.

WITNESS WHEREOF, I have hereunto set my hand and

23 day of June , 1988.

Robert Mapplethorpe (L.S.)

FIRST CODICIL TO WILL
OF ROBERT MAPPLETHORPE

I hereby amend my will dated June 23, 1988 by directing
my executor to make the following bequests (in addition to any
other bequests made in my said will):

$2,500 to TOM PETERMAN;

$2,500 to MICHAEL LUCINE; and

$5,000 to IRIS OWEN.

In all other respects I hereby ratify and reaffirm all
of the provisions of my will dated June 23, 1988.

IN WITNESS WHEREOF, I have on March 7, 1989 signed,
sealed, published and declared the foregoing instrument as a First
Codicil to my Last Will and Testament dated June 23, 1988.

(L.S.)

The foregoing instrument was on said date signed,
sealed, published and declared by said ROBERT
MAPPLETHORPE, as said Testator's Codicil to his
Last Will and Testament dated June 23, 1988.

other respects distribution shall be made hereunder as
if my said wife had predeceased me.

IN WITNESS WHEREOF, I have hereunto set my hand
this 8ᵗʰ day of August , 1963, at 10957
Bellagio Rd. Los Angeles 24.

_____
ALFRED J. HITCHCOCK

The foregoing instrument, consisting of
twenty-five (25) pages, including this
page, was upon the date therein named in
our presence and in the presence of each
of us, signed by ALFRED J. HITCHCOCK,
the testator therein named, and published
and declared by him to us and to each of
us to be his Last Will, and we, and each
of us, thereupon at his request and in
his presence and in the presence of each
other have hereunto set our hands as
witnesses thereto. And we and each of
us declare that we believe said testator
to be of sound mind and memory and not
to be acting under duress, menace, fraud
or undue influence of any person or persons
whomsoever.

BK2313 PG 264

_____ residing at 146 Central Park

The following Will excerpts with signatures reproduced here reveal some of the most intimate and personal
feelings of this mixed bag of famous personalities:

Fred Astaire
W. C. Fields
Ricky Nelson
John Lennon
Elvis Presley
Jim Morrison
Cary Grant
Rock Hudson
Joan Crawford
John Paul Getty
Princess Diana
Frank Sinatra
Jerry Garcia
Henny Youngman
Danny Kaye
Allen Ginsberg
Joe DiMaggio

be paid a reasonable compensation and to be indemnified against all loss, cost or liability in connection with their services. No bond shall be required of any of said trustees, whether acting alone or jointly with other trustees.

EIGHTH: I direct that my funeral be private and that there be no memorial service.

IN WITNESS WHEREOF, I have hereunto set my hand this 6th day of January, 1986, at ___Los Angeles___, California.

Fred Astaire

(b)½   Upon the death of my said brother, Walter
Dukenfield and my said sister, Adel C. Smith and the said
Carlotta Monti (Montejo), I direct that my executors procure
the organization of a membership or other approved corporation under the name of W. C. FIELDS COLLEGE for orphan white
boys and girls, where no religion of any sort is to be
preached. Harmony is the purpose of this thought. It is
my desire the college will be built in California in
Los Angeles County.

(c)   I wish to disinherit anyone who in any
way tries to confuse or break this will or who contributes in
any way to break this will.

(d)   I hereby nominate, constitute and appoint
Magda Michael to be the executor of this, my last will
and testament.

I also wish to bequeath to my friend, Goerge Moran,
formerly of Moran and Mack, the sum of One Thousand Dollars.

IN WITNESS WHEREOF, I have hereunto set my hand
this 28th day of April 1943.

William C. Fields   X
_____
WILLIAM C. FIELDS
TESTATOR

The foregoing Will consisting of five (5) pages,
including this one, was signed and subscribed by the said
William C. Fields, the person named therein, at Los Angeles
California, on the 28th day of April, 1943, in the presence
of us, and each of us at the same time, and was at the time of
his so subscribing the same acknowledged and declared by him to
us to be his Last Will and Testament, and thereupon we, at his
request, and in his presence, and in the presence of each other,
subscribed our names as witnesses thereto

TENTH: I hereby nominate and appoint my brother, DAVID NELSON of Los Angeles, California as the executor of this will. I direct that no bond be required for his services hereunder. I authorize him to compromise any claim for or against my estate and to sell any asset of my estate at any time without the authority of the court. Should my brother be unable to act as executor for whatever reason, I hereby nominate and appoint my friend GREG McDONALD as the executor of this will, also to act without bond.

ELEVENTH: I have intentionally and with full knowledge thereof, omitted to provide for any heirs or other individuals I may leave surviving. In the event that any such person should contest this will, then in such event, I give, devise and bequeath to said person the sum of $1.00 (one dollar) and no more.

IN WITNESS WHEREOF, I have hereunto set my hand this 22nd day of August, 1985.

ERIC H. NELSON

EIGHTH: If any legatee or beneficiary under this will or the trust agreement between myself as Grantor and YOKO ONO LENNON and ELI GARBER as Trustees, dated November 12, 1979 shall interpose objections to the probate of this Will, or institute or prosecute or be in any way interested or instrumental in the institution or prosecution of any action or proceeding for the purpose of setting aside or invalidating this Will, then and in each such case, I direct that such legatee or beneficiary shall receive nothing whatsoever under this Will or the aforementioned Trust.

IN WITNESS WHEREOF, I have subscribed and sealed and do publish and declare these presents as and for my Last Will and Testament, this 12th day of November, 1979.

_____ (L.S.)

THE FOREGOING INSTRUMENT consisting of four (4) typewritten pages, including this page, was on the 12th day of November, 1979; signed, sealed, published and declared by JOHN WINSTON ONO LENNON, the Testator therein named, as and for his Last Will and Testament, in the present of us, who at his request, and in his presence, and in the presence of each other, have hereunto set our names as witnesses.

instrument to be my Last Will and Testament, this ___3___ day
of ___MARCH___, ~~1976~~. 1977

Elvis A. Presley
ELVIS A. PRESLEY

The foregoing instrument, consisting of this and eleven
(11) preceding typewritten pages, was signed, sealed, published
and declared by ELVIS A. PRESLEY, the Testator, to be his Last
Will and Testament, in our presence, and we, at his request and
in his presence and in the presence of each other, have hereunto
subscribed our names as witnesses, this ___3___ day of ___MARCH___
~~1976~~, at Memphis, Tennessee. 1977

*Ginger Alden*_____ residing at __4152 Royal Crest Place__

*Charles F. Hodge*_____ residing at __3764 Elvis Presley Blvd__
Ann Dewey Smith   __2237 Court Avenue__

STATE OF TENNESSEE)

Last Will and Testament

of

JAMES D. MORRISON

I, JAMES D. MORRISON, being of sound and disposing mind, memory and understanding, and after consideration for all persons, the objects of my bounty, and with full knowledge of the nature and extent of my assets, do hereby make, publish and declare this my Last Will and Testament, as follows:

FIRST: I declare that I am a resident of Los Angeles County, California; that I am unmarried and have no children.

SECOND: I direct the payment of all debts and expenses of last illness.

THIRD: I do hereby devise and bequeath each and every thing of value of which I may die possessed, including real property, personal property and mixed properties to PAMELA S. COURSON of Los Angeles County.

In the event the said PAMELA S. COURSON should predecease me, or fail to survive for a period of three months following the date of my death, then and in such event, the devise and bequest to her shall fail and the same is devised and bequeathed instead to my brother, ANDREW MORRISON of Monterey, California, and to my sister, ANNE R. MORRISON of Coronado Beach, California, to share and share alike; provided, however, further that in the event either of them should predecease me, then and in such event, the devise and bequest shall go to the other.

FOURTH: I do hereby appoint PAMELA S. COURSON and MAX FINK, jointly, Executors, or Executor and Executrix, as the case may be, of my estate, giving to said persons, and each of them, full power of appointment of substitution in their place and stead by their Last Will and Testament, or otherwise.

In the event said PAMELA S. COURSON shall survive me and be living at the time of her appointment, then in such event, bond is hereby waived.

I subscribe my name to this Will this 12 day of February, 1969, at Beverly Hills, California.

JAMES D. MORRISON

ARTICLE XIII

It is my intention that no interest be paid on any of the acies provided for in this Last Will or in any Codicil.

ARTICLE XIV

I desire that my remains be cremated, and that there be formal services to note my passing.

I subscribe my name to this Will this 26th day of mber , 1984, at Beverly Hills, California.

_____
CARY GRANT

ADMITTED TO PROBATE

Date **JAN 1 6 1987**
FRANK ZOLIN-COUNTY Clerk-Clerk

By _____ Deputy

FIRST CODICIL

TO LAST WILL AND TESTAMENT DATED AUGUST 18, 1981

OF

ROY H. FITZGERALD (a/k/a ROCK HUDSON)

I, ROY H. FITZGERALD, also known as ROCK HUDSON, a resident of the County of Los Angeles, State of California, do hereby make, publish and declare this to be the First Codicil to my Last Will and Testament which bears the date of August 18, 1981.

FIRST: I hereby delete in its entirety Article FOURTH of my said Last Will and Testament. I purposely make no provision for the benefit of TOM H. CLARK.

SECOND: As amended by this Codicil, I hereby ratify, confirm and republish my Last Will and Testament dated August 18, 1981.

IN WITNESS WHEREOF, I sign, seal, publish and declare this as a First Codicil to my Last Will and Testament dated August 18, 1981, in the presence of the persons witnessing it, at my request on this 23 day of August, 1984.

TENTH: It is my intention to make no provision
herein for my son Christopher or my daughter Christina for
reasons which are well known to them.

ELEVENTH: I direct that my remains be cremated.

IN WITNESS WHEREOF, I have hereunto set my hand and
seal this 28th day of October, 1976.

SIGNED, SEALED, PUBLISHED AND DECLARED
by JOAN CRAWFORD STEELE, the Testatrix,
as and for her Last Will and Testament,

NINETEENTH: If any person who, under the p[ro]v[isi]ons of this my Will, would otherwise be entitled to any g[ift], [be]quest or devise or to any interest in the principal or inco[me] [of] [a]ny portion of my estate or of any trust established here[und]er [s]hall file any objection to the probate of this my Will or s[hall] [i]n any way contest such probate or initiate any litigati[on] [the] [pur]pose of which is to prevent the probate of this my Wil[l] [or to] set aside the probate of this my Will, then such person sh[all], [in] such event, forfeit any and all such gift, devise, bequest [or] [int]erest and the same shall be disposed of as if such person ha[d] [prede]ceased me.

IN WITNESS WHEREOF, I have subscribed and se[aled] [an]d do publish and declare these presents as and for my Last W[ill] [an]d Testament, in the presence of the witnesses attesting t[he] [sam]e at my request, this *22nd* day of *September* , Ninetee[n] [Hun]dred and Fifty-eight.

Jean Paul Getty

I, <u>JEAN PAUL GETTY</u>, of Santa Monica, California, do hereby make, publish and declare this to be <u>a Codicil</u> to my Last Will and Testament, dated September 22, 1958.

FIRST: I hereby amend my Last Will and Testament, dated September 22, 1958, by adding, following subdivision "(c)" of Article "<u>SIXTH</u>" of my said last Will and Testament, a new sub-division "(d)" to Article "<u>SIXTH</u>" of my said Last Will and Testament, which subdivision "(d)" shall read as follows:

(d) I give and bequeath to <u>PENELOPE ANN KITSON</u>, if she shall survive me, Two Thousand Five Hundred (2,500) shares of the common stock, as constituted at the time of my death, of Getty Oil Company or of such corporation as may result from any merger or consolidation, during my lifetime, of said Getty Oil Company and any other corporation or corporations or to which said Getty Oil Company may transfer substantially all its assets during my lifetime.

IN WITNESS WHEREOF, I have hereunto subscribed my name and affixed my seal to this, a Codicil to my Last Will and Testament dated September 22, 1958, this 18th day of June One Thousand Nine Hundred and Sixty.

_____J. Paul Getty_____ (L.S.)

"(2) To PENELOPE ANN KITSON the sum of
One Thousand One Hundred and Sixty-seven
($1,167) Dollars monthly as long as she shall
live."

SECOND: Except as hereinabove modified, I here[by] [r]atify
and confirm my said Last Will and Testament dated Septem[ber] [22,]
1958, as amended by a Codicil dated June 18, 1960 and a [Codi]cil
dated November 4, 1962, a Third Codicil dated December 2[0, 1]962,
a Fourth Codicil dated January 15, 1963, a Fifth Codicil [date]d
March 6, 1963, a Sixth Codicil dated September 16, 1965, [a]
Seventh Codicil dated March 11, 1966, an Eighth Codicil [dated]
January 5, 1967, a Ninth Codicil dated November 3, 1967 [and a]
Tenth Codicil dated February 24, 1969, and as so altered [and]
amended I hereby again publish and declare my said Will [and]
Codicils to be my Last Will and Testament.

IN WITNESS WHEREOF, I have hereunto subscribed [my name]
and affixed my seal to this, an Eleventh Codicil to my s[aid]
Will and Testament, this 28th day of March One Th[ousand]
Nine Hundred and Sixty-nine.

Jean Paul Getty

EXECUTOR *Sarah McCorquodale*   SOLICITOR *Benedict Newland*

I <u>DIANA PRINCESS OF WALES</u> of Kensington Palace London W8 DECLARE this to be

a First Codicil to my Will which is dated the first day of June One thousand

nine hundred and ninety three

1.   My Will shall be construed and take effect as if in clause 1 the name

and address of Commander Patrick Desmond Christian Jermy Jephson were omitted

and replaced by the following:

> my sister Elizabeth Sarah Lavinia McCorquodale (known as The Lady
>
> Sarah McCorquodale) of Stoke Rochford Grantham Lincolnshire
>
> NG33 5EB

2.   In all other respects I confirm my said Will.

IN WITNESS whereof I have hereunto set my hand this *First* day of

February   One thousand nine hundred and ninety six

SIGNED by HER ROYAL HIGHNESS)
in our joint presence and then)   *Diana.*
by us in her presence   )

A Mins
Solicitor
Mishcon de Reya
21 Southampton Row
London WC1.

Paul Burrell
H.R.H's Butler
Flts 8+9
Kensington Palace.

EXECUTOR *Frances Shand Kydd*   SOLICITOR *Benedict Newland*

EXECUTOR *Richard Jardin.*   SOLICITOR *J. G. M. Walsh*
                                         Solicitor

outline of this Will and are not to be considered provisions hereof.

G.   If any provision of this Will shall be invalid or unenforceable, the remaining provisions hereof shall subsist and be carried into effect.

H.   Except as otherwise specifically provided, the validity and construction of this Will and all rights hereunder shall be governed by the laws of the State of California.

SIGNED at _Los Angeles Cal._ , California, on _Sept. 3rd_ , 1991.

Francis Albert Sinatra
FRANCIS ALBERT SINATRA
also known as
FRANK SINATRA

SIXTEENTH

DEFINITIONS

The words "Executor," "Trustee," "child," "children," and "beneficiary," as used herein, shall comprehend both the singular and the plural, and the masculine or feminine shall be deemed to include the other wherever the context of this Will requires. This Will and any Codicil shall be interpreted under the California law as in effect at the date of signature of such document.

IN WITNESS WHEREOF, I have hereunto set my hand this May 12, 1994.

_____
JEROME J. GARCIA

On the date indicated below, JEROME J. GARCIA, declared to us, the undersigned, that this instrument, consisting of sixteen (16) pages, including the page signed by us as witnesses, was the testator's Will and requested us to act as witnesses to it. The testator thereupon signed this Will in our presence, all of us being present at the same time. We now, at the testator's request, in the testator's presence and in the presence of each other, subscribe our names as witnesses.

It is our belief that the testator is of sound mind and memory and is under no constraint or undue influence whatsoever.

EXHIBIT 3e

although not specifically mentioned hereinbefore with relation to any and all such property as if the absolute owner thereof.

IN WITNESS WHEREOF, I have hereunto set my hand and seal to this my Last Will and Testament consisting of three typewritten pages, this 30th day of July, 1991.

[signature: Henny Youngman]

HENNY YOUNGMAN

_____

Signed, sealed, published and declared by HENNY YOUNGMAN, the Testator above named, as and for his Last Will and Testament in the presence of us and each of us, and we at his request, in his presence and in the presence of each other, have hereunto subscribed our names as witnesses thereto the day and year last above written.

[signature] _____ residing at 25 Haverford Avenue
                                                      Scarsdale NY 10583

[signature] _____ residing at 7 Kenneth Court
                                                      Kings Point NY 11024

-3-

Any Executor acting hereunder is further empowered to invest and reinvest surplus moneys of this estate in such types of investments, both real and personal, as may be selected in the discretion of such Executor including corporate obligations of every kind, preferred or common stocks and common trust funds, (including if a corporation shall ever act as Executor any common trust fund of that corporate Executor), subject only to such authorization of court as may be required by law.

My Executor is hereby directed to elect for Federal Estate Tax purposes to have property, in which my wife, SYLVIA FINE KAYE is receiving a qualifying income interest for life as a result of my death, qualify for a marital deduction.

My Executor is specifically authorized to employ as their legal counsel any law with which any Executor is associated, in whatever capacity, and in such event the usual fees shall be paid to said law and the usual compensation shall also be paid to such Executor in the same manner as if he were not so associated, regardless of whether or not, under any arrangements between them, all or a part of such Executor's compensation is to be paid over to such law firm.

IN WITNESS WHEREOF, I have hereunto set my hand this *18* day of *August*, 1983.

Danny Kaye
DANNY KAYE

On the date written below, DANNY KAYE declared to us, the undersigned, that this instrument, consisting of 5 pages including the page signed by us as witnesses, was his Will and requested us to act as witnesses to it. He thereupon signed this Will in our presence, all of us being present at the same time.

At this time DANNY KAYE is over eighteen years of age and appears to be of sound mind. We have no knowledge of any facts indicating that this instrument, or any part

CODICIL
OF
ALLEN GINSBERG

I, Allen Ginsberg, domiciled and residing in the City, County, and State of New York, do make, publish and declare this as the First Codicil to my Last Will and Testament dated the 25th day of July, 1991.

FIRST:
I hereby delete the two lines of text at the top of page 4 in their entirety and replace those two lines with the following language:

> C. To make loans and borrow money for any purpose, including, without limitation, for the payment of any taxes payable by my estate, upon such terms, with or without security, as they in their discretion may determine and to pledge or mortgage any such property as security.

SECOND:
In all other respects I hereby ratify, confirm and republish my aforesaid Last Will and Testament.

IN WITNESS WHEREOF, I sign, seal, publish and declare this as my First Codicil to my aforesaid Last Will and Testament, in the presence of the persons witnessing it at my request, this 26 day of July, 1991.

Allen Ginsberg
—————————————————
Allen Ginsberg

1

ARTICLE III

CASH BEQUESTS

I hereby give and bequeath the sum of One Hundred Thousand Dollars ($100,000) to my nephew, JOSEPH DIMAGGIO (son of my deceased brother, MIKE DIMAGGIO).

ARTICLE IV

BEQUEST OF TANGIBLE PERSONAL PROPERTY

A. I hereby give and bequeath to my granddaughter, PAULA SUE DIMAGGIO, outright, if living, any and all tangible personal property (excluding cash, stocks, bonds and real estate) which I may own at the time of my death. This bequest includes, but is not limited to, household furnishings, silverware, china or linens, automobiles and jewelry together with all prepaid insurance policies on the above items. If PAULA SUE DIMAGGIO shall not survive me, then I give, devise and bequeath to her surviving issue, in equal shares per stirpes, all of my tangible personal property (excluding cash, stocks, bonds and real estate) which I may own at the time of my death. This bequest includes, but is not limited to, household furnishings, silverware, china or linens, automobiles and jewelry together with all prepare insurance policies on he above items.

B. _Alternate Bequest_. If there is no living issue of PAULA SUE DIMAGGIO, then I bequeath any and all of my tangible personal property to my granddaughter, KATHERINE MARIE DIMAGGIO, outright, if living, if

Joseph P DiMaggio

3

John Cassavetes
and
Phil Silvers

The entirely handwritten Wills of director John Cassavetes and comedian Phil Silvers are stark, to the point, and quite revealing about the most intimate thoughts of these two men.

ATTACHMENT 4

June 3, 1988

I, John Cassavetes, being of sound mind. and living at 7917 Woodrow Wilson Drive Los Angeles 90046. Cal. do hereby declare My Last Will and Testament as follows:

I leave all and every thing I own or will own to my beloved wife. Gena Rowlands Cassavetes.

I leave nothing to any one else, whomsoever, they may be.

I owe noone any debt or obligation, other than usual and ordinary bills.

No one has done me a special service that I feel obligated to.

I hereby appoint my wife, Gena Executor of this will. She may at her discretion appoint another executor.

John Cassavetes
June 3, 1988

This document, my only valid will replaces any previous will that might have been drawn. and has been witnessed by my attorney, James Cohen. and my secretary, Doe Avedon Siegel bothof Los Angeles, Cal. Enclosed their witness document. - JC John Cassavetes June 3, 1988 —

Phil Silvers

(July 4th 1984)

This handwritten document will serve as my last will and testament

I request for David Glynn of the firm of Trentbros & Glynn to share the duties of Executor with my eldest daughter Tracey

For carrying out my requests they are to receive and share the sum of Five thousand dollars $2500 each

- Executing the following bequests I leave my entire fortune to be shared equally by my five daughters namely

Tracey, Nancy, Cathy, Candace and Jenny, This legacy includes my ownership of all Stocks and Bonds, Bank accounts, securities and monies in banks and possible partial ownership rights as the Television series "Gilligan Island" - My many awards and documents, photos, and mementoes should be shared equally by my five above mentioned daughters, this is to be supervised by my eldest child Tracey

my further request

To my sister Mrs Pearl Saben of 200 W 59th St New York City × 10019
the sum of Fifteen Thousand dollars $15,000

To my brother Bob Silvers 1130 Brighton Beach Ave Brooklyn N.Y. 1235

Fifteen thousand dollars $500

In the event both the above my Brother and Sister are not alive to accept this Legacy both Sums $30,000 Thirty thousand in Total should be awarded my Nephew Saul Silver
390 First Ave
New York City
N.Y. 10010

fig 2

Phil Silvers

To My friend Leo de Lyon 13147 Hartland Cir. N
Hollywood, Ca 91605 To to I bequest the sum of Five
Thousand dollars $5000 and with this sum my deep respect and
love — To my nurse and constant companion
    Mrs Jean Edward
    10 9 348 Eucaptus.
    apt E   Hawthorne
       Ca 90250

     Phone no. 978-5959
I bequeath to Mrs Edward the sum of Five
Thousand. Dollars $5000 small payment for her

many consideration during my long illness
I have made no reference to my ex-wife Evelyn Patrick
early in our marriage there were some years and there are
five children will attest however for reasons best to the both
of us I leave her nothing mentioned in my also no bitterness
at this writing she is doing very well is her well prepared
profession and I wish her well

   Any reference to the validity of my mental alertness
can be attested by my Doctor of many years

   Clarence M Agress 353-2021 he kept me going when
my physical condition was shaky following a stroke in 1973

    I request my daughter Tracey to inform the
medics of my passing and to arrange my funeral
in Forest Lawn I want a simple coffin and a small
     label Phil Silvers Comedian

I expect David Glynn and TRACY to inform the media and if possible I would appreciate a small eulogue delivered by my friend of many years

Milton Berle. I request my funeral arrangement coffin and head stone not to exceed the sum of Ten thousand dollars $10,000

Good by I go to my rest willingly. The last years were painful but were made bearable by friends. I made through the years especially Ed Traubner who smoothed out many a curve

I go to my end knowing at least as a comedian I was one of a kind

Shalom

Phil

August 15 · 1985

I leave to my daughters, Tracy & Nancy my apartment, 1505. in the west building of the Century Towers 2040 Ave. of The Stars.

All the contents of my apartment shall be divided furniture, photos, awards, equally between them

If they so desire they shall share some of the above with their sisters Cathy, Candy and Laury

I love them all

Phil Silvers

Glossary of Legal Terms

Entire books or volumes of books have been written about the meanings and intricacies of each of the following legal words or phrases. For the purposes of this compendium of Wills, the following simplified definitions should help the reader to understand their usage in this text, but should not be relied upon for any sophisticated legal analysis.

Bequeath—To give a gift of personal property (as opposed to real property) to a person or institution by Will.

Bequest—A gift of personal property (as opposed to real property) made pursuant to a Will.

Codicil—A written and witnessed document that supplements, revokes, or alters certain provisions of a Will and that is executed after the date of the Will, but with all the same formalities.

Conservator—A person appointed by the court to manage and handle the affairs of an incompetent person. A conservator is often appointed as a result of a *conservatorship proceeding* brought before a court.

Construction Proceeding—Case that is brought in court to interpret and apply Will provisions that are unclear or ambiguous.

Copyright—A person's ownership rights in original works authored or created by that person as long as they are fixed in any tangible medium of expression; applies to musical, literary, or visual works.

Devise—A gift of real property (as opposed to personal property) made pursuant to a Will. *Devise* may also be used as a noun to describe the real property that has been gifted. A person or institution that receives the devise is a *devisee.*

Estate—The quantity and nature of the real property (i.e., land and buildings) and personal property, whether intangible (e.g., stocks, bonds, or partnership interests) or tangible (e.g., chairs, paintings, or automobiles), that a person owns or has an interest in. The aggregate of all that is called a person's estate when he or she dies. The word is often applied to the living, who might be doing some estate-planning and preparing for the inevitable.

Executor—Person designated in a Will to administer the estate and to execute the terms of the Will.

Heir—Technically, the person who would inherit the estate if there were no Will; next of kin. *Heir* is often used informally to describe the person who actually inherited part or all of an estate pursuant to a Will.

In Terrorem Clause—*In terrorem* is Latin for "in fright or terror." Used in a Will an *in terrorem* clause threatens the forfeiture of a beneficiary's bequest or interest under a Will should that beneficiary contest the validity of the Will—and lose his suit. Such clauses come in a variety of forms and often do not deter a person from contesting the Will.

Inter Vivos Trust—Trust established by a person during that person's life.

Intestate—Dying without a valid Will. The condition of dying without a valid Will is referred to as *intestacy.*

Last Will and Testament—A written and witnessed document in which a person designates executors, guardians, and/or trustees to administer and dispose of his or her real and/or personal property after his or her death and to take care of family members and others in the manner specified.

Letters of Administration—Certificate issued by the court confirming its appointment of a person, persons, or an institution to administer an estate when the decedent left no valid Will.

Letters of Trusteeship—Certificate issued by a court confirming its appointment of a person, persons, and/or an institution to act as the trustee or trustees of a trust.

Letters Testamentary—Certificate issued by a court confirming its acceptance of a person, persons, or an institution named in a Will to execute the terms of the Will in accordance with the applicable law.

Per Capita—Latin for "by the heads of polls"; method of distribution of estate property when it is made to persons, each of whom is to take in his own right an equal portion of such property.

Per Stirpes—Latin for "by roots or stocks"; method of distribution of estate property when it is made to persons who take as issue, in equal portions, the share that their deceased ancestor would have taken if living.

Primogeniture—Anglo-Saxon concept of law whereby the eldest son has the primary right to succeed to his ancestor's estate.

Probate—Procedure whereby a court accepts the proof of an instrument as the decedent's Last Will and Testament. When the court accepts the validity of such instrument, "the Will had been admitted to probate." The word *probate* also popularly applies to the entire process of an estate administration.

Remainder—The portion of a trust or estate that is left after any life beneficiaries of such trust or estate have died, or their life interest has otherwise terminated. The remainder is a future interest, contingent or vested, or a third party other than the grantor of the property.

Residuary estate—Term used to describe what amount of a person's estate remains for division after the payment of the decedent's and the estate's debts and expenses and any *pre-residuary bequests* or *devises* made in the Will. What is left is divided by the *residuary beneficiaries*.

Testamentary Trust—A trust established under a Will or "testament" of old.

Testate—Dying with a valid Will.

Testator—A male who signs a valid Will.

Testatrix—A female who signs a valid Will.

Trust—An arrangement whereby property is transferred to trustees to be held for the benefit of another person, or other persons or institutions. If the property is transferred pursuant to instructions in a Will, that is a testamentary trust. If the property has been transferred during the life of the grantor or settlor, that is an *inter vivos* trust.

Trustee—Person named in an *inter vivos* trust or under a Will to administer the trust according to its terms.

Will—If you do not know what a Will is by now, please return to the beginning of this book.